Socio-Economic Development in Xinjiang Uyghur Autonomous Region

Alessandra Cappelletti

Socio-Economic Development in Xinjiang Uyghur Autonomous Region

Disparities and Power Struggle in China's North-West

palgrave
macmillan

Alessandra Cappelletti
Xi'an Jiaotong-Liverpool University
Suzhou, China

ISBN 978-981-15-1535-4 ISBN 978-981-15-1536-1 (eBook)
https://doi.org/10.1007/978-981-15-1536-1

Cover illustration: Marina Lohrbach_shutterstock.com

This Palgrave Macmillan imprint is published by the registered company Springer Nature Singapore Pte Ltd.
The registered company address is: 152 Beach Road, #21-01/04 Gateway East, Singapore 189721, Singapore

Introduction

This book is the outcome of a project aimed at understanding transformations and assessing disparities in the quickly changing Xinjiang Uyghur Autonomous Region (XUAR). The oasis mentioned in the title refers to Xinjiang oasis towns, which are the focus of my research, and to a metaphorical oasis characterized by diversity and energy. An oasis which is disappearing and is becoming something else. The intraregional disparities and land acquisition dynamics are part of what is making this change happen.

I am writing this introduction after a long process of taking distance from the research object and findings, which I needed to interpret and analyze on the basis of the new developments in the Xinjiang's context. A mixture of painful and liberating feelings is currently absorbing me. The deep sense of pain is generated by the awareness that it is becoming more and more difficult to reach out the many Uyghur friends, sources and scholars who have been reference persons for this work, as they are in the middle of a controversial process of ideological re-education in Xinjiang's facilities, called by the Chinese government "vocational and education centers".[1] The sense of liberation comes from the fact that this

[1]For an understanding of the official line, see "China Focus: Unveil the truth of Xinjiang vocational, education centers", in Xinhua News Agency, 3rd May 2019. The exact nature and the different kinds of these facilities still need to be assessed. As also academics and intellectuals have been taken there, there must be a whole range of centers classified according to the goal the government wants to reach: "vocational and education centers" are meant for non-educated Uyghurs, while ideological re-education centers could have

work is the outcome of fieldworks, reflection and elaboration over the past ten years, and of an overall reconsideration based on recent developments in Xinjiang. In 2007, I was in the region with a confused and probably naïve idea that Uyghurs and Hans could not coexist because their respective cultures and ethnicities are too different, that Beijing was the oppressor and that Uyghurs were passive victims. Slowly and gradually, I had the chance to realize that Uyghurs have agency, and that this agency could be a key factor in contexts where power relations are unbalanced. Media reports and secondary sources looking at the situation merely from the surface can be biased and are normally unable to see this agency.

The first time I got off the plane in Urumqi, Xinjiang became a kaleidoscopic and complex place I could not manage to stop thinking of. I left my job in a bank and proposed a Ph.D. project on the Xinjiang Production and Construction Corps because I felt the urgency to enter the region with the possibility to stay for long periods of time, eventually get access to its secrets and understand its deep dynamics. The diversity of the social context, in terms of ethnicity, appearances, customs and cultures was striking, and the creeping conflictual ethnic relations I could sense were in a way disturbing; therefore, I decided to turn that superficial and biased initial understanding into something deeper, a knowledge that could help me entering in a kind of empathetic dimension with the situation, in order to interpret it and, eventually, to be able to give a minor but grounded contribution for trying to improve the state of things. The whole process turned into something more important which determined which kind of person I want to be.

Having the chance to get empirical knowledge, experiencing what people in Xinjiang are living in their daily activities and routine, coping with the same problems they have, turned my initial perspective into both an awareness and a responsibility. It never happened to me before to feel so strongly that what we see and feel at a first sight, merely backed by a superficial knowledge collected from readings and news reports, can be as deceiving and biased such as looking only at a few elements

been established for intellectuals, academics, writers, journalists, artists and so on. As the situation is still evolving while I am writing (end August 2019), this is only a hypothesis.

in an unlimited picture. When I have got the feeling that I was like the Zhuangzi's frog in the well, never able to discuss the ocean, and that I needed to open my mind on what I was experiencing, I got a sudden awareness of mechanisms and dynamics that I could not see before. Aprioristic concepts led me to automatically categorizing whatever I was seeing, and this way of keeping the eyes wide shut led me to looking at things by adopting a dualistic perspective. It was only when borders and categories fell down, eyes turned wide open and what surrounded us started to permeate me, that awareness started to grow within myself, and I started to feel the responsibility. Too many people were involved in my project, too many took the risk to help me, and they did not ask anything in return. I had therefore a responsibility, and I now realize that this book reflects merely a partial and limited image of their thinking, it is the outcome of my humble analysis and of my subjective interpretation of facts.

What concerned me in particular is how we think of and understand "development", a teleological incremental process leading toward a goal which is never really reached, a concept which has been conceived and adopted for political purposes in different societies and cultures, at different times in history. Concepts as "urbanization" and "development", closely interrelated and understood as being the pathway to one another, as well as propagandized and instrumentalized to reflect and adjust to new power relations, are analyzed critically, in order to provide an interpretation of how power and its whole range of declinations in human interactions inform our way to understand people's personal trajectory, and how it empirically impacts it.

My hope is that this work provides some useful knowledge on the recent socio-political and economic dynamics in Xinjiang, valuable at least to get an understanding of what is going on at the moment in the region.

Acknowledgements

As I am the only responsible for the positions I took in this work and for its shortcomings, I want to thank many more friends, contacts, interviewees and scholars than those I am allowed to mention here without going beyond the space limitations. The many ordinary people I had chats with and farmers encountered during the fieldwork were of much more help than they can realize.

I was attracted by the region since my bachelor's years, when a colleague of mine, Eloisa Concetti, was working on the Hui district in Beijing and told me once: "You know that in China there is a population claiming a territory for itself, an independent country, that they live in Xinjiang and are called Uyghurs?". She was already familiar with the topic; she already went to Xinjiang for fieldwork. It was the end of the 1990s. It must have been a very different time back then in Xinjiang. When she was there, there was still a harsh struggle, Sufi authorities were at the time—even if underground and persecuted—powerful. They had a strong influence on local communities; their impact on local affairs was deep. And the power struggle had probably still an open ending. Jiang Zemin, the careful and low-profile President, was in charge of guiding China.

While all the shortcomings and problems this manuscript still has are only my responsibility, what is good here, the "hidden gem"—as an anonymous reviewer called it, and I am very grateful to him for the encouragement he gave me—within this work needs to be credited to many people: Two anonymous reviewers, colleagues, but mainly those we were actively involved in this research and who do not have the possibility to speak out anymore.

Prof. Abduresit Jelil Qarluq has been of a constant and generous support, without him I would have never been able to enter into Uyghur society to such a deep extent. He gave me the opportunity to participate in the Sino-German Poverty Alleviation Project in Xinjiang as researcher working on land allocation issues. Without this fundamental experience, my understanding of the dynamics underlying the relations between local authorities and farmers in the Kashgar prefecture would have remained at a rather superficial level, while I would never have grasped core mechanisms internal to Uyghur society. Thanks to this work and research experience I had the possibility to get access areas which in 2012 were still closed to foreigners and Chinese non-residents as Peizawat County, Akto County, and Barin village, to collect material and make interviews to farmers. Without Prof. Qarluq constant and brave help, all the qualitative and sociological analysis related to the development-related issues would have been much poorer. Prof. Marco Buttino deserves a very special mention for his invaluable encouragements and insights on ethnic categories during the early and most difficult stages of the project elaboration.

Sincere thanks are reserved to Prof. Rahile Dawut and Prof. Ekber Niyaz, professor of Uyghur folklore and Archaeology respectively, at

Xinjiang University, for giving support to me throughout the whole process. Professor Niyaz was at the time archaeologist at the Centre for Archaeological Research in Turpan and guided me across the Taklamakan ruins, and the hidden aspect of Xinjiang society and history. Prof. Ilham Tohti made me better understand the current conditions of Uyghurs in the Chinese society, helping me to reflect over the situation of interethnic relations and over the impact of investments and modernization over traditional societies. All my colleagues and friends in Xinjiang and China have been a constant source of inspiration, support and comments during the research process. My Uyghur friends, inside and outside Xinjiang, need a particular mention, since they always did their best to help me in logistic and everyday difficulties, as well as in providing additional meanings to my research and in enriching my thesis, mainly with material and information about their conditions and perceptions, sometimes even at their own risk. I take the opportunity to warmly thank all the many people in China from academia, government, business, art, and other several fields who helped me in many ways, providing information, helping to contact people, and arranging meetings with target groups. Simon James, author of the Xinjiang Video Project, deserves a special mention for his help encouraging me during all the stages of my work. I am grateful for the financial support provided by Università di Napoli "L'Orientale", which granted me with a three-year scholarship which allowed me to pursue my research aims and to carry on my studies in London, Beijing and Xinjiang. My current university, Xi'an Jiaotong-Liverpool University, provided me with the right state of mind and quietness of the Suzhou campus to finalize this project, while my friends helped me to bear the hard times during the research and writing process. I do not have words to really acknowledge the support by Michelangelo Cocco, my husband, a brilliant journalist, who helped me in adopting key categories in political sciences analysis to analyze dynamics and historical events and provided me unique insights on Muslim societies and power dynamics.

The Study

"What is Xinjiang?" is a key question in my research. The geopolitical environment, the historical and cultural *humus* and the religious milieu are all influenced by the cultures of Central Asia, including the Ferghana valley and its Westernmost edge of Samarkand, the Eastern end of the

Oxus River (or Amu Darya), and, more Eastward, the Jiayuguan Pass.[2] Across this vast territory, the influences of the Achemenid, Mongolian and Alexander the Great's empires are still visible in the cultural and social heritage, often merged together into new and original local cultures. Borders are in fact a later arrangement, thus, while studying what today we call Xinjiang, we need to make an effort to consider the broader Central Asian area. The Uyghurs is a diverse population, the result of the intermingling among Pakistanis, Russians, Indian, Iranian and Mongolian peoples. Nestorianism, Manichaeism, Buddhism and various schools of Islam have been simultaneously, or in turn, the local population's faith.

The focal point of this dissertation is on socio-economic disparities in contemporary XUAR, as they have been generated in the development process of the region. A comparative case-study approach has been adopted, with a focus on two regional contexts: Kashgar Prefecture (*Kashi diqu* 喀什地区) and Shihezi sub-prefectural level Municipality (*Shihezi Xianji xingzheng danwei* 石河子县级行政单位). The research has the ambition to represent a small contribution to the broader scholarly literature about intraregional disparities in China, about how the relationship between ethnicity and power has a deep impact on inequalities in certain multi-ethnic societies, and how ethnicity and élite cooptation can be political tools to guarantee the *status quo*. On the background of the relationship between a central power and its peripheral territories, the construction of categories like "ethnic group" and "nation" as developed by Michael Hechter is a major theoretical reference for the whole dissertation.

Xinjiang is one of the twelve provincial-level administrative entities included in the Western territories development strategy (*Xibu da kaifa* 西部大开发) launched in 2000 by Beijing, and it has been target of a massive influx of investments connected to the "19 Provinces and Cities

[2]In Gansu province, the Jiayuguan pass is the first pass at the Western end of the Great Wall of China. Accordingly, to the commonly accepted definition of Central Asia, the concept would include the five independent republics emerged from the Soviet Union: Kazakhstan, Kyrgyzstan, Tajikistan, Turkmenistan and Uzbekistan. Following a broader conceptualization, accepted by UNESCO, other included areas are Afghanistan, North-Eastern Iran, Kashmir, Northern Pakistan, Mongolia, Xinjiang, Tibet and Southern Siberia in Eastern Russia.

support Xinjiang" (*shijiu sheng shi duikou yuanzhu Xinjiang* 十九省市对口援助新疆) central plan, together with the destination of Han Chinese migrants from Inner China in search of a better life. The region represents a challenge in terms of access to archive material, political sensitivity and logistics. It is featured in some specialized touristic publications as a peripheral oases' area on the Silk Road, while the social, economic and political information we have about the territory are often channeled through the official communication apparatus controlled by central authorities, or via statements by Uyghur émigré groups. Both sources are usually unreliable for reasons which do not pertain to the scope of this work, but which can happen to be quickly mentioned in the course of the dissertation.

The research offers new knowledge and a new perspective about this area between China and Central Asia, mainly about the economic and social conditions of its peoples prior to the Xi Jinping administration, and on the challenges the local population and the authorities were facing in a pivotal time in the history of the region (between 2009 when the Urumqi's riots occurred and the ascent to power of Xi Jinping. Through a "research from within", my effort is to give a contribution to those academic researches focused on dynamics underpinning changes and disparities in Xinjiang and China.

The main challenges of this study are basically two: is to study Xinjiang from within China and Xinjiang, and to avoid simply adding new knowledge and notions, but to make an effort in providing new insights and perspectives, new hints for reflection as to how provincial and central government shall find motivations in choosing to develop the region in a more equal and sustainable way, instead of leaning on growth and ethnic factors with too little consideration about the impact on environment and peoples. The whole work is then an attempt to provide a new perspective on the current inequalities existing among the population in Xinjiang.

As a last consideration, we can say that this study might be a contribution to China studies in the discipline of social sciences. The main paradigm for assessing inequality consists in providing a broader and more people-oriented perspective on development issues, taking into consideration two classification systems and questioning them: the World Bank one, based on per capita income, and the UNDP rankings of "human development".

While what is happening in Xinjiang and to Uyghurs is part of a broader national strategy to build a national identity and occurred—and is still occurring—in different ways in other parts of China, responses of people in Xinjiang are different due to local peculiarities, historical path dependencies as well as socio-political and economic factors.

Entrance to the courtyard of a Uyghur rural household (DSCN 2283)

Praise for *Socio-Economic Development in Xinjiang Uyghur Autonomous Region*

"Based on careful fieldwork conducted at the start of the 2010s, this book illuminates the interplay of ethnicity, development, and inequality in Xinjiang during an important period in its recent past. Drawing on her deep familiarity with Uyghur language and culture, Alessandra Cappelletti does specialists in both development studies and Chinese studies a great service by presenting her findings on life and power relations within a complex region, just before dramatically tightening controls began to cause great suffering to its people and block scholarly access to its towns and cities."

—Jeffrey Wasserstrom, *Chancellor's Professor of History, UC Irvine, USA, and co-author of* China in the 21st Century: What Everyone Needs to Know

"A deep dive into my occupied homeland, this highly thoughtful empirical work is as harsh as ice on nude skin. Part of the collective memories of Uyghur people in East Türkistan, it speaks to their souls and sorrows."

—Abdürreşit Celil Karluk, *Professor, Ankara Hacı Bayram Veli Üniversitesi (AHBV), Turkey*

Contents

List of Figures

List of Tables

CHAPTER 1

Previous Scholarship, Methodology and the Concept of Development

1.1 The Kaleidoscopic Dimension of Xinjiang and the Genesis of This Work

Xinjiang Uyghur Autonomous Region is a multidimensional space[1] encompassing a complex variety of identitarian factors, an autonomous region in China, with a geographical and territorial dimension, but also a metaphorical space, loaded with a multiplicity of political meanings and senses of belonging. Writing about Xinjiang today, in summer 2019, as a Western scholar and observer, means drawing a direct link with the intense campaign of ideological reeducation in force in the region and reflecting over the nature and challenges of the Chinese authoritarian regime. We should not make the mistake though of thinking about Xinjiang almost exclusively in connection with Beijing. Xinjiang is much more than that: It is a metaphorical, emotional, interactive and intellectual place where the production of knowledge is usually highly polarized, due to an engrained and well-rooted-in-history political struggle. As scholars, but above all as human beings, we should avoid the epistemological and heuristic fallacies which lead to reinforcing binarisms and oppositions, such as Uyghurs–Hans, Chinese–non-Chinese, oppressors and oppressed. Opening our minds to new perspectives of knowledge is the only way to make progresses in better understanding the world.

[1] Yang et al. (2019).

A. Cappelletti, *Socio-Economic Development in Xinjiang Uyghur Autonomous Region*,
https://doi.org/10.1007/978-981-15-1536-1_1

This study takes into analysis the disparities in the social and economic development in Xinjiang Uyghur Autonomous Region (XUAR), People's Republic of China, in a time span ranging from 1999 to 2016. The original study, my Ph.D. dissertation, analyzed the socio-economic development of the region from 1999 to 2009; therefore, this work required an important process of updating and re-interpreting the situation on the basis of the new conditions. China today is different from the country I lived in 1999 and different also from China in 2009. Standards of life improved, allegedly for all,[2] but in an unequal way, and while all what is "Western" attracted the curiosity and interest of Chinese people until some time ago, today more space is left to the idea of rediscovering the culture and local characteristics of a rich and diverse civilization. Basic needs are not anymore people's first concern. This is also partially true for the area which today we call Xinjiang, "new territory" in Chinese, a vast region lying in the Northwestern part of China, the biggest administrative unit in the country, covering the same land area of Germany, France and Italy altogether. Populated by more than 23 million people mainly belonging to thirteen officially recognized ethnic groups, the majority of them Muslim,[3] Xinjiang borders on eight independent states: Mongolia, Russia, Kazakhstan, Kyrgyzstan, Tajikistan, Afghanistan, Pakistan and India, and internally with Gansu and Qinghai Province on its Eastern border and the Tibetan Autonomous Region (TAR) on the South. Its geography and demography, as well as its natural resources, make the region a geo-political and a highly strategic area for Beijing since at least two thousand years.[4]

This work is focused on social and economic disparities in Xinjiang, in the framework of the more extensive literature on development, identity and dynamics underlying economic and social inequalities in contemporary multi-ethnic contexts. Other countries and political environments

[2] Sun and Guo (2015).

[3] According to *Xinjiang Statistical Yearbook 2017*, the officially recognized minorities living in Xinjiang today are (from the biggest to the smallest): Uyghur, Han, Kazakh, Hui, Kyrgyz, Mongolian, Xibo, Russian, Tajik, Uzbek, Tatar, Manchurian and Daur. 61% of the regional population is Muslim, while the two most represented ethnicities are the Uyghurs and the Hans (46 and 39%, respectively). In these statistical data, the population of the Xinjiang Production and Construction Corps (XJPCC), around 3 million, is not counted.

[4] See Chapter 2.

could have been chosen as well.[5] Reasons why I chose Xinjiang are several: The interaction between "development", "disparities" and "ethnicity" in this frontier region is highly emblematic; center-periphery mechanism and the related socio-economic implications overlap at different levels; Xinjiang is currently undergoing a transformation from a traditional society, based on a familial and state-directed economy, to a "modern" society, where the central state continues to control fundamental economic activities, but at the same time, other actors are striving to obtain their socio-economic space. At the same time, the role of religion, Islam, traditionally constitutive of Xinjiang's society, politics and economy, is being downsized in a deep political effort undertaken by the CCP. While the majority of local Uyghur Muslims perceives the development model which is being implemented in Xinjiang as top-down, Han immigrants hold a different, more positive, perspective: They thank the CCP for taking care of the area by investing and supporting it in a clear path to development. In a region where these forces concentrate and interact to generate or influence change and development, deep dynamics and factors at the basis of disparities can be detected, analyzed and interpreted. This is basically why the area is a perfect object of research.

Another reason is my background of studies on Chinese politics and international relations: The choice of this autonomous region is therefore more suitable than any other areas, on both a methodological level and an analytical level.

A third reason for this choice is that, before the formal beginning of this research in 2009, I had already been in Xinjiang for relatively long spans of time. During these early phases back in 2007 and 2008, she had the opportunity to collect an amount of contacts and material which allowed her to start approaching the issue of interconnections between ethnicity and disparities with a certain level of awareness, in the framework of the more extensive scientific discourse on inequalities and their determinants.

1.1.1 How Did This Work Start?

The genesis of this research work is rooted in a series of journeys to Israel and in the occupied territories of Palestine in different occasions from 2005 to 2008. Simultaneously, I had the chance to go to Xinjiang

[5] For example, Greece and its Muslim minorities in Western Thrace, the Israel and Palestine case, Turkey and its Roman and Kurdish populations in Istanbul.

in 2007 to write reportages for Italian magazines. It was not easy not to compare the two situations. Their resemblance, on which I reflected across the years, was the starting point for the elaboration of a research project on Xinjiang. In the phase of the project draft, an attentive eye was constantly put on the Palestinian situation, mainly on the colonization process in the West Bank. Dru Gladney[6] already analyzed, even if partially, similarities and differences between the two situations. After a careful evaluation of the possibility to elaborate a comparative research project, I realized that too many difficulties and obstacles were on the way. The distance between the two countries and cultures, the complexity of both situations, together with the linguistic and analytical skills required for such a research, were complex enough factors to discourage me from starting such an ambitious work. Thus, I decided to start studying in depth what, in works by Western authors and media, it has often been called the "internal colonisation" process of Xinjiang. The main actors involved are considered to be the Han organization Xinjiang Production and Construction Corps (XJPCC, also called bingtuan),[7] while the primary theoretical framework I relied on is the "internal colonialism" model elaborated by Michael Hechter,[8] who, taking as reference the Welsh and Celtic questions in Great Britain, worked out a comprehensive yet detailed theory of internal colonialism. As a critical voice, I considered Barry Sautman (2000) as an interesting alternative perspective.[9]

After two years of Ph.D. research on the bingtuan system in Naples, London, Beijing and Xinjiang, I had the opportunity to join the Ph.D. dual degree agreement between my home university, Oriental University of Naples, and the Department of Tibetology at Minzu University of China. The occasion was unmissable, since provided the opportunity to work together with a Uyghur tutor, live and study in the region with a

[6] Dru Gladney (2002).

[7] The bingtuan, or Xinjiang Production and Construction Corps (XJPCC), are an economic, political and social administrative unit operating only in Xinjiang. With their own territory and activities, they act independently from the regional government administration. For a more exhaustive explanation, see the related sections in this monograph.

[8] Hechter (1987).

[9] Sautman argues that, for the Xinjiang case, it is impossible to refer to "internal colonization". He mainly considers that the region is not a depopulated and peripheral area (as the "internal colonization" model would require), but a central geostrategic and economic hub which is growing both in terms of population and GDP.

regular student visa and with a research authorization issued by a Chinese institution of higher education. This new situation, together with the new research environment at Minzu University of China, required a reconsideration of the original research project, which is still fundamental in the current work, since Shihezi, one of the two areas chosen as case studies, is in fact the most important bingtuan city in Xinjiang.

The new research proposal was therefore centered on the analysis of intraregional disparities in Xinjiang, mainly on the basis of economic and social data collected during my period of study in China and the fieldwork in the region. The nature of this research required me to enrich my background in China Studies with interpretative and analytical categories from the fields of sociology and anthropology.

The outcomes of this work, which is interdisciplinary and methodologically grounded on information, data and material collected among different social groups in the field, partially contradict the initial hypothesis: Disparities were firstly ascribed to a metaphorical wall between the two cultures and ethnicities, Uyghur and Han, and therefore to the impossibility of an actual communication. Ethnicity emerged, indeed, as the main factor of inequality in Xinjiang. While ethnicity is not a key concept in itself, it becomes such because of the lack of capable Uyghur political representatives and intellectuals proposing a critical perspective. In this context, Uyghurs are easily ethnicized, and "being Uyghur" or "being Han", if not relevant as such, becomes therefore of primary importance. In this way, the social pact between Han and Uyghur elites and establishments[10] becomes more and more solid, and the status quo and connected interests are guaranteed. As a consequence of this ethnicization of the public and political sphere, inequalities in the productive structure of the economy and due to different forms of governance remain well rooted, while dynamics related to economic systems, group cohesion and power struggles are the basis of the unequal distribution of resources and related socio-economic disparities. The concept of ethnicity becomes therefore instrumental and circumstantialist. The implications of the circumstantialist/primordialist debate in the anthropological literature are discussed in Gil-White (1999).

The functional role of the ethnic question in the mechanisms of power relations emerges clearly. Drawing from historical and

[10] Mainly Uyghurs coopted in the Party, government and XJPCC system, a "bridge society" between Beijing and local people in Xinjiang.

anthropological works,[11] ethnicity once again comes out as a political construction, a device which, leveraging on existing differences, tends to strengthen borders and not commonalities and can be easily adopted as a way to gain power, maintain the status quo and consolidate existing social and political roles. According to the situation in the field, a steady social pact and the maintenance of the status quo are then based on a clever use of the "ethnic question".

1.1.2 Historical and Cultural Background[12]

The Chinese Western regions have a history of over 2000 years, associated with trade and exchange, cultural and ethnic diversity, frontier settlements and different kinds of local governments. The classic novel of Chinese literature *Journey to the West* (西游记 *Xiyou ji*) is a fictionalized account of a zoomorphic monk[13] going on pilgrimage to India (then known as the Western regions), a story which left a long-lasting impact on the Chinese collective mind and contributed to the elaboration of a mythology of an allegedly mysterious region. The marriage of Princess Wencheng to the ruler of Tubo (present-day Tibet) during the Tang Dynasty, was a tangible symbol of political and cultural alliance, while Chang'an (present-day Xian) was the national capital and the Eastern starting point of the Silk Road. Another historical link between China's West and its neighbors is the less well-known "Southern Silk Road", that linked present-day Chengdu to India, Pakistan and Burma, via Kunming and Dali, from as early as the third century B.C.

During the Qing Dynasty, large-scale military expeditions to the Northwest, present-day Xinjiang, and the excessive development on the löess Plateau area of Shaanxi, are historical antecedents to the "Go West" campaigns, prior to the twentieth century, used to support the official line that the Western regions are a crucial component of the territorial integrity of the country since antiquity.[14]

[11] Fabietti (2007), Pasquinelli (2005), Remotti and Buttino.

[12] for a more extensive Historical Background, see the first part of Chapter 2 in this book.

[13] Corresponding to the historical character of Xuanzang.

[14] This official narrative is also supported by recent measures taken by the central government, for example, the displacement of the "Jowo Shakyamuni" life-size statue given by Princess Wencheng as dowry to king Songtsen Gambo from a less important position in

The lack of complete historical records and data, together with unreliable official accounts and reports, as well as other political factors, all makes the debate on the Chinese influence in Xinjiang an issue on which general consensus has not been reached yet; therefore, elaborating on the topic is still a sensitive job, among Western as well as among Chinese historians and scholars. It will be interesting to know whether contradictions of views and perspectives, political claims and historical records, will be eventually being absorbed into a consensual and unambiguous historical version in the medium term. According to the available reliable data, the final annexation of Xinjiang into the Chinese Empire took place in 1759, after the war against the Zungar tribes and under the auspices of Emperor Qianlong. Only then, after the suppression of the powerful Zungar nomadic peoples, a systematic policy of integration of the region into Inner China could start, mainly through fiscal and institutional channels. This point in history is of fundamental importance for the integration of Xinjiang into the structure of imperial China. According to the thesis by James Millward (1998), the main channels of inclusion were fiscal and institutional, which means that Xinjiang became an increasingly important source of revenues for the central government and that the whole regional management was mainly entrusted to Han and Manchurian officials, who started to replace the local *amban*.[15]

From 1949 until the fall of Mao Zedong, Beijing's attention and investments were mainly directed toward the Han settlers belonging to the leftist current inside the Communist Party and obedient to the most dogmatic Maoist line, especially during the Cultural Revolution.[16]

During the 1980s and 1990s, central investments and subsidies were primarily addressed to the powerful and influential XJPCC, reestablished by Deng Xiaoping for geostrategic and domestic reasons, after their dismantling in 1979. This situation generated severe unbalances in the

Johkang temple to a more prominent location inside the temple, where the Buddha statue given by the Nepalese Princess Bhrikuti once stood up. This is meant to demonstrate that Tibet had a privileged relationship with the Chinese emperor, a political link prevailing over that with the once powerful Nepalese kingdom.

[15] Manchu word for "high official": Qing imperial residents of non-Han or Manchu origins in charge of working as mediators between the government ranks and the local populations of the same ethnicity.

[16] The works by Donald McMillen are the most detailed and complete on Xinjiang during Mao.

economic and social development of the region, with *bingtuan* residents receiving the major advantages of the central investments and the rest of the population benefitting only on a lesser extent.

1.2 Previous Research

1.2.1 Xinjiang Economic Situation

While attention and interest of Western scholars for Xinjiang have been mainly focused on historical, anthropological, political and ethnic issues, not much has been written on the contemporary economy and society of the region. This is also due to the fact that the area became an economic center only recently, one of the main targets of national investments, as well as a crucial territory for implementing different types of development projects. The central government is considering Xinjiang as a valuable bridge to Central Asian resources and markets where the economy needs to be boosted, and political and government measures need to be more attentive to social and developmental aspects.

Among Western authors, Calla Wiemer (2004) argues that the province is one of the areas more subsidized by the central government in the whole country and that Beijing can claim outstanding achievements in the development of Xinjiang's economy over the 1980s and 1990s. In terms of GDP growth rate, the author underlines that Xinjiang, in comparison with the other provinces and with the national-level data, "is extremely well off". Simultaneously, the author recognizes the pervasive economic presence of the *bingtuan*, whose "activities range from processing agricultural commodities to producing steel, from extracting minerals to providing electricity and water, and from educating students numbering in the hundreds of thousands to conducting scientific research".[17] As far as the Uyghurs–Hans relations are concerned, deep regional inequalities are assessed in terms of resource distribution and job opportunities, disparities which mainly follow ethnic lines. The role of the state in the regional economy is recognized as a leading one, and Xinjiang is thus seen as beneficiary of net transfers, in a high ranking, just after Guizhou, Beijing, Yunnan and Shaanxi. At the same time, unemployment, unbalanced ratio between expenditures and revenues,

[17]pp. 169–170.

a still heavily planned management of the regional economy and a modest internal output are still severe problems. In summary, Wiemer sees Xinjiang as a territory with great potentials, but with a future which depends on how the economic policies will be able to reduce the role of the state and to develop the private sector in a sustainable way, at the same time narrowing the gap between rich and poor. This is the same position as Li (2018), who writes that the development projects are indeed very successful in terms of economic results, but an effort needs to be made, from the side of the government, to redistribute wealth in a more equal way.

Nicholas Becquelin (2004) considers the political and economic dimensions as inevitably intermingled. On this basis, he argues that the economic policies implemented by Beijing in Xinjiang are aimed at fostering the *bingtuan* and at consolidating the territorial integration and political stabilization of the region, mainly through transferring Han migrants. He also highlights the massive fiscal transfers that from Beijing are directed to the area and underlines the large deficit interesting the regional budget, assessing the tight grip of the center on its periphery. The *bingtuan* are considered an elephantine structure, generously subsidized and funded, mainly a political entity hiding under the appearance of a business corporation, with the target of controlling and sinicizing the local population. His conclusion is that Xinjiang economic structure, which was at the time of his research still characterized by a predominance of heavy industry, fits the picture of a peripheral area, the main function of which is to supply the core with raw resources and industrial products, while most of its manufactured needs are satisfied through imports from the most developed areas of the country. In addition, he also tries to provide some ideas on the "staged development" strategy implemented by the central government, raising questions on whether it is likely to placate the alleged increase in ethno-nationalist sentiments, if it is apt to fulfill the ultimate strategic objectives of the central authorities.[18]

The work by James Millward (2007) is an attempt to piece together the different historical events and phases of the region since prehistory, while in his 1998 study he carries on an in-depth analysis of the Qing fiscal system, and of the path through which Xinjiang came to be integrated in a broader national entity, being involved in the central tax-paying system.

[18] Becquelin (2000, 2004).

Literature by Chinese authors can be considered in line with the central narrative: The central government is willing to improve the life conditions of the population of all ethnic groups in Xinjiang. This task comes out to be partially achieved via the central investments pouring into the region, while, according to these authors, it will reach its climax during the next years. Issues like the sinicization process, the perception of increased marginalization by the Uyghur population, the unequal distribution of wealth are usually not taken into analysis. In some studies[19] and journalistic works, a different perspective is adopted: The admission that there are some issues related to the development process in the region leads to the attempt to sketch tentative suitable solutions. For instance, an issue raised is that Xinjiang cannot be considered equal to the Eastern coastal provinces; thus, a more focused development model should be outlined and implemented considering the region's special geographic, cultural and social environment. Secondly, the suitability of the banking system is questioned, since it would probably not be apt to support the planned development, and, thirdly, the ethnic question is not being addressed in a proper way.[20] One of the major critics of the development model in Xinjiang is Tohti (2005), who underlines contradictions and inconsistencies between the stated goals of Beijing, the alleged achievements and the situation on the ground in Xinjiang. Focusing mainly on the disparities in income distribution and job opportunities between Hans and Uyghurs, the author claims that an increase in political participation, a major role in the decision-making process and a more equal resource distribution would surely improve the quality of interethnic relations, while the current state of affairs, characterized by social marginalization and religious repression in Uyghur society, is eventually putting in danger the stability of the whole region, as it would have been soon recognized as a nationwide recognized problem. At the same time, Tohti acknowledges that the diffusion of a market economy system is giving an opportunity to young Uyghurs moving from the countryside to urban realities[21]: The possibility to establish their own businesses and

[19] Bennian Wang (2008) and Aqim (2003).

[20] *Liaowang* 嘹望, *Fenghuang Zhoukan* 凤凰周刊, *Caijing* 财经 *e Caixin* 财新 are the magazines which publish the critical voices.

[21] According to the census data, from 80 to 90% of the Uyghur population in Xinjiang lives in the countryside.

to find jobs which, even if hard and underpaid, could help to improve their self-awareness about the conditions of their fellows and to claim the need to participate in the building a new society[22] was considered a positive process in Uyghur society. Thus, despite acknowledging discrimination and marginalization, Ilham Tohti assumes that a historical opportunity to claim for equal rights is eventually given to Uyghurs and that they should be ready and intelligent enough to catch this chance.

1.2.2 Xinjiang Social Issues

Michael Dillon (2004) argues that Islam, especially Sufism, the most heterodox branch of the Muslim faith, shall be considered as a religious and political thought which pertains to the fundamentals of Uyghur society. Sufism, a syncretic mystical creed which is very popular across all Central Asian countries, has always been intermingled with local politics since its first appearances in the seventh century. For this reason, its adherents have often been considered as challengers to the established powers, mainly for its subversive and revolutionary concepts which used to catalyze those who were not satisfied with the current state of affairs. According to what Dillon elaborates, Sufism is well rooted in Xinjiang society, where it is listed among those "illegal religious activities" forbidden by the Chinese central and local government. Its popularity notwithstanding, all its followers practice it in secret in order to avoid persecution. When questioned about Sufism, Uyghurs do not hesitate to confirm the popularity of this branch of Islam in Xinjiang, even if it is very hard to meet Sufi leaders and followers due to their sensitive status. At the same time, some Uyghur intellectuals and artists can elaborate the importance of Sufism among their peoples and in the history of the area.[23] According to Dillon, the outbreaks of violence and the expressions of discontent among Uyghurs are essentially prompted by religious inputs and watchwords; thus, they are not directly linked to ethnicity, independence or nationalistic claims, or socio-political injustice. Bovingdon (2010) holds a different perspective: The author tends to adopt a nationalistic perspective to read Uyghur discontent, including violent riots and any other form of dissent. In his

[22] Personal communication at Minzu University of China, November 2010.

[23] Among them, the famous *duttar* player Abdurehim Heyit, and Prof. Yasin at Minzu University of China in Beijing.

overall interpretation of the situation in XUAR, the value of locality and geographic affiliation, religious principles and watchwords, together with clan-based demands, are scaled down. Contextually, socio-economic discrimination is not considered in Bovingdon analysis. In his outstanding survey of Uyghur society and self-identification, analyzed taking the Northern Xinjiang city of Ghulja as case study, Justin Rudelson (1997) poses a challenge to those authors who emphasize the nationalistic character of Uyghur discontent. During his in-depth field research in the Ili area,[24] Rudelson discovered that those Uyghurs he interviewed identified themselves on the basis of their geographical origin, usually the oasis where they were born and where the whole enlarged family was still living. This clan-based and oasis-limited definition of identity, attested by rich fieldwork materials, is presented as the proof that there is no nationalism among Uyghurs, since there is no unitary identitarian perception and no sense of a unitary nation. According to Rudelson, Western scholars applied the nationalistic label to movements and social phenomena which are in reality motivated by local power struggles.

Prof. Dru Gladney, from his perspective of a social anthropologist, worked a lot on Uyghurs and Hui and on China's Muslim minorities in general. On the social situation of the Uyghurs, he adopts a more political perspective to assess the de facto perception, prevalent among the overall population, to belong to a same unitary ethnic entity. According to Gladney, this results from the adoption of measures of *affirmative action* taken by central authorities. Following this argument, the sense of a unitary ethnic affiliation became deeper and deeper since the Communist takeover in 1949.

The French researcher Nicholas Becquelin, who started his research on XUAR focusing on the Xinjiang Production and Construction Corps, a currently a Hong Kong-based senior Asia researcher for Human Rights Watch, wrote two notable articles on Xinjiang (2000, 2004), in which he adopts a more sociological angle of analysis: In brief, he argues that the long-term strategy of the central authorities has always been to subdue Uyghurs through military and political measures matching both discrimination and assimilation. With a deeply critical perspective toward Beijing, he argues that the Xinjiang Production and Construction Corps can be

[24] A Kazak autonomous prefecture in Northern Xinjiang with Ghulja (Yining in Chinese) as chief city. Uyghurs are 16% if the population, and they are mainly concentrated in Ghulja.

considered as the main channel of colonization of the area. Together with all the political steps adopted targeting at a "staged development" of the region, the Corps are responsible for the current wretched conditions of the Uyghur population and for the weakness of Uyghurs inside the Chinese state. The US-China expert Calla Wiemer, in her essay written for the Starr volume (2004), analyzes Xinjiang's economy in its internal dynamics and in its relationship with the central authorities. Her conclusion is that, despite the region is one of the most heavily subsidized by Beijing, the annual revenues are not sufficient to cover the budget deficit at the end of each year. She points to the Xinjiang Production and Construction Corps as the first responsible for this unbalance and to the mismanagement of public funding and subsidies by local authorities. Her final assumption and suggestion are that an expansion of the private sector, a better involvement of Uyghurs operators and a more rational handling of financial and natural resources would help the region to develop in a more balanced way and to become a real hub between Central and Eastern Asia. In her analysis, she considers unemployment among Uyghurs as a social disease which needs to be treated at the soonest, as well as those phenomena of ethnic discriminations perpetrated by the Hans. Always in Wiemer's view, what is at stake is the political and social stability of the whole country.

The Uyghur scholars Ilham Tohti and Abduresit Jelil Qarluq, both of them former professors at Minzu University of China in Beijing, at the Department of Economics and Sociology respectively, share the same opinion on the fact that, in several fields of Chinese society, Uyghurs claims for equal rights and job opportunities are disregarded and not considered as serious social needs by government authorities. Moreover, the two scholars assume that Uyghurs are not properly involved in the development process which is interesting in China since the end of the 1970s and the region since at least 2010.

Ilham Tohti, in his works in Chinese and Uyghur languages and during his classes, focuses on religious discrimination, which he maintains to be in force only for Uyghurs and not for the other Muslim minorities in China. Moreover, Xinjiang is watched by the central authorities with a suspicion which is not shared with other Chinese regions where consistent Muslim communities live, like Ningxia and Yunnan. The most evident outcome in Uyghur society, in his view, is the impossibility to practice Islam according to Uyghur traditions. Even if job opportunities are assessed as not being equal for Hans and Uyghurs, in Tohti view the job market is starting to welcome Uyghur workers for low paid and low status jobs, giving them the opportunity to move in big cities from their countryside villages and to start questioning their conditions and their rights as Chinese citizens and workers. The third concern is about discontent and dissatisfaction among Uyghurs, which in Tohti's view could lead to sudden outbreaks of violence.

An interesting analysis of rural–urban migration and of conditions of Uyghur workers in the mainland by Prof. Qarluq puts into evidence their difficulties and the discriminations they are subjected to, through several reality-drawn examples and case studies. The studies on Uyghur intellectuals and HIV in Xinjiang by this author are some of the most outstanding sociological works, based on in-depth field researches, available on Xinjiang. The most recent sociological works on Xinjiang are constituted by articles written by young scholars on particular aspects of Uyghur society: from education to unemployment, from discrimination in the work environment to identitarian issues.

Among Han Chinese scholars, Ma Rong is the most prominent sociologist dealing with Northwestern minority issues. His works are detailed analysis and monitoring of the conditions of minority groups in Northwestern China. Ma argues that preferential policies for minorities are a source of socio-economic instability, since the Han population feels disadvantaged in comparison with its Uyghur counterpart. Its positions are contested by Barry Sautman, Professor at the Hong Kong University for Science and Technology, who argues that only improving and supporting the rights of minorities, together with preferential policies, socio-political stability can be guaranteed. Prof. Yang Shenming, former Director of the School of Ethnology and Sociology at Minzu University of China, after several fieldworks in China, argues that in Xinjiang, there is no interethnic problem, but tensions and riots are caused by Uyghur émigrés groups, led mainly by Rebiya Kadeer (the leader of the World Uyghur Congress in Washington) and Western human rights advocates. Works on Uyghur society by Chinese authors are basically aligned on this interpretation.

1.2.3 Notes on Ethnicity as Determinant of Development Disparities: Some Reference Works

Development and growth have been extensively studied since the 1950s (ref. Rostow 1952, 1971, 1990; Harrod 1973; Domar 1952, 1957; Lewis 1955; and Solow 1956). Since the beginning of the industrialization and globalization processes, the connection between economic growth and development started to represent a source of inspiration for economists and sociologists. Research on phenomena like raising and decreasing trends in economic indicators, as well as the determinants of growth, resulted in a more and more formal corpus of scientific literature and in the elaboration of different models of economic growth. Discriminants and indicators of economic growth have been extensively identified, researched and understood in their interconnections, and the impact of economic growth on societies has been assessed, when it started to become clear that growth did not necessarily coincide with development, not to mention "even development". Scholars and economists made a deep effort to reflect and elaborate on different concepts of "development", attracting the attention of the broader scientific community as well as that of the public opinion: Formal as well as more descriptive and jargon-free "development models" started to be elaborated. A step forward was made when empirical studies proved that growth and development not always meant that equality[25] was eventually reached. Economists and other scholars in the field of "economy of development" and "sociology of development"—more generally, "development studies"—started to question and dispute the different development models. At that point, "sustainable development", "development without inequalities", "equal redistribution and access to resources", "equality through development" all became subjects of scholars' inspiration as well as dynamic research topics. Equal access to education, housing, mobility, credit and health services, as well as a sort of development which is respectful of environmental issues and social needs, became objects of research for a growing number of scholars. What "sustainable development" is and how development can be sustainable, how a country can achieve development goals if local and intraregional inequalities still exist, started to appear on scholarly articles and publications. An effort to propose a formal calculation of the level of development and inequalities was undertaken by the two economists Mahbub ul Haq and Amartya Sen.[26]

The literature on development inequalities which fits our study the most is centered on the "determinants of development inequalities".

[25] See the rich literature on the case of the Italian Mezzogiorno.

[26] See below for the theory of "capabilities".

Hirschman (1958) and Kuznets (1963) launched a new branch of research focusing on determinants of inequality. Kuznets argues that there is an inverted U, a shape curve between growth and inequality, which means that higher growth is associated with a higher level of inequality in the short run, but on a long-term basis, the level of disparity tends to decrease. Following this first assumption, different determinants have been considered as potential cause of inequality: The impact of education on inequality is analyzed in Gregorio and Lee (2002), while the negative impact of a high level of macroeconomic volatility is assessed by Breen and Garcia-Penalosa (2005). The importance of a well-functioning fiscal system and tax collection mechanism for equality is analyzed in Gerry and Mickiewicz (2008), where the authors argue that this relationship is significantly stronger under authoritarian regimes than under democracies. While the Marxist perspective of Thomas Piketty and Jean-Paul Fitoussi provide an extensive and in-depth critical view on capitalist societies, the political determinants of inequality as such started to be a subject of scientific analysis only in the last two decades: The authors who claim that democratic systems present a higher level of capital redistribution to the poor with decreasing inequality as a result are Bollen and Jackman (1985), Lee et al. (1998), Rodrik (1999), and Reuveny and Li (2003). A stronger role of efficiency rather than policy is assessed by Sala-i-Martin (1996), Benabou (1996), and Rodríguez-Pose and Bwire (2004). These authors claim that the type of regime cannot directly influence inequality. The impact of institutions on disparities is analyzed by Engerman and Sokoloff (1997, 2000) and Chong and Gradstein (2007), while how ideology can impact inequality has been explored by Milanovic et al. (2001), while Gupta et al. (2002) focus on the role of corruption on inequality and poverty.

An outline of the literature on the impact of colonization and early institutions on disparities can be found in Acemoglu et al. (2005), while the connection between cultural features—mainly family ties, trust, social capital and religion—and development inequalities has been outlined by Guiso et al. (2006) and Fernandez (2011). Works exploring geography and inequality are listed in Sachs and McCord (2008) and Nunn and Puga (2012).

The ethnic factor and its significance on disparities is studied in Clarke et al. (2003): After the analysis of a panel data for 91 countries from 1960 to 1995, these authors assume that in countries where ethnic heterogeneity is larger, people are less interested in redistribution, and thus, inequality is deeper. The same thesis is argued by Partridge and Rickman (1998), while Mushchinski and Pockering (2000) research the influence of tribal culture characteristics on income inequalities in North America. Alesina et al. (2011), Englebert et al. (2002), and Michalopoulos and Papaioannou (2016) show that ethnic partitioning is associated with a lower level of development and higher degree of civil conflict. Ashraf and Galor (2011, 2013) study the effects of cultural and genetic diversity in the process of economic development before and after the Industrial Revolution and trigger an interesting discussion among economists focusing on development dynamics.[27] The contribution of ethnic disparities to inequality is analyzed in Anand (1983) and Glewwe and Van Der Gaag (1988). The perspective of Micheal Hechter on ethnicity, and inequality will be taken into consideration here below.

The author's assumption is therefore that "economic growth" and "development" (considered as the political powers and measures which make growth be the driving force for structural transformations, like in GDP composition, urbanization processes, health, educational and welfare measures and so on) are not necessarily connected. The two concepts do not necessarily, nor simultaneously, include all the social actors living in a certain territory, and in this specific case, we can argue that there is "uneven development". "Ethnicity" is one of the possible determinants of uneven development, and it can impact negatively on the access to political power and resources.

1.2.4 *Internal Colonialism and Ethnicity*

Michael Hechter's model of "internal colonialism"—a theoretical development consistent with Immanuel Wallerstein's theses—demonstrates that the British rule toward the peripheral areas of Scotland and Wales had all the characteristics of a colonial domination. In an effort of theorizing the "internal colonialism" model, Hechter (1975) proves that class affiliation and religious creed, considered as social categories organizing society into groups with coinciding or conflicting interests, have been main determinants of access to capitals and resources at least until the French Revolution. The author's idea is that, after the beginning of the nineteenth century, ethnic affiliation replaced social class and religion,

[27] D'Alpoim Guedes et al. (2013).

becoming in this way the main determinant of inequality. Through the analysis of the center-periphery relation—between the British establishment and the selected case studies, Scotland and Wales—Michael Hechter proves that the new poor and discriminated are all those who do not belong to the dominant ethnicity. There is still a coincidence between class and religious affiliation with inequality; therefore, the old divide can still be identified in the new classifications: Members of minorities come out to be at the lowest levels of society, since the majority of them still belong to the working class and to poorest social strata. The main assumption of Michael Hechter is that victims of inequality remain the same over the centuries, only labels to identify the change. The reason for this different labeling shall be understood in light of the changed European historical and political environment followed to the French Revolution and of the opening of the contemporary era. While this ethnic divide is seen as a political tool for social control in the hands of central powers, its potential danger as a source of socio-political instability is also recognized. In Hechter's thesis, training a compliant minority establishment is a central political strategy which allows the colonial government to better control its peripheral peoples' discontent. As we will see in the conclusive section of this dissertation, an analogous situation has been found out in Xinjiang. In formulating the "internal colonialism" model, Hechter maintains a circumstantialist concept of ethnicity. In his assessments, ethnic categories are porous political categories, useful for central powers to build a taxonomy of their populations, assign a dominant position to a carefully selected ethnic group, which shall be the most compliant possible to the government line. The main target of central powers comes out to be the submission of all the other ethnicities in the name of an alleged cultural and economic superiority, the exploitation of resources and economic potentialities in its peripheral territories, the avoidance of destabilizing social problems and open conflicts. If these mechanisms happen in a society, it can be reasonably argued that "internal colonialism" occurs.

By taking Hechter's assumptions as a pivotal theoretical reference, ethnicity is understood as the main determinant of inequality, and the existence of a "bridge society" is argued. This is basically an establishment of compliant minority nationals acting as middlemen and deterrent against possible violent outbreaks of social discontent, and it exists in Xinjiang, where a small elite of Uyghurs shares the same interests as those of the Han establishment.

1.2.5 Capabilities and Human Development Index (HDI)

Indicators adopted to measure the HDI are adopted in this study, and the effort goes in the direction of obtaining an immediate knowledge of the social situation and possibility to access resources by different social strata in the two selected areas. The concept of "capabilities", as understood by Sen, is taken into account to understand how economic and social inequalities surface as social and economic phenomena which potentially endanger the political and social stability.

The whole work by Mahbub ul Haq, the Pakistani economist who theorized the HDI, in an effort to give a numeric value to development, has the explicit purpose to shift the focus of development economics from national income accounting to people-centered policies. Nobel laureate Amartya Sen studies on "capabilities" and "functionings" provided the foundations and conceptual framework for the elaboration of

Fig. 1.1 Information plaque related to a past Poverty Alleviation and Development Program in a village close to Kashgar (Picture taken by the author)

the HDI conceptualization. While Haq was sure that a simple composite measure of human development was needed in order to convince the public, academics and policy-makers that they could and should evaluate development not only by economic advances, but also by improvements in human well-being, Sen initially opposed this idea, but he agreed in helping Haq to develop the HDI-related researches. Sen was still worried that it was difficult to capture the full complexity of human capabilities in a single index, but Haq persuaded him that only a single number would shift the attention of policy-makers from their concentration on strictly economic values to human well-being. Both these scholars eventually supported and finalized a concept of development which is more inclusive than the concept elaborated by the classical theory, focusing on how the needs of a multi-faceted human being are identified and satisfied and trying to understand when it is possible to say that a society is really developed, across and beyond the growth models (Fig. 1.1).

1.3 Research Problem and Questions

1.3.1 Research Problem

Xinjiang is one of the fastest developing regions in Northwestern China. Nevertheless, if we consider it from a national perspective, it still lags behind the Southern and North-Eastern coastal provinces. This study aims at analyzing the intraregional disparities in terms of development achievements in one region, XUAR. Part of the population still lives in poverty, having an income at its disposal which is considered to be below the minimum subsistence level by both international and Chinese standards. Another part of the population, mainly concentrated in urban areas, is, on one side, considerably well-off. This current situation is acknowledged by both Chinese national and local authorities, in whose reports it can be read that in some areas in Southern Xinjiang, especially in Kashgar and Khotan prefectures, there are counties where four members' families live with a single income of 600 RMB per year. On the other side, cities like Urumqi and Shihezi are considerably developed and well-off, and all the services and facilities characteristic of the richest urban areas in Inner China are available, while salaries and job opportunities are quickly increasing. An analysis of the disaggregated data and a quick look at the region map clearly show that the disparities inside the region seem to follow ethnic borders: The areas where the majority of Uyghurs live are poverty-hit ones, while the Han population is living where incomes and development levels are higher.

1.3.2 Research Question

This "discrimination following ethnic lines" does not entail a real ethnic struggle, but leverages on a solid "socio-political pact" between the Han establishment and a Uyghur elite, which acts as ally in order to preserve the status quo. Adopting a circumstantialist approach, I consider ethnicity as an analytical category which defines the extent to which a certain population is close to power, mainly in its lifestyle, mind-set, and cultural and political traditions. Those who are more distant from the "dominant ethnicity" belong to the discriminated and weakest ethnic groups, while those who comply with values and ideas of the dominant powers are members of the prevailing ethnicity. "Ethnic affiliation" becomes then a kind of label, an indicator of status and position which a person occupies in his/her society. While we agree with the widely accepted assumption according to which ethnicity is a construction, we also recognize the pregnancy and the emotional implications connected to identity values and the fact that they are often instrumentalized for political reasons.

The dynamics determining the unequal development in Xinjiang are therefore the research focus of this work.

1.3.3 Ethnicity and Inequality

One of the main determinants of inequality came out to be ethnicity, but at the basis of this concept, there are not diversity and identity issues, but power relations and political vision. The lack of a Uyghur political class allows the concept of "ethnic identity" to gain more and more importance, since there is not a theoretical discourse based on economic and social issues, and a real political vision based on the claim for equal rights as citizens of China still needs to be elaborated. In this framework, the best tool in the hands of the most powerful group to consolidate the control on an area and on a population is ethnicity, which, in Xinjiang, becomes the channel to strengthen the social pact existing between the Han and the Uyghur establishments and to maintain the status quo. Once again, ethnic categories appear to be a construction, a useful tool to be used when circumstances require it, a watchword to rise with an instrumental mind-set. While Han and Uyghurs are all citizens of the same country, with same rights and obligations, those who discriminate are not necessarily Han, but those who have power and a status to consolidate inside the Chinese national, regional or local context. Those who suffer discrimination are not the Uyghurs, but those who do not comply with the central government project and who are bearers of a different political and social model. The geography of discrimination, as it comes out from this study, and especially from the fieldwork, mainly follows ethnic lines because they delineate power relations. Our effort will then be focused on demonstrating that ethnicity borders are volatile that the different allocation of resources is caused by a pervasive power conflict supported by ever-changing alliances among the most influential socio-economic groups. Ethnic identity is then a useful political category which helps Beijing, on one side, to implement unpopular and repressive political measures, while it becomes a useful category for those Uyghurs who claim more power and benefits in exchange of compliance, following a conservative mind-set. They can claim more ethnic preferential policies, as well as more benefits for themselves as middlemen between the establishment and the Uyghur population. The role of institutions, governance and social values is also considered central in the context of this work.

Bibliography

Acemoglu, D., Johnson, S., and Robinson, J. A. (2005), "The Rise of Europe: Atlantic Trade, Institutional Change and Economic Growth", in *American Economic Review*, vol. 95, pp. 546–579.

Alesina, Alberto, Easterly, William, and Matuszeski, Janina. (2011), "Artificial States", in *Journal of the European Economic Association*, vol. 9, pp. 246–277.

Anand, Sudhir. (1983), *Inequality and Poverty in Malaysia: Measurement and Decomposition*, Oxford University Press.

Aqim, Yusup. (2003), *Study on Some Questions Concerning Xinjiang Economy*, Xinjiang People's Press.

玉素甫.哈其木, 新疆经济发展若干问题研究,新疆人民出版社,乌鲁木齐2003.

Ashraf and Galor. (2011), "Dynamics and Stagnation in the Malthusian Epoch", in *American Economic Review*, vol. 101(5), pp. 2003–2041.

Ashraf and Galor. (2013), "Genetic Diversity and the Origin of Cultural Fragmentation", in *American Economic Review*, vol. 103(3), pp. 528–533.

Becquelin, Nicholas. (2000), "Xinjiang in the Nineties", in *The China Journal*, No. 44, pp. 65–90.

Becquelin, Nicholas. (2004), "Staged Development in Xinjiang", in *The China Quarterly*, vol. 178, pp. 358–378.

Benabou, Roland. (1996), "Equity and Efficiency in Human Capital Investment: The Local Connection", in *Review of Economic Studies*, vol. 63(2), pp. 237–264.

Bollen K. A., and Jackman R. W. (1985), "Political Democracy and the Size Distribution of Income", *American Sociological Review*, vol. 50(4), pp. 438–457.

Bovingdon, Gardner. (2010), *The Uyghurs: Strangers in Their Own Land*, Columbia University Press.

Breen, Richard, and Garcia-Penalosa, Cecilia (2005), "Income Inequality and Macroeconomic Volatility: An Empirical Investigation", in *Review of Development Economics*, vol. 9(3), pp. 380–398.

Buttino, Marco. (1997), *L'URSS a pezzi. Nazionalismi e conflitto etnico nel crollo del regime sovietico*, Paravia.

Buttino, Marco. (2003), *La Rivoluzione Capovolta. L'Asia Centrale tra il crollo dell'impero zarista e la formazione dell'Urss*, L'Ancora del Mediterraneo.

Buttino, Marco, Ercolessi, C., and Triulzi, A. (2000), *Uomini in armi. Costruzione etnica e violenza politica*, L'ancora del Mediterraneo.

Chong, Alberto, and Gradstein, Mark. (2007), "Inequality and Institutions", in *Review of Economics and Statistics*, vol. 89(3), pp. 454–465.

Clarke, George, Xu, Lixin et al. (2003). "Finance and Income Inequality: Test of Alternative Theories", in Policy Research Working Paper Series 2984, The World Bank.

D'Alpoim Guedes, Jade, Bestor Theodore, C., Carrasco, David, Flad, Rowan, Fosse, Ethan, Herzfeld, Michael, Lamberg-Karlovsky, Carl C., et al. (2013), "Is Poverty in Our Genes?", in *Current Anthropology*, vol. 54(1), pp. 71–79.

Dillon, Michael. (2004), *Xinjiang—China's Muslim Far Northwest*, RoutledgeCurzon.

Domar, Evsey. (1952), "A Theoretical Analysis of Economic Growth", in *The American Economic Review*, vol. 42(2).

Domar, Evsey. (1957), *Essays in the Theory of Economic Growth*, Palgrave.

Engerman, Stanley L., and Sokoloff, Kenneth L. (1997), "Factor Endowments, Institutions, and Differential Paths of Growth Among New World Economies: A View from Economic Historians of the United States", in Stephen Haber (ed.), *How Latin America Fell Behind*, Stanford University Press.

Engerman, Stanley L., and Sokoloff, Kenneth L. (2000), "Inequality, Institutions, and Differential Paths of Growth Among New World Economies", in Claude Menard (ed.), *Institutions, Contracts, and Organizations*, Edward Elgar.

Englebert, Pierre, Tarango, Stacy, and Carter, Matthew. (2002), "Dismemberment and Suffocation a Contribution to the Debate on African Boundaries", in *Comparative Political Studies*, vol. 35(10), pp. 1093–1118.

Fabietti, Ugo. (2007), *L'identità etnica, storia e critica di un concetto equivoco*, Carocci (first ed. 1998).

Fernandez, R. (2011), "Does Culture Matter?" in J. Benhabib, M. O. Jackson, and A. Bisin (eds.), *Handbook of Social Economics*, vol. 1/A, North-Holland, pp. 482–508.

Fitoussi, Jean-Paul, Sen, Amartya, and Stiglitz, Joseph E. (2010), *Mismeasuring Our Lives: Why GDP Doesn't Add Up: The Report*, New Press.

Gerry, Christopher J., and Mickiewicz, Tomasz Marek. (2008), "Inequality, Democracy and Taxation: Lessons from the Post-Communist Transition", in *Europe-Asia Studies*, vol. 60(1), pp. 89–111.

Gil-White, F. J. (1999), "How Thick Is Blood? The Plot Thickens...: If Ethnic Actors Are Primordialists, What Remains of the Circumstantialist/ Primordialist Controversy?", in *Ethnic and Racial* Studies, vol. 22(5), pp. 789–820.

Gladney, Dru C. (1991), *Muslim Chinese: Ethnic Nationalism in the People's Republic*, Harvard University Press.

Gladney, Dru C. (1998), "Internal Colonialism and the Uyghur Nationality: Chinese Nationalism and Its Subaltern Subjects", in *Cahiers d'Etudes sur la Méditerranée Orientale et le monde Turco-Iranien* (25).

Gladney, Dru. (2002), "Xinjiang: China's Future West Bank?", in *Current History*, vol. 101(656), p. 267.

Glewwe, P., and Van Der Gaag, J. (1988), "Confronting Poverty in Developing Countries", Papers 48, World Bank—Living Standards Measurement.

Gregorio, J. D., and Lee, J. (2002), "Education and Income Inequality: New Evidence from Cross-Country Data", in *Review of Income and Wealth*, vol. 48, pp. 395–416.

Guiso, Luigi, Sapienza, Paola, and Zingales, Luigi. (2006), "Does Culture Affect Economic Outcomes?", in *Journal of Economic Perspectives*, vol. 20(2), pp. 23–48.

Gupta, Sanjeev, Davoodi, Hamid, and Alonso-Terme, Rosa. (2002), "Does Corruption Affect Income Inequality and Poverty?", in *Economics of Governance*, vol. 3(1), pp. 23–45.

Harrod, Roy. (1973), *Economic Dynamics*, Springer.

Hechter, Michael. (1975), *Internal Colonialism: The Celtic Fringe in British National Development, 1536–1966*, University of California Press.

Hechter, Michael. (1987), *Internal Colonialism: The Celtic Fringe in British National Development*, University of California Press.

Hirschman, Albert O. (1958), *The Strategy of Economic Development*, Yale University Press.

Kuznets, Simon. (1963), "Quantitative Aspects of the Economic Growth of Nations, VIII: The Distribution of Income by Size", in *Economic Development and Cultural Change*, vol. 11, pp. 1–92.

Lee, Y., Amaral, L. A. N., Canning, D., Meyer, M., and Stanley, H. E. (1998), "Universal Features in the Growth Dynamics of Complex Organizations", in *Physical Review Letters*, vol. 81(15), p. 3275.

Lewis, Arthur W. (1955), *Theory of Economic Growth*, Routledge.

Li, Yuhui. (2018), *China's Assistance Program in Xinjiang*, Lexington Books.

Ma, Rong. (2002), "The Western Development Program, Transfer of Labour Force and Education of Minority Nationalities", in *North-West Minorities Research*, 1.

马戎,西部大开发:劳动力流动与少数民族教育,西北民族研究,2002年,第1期.

Ma, Rong. (2006), "Education of Ethnic Minorities in Contemporary China", Paper presented at the International Symposium on China's Positive Policies in Minority Education: Plural Perspectives, Dickinson College, USA (April 14–15, 2006).

McMillen, Donald H. (1979), *Chinese Communist Power and Policy in Xinjiang, 1949–77*, Westview Press.

McMillen, Donald H. (1982), "China's Political Battlefront: Deng Xiaoping and the Military", Research School of Pacific Studies, Australian National University.

McMillen, Donald H. (1984), "Xinjiang and Wang Enmao: New Directions in Power, Policy and Integration?", in *The China Quarterly* (99), Cambridge University Press.

Michalopoulos, Stelios, and Papaioannou, Elias. (2016), "The Long-Run Effects of the Scramble for Africa", in *American Economic Review*, vol. 106(7), pp. 1802–1848.

Milanovic, Branko, Gradstein, Mark, and Ying, Yvonne. (2001), "Democracy and Income Inequality: An Empirical Analysis", CESifo Working Paper Series No. 411; World Bank Research Working Paper No. 2561.

Millward, James. (1998), *Beyond the Pass: Economy, Ethnicity and Empire in Qing Xinjiang, 1759–1864*, Stanford University Press.

Millward, James. (2007), *Eurasian Crossroads: A History of Xinjiang*, Columbia University Press.

Mushinski, D. W., and Pickering, K. (2000), "Inequality in Income Distributions: Does Culture Matter?", in *Journal of Economic Issues*, vol. 34(2), pp. 403–412.

Nunn, Nathan, and Puga, Diego. (2012), "Ruggedness: The Blessing of Bad Geography in Africa", in *Review of Economics and Statistics*, vol. 94(1), pp. 20–36.

Partridge, Mark, and Rickman, Dan. (1998), "Regional Computable General Equilibrium Modeling: A Survey and Critical Appraisal", in *International Regional Science Review*, vol. 21, pp. 205–248.

Pasquinelli, Carla (ed., 2005), *Occidentalismi*, Carocci.
Piketty, Thomas. (2014), *Capital in the Twenty-First Century*, Belknap Press.
Remotti, Francesco. (2007), *Contro l'identità*, Laterza (first ed. 1996).
Remotti, Francesco. (2010), *L'ossessione identitaria*, Laterza.
Reuveny, Rafael, and Li, Quan. (2003), "Economic Openness, Democracy, and Income Inequality: An Empirical Analysis", in *Comparative Political Studies*, vol. 36(5).
Rodríguez-Pose, A., and Bwire, A. (2004), "The Economic (In)efficiency of Devolution", in *Environment and Planning A*, vol. 36, pp. 1907–1928.
Rodrik, Dani. (1999), "Where Did All the Growth Go? External Shocks, Social Conflict, and Growth Collapses", in *Journal of Economic Growth*, vol. 4(4), pp. 385–412.
Rostow, Walt Whitman. (1952), *The Process of Economic Growth*, Norton.
Rostow, Walt Whitman. (1971), *Politics and the Stages of Growth*, Cambridge University Press.
Rostow, Walt Whitman. (1990), *Theorists of Economic Growth from David Hume to the Present*, Oxford University Press.
Rudelson, Justin Jon. (1997), *Oasis Identities: Uyghur Nationalism Along China's Silk Road*, Columbia University Press.
Sachs, J., and McCord, G. C. (2008), "Geography of Regional Development", in S. Durlauf and L. Blume (eds.), *The New Palgrave Dictionary of Economics Online*, Palgrave Macmillan.
Sala-i-Martin, Xavier X. (1996), "The Classical Approach to Convergence Analysis", in *Economic Journal*, Royal Economic Society, vol. 106(437), pp. 1019–1036.
Sautman, Barry. (2000), "Is Xinjiang an Internal Colony?", in *Inner Asia*, vol. 2(2), pp. 239–271.
Sen, A. K. (1981), *Poverty and Famines: An Essay on Entitlement and Deprivation*, Oxford University Press.
Sen, A. K. (1984a), "The Living Standard", Oxford Economic Paper 36.
Sen, A. K. (1984b), *Resources, Values and Development*, Basil Blackwell.
Sen, A. K. (1985), *Commodities and Capabilities*, North Holland.
Sen, A. K. (1987), *The Standard of Living*, Cambridge University Press.
Sen, A. K. (1992), *Inequality Re-examined*, Clarendon Press.
Sen, A. (1997), "Human Capital and Human Capability", in *World Development*, vol. 25(12), pp. 1959–1961.
Sen, A. K. (1999), *Development as Freedom*, Oxford University Press.
Sen, A. K., and Foster. (1997), *On Economic Inequality*, Clarendon Press.
Solow, Robert M. (1956), "A Contribution to the Theory of Economic Growth", in *Quarterly Journal of Economics*, vol. 70(1), pp. 65–94.
Sun, Wanning, and Guo, Yingjie. (2015), *Unequal China*, Routledge.

Tohti, Ilham. (9.12.2005), "The Development of Xinjiang Economy and Interethnic Relations", Lecture at Minzu University of China.
伊力哈木土赫提,新疆经济发展与民族关系,2005年12月9日在民族大学的演讲.
Ul Haq, Mahbub. (1976), *The Poverty Curtain: Choices for the Third World*, Columbia University Press.
Ul Haq, Mahbub. (1996), *Reflections on Human Development*, Oxford University Press.
Wang, Bennian. (2008), *Economic Research of Xinjiang*, Haiyang Press.
王本年,新疆经济探微,海洋出版社,北京2008.
Wiemer, Calla. (2004), "The Economy of Xinjiang", in Starr Frederick (ed.), *China's Muslim Borderland*, M.E. Sharpe.
Yang, Jun, Li, Yi, Hay, Iain, and Huang, Xianjin. (2019), "Decoding National New Area Development in China: Toward New Land Development and Politics", in *Cities*, vol. 87, pp. 114–120.

CHAPTER 2

Xinjiang Economic Development

2.1 From Special Economic Zones to the Belt and Road Initiative

During the Deng Xiaoping's Opening and Reform period in the 1980s, the Chinese leadership started to reflect over possible ways for a rapid economic growth in order to lift the maximum amount possible of Chinese people out of poverty and accumulate capitals aimed at building an economic power which could be competitive in an international community.[1] Whit this in mind, specific locations had been identified as pilot areas for investments in the coastal provinces of Eastern and Southern China. Special Economic Zones (SEZs) became quickly the symbol—worldwide—of the "Chinese economic miracle". Those coastal areas were meant to be experiments which, if successful, could have been reproduced in other, less developed, provinces of China.[2]

[1] Hsu (2000, pp. 942–949).

[2] For an extensive and in-depth study on China's SEZs and the development model behind this idea, see Yitao and Lu (2018).

This chapter is a development, and a substantial updating, of the book chapter "Kashgar and Shihezi: Socio-Economic Disparities and Development Gap", in Hayes, Anna, and Clarke, Michael (eds.) 2016, *Inside Xinjiang: Space, Place and Power in China's Muslim Far Northwest*, Routledge.

A. Cappelletti, *Socio-Economic Development in Xinjiang Uyghur Autonomous Region*,
https://doi.org/10.1007/978-981-15-1536-1_2

As mentioned, the reason for establishing such zones was to create a competitive economic power at the international level, by putting the country "on track" to catch up with the development reached by advanced economies, with the aim of generating a rapid economic growth regardless—at least in a first experimental phase—of income and welfare disparities across regions. In 1984, the then Premier Zhao Ziyang stated that coastal regions were pivotal areas for the development of the whole country, and predicted that Xinjiang and other Western and interior provinces would have needed to wait until the 1990s in order to receive the investments necessary for generating growth.[3] Because approximately 70% of China's ethnic minorities[4] are concentrated in Western and interior regions and provinces, the uneven development path taken during the Reform era mostly affected minority-populated areas. Disparities are even clearer if we think that ethnic minorities have been living in more than 80% of the poorest counties in China.[5] Since the years 2000s, Xinjiang Uyghur Autonomous Region (XUAR) became one of the key areas in the Western part of the country for liberating productive forces and generating economic activities, mainly thanks to the Great Development of the West[6] as well as to the foreign policy grand scheme Belt and Road Initiative (BRI), which was launched in 2013 but entailed a long preparation in the region, which is the Chinese gate to the West as well as a crossroad of trades and thoughts.

2.2 Regional Characteristics and Resources

2.2.1 Geographic Position

Xinjiang is located in the Northwestern part of China; its size of 1.664.900 million square kilometers makes it the largest province-level administrative unit in the country, representing 1/6 of the total national territory, with 5600 km of international frontiers with Mongolia on the North-East; Russia, Kazakhstan, Kyrgyzstan and Tajikistan on the

[3] Yang (1990).

[4] The population of China is classified into 55 ethnic minorities and one majority, the Han, representing 92% of the total population.

[5] The study by Bhalla and Qiu (2006) covers a number of key aspects of underdevelopment in China's minority areas.

[6] See below in this chapter.

West; and Afghanistan (Wakhan Corridor), Pakistan and India on the Southwest.

A dispute about part of the international border with the Indian part of Kashmir still needs to be settled, this is why authors such as Chaudhuri (2005) write POK: Pakistan Occupied Kashmir. All the other until-recently pending disputes on international borders have been solved.[7] The province borders internally, from South to North, with the Tibetan Autonomous Region and with Qinghai and Gansu Provinces. Xinjiang is one of the five administrative units in the PRC with the status of an autonomous region.[8]

Almost two-thirds of the total area of Xinjiang consists in inhabitable deserts and high mountains. Only about 1.8% of its territory is cultivable land, 34% of which is used for pasture, while forests occupy 2.2% of the regional area.[9] The continental location and mountain system of this Central Asian part of China heavily influences the hydrographic and climatic conditions of the region: On its South, the region is protected by the Karakorum and Kunlun ranges; on the Southwest by the Pamir; and on the North-East by the mountains of the Altai area. Xinjiang is divided into two major geographical regions by the Tian Shan mountain ranges, which cross its territory horizontally: Zungharia on the North and the Tarim Basin on the South. Most of the rivers (more than two hundred) and small lakes of the region depend upon the snow melting from the high mountains, waters which eventually disappear in the desert, with the Irtysh—reaching the Arctic Ocean—as the only exception. Numerous small saltwater lakes are scattered throughout the region.

The climate is extreme continental, generally very dry, with annual rainfalls averaging 100 millimeters in Zungharia and only 50 millimeters in the Tarim Basin. The lowest temperatures might reach minus 50 degrees centigrade South of the Altai Mountains, while in the Turpan Depression in the East (the second place under the sea level in the world after the Dead Sea), summer temperatures can reach 52 degrees centigrade. Zungharia is surrounded by three mountain ranges: the Alatau

[7] Fravel (2008, pp. 102–103).

[8] The other province-level autonomous units are: Ningxia Hui Autonomous Region, Inner Mongolia Autonomous Region, Tibet Autonomous Region and Guangxi Zhuang Autonomous Region.

[9] For these data, I mainly rely on *Xinjiang Statistical Yearbook 2010* and *Xinjiang Statistical Yearbook 2017*.

mountain range, on the Northwest; the Tian Shan on the South; and the Altai on the North-East. It largely consists of steppe and semi-steppe areas—except for the fertile Ili Valley on the West—historically exploited as pasture land. Recently, the production of cereals has become increasingly important in the area, and vast oil reserves have been discovered. The Tarim Basin is also surrounded by mountains: the Tian Shan on the North, the Pamir on the West, the Karakorum on the Southwest, the Kunlun on the South and the Altyn-Tagh on the South-East. The Taklamakan, the second largest desert in the world after the Sahara, covers vast areas of the Tarim Basin, while the oasis settlements with oasis agriculture are located along the desert edge, not far from the foot of the mountains, usually protected by forest belts.

On the Northern side of the Taklamakan Desert lays the Turpan Basin, which is bounded with the Eastern Tian Shan ranges. The archeological excavations in Kroran/Loulan and Ordek/Xiaohe revealed that human settlements were situated deeper in the Taklamakan about 4000–3000 years ago.[10] Water, at that time, was available also in those now desert areas. At a certain point in the geological history of the region, dramatic climatic and ecological changes rendered those settlements not suitable for human living anymore, and thus, people were pushed to move closer to the desert edge. While these oasis settlements are entirely dependent on the availability of water, mostly supplied by the melting snow from the high mountains, important underground reserves have been recently discovered. The economy of the Tarim Basin is mainly based on agriculture, especially wheat, maize, rice, cotton and fruit. Sericulture, traditional handicrafts, trade, mining (coal and oil mainly) and forestry also play an important role in the local, and also national, economy.

In addition to these two large areas, there are two smaller regions which are worth to be mentioned. The Turpan Depression on the East, which also borders with large mountains: the Bogda range on the North, the Tian Shan on the West, and the Quruq Tag on the South. The Flaming Mountains[11] close to Turpan divide the region following an East–West axis. The Southern part is situated below the sea level and is extremely hot

[10] Archaeological sites in the Taklamakan desert, the so-called sand buried cities and a number of necropolises, testify that human settlements were once flourishing in today's Xinjiang desert areas.

[11] Name deriving from the aspect of these mountain ranges which resemble flames against the sky.

during summers. The rate of evaporation exceeds precipitation in most areas of this region. Oasis agriculture gets irrigation from mountain rain and melted snow by complex underground systems, the *karetz*,[12] mostly producing fruits, grapes and melons. The Ili Valley in the North-East is separated from the rest of the region by the Borohoro Mountains on the North-East and the Tian Shan on the South, while it has no natural barriers on the West. The land in the Ili Valley is much more fertile and suitable for agricultural production than in the rest of the regional territory, since it receives significant amounts of rainfall. Two-thirds of the pastureland in Xinjiang is situated in the North, but some Northern areas are also specialized in agricultural production, and also have important industries, including textile production, machine industry and mining.

Because of its geostrategic position between China, Russia, Central and South Asia, Xinjiang has always been an important trading spot on the Silk Roads and therefore, more recently, a vital center for cross-border activities as well as a key logistic and trading hub in the framework of the BRI.[13]

2.2.2 Demographic and Administrative Profile of Xinjiang

Just to provide a comparative perspective, according to the data found in *Xinjiang Statistical Yearbook 2010*, the total population in the region, in 2009, was 21.586.300 people.[14] While in 1955 a total of 5.117.800 people lived in the region (the increase over 2009 had been of 23.7%), the yearly increase from 2008 had been of 1.3%. In 2009, 13.169.433 people within the registered population were ethnic minorities (少数民族 *shaoshu minzu*). Xinjiang is home to 13 recognized ethnic groups (see Table 2.1): Uyghur, Han, Kazakh, Hui (Dungans for non-Chinese speakers), Mongolian, Kyrgyz, Xibo, Tajik, Uzbek, Daur, Manchurian, Tatar and Russian. There is also a small percentage of the population belonging to other recognized ethnicities, but since the numbers are too small, they are not relevant in the region's demographic context. The main ethnic group is the Uyghur, with 10.019.158 people (46.42% of the total), in 2009. The second largest ethnic group, the Han,

[12] Millward (2007, p. 312).

[13] An interesting study on the characteristics and potential of the BRI is Shaun et al. (2019).

[14] Table 0301.

Table 2.1 Ethnic groups in XUAR. Data 2016 (*Xinjiang Statistical Yearbook 2017*, Table 3.8)

Population	*Units*	*Percentage (%)*
Total population	23.023.200[a]	100
Uyghur	11.449.000	47.74
Han	8.269.500	34.48
Kazakh	1.586.700	6.6
Hui	1.020.100	4.25
Kyrgyz	204.200	0.85
Mongolian	179.200	0.75
Xibo	43.100	0.2
Russian	11.800	0.05
Tajik	50.500	0.21
Uzbek	18.800	0.08
Tatar	5.100	0.021
Manchu	27.700	0.12
Daur	6.900	0.03
Other	150.600	0.63

[a]Numbers about the total population vary across the statistical yearbook, and often do not match. The author explained the problems about China's statistical yearbooks, and about numbers and percentages which do not match across the different parts of the same yearbook, or the same sections in different years' yearbooks, in this chapter when dealing with the Gross Domestic Product (GDP)

accounted for 38.99% of the population (8.416.867). What is worth noting is the increase of the Han population, which in 1945 represented a mere 6.2% over the total.[15] In reductive terms, Xinjiang is divided between Muslims, most of whom speak Turkic languages, and non-Muslim Han Chinese immigrants. While the Muslim population is predominant, it still does not constitute a single solid identity since there are plenty of linguistic and cultural differences across Muslim ethnic groups living in the region. The region is administered through eight prefectures: Turpan, Hami (Kumul), Aksu, Kashgar, Khotan, Altay, Tacheng and Ili (Ghulja). There are five autonomous prefectures where ethnic groups other than the Han and Uyghur are the majority of the population: Kizilsu (Kyrgyz), Changji (Hui), Bortala (Mongol), Bayangol (Mongol) and Ili (Kazakh). These administrative divisions are further divided into counties, autonomous counties, prefecture-level cities and other smaller units. The ethnic composition of the region has

[15]Chaudhuri (2005, p. 5).

been oversimplified by modern Chinese ethnographers working within the guidelines set by the Chinese Communist Party[16] on the basis of the concept of "nationalities" shaped in the Soviet Union under Stalin. The actual complexity of ethnic identities in the region is revealed in the comprehensive work of Thomas Hoppe, based on his fieldworks in the region.[17] Until 1949, over 70% of the Xinjiang's population lived in the South and only 25% in the North. The situation changed dramatically because the new CCP authorities adopted a strategy focused on developing the North and neglecting the South, an idea which mainly derived from Emperor Qianlong of the Qing Dynasty, who gave shape to this concept by putting in place the related policies in the region.[18] Due to the uninterrupted waves of migrants coming from Inner China from the 50s onward, either for settling in the region or for seasonal jobs, and to the fast economic development in the Northern part of Xinjiang (especially based on heavy industry and oil), by 1980 the population in the North exceeded the numbers of the South.[19]

2.2.3 The Uyghurs

Xinjiang Uyghur Autonomous Region is named after the Uyghurs, the population which represents the majority and who is entitled to benefit from preferential policies.[20] Uyghurs are sedentary and semi-nomadic agriculturalists living in oases, craftsmen and traders, united as a group by language and cultural elements, as well as closely related to the other Turkic

[16] Mainly Fei Xiaotong, one of the most prominent Chinese sociologists.

[17] Hoppe (1995, p. 16).

[18] Zhang and Cappelletti (2012).

[19] Chaudhuri (2005, p. 5), citing Yuan (1990).

[20] Chinese minorities are entitled to benefit from preferential policies which have been designed and enforced in the 1950s following the Soviet Union model of governance related to national minorities (on this topic, see Martin 2001). In China, national minorities enjoy preferential policies such as the possibility to have more children than the Han; to get a higher Gaokao mark (usually 10 points); facilitated access to credit in some specific circumstances (e.g., in some areas, favorable mortgages for young married couples or advantageous loans to open new businesses); in autonomous regions and other administrative units where a certain ethnic group represents the majority (for instance, in Xinjiang), they need to appoint a number of officials of that minority which matches a certain quota, a percentage which matches the percentage of that population in that territory (in Xinjiang almost 48% of local government officials need to be Uyghur); right a bilingual education and other similar advantages.

peoples in Xinjiang and in the whole of Central Asia. In fact, they are a combination of Indoeuropean, Mongolian and Turkish populations—as it is reflected in their language and customs—with a different range of religious affiliations (Sufi, Hanafi Sunni, Shia, Christianity and so forth) and without a clear-cut identity.[21] This derives from their history as well as geographical positioning between China and Central Asia. In Inner China, there are significant Uyghur communities in the provinces of Gansu, Guangdong, Hunan and in cities such as Beijing, Shanghai and Tianjin. Abroad they mainly live in Central Asia (Kazakhstan, Uzbekistan, Kyrgyzstan), Turkey, Saudi Arabia, Germany, Sweden, Australia and in the United States. Due to the practice of quickly adopting the nationality of the hosting country, nowadays it is difficult to assess the number of Uyghurs living abroad, but, according to scholars such as Michael Dillon and James Millward, over one million of them are currently living out of China.[22] While there are authors who write about "Uyghur nationalism",[23] there are debates concerning whether this ever existed and, if this would be the case, when and in which form, and whether it should be considered as a recent phenomenon or something with deeper historical roots. As Justin Rudelson argues in his book,[24] in the past these oasis dwellers tended to identify themselves with the particular oasis town of the clan, rather than with an abstract concept of Uyghur nation. This said, especially as a result of Chinese policies on nationality emulated from the Soviets, as well as under the influence of the Muslim populations of Central Asia, there is a growing perception of a Uyghur identity, especially in the Altisheher[25] region, bordering Pakistan and Afghanistan, where the majority of Uyghurs live.

The attribution of these ethnic terms needs to be constantly questioned and challenged, as it is based on policies ascribing "nationalities" to all ethnic groups of the Soviet Union under Stalin, which were later adopted by CCP leaders. In reality, ethnic divisions in Xinjiang are far from being clear-cut and there are also marriages which cut across ethnic

[21] See Thum (2012, 2014) and Rudelson (1997).

[22] Dillon (2004, p. 51) and Millward (2007, p. 345). For a historical anthropology of the Uyghurs, see Beller-Hann (2007).

[23] See for instance Bovingdon (2010).

[24] Rudelson (1997).

[25] Altisheher in Uyghur language means "six cities". The term is used as a toponym and it has a long history in the historical written sources, indicating the oases of Kashgar, Yenghissar, Yarkand, Khotan, Uch Turpan and Aqsu in Southern Xinjiang.

lines, particularly among the educated urban classes, as well as cases of young people with parents from the Han nationality and from a minority, choosing the minority to enjoy the above-mentioned preferential policies.[26] Because of the massive numbers of Han migrants who moved to Xinjiang after the 1950s, and of the feeling—widespread among the population—of quickly becoming "foreigners in their own land", Uyghur individuals and communities, as a form of identitarian reaction, started identifying themselves as members of an ethnic group, and often wear clothing, headgear and, for men, beards, in a fashion that clearly marks them as Uyghurs. A more in-depth analysis reveals that tribal allegiances are still more important than ethnic or national affiliations, and deeply determine social, cultural and political patterns within Uyghur communities. Slightly different dressing styles and ways of speaking can still reveal the identification and affiliation with one group or another.

The distribution of ethnic groups on the regional territory is uneven: only 1/5 of the Uyghur population lives in Northern Xinjiang, where the majority of Hans live, while Southern Xinjiang, where 4/5 of Uyghurs lives, has only 33.3% of the Xinjiang urban centers and 35% of the total urban population in the region. This means that the majority of the Uyghur population—more than 80%—is mainly settled in the rural areas of Southern Xinjiang, a territory which is considered, by the mainstream society, as traditional, poor and backward.

2.3 Historical Outline Since the Collapse of the Qing Dynasty

2.3.1 The "Great Game" and the Warlords' Period[27]

From the late nineteenth century, Xinjiang became the center of the "Great Game".[28] The region became receptive to European influences, especially in periods when the governance system was more

[26]This happens because young people under 18 years old, with a parent which is Han and the other from a national minority, can choose the nationality they prefer to be officially identified with.

[27]An exhaustive overview of the history of the region from prehistoric times to the nineteenth century can be found in Millward (2007).

[28]See Peter Hopkirk works.

decentralized, and the control of the empire loosened. The final defeat of the Muslim rebellions in Eastern Turkestan[29] did not change the fact that the region remained part of the wider Islamic world. This became particularly evident during the first decades of the Republican era (1912–1949), which followed the demise of the Qing Dynasty. The so-called warlord period saw the rule of three long-serving governors: Yang Zengxin (1912–1928), Jin Shuren (1928–1933) and Sheng Shicai (1933–1943).[30] During this era, a certain degree of independence was guaranteed, since the warlords disregarded the weak and contentious center, conducting the internal politics with a high degree of arbitrariness. They collected their own taxes, created their own military forces and built up a Han-dominated group of loyal administrators, among whose many Hui officials were recruited. A certain degree of independence was left to native leaders as well: they continued to deal with local affairs, and to be acknowledged as authorities by local communities, in this way indirect rule was perpetuated until today. Under Governor Yang, the Qing administrative system was maintained with only a few changes and, on the lower administrative level, the *begs*[31] continued to hold power and authority in some areas. Governor Yang's rule was characterized by an excessive fear of revolt, distrust of his subordinates and anxiety toward the reformist and egalitarian influences coming from Western Turkestan.[32] Episodes of corruption and abuse of power among government officials were common, and the economic situation rapidly deteriorated. This was partly due to the fact that the generous subsidies from the Qing imperial center ceased to reach the regional treasury, and, contextually, the trade volume with Russia declined. Exploitative economic policies contributed to the general impoverishment and discontent across the society. Yang's unpopularity grew not only among Muslim populations but also among Han Chinese, and it was one of them who eventually assassinated him.

Yang successor Jin Shuren pursued similar policies, leaving the administrative system inherited from the late Qing Dynasty untouched and

[29] Kim (2004).

[30] Forbes (2011).

[31] Native authorities, Benson (1998).

[32] Mainly the Jadidist movement. On this reformist movement, see the works by Adeeb Khalid.

stepping up the measures of surveillance and censorship. Misguided and exploitative practices, such as the dramatic increase of land taxes and inflation, caused by the issuance of an incredible large circulation of paper money, led to a further deterioration of the economic conditions in the region. Jin initial isolationism, close to xenophobia, was characterized by good relations with Soviet Russia and opened the way to Soviet penetration into Xinjiang and to an increase of the Soviet political influence in the area.

The 1930s and 1940s saw several Muslim insurgencies, growing nationalism among the Turkic-speaking populations and a stronger Soviet economic and political influence. The series of Muslim rebellions, led by Uyghur independentist leaders such as Khoja Niyaz and Yulbars Khan,[33] which shook the region in the early 1930s, were triggered by the policies of Jin Shuren: the annexation of the Qumul Khanate clashed with much of the population's expectations, since Qumul was the last symbol of Islamic autonomy. In his analysis of the causes of these rebellions, Andrew Forbes attributes a particularly important role to regional factionalism. In his works, he highlights continuities in the divided political loyalties of the three main regions from the imperial times to the Republican era: Due to historical reasons, the Qumul-Turfan area in Eastern Xinjiang remained generally closer to the Chinese on the East, as did the Han Chinese and Hui population in the North. On the other side, the Taranchi population, the Turkic-speaking Muslims settled in the North from the Tarim Basin,[34] increasingly came under Russian influence. At the same time, regions with a traditional history of close relations with China were not exempt from rebellions, as testified by the Qumul and Turfan upheavals in the early 1900s, but it was the South, with Kashgar as its center, which emerged as the stronghold of conservative Islamic traditionalists, who opposed both the Chinese rule and the socialist ideology.[35] It was at this point that, as a culmination

[33] On these Uyghur revolutionary leaders, see Forbes (2011).

[34] Taranchi ("farmer" in Chagatai Uyghur. Chagatai is the common predecessor of modern Uzbek and Uyghur, an extinct Turkic language that was once widely spoken in Central Asia and remained the shared literary language there until the early twentieth century) was the name used for those Turkic Muslims transferred from the Tarim Basin by Zunghars and the Qing Dynasty to farm in the Yili Valley up North. Millward (2007, p. 118).

[35] Sheel (1989) on the origins of the revolutionary movement in Xinjiang.

of the uprisings, the short-lived Islamic Republic of Eastern Turkestan of 1933 and 1934 was declared with Kashgar as its center, with a leadership dominated by anti-Han, anti-Tungan and anti-Soviet sentiments. The rebellions in the South were brought under control mainly by Soviet interventions from 1934 to 1937.

For reasons related to the ongoing world war, in 1942 Governor Sheng Shicai broke with the Soviets and started to support the Guomindang government. Muslim discontent with the Chinese rule flared up again, this time in the North, where it was secretly encouraged by the Soviets, trying to force Sheng to guarantee economic privileges to the USSR in the area called "Three Regions".[36] With the Soviet military support, the Eastern Turkestan Republic was established in Ghulja (Ch. Yining) in 1945. While the rebellion occurred ten years earlier in Kashgar had a primarily Islamic character, linking together Turk and Chinese-speaking Muslim groups against the non-Muslim Hans, this second uprising had more a pan-Turk character. The Ili rebellion (1944–1949) had a mostly progressive leadership which distanced itself from conservative Islamic forces, and opposed the Nationalist Government.[37] This explains why the Chinese Communist Party interpreted it not as a separatist movement of the Turkic-speaking Muslims of Xinjiang, but as a manifestation or their support to the Chinese Communists. The late 1940s saw the emergence of regional governments, ending with the incorporation of the whole region into the People's Republic of China in 1949.

2.3.2 Post-1949 Xinjiang

The PLA's troops led by commander Wang Zhen[38] entered Xinjiang in mid-October 1949, accessing a relatively "new territory",[39] where

[36] Ili, Altay and Tarbagatay districts in Northern Xinjiang.

[37] Benson (1998).

[38] For a CCP account on Wang Zhen, see Weiping and Hanlin (2008). According to Uyghur scholars who prefer to remain anonymous, the commander was a bloodthirsty politician who did not hesitate to kill women and children when he encountered any kind of resistance in Uyghur villages. Due to the sensitivity of recent historical events in the region, and to the impossibility to get access to the regional archives, it is hard to assess how much of Wang Zhen was in reality a hero, as the CCP propaganda depicts him, or an unscrupulous commander.

[39] The literal meaning of Xinjiang 新疆 is "new territory".

populations with a different culture, customs, language and religion lived together since centuries. As mentioned, the Han population at the time was less than 6% of the total.

Quite surprisingly, when Wang Zhen led his PLA units into Southern Xinjiang, he apparently did not encounter any resistance.[40] From the Southern districts, he moved northward, where he was in charge of managing the nomadic populations and of purging the military and political leaders suspected of ethnic separatist ideas.[41]

The first urgent task for the Chinese government in the area, as well as in the whole Chinese territory, was to position itself in the new context and redefine power dynamics and balances mainly redistributing positions of authority, with the aim of handling a complex transitional phase as well as a difficult relationship with the enemies. The power apparatus and the mechanisms of state control needed to be reorganized according to the new CCP guidelines coming from the center and to the just changed socio-political conditions. What James Millward calls "the transition from a Qing dynastic empire to a Chinese nation-state",[42] which started in the Eighteenth century, is a process which became then clear in its full complexity, and started to represent an urgent issue for the new establishment.[43]

Wang Zhen was the man in charge of reorganizing the political, administrative and social structure of the region on the basis of the new CCP directives. The measures which Wang Zhen implemented in Xinjiang represent the basis of the current CCP policies and mainly consisted in: establishing a solid bingtuan[44] system on the basis of the old

[40] Millward (2007, p. 232).

[41] The South of Xinjiang has always been less politicized, more profoundly religious and less developed than the Northern part due to the strategic plans of the Qing Dynasty and the CCP.

[42] Millward (1998, pp. 74–75).

[43] Anderson (1983) provides a critical and exhaustive understanding of these nation-building processes. Similar processes and cases can be found in relation to the Byzantine Empire, and the Turkish and Greek states.

[44] The bingtuan is a political, economic and military organization which controls part of the XUAR territory. Today the whole structure is composed by 14 divisions and 175 regiments, it administers 5 municipalities (one of them is Shihezi), and it has its own health, legal and education systems (with hospitals, courts and universities with high-quality standards). For a complete review of works on the bingtuan system, see the related chapter in this book. Zhang and Cappelletti (2012).

tuntian[45] network in order to create a defense force in case of internal turmoil or attacks from abroad, as well as to attract more Hans in the region; educating minority cadres to take positions in the CCP ranks and become the middlemen of Beijing in the region; conceiving and operationalizing a deep political work within the society at all levels, mainly adopting education and propaganda tools to dilute the religious identity of local Uyghurs, and to implement measures of collectivization aimed at replacing the Uyghur traditional leadership; reforming the education system in order to promote the teaching of Chinese language.[46]

As they consolidated control over parts of Xinjiang, the new Chinese authorities, in the spring of 1953, started establishing "autonomous areas", beginning with the lowest levels of the administrative hierarchy (township, *xiang* 乡 and district, *qu* 区) and gradually moving up to prefectural level (*zhou* 州) by 1954, when the Ili Kazakh Autonomous Prefecture was created, incorporating the districts of Yili, Tarbagatay and Altai. In October 1955, the process reached the provincial level and Eastern Turkestan became an autonomous administrative unit in China, officially renamed Xinjiang Uyghur Autonomous Region (Ch. *Xinjiang Weiwuer Zizhiqu* 新疆维吾尔自治区). Saifuddin Azizi, a Uyghur Party official from an influential traders' family in Artush, became the first Chairman of the XUAR People's Council, but the real power laid in the hands of Wang Enmao,[47] a Long March veteran who replaced Wang Zhen at the regional top military position as commander of the Xinjiang Military Region and who had also served as First Secretary of the Xinjiang office of the Chinese Communist Party, as well as member of the XUAR People's Council.

The concept behind these autonomous areas has to do with the PRC policies toward non-Han people on a national level. Developed in the years leading up to and immediately following the formation of the PRC, the idea was to both to distance the Party from the assimilationist attitude of the Guomindang (GMD)[48] and to avoid encouraging separatism in key frontier areas. The Chinese People's Political Consultative Conference, held in September of 1949, passed a Common Programme which guaranteed the equality among "nationalities" (Ch. *Minzu* 民族),

[45] Zhang and Cappelletti (2012).

[46] On Uygur society before 1949, see Hann (2008).

[47] McMillen (1984).

[48] Millward (2007), Ch. 5.

and announced that areas with large concentrations of non-Han peoples would enjoy an autonomous status, though their territories would remain inalienable parts of the PRC. One of the key tasks of the new Chinese government was to identify which groups, within China's vast and diverse ethnic landscape, would qualify as "minority nationalities" (*shaoshu minzu* 少数民族), and would consequently be eligible to be granted with a special status and preferential policies within the society, with an autonomous administrative area where the official and educational use of a non-Chinese language, the promotion of local cultural characteristics, a certain number of local officials belonging to the minority which represents the majority in the area in the regional government system (superior—a certain percentage—to that of officials of other nationalities) and other rights were going to be guaranteed.

The process of selection of recognized ethnic groups involved official teams of ethnographers and sociologists conducting fieldwork and mapping the territory, teams committed to applying Stalin's definition of "nation" as "a historically constituted, stable community of people, formed on the basis of a common language, territory, economic life and psychological make-up manifested in a common culture".[49] After the missions undertaken by the Chinese ethnographers and sociologists, by 1955 around five hundred groups had already applied for the legal status of national minority. The authorities of the Commission for Nationalities' Affairs (民族事务委员会 *Minzu shiwu weiyuanhui*, known today as the State Ethnic Affairs Commission) eventually acknowledged 55 "national minorities", which, with the Han, represented the 56 official nationalities of China. In Xinjiang, the process of identification of nationalities generated thirteen groups.[50]

In the early half of the 50s, the pastoral areas, mainly steppe, populated by Kazakhs were mostly excluded from the Communist agrarian reform, mainly because they were not considered suitable for cultivation. Only after Mao's directive of July 1955 which ordered a faster pace of collectivization, reform measures in the pastoral areas of Xinjiang were implemented.[51] In the autumn of 1958, the regional government

[49] Sentence by Stalin in a 1953 speech, quoted in MacKerras (1994, p. 141).

[50] See the section on Xinjiang's population at the beginning of this chapter. For the concept of ethnicity, see the conclusive chapter in this book.

[51] McMillen (1979, p. 154).

started to establish communes in the agricultural areas of Xinjiang. In six months, around 93% of the agrarian population and 70% of the pastoral herdsmen were included in the commune system. A large number of agricultural laborers were engaged in labor-intensive capital production[52] in the communes. According to the available historical sources, the regional leadership soon became aware of the difficulty for minority nationals to accept universal collectivization, and started to slow down the process. The pastoral areas in the North of Xinjiang were more heavily impacted by the process than the grain-producing Tarim Basin in the South,[53] this is why policies were softened especially in that area.

In the 50s, the central government invested heavily in capital construction in Xinjiang. During this period, the bingtuan and local army units restored the old transportation network and built new highways turning Urumqi into a transportation hub. The Urumqi-Korla and the Kashgar-Tashkurgan highways were renovated in 1958. The construction of the Xinjiang (Urumqi)-Lanzhou railroad started in 1955 and was concluded in early 1961. In 1949, the gross value of industrial output was 81 million RMB, which increased to 446 million RMB in 1957 and to 636 million RMB in 1965.[54] During the first FYP (1953–1957), 63.1% of the total state capital investment were directed to the interior regions of China, and 68% of the 694 industrial projects were implemented in Central and Western provinces. This trend continued during the third and fourth FYP periods (1966–1975). From 1965 to the early 1970s, the central government started the implementation of a massive secret plan, known as the Third Front policy (*sanxian jianshi* 三线建设), aimed at developing modern industries in parts of the country which were considered to be safe from possible invasion and bombing by the USSR. In Xinjiang, military and nuclear industries were built up or expanded under this policy umbrella, but the need for basic industries was overlooked.

The Han population, especially migrants from Inner China settled in the region as bingtuan residents, was particularly close to the Mao's

[52] An in-depth account on the agricultural reform in Xinjiang in the 1950s can be found in Warikoo (2016).

[53] Ibid., pp. 140–143.

[54] Ibid., p. 166, Table 11.1.

leftist positions, while the regional leaders were labeled as rightists. During the Cultural Revolution and the turbulent years preceding Mao's death, the clashes between these two factions became more and more violent, causing more deaths of the Uyghur revolts altogether.[55] During those years, a difficult-to-define number of mosques and madrasas[56] have been destroyed.

Following the death of President Mao Zedong, the Reform era of the 1980s had a deep impact on the socio-political and economic situation in the region. The new historical context opened the way to a period of relative freedom, development of the market economy and new ideas from the West. While the bingtuan system was dismantled in the other Chinese provinces and regions,[57] in Xinjiang the organization became stronger, and acted as catalyst for new waves of migrants. At the same time, archive pictures of the period[58] show Muslim minorities, mainly Uyghurs, marching freely on the streets of Urumqi to demonstrate against discrimination and to call for more religious freedom.

The situation changed completely after 1989: During the 1990s, there was a stiffening and strengthening process of the policies related to language, religion and political representation, the direction of which was clearly toward a more accentuated "sinicization", or integration of the region into the Han core. Key religious sites were closed, religious and popular festivals prohibited,[59] while a difficult-to-define number of mosques have been destroyed or closed.[60] The result of those politics

[55] Millward (2004).

[56] Koranic schools.

[57] They were not established only in Xinjiang, but also in other 13 provinces and regions. For instance, see He and Shi (1994).

[58] Visible in Dru Gladney (1991).

[59] The most important *mazar* (tomb of saint) in Southern Xinjiang named Ordam was eventually closed in 1997, and the annual festival which was taking place there, attracting up to twenty thousand pilgrims a day, was not allowed to be performed anymore. Officially, Ordam Mazar is now an archeological site in the Gobi/Taklamakan desert, preserved by the Department of Cultural Affairs of Yuepuhu County; in fact, it is not accessible due to the permanent presence of the police. On Ordam Mazar, see Minoru Sawada (2001a, b), Jarring (1935), and Dawut and Harris (2002).

[60] In the whole region, it is still possible to see big and small mosques closed with a padlock. As a reference, see Kuo (2019).

consisted mainly in an increased number of violent incidents across the whole region, from explosions in buildings and buses in Urumqi and in other main urban centers,[61] to the Ghulja events of 1997.[62]

2.3.3 *Twenty-First Century Xinjiang*

The history of twenty-first-century Xinjiang is significant mainly for the fast implementation of developmental policies, eventually aimed at the ultimate stabilization and integration of the region into the Han core. The main narrative promoted by the Chinese government through media and White Papers is that everything related to the Han culture is associated with modernity and comfort, while whatever is linked to Uyghurs and their culture means backwardness and underdevelopment. This "minoritization" process is pursued since the 1990s, and it is evident even to tourists traveling to the region: Every monument hosts a performance by Uyghur dancers and musicians, an ethnicity which is represented as the symbol of good craftsmanship and of an exotic way of life.[63] Considered as unapt to live in a modern context, Uyghurs are associated either with a remote, exotic and fictional past or with burglary and crime perpetuated in Chinese cities. Efforts to open the region to foreign investments and trade have been made since the 1980s: In January 1988, the State Council approved a nine-point preferential policy for the region, which has the merit of having brought a rapid growth in foreign trade. Five cities—Aksu, Korla, Changji, Turpan and Hami—have been exempted from customs duties along with those—Urumqi, Yining, Shihezi and Kashgar—which were already enjoying this facilitation. Procedures for border trade were simplified and the regional government was given more power to deal with foreign partners. The most remarkable change in Xinjiang's export items in the 1980s was that the primary products like agricultural and mineral raw materials of the 1950s and early 1960s were replaced by light industry products and processed commodities. By the end of the 1980s, commercial activities had already started to flourish along the borders of the Ili, Tacheng, Altai, Kizilsu and Kashgar

[61] Witnesses accounts have been collected by the author from 2007 to 2012.

[62] Called Ghulja massacre by the Uyghur political groups outside of China, due to the censorship and sensitivity of the issues, there are no reliable reports on the events. Millward (2004) and Dillon (2004, pp. 125–126) provide some accounts.

[63] See Schein (2000).

prefectures. In 1989, the region extended its commercial activities to other Soviet republics beyond Central Asia, establishing trade relations with Mongolia and Eastern Europe. From 1992 onward, Central Asian countries accounted for more than half of the region's foreign trade.

After the initial stages of the plan for the development of the West (西部大开发 *Xibu Da Kaifa*) in 2000,[64] aimed at promoting the infrastructural and economic development of the Western and interior regions of China, the 11 September 2001 attacks changed the whole situation. It was only then that the Chinese government acknowledged in front of the rest of the world that the country was suffering from a terrorist threat domestically, and that all the raids carried on in Xinjiang during the previous decades had, in fact, terrorist origins. Beijing changed its terminology related to Uyghur discontent: Uyghur became terrorists, and their protests became closely related to international Islamic terrorism and separatism. The Uyghur Turkestan Islamic Party (TIP)[65] would have alleged links to Al Qaeda and Hizb ut-Tahrir. The main narrative became in a certain sense ambiguous: When the government pointed at attracting investments and business activities in the region, the terrorist threat was scaled down, while when there was the need to justify crackdowns on Uyghurs, a renewed terrorist threat reappeared in the official discourse.

With the goal of developing a spirit of collaboration, and starting to set up confidence-building measures, a regional cooperation organization, Shanghai Five, was established after the meeting of the presidents of China, Russia, Kazakhstan, Kyrgyzstan and Tajikistan, held in Shanghai on 26 April 1996. After the sixth anniversary of the foundation of this regional organization, a newly named Shanghai Cooperation Organization (SCO) was established in Shanghai in June 2001, allying China, Russia, Tajikistan, Kyrgyzstan, Uzbekistan and Kazakhstan against terrorism, while in Xinjiang increasingly repressive policies were matched with new economic stimulus. The eastward expansion of NATO, the strengthening of the US-Japan security alliance and common aspirations regarding a multipolar world, brought China and Russia closer. During the St. Petersburg summit in June 2002, a trade component was added to the mainly security-focused activities of the SCO.

[64] Goodman (2004).

[65] Reed and Raschke (2010).

The Urumqi demonstrations of July–September 2009, during which at least 200 people died,[66] gave the final push to the developmental policies promoted by the center: the "19 provinces and municipalities help Xinjiang" plan (Ch. *Shijiu shengshi yuanzhu Xinjiang*), and the establishment of two Special Economic Zones (SEZ) in Kashgar and Korgas in 2010, represent, despite occasional episodes of violence toward Han immigrants especially in Southern Xinjiang,[67] the almost complete incorporation of the region in the allegedly modern Han Chinese context, and its preparation to join the soon-to-be-launched China-proposed Belt and Road Initiative.

2.4 Macroeconomic Profile

The regional macroeconomic profile of Xinjiang has been shaped by Beijing's policies at least since the 1950s, when the region came under the control of the Chinese Communist Party and Wang Zhen. At the same time, many of these policies had indeed been inherited from the Qing Dynasty. We can then say that the regional economic performance depends on a top-down process which sees national authorities defining directions and targets, and generating major fluctuations in the macroeconomic dynamics. Large-scale schemes and fiscal facilitations, encouragement of migrations and investments from Inner China, launch of foreign policy initiatives involving Central Asia all have a strong impact on XUAR economy. As it happens in the theory of "quantum entanglement"—a physical phenomenon that occurs when pairs or groups of particles are generated, interact or share spatial proximity in ways such that the quantum state of each particle cannot be described independently of the state of the others, even when the particles are separated by a large distance—what Beijing decides and what happens in the center have an impact on China's Muslim Far Northwest.

In consideration of these broader dynamics, the BRI—launched in 2013—represented a watershed in the economic development in Xinjiang, not only because of the investments targeting the region after the announcement of this foreign policy scheme, but in particular due

[66] Millward (2009). The number does not exceed 200 because in the case of more than 200 deaths the UN observers would have been entitled to request a visit to the region.

[67] On economic development and the recent episodes of violence, see the conclusive chapter in this work.

to the socio-economic and political changes that Xinjiang experienced in the years previous to its implementation. In order to provide a sense of these changes, it is useful to look at the performance of the regional economy in a time period spanning from 2009 to 2016.[68]

2.4.1 Xinjiang Development in the 1990s

During the latter half of the 1980s, the Chinese central government announced its intention to "seize an historic opportunity", launching an ambitious policy to "open up Xinjiang to the world[69]". Beijing long-term plan consisted in setting up SEZs, expanding border trade and pouring massive investments into infrastructure and capital construction in the region, in line with the strategy originally designed for coastal China, and praised for its alleged potential spillover effects. The central authorities declared that the province would become a regional powerhouse, basically thanks to massive investments both in the cotton-producing areas and in social infrastructure projects which would have risen the living standards of the whole population. In fact, economic zones were set up in Xinjiang, mainly in Urumqi, Shihezi, Bole, Yining, Changji, Wujiaqu and Tacheng. Despite these areas in Northern Xinjiang were officially proclaimed as of the same kind as those in the coastal provinces, in reality they were mainly "new development areas" (xin kaifa qu 新开发区), "border economic cooperation areas" (bianjing jingji hezuo qu 边境经济合作区) and "economic and technological development zones" (jingji jishu kaifa qu 经济技术开发区). In line with the policy of "developing the North, and leaving the South aside",[70] all those areas are located in Northern Xinjiang, while Southern Xinjiang registered the lowest living standards on a regional level, and in some of its districts even on a national basis. In these areas of new development, the same preferential fiscal régimes of the SEZs established in

[68] The last available data from the statistical yearbooks are those related to 2016.

[69] According to the interviews conducted by the author, the 1980s have been a time of openness and dynamism in the region, when local people could still have a role in the decision-making process by staging protests and demonstrations on the streets for any kind of reasons. The political climate changed across the country after the facts of Tiananmen in 1989.

[70] Zhang and Cappelletti (2012).

the late 1970s had been applied. For instance, in June 1992, it was announced that the tax-sharing regulations enjoyed by coastal provinces would be applied to nine additional provinces and cities, including Xinjiang. Despite the emerging SEZs, foreign direct investments' inflow in Xinjiang remained extremely limited. This might be due to the remoteness of the region and to the frequent security alerts occurring for during the whole of the 1990s.

As additional measures, ethnic minority regions like XUAR would have been entitled to keep 80% of local taxes, against the usual 50%. If we consider the situation on a national basis, we can observe that Xinjiang was chosen by the central government as a special area, entitled to benefit from fiscal transfers from the central government, an exceptional place to be dealt with in a non-standard way. The commitment of the central government for developing the region can be assumed from two main indicators: Between 1991 and 1994, the province Gross Domestic Product (GDP) doubled from 7.5 to 15.5 billion RMB, with investments in infrastructures leaping from 7.3 to 16.5 billion RMB.

This developmental push was conceived with a close attention on keeping much of Xinjiang's economy tightly under the control of the national central state, outlining an idea on regional development which was different from those criteria underpinning the government strategy for Eastern China. Xinjiang's industries, up to now, remain predominantly state-owned, representing an anomaly in the national context. In 1996, 84% of the region's industrial assets were still publicly owned, one of the highest ratios in China. At the same time, Xinjiang's foreign direct investments were extremely low, with the region ranking 28th out of the 31 provinces in 1998 (0.05% of China's total). At the time, the fixed yearly subsidy provided by the central government amounted to 2 billion yuan, while another subsidy offsetting the remaining budget deficit. According to official statistical data, in 1998 the total transfer of capital from Beijing to Xinjiang amounted to 8.06 billion yuan. Such subsidies ranked Xinjiang as the fourth province most dependent on central subsidies, together with Tibet, Qinghai and Ningxia. It is also notable that while the budgetary revenue of Xinjiang almost tripled, between 1990 and 1998, to 6.54 billion yuan, budgetary expenditures grew faster over the same period, reaching 14.6 billion yuan. Even if data on Xinjiang budget deficit, fiscal transfers and subsidies from Beijing are considered politically sensitive, we can still say that, relying on officially released figures, large budget deficits still leave the provincial government highly dependent on Beijing's financial aid and support.

The beginning of the twenty-first century has been characterized by a ubiquitous and overall rhetoric of economic growth, development and welfare for all the nationalities in Xinjiang. Development projects and programs ranging from economic stimuli to exchanges in the educational field started to be implemented and they are still ongoing. The declared intentions behind these projects consisted in a fast economic growth which would have constituted an advantage to all the nationalities in Xinjiang, in the framework of a political view and an institutional mind-set focused on economic growth but with an allegedly closer attention to a more general and comprehensive concept of development. The main features of the development model implemented in Xinjiang are (a) a particular focus on capital-intensive sectors like real estate, large-scale infrastructures, agricultural and industrial enterprises, large-scale environmental systems; (b) programs and exchanges in the education field; (c) measures to encourage a deeper integration of the region into the Han core, and of the Uyghur population into a predominantly Han nation-state.

2.4.2 *Gross Domestic Product (GDP)*

The Statistical Yearbooks published by the National Bureau of Statistics of China are a useful source of official data and figures, which, due to the specific processes related to their compilation and the political aspects involved, need to be used with consideration.[71] The Xinjiang-related Statistical Yearbooks have been consulted at the National Library in Beijing and through the China Statistical Yearbooks Database (CSYD) called China Data Insights. During this process, I observed that data and figures concerning the GDP total value, as well as the related disaggregate records, are not consistent in tables of the same Yearbook and across different Yearbooks. This means that numeric figures related to the same item, for instance "GDP total value", differ according to the table of reference in the Yearbook, while data provided through percentages are generally more consistent. The process of double and multiple checking through interviews, participant observation and analysis of other primary

[71] Orlik (2011) and Wiemer (2004, p. 415, note 3) offer interesting insights on this issue.

sources is fundamental to confirm or either assess the variations across the collected information.

After consultations with Chinese journalists and academics working with statistical data, and following a multiple check process, I relied mainly on Xinjiang Statistical Yearbooks up to the year 2017 for realizing the graphs below in this chapter.

According to Statistical Yearbooks, from 2009 to 2016 the GDP of Xinjiang saw a constant progressive increase. In 2009, it was 427.705 billion yuan, with a registered increase of 8.1% over the previous year, a value coherent with the national data, 8.7%. In 2016, it amounted to 965.000 billion yuan, 3.1% more than the previous year, a lower percentage increase than the national-level one: 7.4%.

On a national level, Xinjiang ranked 25th in the list of the Chinese regions elaborated on the basis of the GDP added value, followed by Guizhou, Gansu, Hainan, Ningxia, Qinghai and Tibetan Autonomous Region (TAR). In 2016, it was ranked 26th before Gansu, Hainan, Ningxia, Qinghai and Tibet. While in 2009 Xinjiang was the second region with less GDP increase rate (8.1%) over the previous year, positioned at the 30th place in the interregional list ahead of Shanxi Province, in 2016 it raised to the 16th position. In 2009, the added value of the primary industry was 75.974 billion yuan, up by 4.5% over the previous year; that of the secondary industry was 192.959 billion yuan, up by 8.5%, while that of the tertiary industry reached 158.772 billion yuan, up by 9.2% over the previous year. In 2016, the added value of the primary industry was 164.900 billion yuan, 5.5% over the previous year; the secondary industry was 364.700 billion yuan, with a 1.4% increase over the previous year; the tertiary industry was 453.370 billion yuan, a 4.2% increase over the previous year.

In 2009, the per capita GDP, based on the permanent population, was 19.942 RMB (around US$2.920 considering the exchange rate at the time) for a total population of 21.590.000, up by 6.5% over the previous year. The intraregional ranking was low: 21 on 30 in terms of per capita GDP and 24 in terms of total population. In 2016, data change substantially: The per capita GDP raised to 40.564 (around US$5907.78 at the current exchange rate) for a total population of 23.980.000, with an increase of 1.3% over the previous year. The intraregional ranking did not register any relevant variation.

In 2009, the total consumer price index was up by 0.7%, registering an increase of 2.1% over the previous year. In 2016, it was 101.4, and

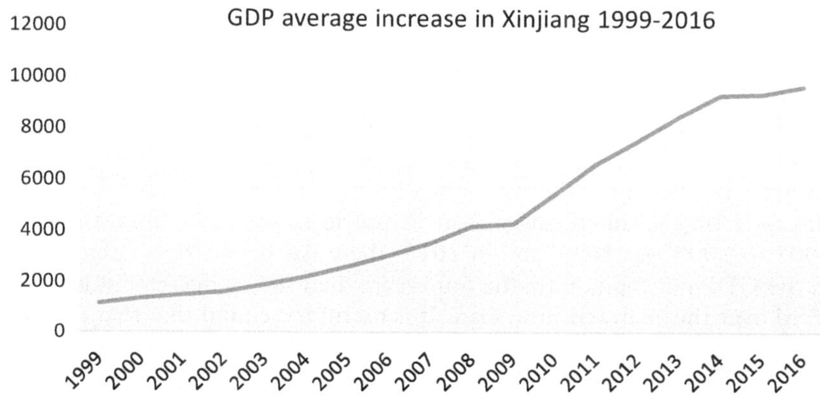

Fig. 2.1 GDP increase in Xinjiang 1999–2016 (100 million RMB)

the increase over the previous year was 2.2%. Considering the above figures, and confronting the data related to Xinjiang with those issued by other regions, the macroeconomic performance in XUAR can be considered satisfactory, and trends, annual increase rates and so forth are actually showing an ascending tendency. Xinjiang cannot thus be considered one of the poorest regions in China, but it still positions itself in the mid-low ranks in the intraregional statistics (Fig. 2.1).

According to the statistical data, the GDP average growth rate was 12%, in line with the national figure of 12% over the same time span. Nicholas Becquelin[72] argues that during the 1990s Xinjiang experienced a process of rapid and sustained economic growth (more than 10% per year on average), mainly due to the development policies implemented and developed at a regional level in 1992, following the first official calls to "Open Up the North-West", a development scheme aimed at investing in the Western regions. This GDP average growth rate was sustained in the 20 years from 1999 to 2019, mainly due to important investments in infrastructures and real estate, and to development plans which will be taken into analysis below in this chapter, as well as to the launch of the foreign policy scheme BRI, in 2013.

[72] Becquelin (2004, p. 363).

2.4.3 *Per Capita GDP*

The trend in the GDP performance in Xinjiang appears in Fig. 2.2 (1999–2016).

The increase rate of the per capita GDP in Xinjiang is 11%, slightly below the national figure of 12% for the same time span. Interestingly enough, in 2009 the GDP per capita increase rate over the previous year was only of 1%, much lower than in previous years (the increase from 2007 to 2008 was 16%), and in 2015, there has been a decrease of −2% in the GDP per capita rate, the only year when such a decrease was registered over the analyzed time span. It is useful to remind that that was the time when the "Strike Hard Campaign against Violent Terrorism" (*yanli daji baoli kongbu huodong zhuanxiang xingdong* 严厉打击暴力恐怖活动专项行动), launched in 2014, became operational, and the first ideological reeducation facilities were established in the region.

Nicholas Becquelin, quoting Wen Jun and Hu Angang (2001),[73] writes of an "outstanding economic growth" in Xinjiang, in line with Calla Wiemer assessments. Wiemer argues that "the PRC can claim

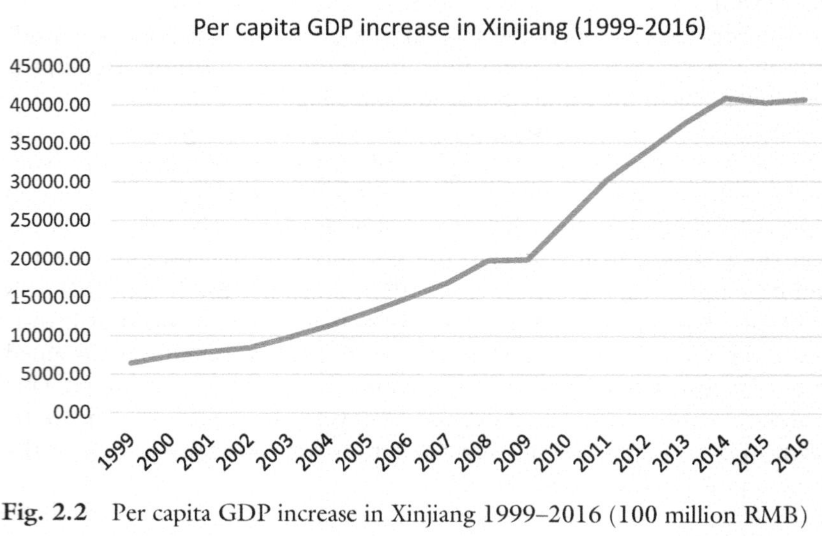

Fig. 2.2 Per capita GDP increase in Xinjiang 1999–2016 (100 million RMB)

[73]Becquelin (2004, p. 359), citing the work by Wen Jun and Hu Angang (2001).

striking achievements in the development of the region's economy over the last two decades".[74] In Becquelin (2004), we read: "From an economic standpoint, Xinjiang is highly atypical among the interior and Western provinces, as the only province with a GDP per capita above the national average (at the 12th position in provincial rankings). These economic achievements stand out more dramatically when considered against the wide interregional variation existing in China, since the first eleven ranking positions were occupied by coastal provinces". On the same note: "By the standards of inner China, - Wiemer[75] continues - Xinjiang today is extraordinarily well off". In particular, this author refers to the 10.3% GDP regional growth rate related to the 1978–2000 period, against the figure of 9.5% on a national scale. The rapid growth of the region's population is accounted as the main reason for the not consistent GDP growth margin on a per capita basis, since the regional data remain 8.4%, in fact not too different from the national figure of 8.1%. In the same analysis, Wiemer underlines, taking the 1990–2000 period as reference, a decreasing trend in relative terms, if the region is compared with the rest of China: Xinjiang annual per capita GDP growth stood at 7.8%, while the figure for China as a whole was 8.9%. Moving onward, in 2009 the annual per capita GDP was 19.942 yuan/person, with Xinjiang ranking 21st in the list of the 31 Chinese provinces, and 25th if we consider the overall GDP data.[76] This shift in GDP and growth parameters at the edge of the twenty-first century is worth of further analysis. Xinjiang's growth in the 1990s has been slower than other provinces, and the region was at the same low positions as Tibet, Gansu and Qinghai, all in the Northwestern part of China. What we can assess for the moment is that in the geographical context of Northwestern China, Xinjiang is still a faster-growing economy, but the speed of its growth is still slower than the coastal provinces and the national one.

[74] Wiemer (2004, p. 164).

[75] Wiemer (2004, p. 164).

[76] *Xinjiang Statistical Yearbook 2010*. The region is followed respectively by Guizhou, Gansu, Hainan, Ningxia, Qinghai and Tibet.

2.4.4 GDP Composition by Sector and Increase Rate

The composition of the three industries at the regional level in 2009 was: 17.8:45.1:37.1, and in 2016, it was 17.1:37.8:45.1. While the proportion of the agricultural sector remained stable, there has been an evident switch between industry and services: the increased attractiveness of the touristic sector for the Inner China's market and the enhanced importance of the logistics sector connected to the BRI and to the different economic corridors passing through Xinjiang, both contributed to the rise of the third sector. Interestingly enough, in the intraregional ranking table, in 2009 Xinjiang positioned itself 21st, 26th and 26th for its contribution to the regional economy's primary, secondary and tertiary industry, respectively. This contribution seems noticeably more substantial in 2016, when Xinjiang ranked 3rd (after Hainan and Heilongjiang), 25th and 19th in the three sectors, respectively, registering an important increase as far as the agricultural sector is concerned, and, on a lesser scale, of the service sector. As it is highlighted in Chapter 5 of this work, the process of transformation of small-plot agriculture into large-scale agribusiness, which started at the end of the years 2000s in the Southern part of the region, was precisely aimed at enhancing the productivity of the limited fertile land available in the region, as well as at increasing the output of the agricultural sector. These data demonstrate that this target has actually been reached. As mentioned, the increased contribution of the service sector can be linked to the raising numbers of tourists from Inner China and to the demand of related services, as well as to the logistic, trade and satellite activities generated by both development programs and the BRI in the region.

2.4.5 Primary Sector

The primary sector reported an 11% average increase rate from 1999 to 2016, a better performance in comparison with the national figure of 9% over the same time span. In 1999, the agricultural sector in Xinjiang accounted for 23% of the total regional GDP, while in 2009 it dropped to 18%, and in 2016 to a mere 13%, a national-level tendency which affects all Chinese regions and provinces and is due to the rapid increase in the contribution of the second and third sectors. At the national level, in 2009 the sector contributed to the total GDP value for 10.3%, and in 2016 it counted for 4.4% (Figs. 2.3 and 2.4).

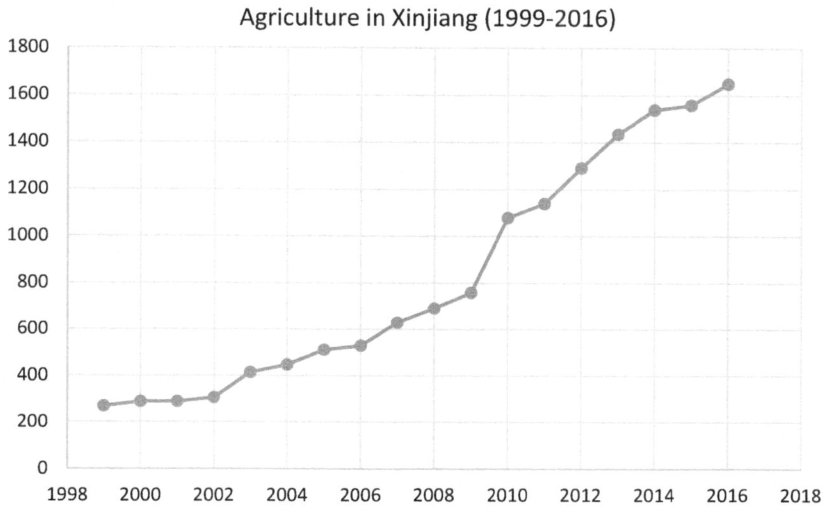

Fig. 2.3 Increase of the primary sector in Xinjiang—100 million RMB

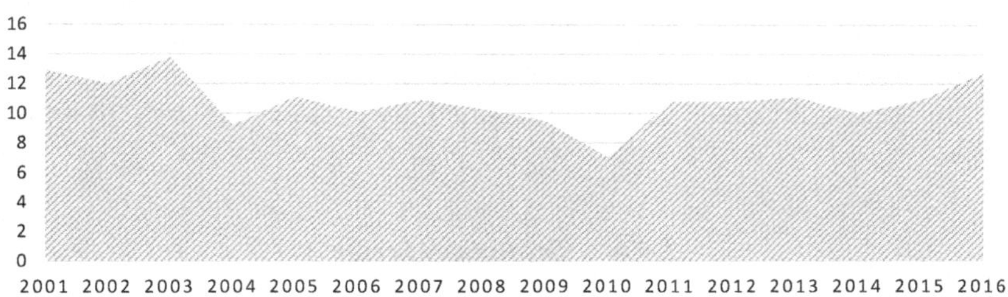

Fig. 2.4 Share of the contributions of the primary industry to the increase of the GDP in Xinjiang (%)

The total land area of the region consisted in 167 million hectares in 2009, and in 2016, it was reduced to less than 7 million hectares.[77] In 2009, only 41 million were cultivated, and about 68 million hectares,

[77] *Xinjiang Statistical Yearbook 2010* and *2017*. This decrease can be understood by looking at the policies on land use and at the strategic goal of the regional government to reduce the amount of land used for agriculture, reduce the workforce employed in the first sector and enhance the productivity of the reduced land by establishing an agribusiness sector.

41.2% of Xinjiang's total area, had been assessed as suitable for further developing agriculture, forestry and animal husbandry. Out of the 68 million hectares, 48 were natural grassland for grazing, 9 were available for reclamation, and over 4 million ready to be cultivated, while the rest consisted in man-made pastures. These numbers were significantly reduced in 2016, with 6.3 million of total cultivated land. Xinjiang is one of China's five major grazing areas. In addition, approximately 4.8 million hectares of land are available for forestry, including 1.5 million hectares suitable for forest products, with reserves of approximately 250 million cubic meters of timber. 1.2 million hectares are earmarked for construction.

Both in 2010 and in 2017, the land utilization rate is attested at a mere 38.64%; therefore, it is easy to understand the central government's policy of focusing on the region's land reserves and to their considerably high potential. In the *Xinjiang Statistical Yearbook 2017* (Table 6.1 "Natural Resources"), the land "yet to be used" in the region is reportedly assessed at 102.165.100 hectares, with a land utilization rate of still at 38.64%.

Xinjiang is a leading cotton-growing region, contributing to more than one-third of the national production. 2010s statistical data show that in 2009 grain crops are sown on 43% of the total cultivable area, whereas cotton is produced on 30% of it. 2016s data are different: 13% of the total cultivated area was destined to cotton and 14% to grain crops.

2.4.6 Secondary Sector

The secondary sector grew at a rate of 13% in the selected time span, taking into consideration that a relatively high percentage of this growth is represented by the dominant extractive and disproportionately large construction sectors. The national figure for the same period is 12%. In 2009, the sector contributed 45% to the regional GDP, more or less in line with the national figure of 46.3% in the same year. In 2016, the secondary sector contributed to the regional GDP for 31.6%, in line with the national figure of 31.7%. At both the regional and national levels, construction and heavy industry have a big share in shaping the total GDP (Fig. 2.5).

Oil, coal and gas represent the key component of the commodities' production in Xinjiang and make the extractive industry a prominent

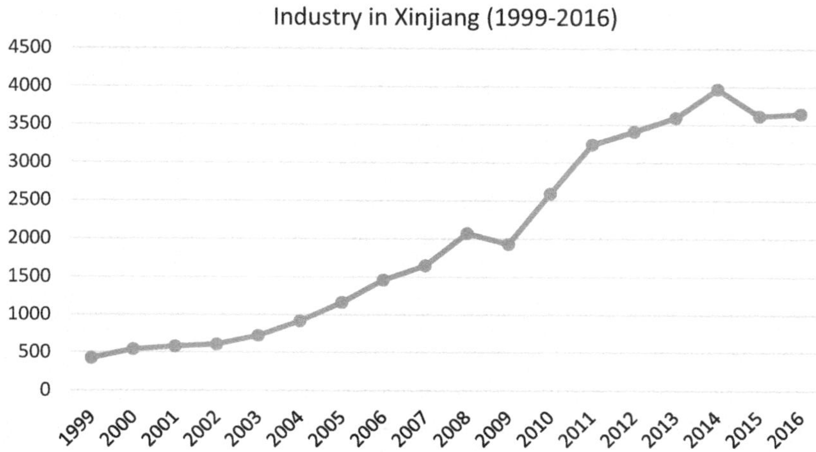

Fig. 2.5 Increase of the secondary sector in Xinjiang—100 million RMB

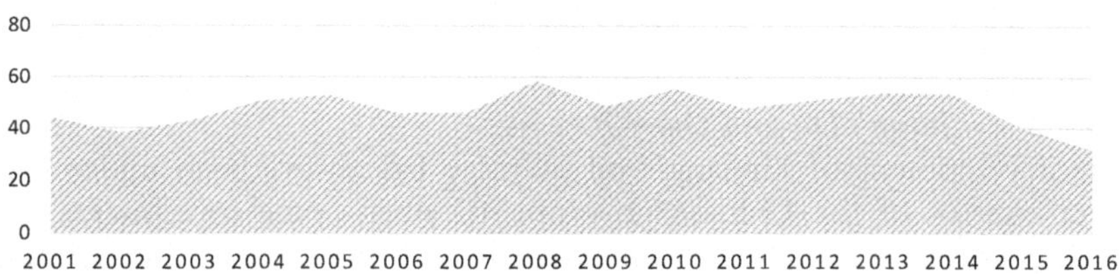

Fig. 2.6 Share of the contributions of the secondary industry to the increase of the GDP in Xinjiang (%)

part of the region's economic activities. In the Statistical Yearbooks, these commodities are included in the secondary sector. Chaudhuri (2005)[78] argues that the dominant role of heavy industries and the underdevelopment of light industries are the major weaknesses of Xinjiang's industrial sector (Fig. 2.6).

2.4.6.1 Resources

China is a fast-growing economy with one of the biggest populations in the world, which overtook the United States as the world's largest crude

[78] P. 26.

importer between 2010 and 2015 (the two countries account for almost a third of world oil consumption) and in 2010 surpassed Japan and raised to the second position just after the United States.[79] Since 1993, the country became a net importer of petroleum products and, since 1996, of crude oil. At that time, the importance of Xinjiang's reserves, as well as its proximity to the resources-rich Central Asian countries, increased considerably. The reliance on imports rose by 15% in 2002 (when it reached 71 million tons), at that time of heightening concerns about the Chinese economy starting to live under the threat of fluctuating oil prices. On 4 February 2002, *Xinhua News Agency* published a report titled "Xinjiang's 'black and white'[80] strategy boosts economy and living standards", it is predicted that the region "will become the energy base of the country for the 21st century", referring to the proved reserves of petroleum amounting to over 2.5 billion tons, and to the 700 billion cubic meters of natural gas reserves. Xinjiang is currently the second largest crude oil producer in China: It became so in 2008, when the output reached 27.4 million tons, 1 million tons more in comparison with 2007.[81] In the same year, 30.6% of the total energy production in the region was of crude oil.[82] This large oil-producing area has a combined capacity of 20 million tons per year.[83]

2.4.6.2 Xinjiang's Oil and Other Resources

The development of Xinjiang's oil industry has always been under the strict control of the Chinese government, albeit some investments by foreign oil companies have been allowed. The main Xinjiang oilfield at Karamay (meaning "black oil" in Uyghur), part of the Junggar Basin and close to the border with Kazakhstan, where the headquarters of the Xinjiang Petroleum Administrative Bureau (Xinjiang Shiyou Guanli ju 新疆石油管理局) have been established, was opened in 1955,[84] when

[79] "China passes Japan as Second-Largest Economy", by David Barboza, in *The New York Times*, 15 August 2010.

[80] The "black and white" strategy is a government plan to make Xinjiang economy focus on basically two sectors: crude oil and cotton.

[81] "Xinjiang Becomes China's Second Largest Crude Oil producer", *Xinhua News Agency*, 2 January 2009.

[82] *Xinjiang Statistical Yearbook 2010*, section 15.1.

[83] "Exxon, Shell, Gazprom Buy 15% each in China Pipeline", *Bloomberg*, 1 July 2002.

[84] With the technical and financial support of the Soviets.

the city started to grow into Xinjiang's main petrochemical refining center. The Xinjiang Petroleum Administrative Bureau, the state body responsible for prospecting for oil and managing the oil industry, has shifted its exploration activities from field to field for decades, in search of commercially exploitable oil sources. By late 1998, the focus of those prospections moved to Karamay. At that time, the new discoveries of oil and gas, together with an ambitious investment program conceived by the local government, already led to the official assumption that the oilfield would have been at the forefront of regional and also national development in the early years of the twenty-first century.

Although most extraction of oil and natural gas has so far taken place in Northern Xinjiang, Chinese (and, since 1994, foreign) firms have focused their prospection efforts on the Tarim Basin, despite the formidable obstacles related to drilling in the Taklamakan Desert. Claims of new findings are published frequently, and Chinese estimates of Xinjiang's petrochemical reserves climb higher and higher.

In 2008, the total output of natural gas was attested at 3.42 billion cubic meters, representing 24.8% of the total regional energy consumption. While PetroChina doubled its annual gas output in Xinjiang to 30 billion cubic meters by 2015, Sinopec wants to increase its output nearly five times to 5 billion cubic meters a year. The region represents the source of almost 30% of China's total natural gas output.

Estimates put Xinjiang's coal reserves at about 38% of the national total. Coal production in the Northwestern autonomous region surpassed 100 million tons in 2010, Xinjiang Daily, citing local authorities, reported on 11 January. In 2008, 46.5% of the total energy consumption was represented by coal, and in 2016, the share of coal raised to 54.3% of the total energy consumption. The region is rich in coal mines and the high consumption of this easily available resource made Urumqi one of the most polluted cities in China.

In August 1996, the Institute of Remote Sensing Applications, a specialist organ of the Chinese Academy of Social Sciences, reported that the analysis of satellite and other remote-sensing data suggested the possibility that there may be large-scale gold deposits on the West of the Tian Shan Mountains. Gold prospecting began in the Kizilsu Kyrgyz Autonomous Prefecture in 1998, after agreements on cooperation had been signed by the local mining department, the Australian mining company Broken Hill Proprietary and Barrick Resources from Canada. The prefecture, located at the point where the Tian Shan and the Kunlun mountain ranges meet, is on the Pamir River, and it is thought to be the most likely site for gold. Kizilsu is an area of particularly harsh climate that has made it extremely difficult for prospecting. Since the gold reserves represent a sensitive topic, the results of the explorations and the data about them are unknown. The region also has substantial reserves of nonferrous metals such as copper and nickel, which, due to the fact that discoveries are recent, are difficult to assess in terms of figures.

After 17 years of work, in 2009 Chinese geologists discovered the country's first 10,000-ton level leaching sandstone-type uranium deposit in the Yili Basin, which is in the Northwestern Xinjiang Uygur Autonomous Region. Yili became then the country's largest source of leaching sandstone-type uranium deposits. General engineer Wang Cheng declared that the deposit would produce more than 300 billion yuan (about 40 billion US dollars) worth of uranium, coal and associated minerals, with coal resources totaling to more than 4 billion tons. He said the find would boost the development of an existing large-scale coal and electricity production base in the region. Recent discoveries of iron, copper, zinc, mica, asbestos and limestone reserves make the region a key mineral ore.

2.4.6.3 Infrastructural Projects

The development of petroleum industry in Xinjiang largely depends on improved transportation and delivery systems: The Karamay-Urumqi oil pipeline was built already in 1982, but major construction works on oil and gas pipelines in Xinjiang started in the 1990s. From 1993 to 1996, the Lunnan-Korla, Shanshan-Urumqi, Cainan-Shixi-Karamay, and Tazhong4-Lunnan pipelines were completed. In order to deliver Xinjiang natural gas to the Eastern provinces (西气东输 *xiqi dongshu*, meaning that the Western gas would have to migrate to the East), in the mid-2000s the central government started the construction of a 4000-km-long pipeline from Lunnan to Shanghai via Jingbian in Shaanxi Province. As part of a long-term plan to connect this energy artery with major oil- and gas-producing areas of Kazakhstan and Russia, at the time China had already signed deals with the government of Kazakhstan for the construction of a 3000 km pipeline across the country. Under this light, the significance of the BRI becomes more clear.

In 2004, around two-thirds of China's oil imports, mainly from the Middle East and Africa, had to pass through the Straits of Malacca, where they were vulnerable to piracy, terrorism or US blockades.

Chinese leaders thus urgently wanted to develop more secure, continental sources of energy. The same political calculus evidently applied to the flagship project called "Great Development of the West" and to the current China-Pakistan Economic Corridor (CPEC) which is being developed under the BRI umbrella.[85] According to the "2010 SINOPEC Annual Report and Accounts", "new discoveries were made following the exploration of Tarim Basin's Maigaiti Slope, Tahe Oilfield and Jiyang Depression". Those oilfields in Xinjiang are all located in the Southern part of the region, far from the already known and normally exploited fields or the North (mainly close to Karamay). According to Professor Guo Haitao, researcher at the Chinese University of Petroleum (*Zhongguo Shiyou Daxue* 中国石油大学) in Beijing, whose interview by *Le Monde* has been published in English translation by *TIME* magazine,[86] Xinjiang comes out as crucial for the national strategy on natural resources. A pipeline of more than 2.800 km already connects Atyrau in Northwestern Kazakhstan to Alatau Pass in Xinjiang and then in the region to the PetroChina Dushanzi Petrochemical Company, a pipeline which has been operating smoothly since May 2006 replacing rail shipments of Kazak oil. In May 2019, the pipeline has sent 119 million tons of crude oil from Kazakhstan to China, with a trade value totaling 443.8 billion yuan (approximately 64.2 billion US dollars). These infrastructures allow oil imported from Central Asia and produced in Xinjiang to be delivered to coastal industrial provinces in Eastern China, since the oilfields closer to these dynamic coastal zones in the North-East are emptying. In 2019, China has imported 3.7 million tons of crude oil, worth 10.4 billion yuan, during the first four months via the Alatau Pass.

The pipeline helped diversify Kazakhstan's crude oil exports, ensured the crude oil supply for two major refineries in Eastern Kazakhstan, and expanded China's crude oil import channels. Under the BRI, energy cooperation between the two countries has been strengthened.

"In the East, reserves of black gold are declining after decades of exploitation. The petroleum of Xinjiang offers a very real margin of

[85] If the CPEC will be successfully finalized—and this depends on how the Chinese government will cope with the political and economic risk connected with the situation in Pakistan and the CPEC-related projects—it will allow imports of oil and gas from the Arabian Sea through the land route Gwadar-Kashgar, in Xinjiang, and then directly to the more developed Eastern parts of China, avoiding the US-influenced Strait of Malacca.

[86] *TIME World*, "In China's Wild West, a 'Black Gold' Rush Takes Place", 23 May 2011.

development", argues Dr. Guo. "The high prices of imported oil are a heavy burden, and China has to change its rate of energy consumption, become more efficient, and reach an equilibrium with available oil stocks".[87]

In the five-year plan adopted in March 2011, which guided Beijing strategic choices until 2016, there was the anticipation of a reduction in the historical dependence of the national energy consumption on carbon—which at the time counted for two-thirds of China energy needs—by relying more on alternative and renewable energy. New investments in oil prospections, mainly in Xinjiang and Inner Mongolia, were also predicted, within the framework of the five-year plan.

2.4.7 *Tertiary Sector*

This sector registered an average annual growth of 13%, in line with the national-level increase of 13% over the same time span (Fig. 2.7). Its weight on the total GDP at the regional level increased recently, as it is shown in the Fig. 2.8.

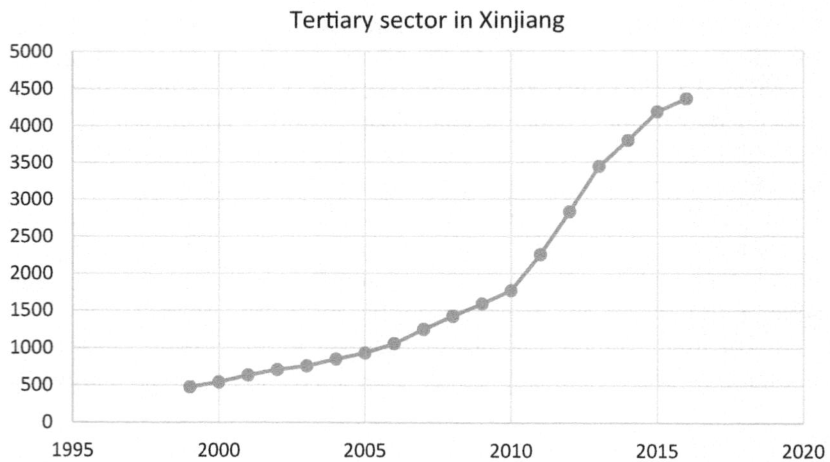

Fig. 2.7 Increase of the tertiary sector in Xinjiang—100 million RMB

[87] Ibid.

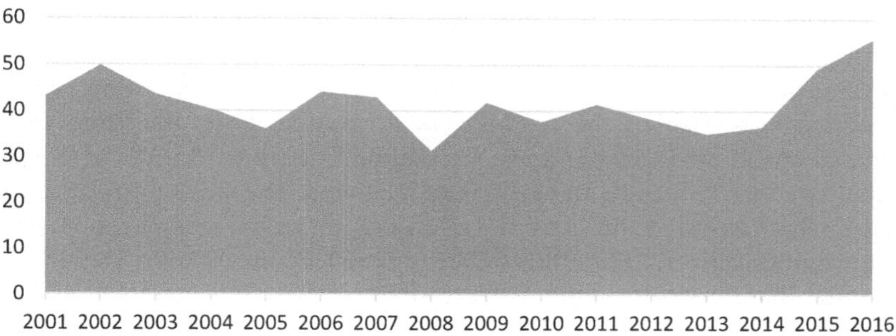

Fig. 2.8 Share of the contributions of the tertiary industry to the increase of the GDP in Xinjiang (%)

In 2016, the tertiary sector in Xinjiang accounted for the 55.6% of the total GDP, while, on a national level, it weighed 58.2%, absorbing surplus labor from the primary sector in all Chinese provinces and regions. Taking the time span 1978–2001 as reference, Chaudhuri (2005) argues that surplus labor from the primary industry in Xinjiang has gradually been absorbed by the tertiary sector. In absolute terms, the tertiary industry share on the total regional GDP value in the selected time span increased dramatically, registering, by 2001, a major increase of 72% in the employed labor force.[88]

2.4.8 *Agriculture, Industry and Services*

All three sectors registered a progressive increase in absolute terms over the chosen time span, and, if we take into account the GDP composition by sector, we can see that agriculture and services show bigger percentages in the regional GDP over time, while the relative weight of industry on the GDP declined. If we compare the figures of the secondary sector with data related to the year 2000, the increase in absolute values was relevant: The production of secondary commodities in Xinjiang stood at the time at 43%, against a national figure of 50.9%. This predominance of the secondary sector in the year 2000 was in line with the national figure, and, according to the classical concept of a developed economy,

[88]Chaudhuri (2005, p. 14).

Xinjiang, and the whole of China, was still a developing economy going through a phase of industrialization.[89] In 2001, heavy industry counted for almost 2/3 of Xinjiang's GDP, with oil and gas exploitation representing almost half of the region's fiscal revenues.[90] In the same year, services stood at 35.9% vis-a-vis the national figure of 33.2%. This was mainly due to Xinjiang's vast distances relative to the small population, a factor which boosted the share of GDP deriving from transport, post and telecommunications. The 2009s 37% regional figure vis-a-vis the 43.4% national share does not imply a decrease in services, but mainly a relative increase in the other sectors.

In the analysis and interpretation of these data, we need to take into consideration that part of the regional production is necessarily not computed in the final GDP-related figures: Broad segments of the grey and underground economy, as well as corruption and system-malfunctioning dynamics failing in correctly registering and declaring earnings, surely play a role in the accuracy of our computations. During our fieldwork, we could assess that data concerning the primary and tertiary sectors might be underestimated, mainly for the outstanding impact of shadow economy on the agriculture-related works, as well as on transportation and logistics. Due to the lack of estimates on the extent of the underground market in Xinjiang's economy, it is impossible to get an idea of an approximate margin of error in official figures.

2.4.9 Central, Provincial/Regional, Local and International Investments

In 2009, XUAR ranked 25th among the provinces and regions listed in the table "Total Investment in Fixed Assets in the Whole Country",[91] while in 2016 it ranked 23rd. Data and figures related to 2009 show the total investments in fixed assets (*guding zichan touzi* 固定资产投资)

[89] We cannot uncritically rely on data provided by the Chinese central government though, since as long as China was classified as a "developing country", international funding for development, mainly from United Nations (UN) and World Bank (WB), is easy to be obtained. China is still now, in 2019, considered a developing country by the World Trade Organization (WTO), a status which allows Beijing to claim a preferential treatment in international trade.

[90] Becquelin (2004, p. 362).

[91] XJSY, table 2001.

amounted to almost 283 billion RMB, vis-a-vis the 1999 figure of 53.465.000.000 RMB: The 1999 figure increased five times, registering an average annual growth rate of 18.6%. In 2016, the total investments in fixed assets increased to almost 100 billion RMB.

The sources of investments are illustrated, from 1999 to 2016, in Figs. 2.9, 2.10, 2.11, 2.12, 2.13, 2.14, and 2.15.

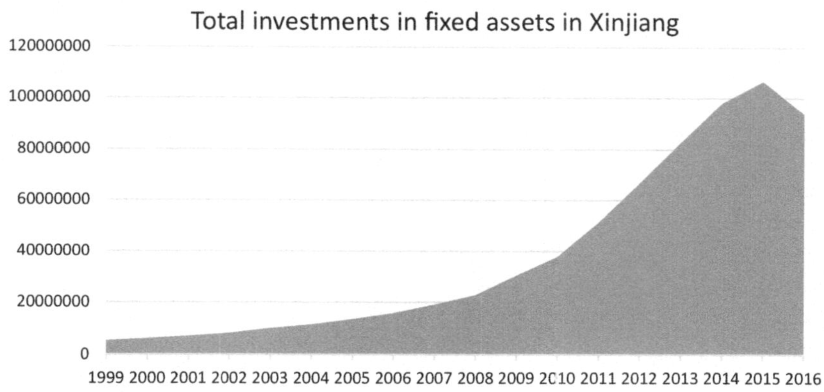

Fig. 2.9 Total investments in fixed assets in Xinjiang (1999–2016, 10.000 RMB)

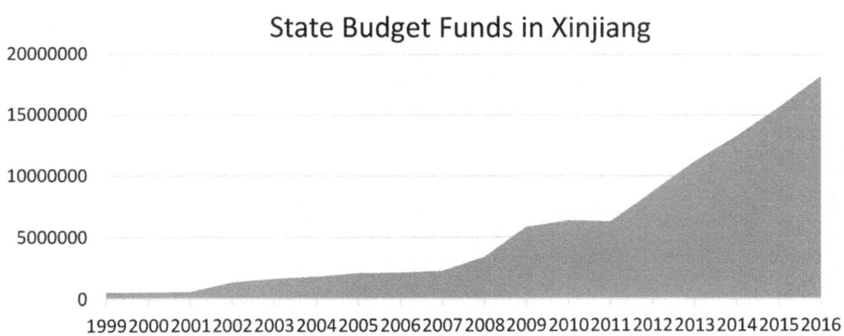

Fig. 2.10 State budget funds in Xinjiang (1999–2016, 10.000 RMB)

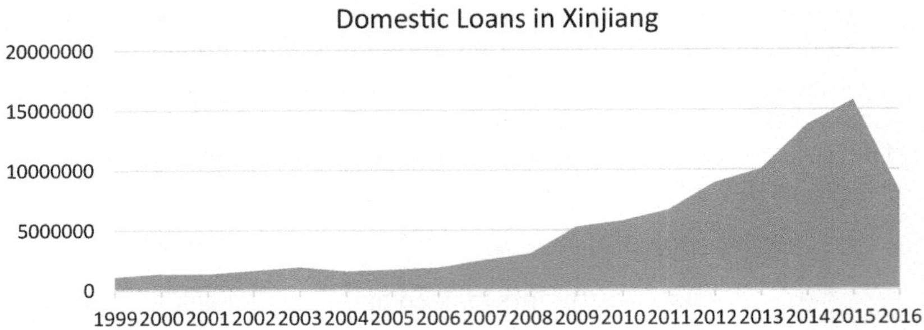

Fig. 2.11 Domestic loans in Xinjiang (1999–2016, 10.000 RMB)

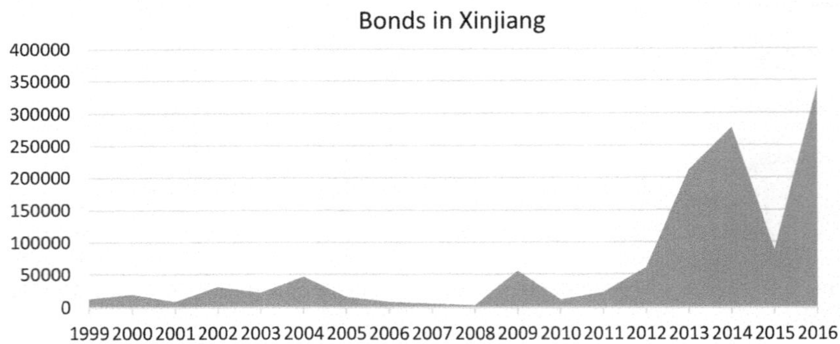

Fig. 2.12 Bonds in Xinjiang (1999–2016, 10.000 RMB)

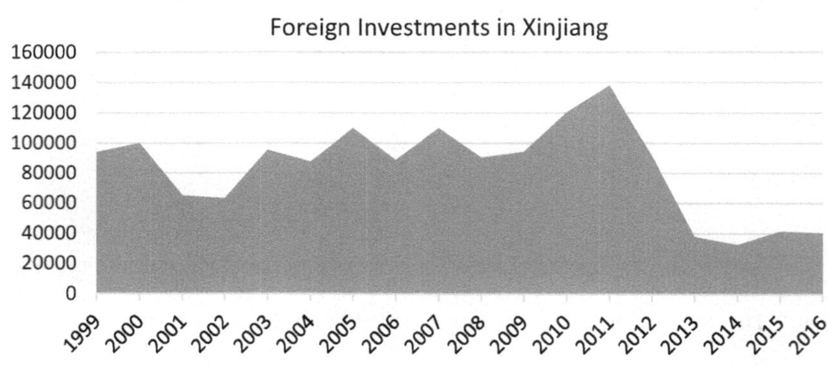

Fig. 2.13 Foreign investments in Xinjiang (1999–2016, 10.000 RMB)

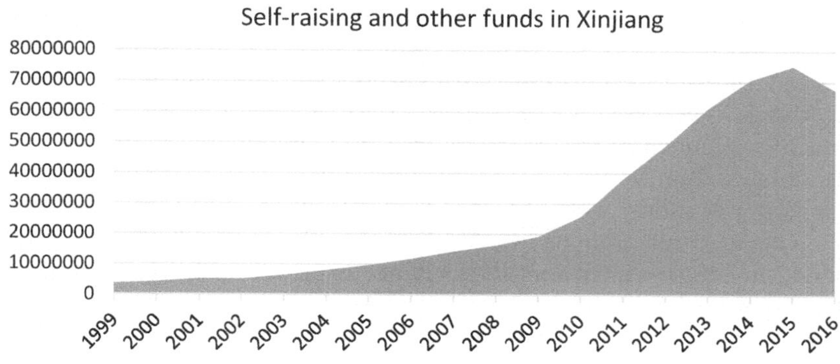

Fig. 2.14 Self-raising and other funds in Xinjiang (1999–2016, 10.000 RMB)

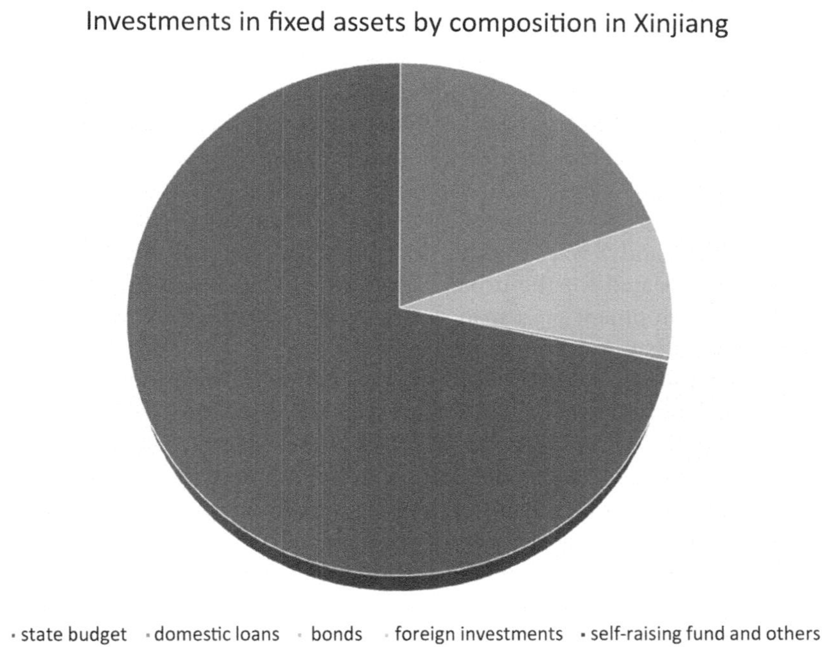

Fig. 2.15 Investments in fixed assets by composition (2016, 10.000 RMB)

In Fig. 2.14, the item "Self-raising and other funds" is dominant (72%) and represents SOEs' profits which are reinvested in fixed assets, instead of being redistributed to stakeholders. In Chinese Statistical Yearbooks, they are categorized as "State Budget Funds", a concept which is intended differently from what we commonly mean in Western economies. Bonds are not yet relevant in terms of investments since Xinjiang's economy still over-relies on bank credit, despite the fact that China is gradually going toward a direct financing model. On the other hand, the business environment is still not attractive for foreign investors: The legal system does not guarantee foreign firms properly, and business conditions remain not tempting, mainly because of the overwhelming presence of state capitals. Due to political and security concerns, the Chinese government normally does not encourage foreign firms to enter the Xinjiang's market, and the recurrent alerts tend to represent an obstacle for investors from outside of China.

In 2009, the investments in fixed assets understood in terms of urban–rural divide showed such a composition: 89.7% of capitals targeted urban development, 8.3% real estate development and 10.3% rural development. In 2008, 89.6% of investments targeted urban development, 10.1% real estate and 10.4 rural development. According to figures and data published in 2000, 91.2% of capitals were earmarked for the development and implementation of the urbanization process, 10.3% for real estate and 8.8% for rural development. The majority of investments was allocated for the urbanization process, followed by real estate and rural development, in a span of time, 1999–2009, which was key for the regional urbanization process (Fig. 2.16).

In line with the national trend, the proportion of investments in fixed assets in relation to Xinjiang GDP tended to decrease from 2000 to 2009: 66.1% in 2009, 54% in 2008 and 44.8% in 2000. We can therefore assume that items shaping the regional GDP are becoming more diversified.

What economists usually argue is that the region registers a constantly growing deficit toward the central government.[92] A huge amount of special subsidies and funding are invested in large-scale projects, while smaller injections of capitals are guaranteed by the launch of development projects jointly funded by foreign governments, NGOs and the Chinese government.

[92] For instance, see Wiemer (2004), Ch. 6.

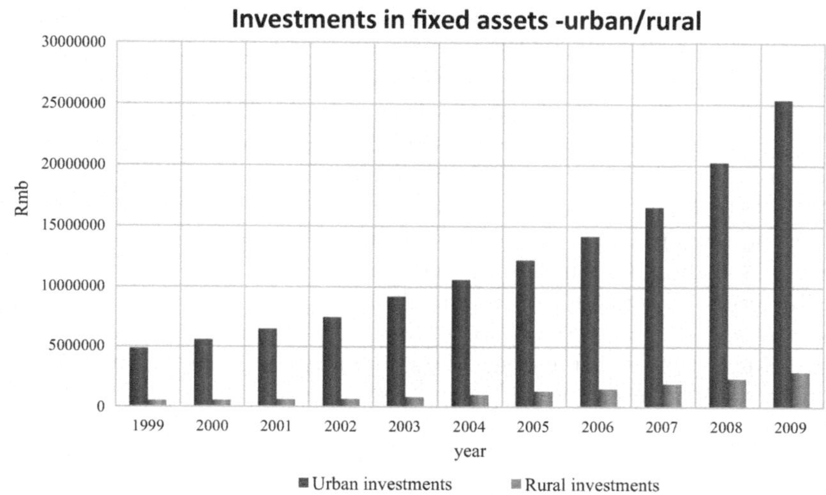

Fig. 2.16 Investment in fixed assets—rural/urban (1999–2009)

This said, data show that, together with Ningxia, Qinghai, Gansu, Tibet, Guizhou and Hainan, Xinjiang apparently still lags behind as beneficiary of central investments. Even if the trend is positive and figures related to a long time span report an increase, these provinces still remain in the last positions. In order to better comprehend the situation, we should take a look at the patterns of subsidies and transfers from Beijing, at special development projects and special funding addressed to autonomous regions.

2.4.10 Urban–Rural Divide and Increase in the Agricultural Output

One of the phenomena which are worth considering in the framework of this work is the persistent rural–urban divide in XUAR, as well as the substantial increase in the agricultural output.

The urban–rural divide is still significant in Xinjiang. In 2016 data, the per capita disposable income of urban households was 28.463 RMB, with the region ranking at 17th but still well below the national average of 53.980 RMB. In terms of total investment in fixed assets, it ranks 25th (before Gansu, Shaanxi, Shanxi, Inner Mongolia and Guizhou).

The per capita annual living expenditures for consumption in rural areas are pretty high, 21.229 RMB, with the region ranking 12th among the other regions and provinces. In terms of annual per capita disposable income of rural households, it amounts to 10.183 RMB (less than half of the urban correspondent value) and places the region at the 23rd position among other provinces and regions (national average 12.363 RMB). 8277 RMB is the annual per capita living expenses of rural households, a very low figure which positions Xinjiang at the 26th place (just before Shanxi, Guizhou, Gansu, Yunnan and Tibet).

In terms of agricultural output, all measures implemented in order to increase it—transforming small-plot oasis farming into large-scale agricultural ventures, building a low-intensity labor agribusiness characterized by a heavy use of chemicals[93]—apparently helped to reach the targets. In 2016, the Gross Output Value of Agriculture, Forestry, Animal Husbandry and Fishery was 296.970.000.000 RMB, with the region ranking 19th at the national level. The output value increase rate in 2015 over 2014 of Agriculture, Forestry, Animal Husbandry and Fishery was 6%, placing the region in the 3rd position in the ranking (14th in 2009). As far as cotton, natural gas and crude oil production is concerned, Xinjiang ranked 1st, 3rd and 4th, respectively.

2.5 Infrastructures and Foreign Direct Investments (FDIs)

2.5.1 Infrastructures

A major hindrance to Xinjiang's economic development is represented by the structural characteristics of its territory, which mainly consists in either mountain or desert. Up to the twentieth century, large parts of Xinjiang were crossable only by camel caravan.[94] Moreover, in 1903, with the completion of the Trans-Siberian Railway, Xinjiang's role as a transit corridor between East and West diminished. In the 1930s, a major achievement in infrastructure development was the construction, thanks to Soviet loans, of a road from Horgos Pass, via Urumqi, up to

[93] See Chapter 5.

[94] A firsthand account of a 1935 journey can be found in Fleming (1936).

Hami, then extending further eastward to the Gansu Highway. This infrastructure permitted motorized transport finally to replace camel caravans in linking Xinjiang with the rest of China. All Soviet armaments and equipment provided for fighting the Japanese reached Inner China across this road.[95] Because of the size of the region, domestic air travel within Xinjiang became essential, and almost all the Chinese air companies opened routes from Beijing to Urumqi, and between Urumqi and other urban centers in Xinjiang. A direct flight route Beijing-Kashgar operated by Air China has been opened in 2010, while new airports in new growing cities such as Tumushuke and Aral have been opened in the framework of different investment stimuli. Xinjiang is normally connected to other countries with flights from Urumqi to Istanbul, Moscow, Tehran and Almaty. Borders with the Central Asian neighbors have been reopened only in the 1980s, and bus and train routes connecting the region to Central Asian republics, Mongolia and Russia have been opened since 1989. Buses and trains also connect the major oases within the region: The Taklamakan Highway was completed in 1995, providing a central North–South transport axis across the desert. In May 1999, the extension of a rail link between Korla and Kashgar was completed. Both transport routes have their starting point at the Han-dominated town of Korla, which in turn is connected with the major East–West transport lines linking the region with the rest of China. In addition, the freight capacity of the railway reaching Xinjiang from Inner China was doubled, and the province's central highway was extended by 500 kilometres between Turpan, Urumqi and Kuitun. In June 2011, the railway segment connecting Urumqi and Kashgar reached Khotan in Southern Xinjiang. A turning point in the modern history of Xinjiang, as well as a decisive step toward the eventual transformation of the demographic balance in the region, has been the rail link Beijing-Urumqi through the Lanzhou-Xinjiang high-speed railway, a train reaching 300 km/h, the same concept of the Beijing-Lhasa high-speed connection. Construction works started in 2009 and, according to the news circulating in 2012, 3450 km would have been covered in less than 12 hours by 2014. In 2014, the passenger transport started operating.

[95]Wang Shuanqian (1999), Chs. 1–3. The Horgos Pass between China and Kazakhstan has been turned into a special economic border area in the framework of the BRI.

These large-scale and capital-intensive infrastructural projects are all aimed at increasing the economic integration of Southern oases, previously linked to the North by merely a single and not always practicable road. Enhanced economic integration brings also the possibility to exercise control over remote areas which were previously enjoying a high degree of independence. Geographical and political reasons make the communication network not much stable and not particularly efficient,[96] with mobility depending on both seasons and the contingent political situation.

Together with the establishment of a Special Economic Zone and commercial hub at Horgos Pass, at the border with Kazakhstan, other fundamental infrastructural projects have been realized.[97] For instance, hydroelectric power plants have been built across the whole region: Works for the construction of a huge dam started in 2012 in the Kashgar Prefecture, an area hit by an endemic problem of water scarcity. Although underground waters are abundant in the prefecture, farmers lack an effective system for collecting underground water as well as the proper equipment to rationalize its usage. A Beijing-based company conducted the negotiations with the Water Resource Bureau in the Kashgar Prefecture and started to collaborate with local authorities to devise possible collaborations and synergies.[98]

Telecommunications are developed as in the other parts of China, with Internet and phone restrictions enforced only in case of unrest. For instance, after the 2009 riots, communications with other countries have been impossible for ten months, and in some closed areas[99] of Southern Xinjiang, this problem represents a daily reality.

[96] For the problems on the communication network, see Dillon (2004, pp. 42–43).

[97] A lot of them, especially those not yet finalized by 2013, have been included in the BRI.

[98] The KFW project I was part of as consultant, in a research team led by Professor Abduresit Jelil Qarluq, was exactly addressing this problem and trying to match famers' needs by installing water-saving equipment as well as machinery to rationalize the use of available waters.

[99] In Southern Xinjiang, there are some villages which are surrounded by checkpoints and accessible only by residents, while Chinese non-residents and foreigners need special permissions. This can be due to a different number of reasons, ranging from military settlement to the presence of natural resources such as uranium and gold, and also to political issues related to tensions between the local people and authorities in those specific areas.

2.5.2 *Foreign Direct Investments (FDIs)*

Up to 2013, foreign enterprises and investors had been encouraged to enter the region's market, and they could enjoy simplified processes and fiscal facilitations for their business operations. At the time, Xinjiang was a key area for Beijing, and all the necessary steps were taken to turn it from a drowsy peripheral area into an international industrial, logistic and trade hub. One of the stated goals of central authorities was to transform Kashgar into a vibrant center, namely into a "Dubai of Central Asia".[100] Just before 2013, when the Xi-Wen administration went to power, signals of increasing interest in the business environment of the region by foreign businessmen started to be reported by financial media and news services. Allegedly, FIEs and JVs became increasingly attracted by the unexploited business potential hidden in Xinjiang. The factors which played a major role in attracting the interests of foreign investors basically were: (a) the geostrategic location of Xinjiang, in between the Chinese superpower and the markets and resources of Central Asia; (b) the fiscal facilities accorded by the Chinese government; (c) the expanding internal market; and (d) the low cost of labor. As a matter of fact, if we consider the total output value of construction enterprises with funds from Hong Kong, Macao, Taiwan and foreign JVs, they accounted for 0.005 and 0.0024% of the total value, in 2008 and 2009, respectively. Since 2000, when the *Xibu Da Kaifa* started to be implemented, the capital-intensive sectors of real estate, infrastructural and large-scale construction works boomed, but still did not act as a magnet for foreign investments. In 2009, enterprises with capitals from Hong Kong, Macao and Taiwan were 4 out of 1345, they employed 579 people, while the enterprises funded exclusively with Hong Kong, Macao and Taiwan capitals were only 3 and they were employing 536 workers. One single share-holding corporation (Ltd.) with capitals from Hong Kong, Macao and Taiwan was in the market, together with only two foreign-funded enterprises. After 2009, there had been a renewed interest in the region by foreign investors, in particular by Turkish actors.

In April 2012, the Turkish Prime Minister Recep Tayyip Erdogan, during an official visit to China, declared that Turkey was planning to build an almost 5000-kilometer-long rail network in Xinjiang, with the

[100] Slogan which was very common at the time across the city and the region, as well as in airports and many public places. See Cappelletti (2014).

cooperation of Chinese firms. The project of a modern "Silk Road",[101] which had been discussed for twenty years but not strategized and implemented,[102] was considered highly significant for China's trade with Turkey, the Caucasus and Central Asian countries, as well as for the stability of the whole region. The official data related to Xinjiang's involvement in the plan and the related strategic issues have never been disclosed nor defined, but the idea of a "Silk Railway"[103] linking China and Europe, to expand the economic integration and increase the level of trade among countries in the whole of Eurasia,[104] emerged quite clearly from programmatic documents.

In 2016, companies from Hong Kong (209), Taiwan (23), Japan (9), United States (31), Canada (12), Germany (7), Turkey (9), UK (6), Australia (14), Russia (9) and South Korea (29) invested in the region.

On 19 April 2012, financial media reported that Shanghai Volkswagen, the German carmaker Volkswagen AG's joint venture in China, was planning to set up an assembly plant in Xinjiang Uyghur Autonomous Region to be closer to markets of Northwestern China and Central Asia.[105] The plant was set up in Urumqi Development Zone and become operational in 2013, with the goal of producing 50.000 small sedans annually, according to Mr. Li Yi, officer at the Trade and Investment Bureau of Urumqi's Development Zone.[106] Italian and Greek enterprises are also present in the region: In Changji Development Zone, a US joint venture is producing high-quality European-style home furniture for the Chinese South-Eastern coastal market. In Urumqi, a Greek enterprise produces *dolmades*, the typical Greek rice rolls in wine leaves, with ingredients from the local Turpan area. This product is sold in Greece as a made-in-Greece product. An Italian-invested touristic enterprise, Zhangjiakou Saibei Duoleimeidi Ski and Leisure Co., collaborates with Tianye Ltd. for the construction of ski resorts in the Altai region, sites conceived for the booming touristic market in Inner

[101] Shah and Reed (2012) and Kuchins and Starr (2010).

[102] This happened in 2013 with the launch of the BRI.

[103] Colacoglu (2012) and Lin (2011).

[104] On the potential for economic integration and norms setting in Central Asia, see Schiek (2017).

[105] A Ford factory was established in the region in the 1930s, see Clark (2011).

[106] Interview by the author in August 2012.

China as well as for the expat community. Another Italian company, Ing. A. Rossi Group, which produces complete processing lines for the food industry and exports globally, is designing and manufacturing machineries for processing tomatoes from the *bingtuan* area of Changji into tomato sauce. According to a news appeared on the Italian financial daily *Il Sole 24 Ore* on 4 May 2012, the Italian group Italcementi became the third shareholder, as well as strategic partner, of West China Cement, with 6.25% of the total shares.

The terms of the deal imply that the Italian group is entitled to have a representative in the Board of Directors of West China Cement. Italcementi is a holding company active in Shaanxi and Xinjiang with an actual capitalization of approximately 780 million euros and a productive capacity of around 20 million tons of cement, listed in the Hong Kong Stock Exchange since 2010. At the end of 2012, its productive capacity rose to 24 million tons thanks to 15 cement mining sites, including Fuping and Shifeng in Shaanxi. The Italcementi-West China Cement deal was finalized on 28 June 2012 with the financial assistance of CITIC Securities International.[107] The limited presence of foreign firms in Xinjiang shows that it has always been difficult to attract foreign investments in the region, and, since the Xi-Wen administration replaced the Hu-Wen leadership in 2013, attracting foreign capitals stopped to be a Chinese government-stated goal, both for political and for security-related reasons.[108]

Therefore, the international business community did not show a strong confidence toward the governmental plans so far, and, while just a few foreign enterprises already considered Xinjiang for investments, the region is still considered as a "not safe" environment for investments, and operators are still "watching". Here below, we make an effort to consider a few key factors which are impacting on the international business community in relation to the region's industrial and commercial environment.

[107]Press release: "Gruppo Italcementi finalizza accordo con WCC" [Italcementi Group Finalises Agreement with WCC], in: http://borsa.firstonline.info/NisViewer.ashx?file=0165-28-2012.pdf&year=2012&filetype=comunicati (accessed on the 12 November 2012).

[108]With the administration of Xi Jinping, the investment environment in the region became less attractive, mainly because of the "Strike Hard Campaign against Violent Terrorism" launched in May 2014.

1. The lack of effective legal guarantees for international investors—who need a system with a transparent and effective legal framework—is one of the major problems of the investment environment in Xinjiang. The widespread corruption among local authorities and élites constitutes an element which combines with the often too vague laws and regulations, creating a sense of uncertainty and diffidence within and among business communities.
2. The second problem is the distance from the coast: Urumqi, the regional capital, is the closest city to the most distant area from the sea in the world, and this makes the transportation of goods and raw materials difficult and expensive. Distance from markets in Inner China is also a liability, while the closest markets are in the Central Asian neighbors, scarcely populated countries, with an economy mainly based on the export of resources, and with uncertain legal systems. If the problem of insufficient infrastructures is successfully solved, the investment environment has the potential to become more attractive for foreign companies.
3. Lack of professionals and expertise represents the fourth problem, since measures and actions to train a new class of local employees and professional have started only recently.
4. Moreover, Xinjiang remains a volatile political and social environment, because of local discontent periodically resulting in outbreaks of violence, and of the presence of radical Islamists in some areas of the region. Investments with a long-term perspective require an appropriate socio-economic equilibrium: Riots and terrorist alerts are occurring on a regular basis and provoke Internet blockages and the creation of checkpoints at the entrance of cities and villages, slowing down the traffic. Worth of mentioning are the many areas closed to both Chinese nationals and foreign citizens in Southern Xinjiang, and along the border with the former Soviet Union. Mainly located in the Khotan Prefecture, Kashgar Prefecture (among the others: Peyzawat County, Baren Village, Maralbashi County) and Kyzil Kyrgyz Autonomous County, these territories are inaccessible for different reasons, ranging from the presence of a deeply religious population or of labor camps, to quicksands or the alleged storage of nuclear and traditional weapons by the Chinese army. The border with the Indian controlled Kashmir, in the Khotan Prefecture, is still not settled, while those with Afghanistan and Pakistan are heavily militarized and patrolled

all the year long. Closed areas also include important saint shrines (the most important one, Ordam Padishah Mazar in the Kashgar Prefecture, has been inaccessible since 1997) and areas considered dangerous for the presence of extreme weather phenomena like severe sandstorms. Other issues, like environmental degradation and the effects of nuclear tests realized in the Lop Nor Desert, together with probable presence of uranium deposits in underground tunnels in Southern Xinjiang, are of concern for foreign businessmen, but they still constitute elements of potential instability and they are not handled with due transparency by the Chinese government.

2.6 "Large-Scale Development of the Western Regions" (西部大开发 *Xibu da kaifa*)

At the end of the 1990s, the Jiang Zemin-Zhu Rongji administration acknowledged that times were mature to start dealing with underdevelopment and inequalities in the Chinese Central and Western regions, as well as with contradictions and tensions in Xinjiang. This awareness matched with the chance to exploit the variegated and profitable economic potentials of XUAR, in a moment when China, due to its booming growth, started to become a country in constant need for natural resources. A new long-term development plan for Western and Central regions in China was envisaged, a scheme entailing influxes of capitals mainly in six provinces: Shanxi, Anhui, Jiangxi, Henan, Hubei and Hunan, areas where 30% of the Chinese population and one-third of the overall total rural population used to live. Xinjiang was included in the plan, and Beijing needed starting to cope with phenomena of political instability and rebellions such as the revolts of Baren (1990) and Ghulja (1997)—allegedly among the bloodiest ones[109]—with the intention of solving the "Xinjiang problem" for good. A number of political and strategic assessments were at the basis of the Chinese government

[109]The municipality of Baren, in Akto County, is still closed to foreigners and non-residents, while the city of Ghulja, in the Ili region in Northern Xinjiang, is patrolled by police forces and the army on a daily basis. Around 8 o'clock in the evening, a curfew-like condition occurs, with market stalls usually opened along the whole night which are forced to close, people disappear on the streets, while militaries patrol the empty streets (personal observation in June 2008).

choices: the collapse of the Soviet Union in 1991 and the creation of independent Central Asian Republics; the revival of Islamic extremist groups in the area[110]; together with the new nationalist movements and wars in the international context, all these situations outside of China have been considered by the central government in elaborating plans of development for Xinjiang. Internal issues mainly reflected international events: The impact of Islamic movements and nationalist ideas on the local Uyghur population was source of major concern for Beijing, while internal discontent for the poor conditions of the majority of the population could act like a magnet for those reluctant to give their consensus to Beijing, as well as for those social groups who were not properly represented in the government setting. At the same time, the Jiang Zemin and Zhu Rongji administration was concerned about rebalancing disparities in development levels among regions: At the eve of the twenty-first century, China still presented a highly unbalanced distribution of wealth, with the South-Eastern coastal provinces and their SEZs out in front, and the Central and Western regions representing the tail lamp. The Hu-Wen administration has been appreciated for having put these issues at the top of Beijing political agenda, and, despite the critical voices blaming the leadership of grim populism, launched a development plan which opened the way to a series of measures and policies aimed, for the first time in the history of the region, to solve the "Xinjiang problem" for good. This was the foundation of today's BRI.

The "Large-Scale Development of the Western Regions" was a project outlined and approved by the Chinese Communist Party Central Committee (CPCC) in September 1999, and started to be implemented in 2000, partially representing the response of the Chinese government to the tensions looming from outside the Xinjiang's borders and to the incumbent internal potential turmoil.[111]

[110] Ahmed Rashid (2002) and Jason Burke (2004).

[111] According to five Han Urumqi residents interviewed by the author and who accepted to speak under the condition of anonymity in 2005 and in 2007, respectively, during the 1990s in the streets of the Xinjiang capital, there was one explosion a week at least, the typology of which ranged from explosives in buses to the collapse of buildings following suicide attacks. These incidents did not receive coverage on the international media because of the reluctance of the Chinese government to release the news, and for the absence of foreign journalists in Xinjiang, but the major events have been listed in a dedicated White Paper on terrorism in China compiled by the central government after 9 September 2001.

After two decades of economic stimulus, unique fiscal and commercial policies and assisted development measures in the Eastern provinces, which attracted foreign and internal capitals, it was then the turn of the Western regions.

In September 1999, a document issued by the plenary session of the Central Committee, the "Deliberations on some urgent problems of opening and development of State-owned enterprises" (中共中央关于国有企业改革和发展若干重大问题的决定 *Zhonggong zhongyang guanyu guoyou qiye gaige he fazhan ruogan da wenti de jueding*), contains the first mention to the *Xibu Da Kaifa* strategy.

The "Outline of the 15th Five-Year Plan on the National Economic and Social Development in the People's Republic of China" (中华人民共和国国民经济和社会发展第十个五年计划纲要 *Zhonghua Renmin Gongheguo Guomin Jingji he Shehui Fazhan dishige Wunian Jihua Gangyao*), issued in March 2001, contains, again for the first time, a detailed outline of measures and policies for the implementation of the program. According to this document, the experience accumulated in the recent past acted as leading principle, mainly the three stages that China went across in the previous 50 years: "to establish the foundations", "accelerate development" and "promote modernization under every aspect", would be the main directions for the whole project. The section of the document concerning the *Xibu da kaifa* can be understood more as a declaration of general intents than an operative schedule for the gradual implementation of the project. In October 2005, the Qaidam Basin in Qinghai, rich in oil, natural gas and minerals like asbestos, borax and gypsum, became a test area at a national level, and, in the framework of the *Xibu Da Kaifa*, the basin's large mineral deposits triggered a great deal of investment interest.

Another declaration of intents follows with the "Eleventh Five-year Plan for the Large-Scale Development of the Western Regions"

In May 1997, a bomb exploded on a Beijing bus, killing two and injuring a hundred people. No vindications were issued, but, according to the Chinese public security departments, this kind of events all consisted in terrorist attacks conducted by Uyghurs trained in Pakistan and Afghanistan. According to one Uyghur witness who at the time was in his twenties, it was rather common for young Uyghurs to have the possibility to use drugs like heroin and opium smuggled from Yunnan Province, and to fabricate explosives at home. The existence of special camps to train Uyghurs fighters for a Holy War in Afghanistan and in the whole of Central Asia has been assessed by Reed and Raschke (2010), and already acknowledged by the majority of Xinjiang scholars.

(西部大开发 "十一五" 规划 *Xibu da Kaifa "Shi yi wu" guihua*) issued in December 2006, where, in general terms, the main goals of the project are stated: (1) to promote a fast economic development; (2) increase the standards of life; (3) give a contribution for the preservation of the environment and the regional ecology; (4) redistribute wealth and services among the population; (5) in order to go a step further in building a harmonious and socialist society. While in 2009 Guangxi Zhuang Autonomous Region and Gansu Province were the main target areas for investments, in 2010 it was the turn of Qinghai, Ningxia and Xinjiang. On 23 May 2011, *Xinhua News Agency* reported on six main metals discovered in Qinghai, and identified by the Council of State as potentially becoming the basis of the region's industrial structure, in the framework of a document aimed at providing the guidelines for an overall plan for Qinghai Province.

In 2010, several other policies and measures related to the *Xibu da Kaifa* were implemented: The visit to Ningxia Hui Autonomous Region by Hu Jintao was matched with speeches on the successes of the plan, and on the new direction, it was going to take in the future, becoming in this way more and more important in the framework of the 12th Five-Year National Plan on Economic and Social Development. In that occasion, a fundamental principle and political direction were underlined: "to open up a new broad space of development for our country" (为我国发展开拓新的广阔空间 *wei wo guo fazhan kaituo xin de guangkuo kongjian*).[112] State support and encouragement to China's new rich willing to reinvest their accumulated capitals were stated and identified as a national goal and as one of the most important inputs for a better implementation of the plan.[113] Over time, great economic successes were proclaimed in Guangxi, Sichuan and Gansu, up to 10 years after the implementation of the plan. Interestingly enough, from 17 to 19 May 2010, a Xinjiang Working Forum (中央新疆工作座谈会 *Zhongyang Xinjiang gongzuo zuotanhui*) was organized in Beijing. The speech by Hu Jintao represented a clear schedule devised by the government to govern Xinjiang from an economic standpoint, with the targets of achieving a "leapfrog development" and a "lasting stability". In realizing the working program, the leadership in Beijing acknowledged that the nation-building process in Xinjiang was still far from being accomplished and still required political, cultural and social measures aimed

[112] Something which happened and was branded later with the BRI.

[113] See the later developments and the launch of the BRI as a finalization of this concept.

at building a socialist nation guided by the CCP and at consolidating the Party structure.[114] The acknowledgment that these goals were not achieved yet could be interpreted as a sort of admission, from the side of the authorities, of failure. In an attempt to eventually put an end to the process of "building the nation" with Chinese characteristics, the Xinjiang case was of utmost importance. The region, with its Muslim majority and proximity to Central Asia, was, and indeed is, still considered as one of the less integrated into the Chinese Han core, and the *Xibu da kaifa* was considered of great importance for the region incorporation/assimilation into the broader national context. The policy document released by the Working Forum stated that by 2015 the per capita GDP in Xinjiang would have reached the value of the average per capita GDP at a national level, and indeed, it did, since the 2015 per capita GDP in the region amounted to 40.036 RMB and the national value was 49.992 RMB; moreover, rural and urban incomes and the per capita social services would have reached the Eastern regions' average level, a projection which turned to be true. The overall assessment of the work done up to that moment stated that basic economic conditions in the region already improved, the self-capacity for development also developed, while, from a central government perspective, progresses had been made also in relation to the unity of nationalities (a key point in Beijing's agenda), and social stability had also improved. 2020 comes out as a watershed: Great progresses are foreseen in the fields of (1) coordinated development; (2) prosperity for the people; (3) protection of the environment; (4) harmony among nationalities; (5) social stability; (6) borders' protection; and (7) progresses in cultural issues, while the "struggle aim"[115] is defined as to achieve the construction of a "comparatively well-off society" (小康社会 *xiaokang shehui*) in every aspect of the daily life. The speech delivered by President Hu Jintao was followed by talks by Prime Minister Wen Jiabao and the CCP Political and Secretary of CPC Central Political and Legislative Committee, Zhou Yongkang, the man in charge of the state security apparatus. Urbanization and a shift from a traditional toward a modern society are the main political

[114] I here use the expression "nation building" as it has been understood by Millward (1998), and in the framework of the debate which was common in China at the time, about the transition from a "multinational" to a "nation state". On this topic, see the works by Ma Rong (2006, 2011).

[115] Expression adopted from the revolutionary jargon.

points which have been made clear as the future path of development for Xinjiang's society. These very high profile 2010 talks highlighted the growing importance of Xinjiang, of the often mentioned Xinjiang Production and Construction Corps, as recipients of financial investments, and of Xinjiang as a key area for the future strategic goals of the Chinese government.

The main configuration of Xinjiang's economy, with its export-oriented vocation, is the plan's core, because of the necessity, in line with national goals, of increasing the internal demand and moving toward a more dynamic and open economy, with an encouraging business environment. The planned engineering projects envisaged for the Western regions were 23, for a total investment of 682.200.000.000 RMB, and, back in 2012, were still in the implementation phase. The only project planned for Xinjiang was the Kensiwate Dam, under the Shihezi administration, which would have acted as a water reservoir for the whole urban area of Urumqi. Sinohydro Corporation was the contractor in charge of the project, China's powerful and internationally renowned leading state-owned dam builder.

During several high-level talks on the successful implementation speed of the *Xibu Da Kaifa* held in Beijing, issues such as environment and the increase of life standards, sedentarization of nomads and afforestation measures, had been discussed. Following the inclusion of Hainan Province and Guizhou Province among the plan's beneficiaries, on 8 August 2011, the Dushanzi area, within the bingtuan municipality of Kuitun, became a Special Economic Zone. The exact naming is "national economic and technological development area" (*guojia ji jingji jishu kaifa qu* 国家级经济技术开发区), with oil extraction and chemical engineering, equipment manufacturing, traditional industry, animal husbandry and agriculture (mainly grain), as the main productive activities. Since then, Kuitun has been elected as a key industrial basis for the large-scale extraction and processing of mineral resources on a national level. According to a five-year schedule (2011–2015), the State Grid Corporation of China was planning to build two high-voltage electricity engineering systems, one from Hami to Henan Province, to be completed in 2012, and the other one from Hami to Chongqing across the whole of Inner China, which were ready in 2014.

In November 1983, the Horgos Pass was officially reopened by the Chinese State Council, after having been closed by the Maoist administration. As the main overland channel for the passage of peoples and goods in the area, it became again the international natural gateway and bridgehead for economic and cultural communication, as well as for the development of the relationship between China and the bordering countries. In 2004, the two governments of China and Kazakhstan jointly signed a protocol on the establishment of a Sino-Kazakh international border cooperation center in the Horgos area, while the two heads of State promoted and encouraged the construction of a factory as an early measure toward the creation of the first international cross-border free trade frontier port in China. In May 2005, during a special conference held by the central government on Xinjiang, the establishment of two new Special Economic Zones, one in Kashgar and the other at the Horgos Pass, was proposed. Ad hoc policies and flexible measures were endorsed, since the two areas had been identified as the door for the Chinese expansion westward, as well as two important new hubs of economic development for the whole region. On 8 October 2011, the Web site of the Chinese government issued a statement named "An outline on the support by the State Council for the creation of a zone of economic development in the Kashgar and Horgos areas".

The document focused on seven important characteristics shared by the two places: strategic location, similar needs, fundamental principles, border environment, industrial layout, preferential policies and organizational leadership. At the same time, the Chinese government adopted ten large-scale measures for the provision of financial allowances, in order to increase the degree of political support for the economic development of Kashgar and the Horgos Pass. The establishment of these two new economic zones became an important window toward the West, promoting at the same time the areas in the fast regional development process. In the same document, the program schedule was outlined, listing the following targets for 2015: the construction setup for building the basic facilities in the two Special Economic Zones; the initial construction of a space layout and of an industrial system with a "scientific logic, distinct characteristics, functional organization, and coordinated development", all aimed at establishing solid bases for a better growth in the new economic zones. By 2020, the overall economic potential of the Kashgar and Horgos SEZs should have become operational, together with their competitive industrial power, with the aim of promoting the advancement and generating spillover effects from the fast development of the region.

Kashgar economic development zone (喀什经济开发区 *Kashi jingji kaifa qu*) extends over an area of approximately 50 square kilometers, which also includes a territory under the Xinjiang Production and Construction Corps. A territory of 40 square kilometers belongs to

Kashgar Municipality, and 10 square kilometers to the Irkeshtam Pass at the border with Kyrgyzstan. The other new economic development zone established at the Horgos Pass, at the border with Kazakhstan, covers an overall territory of 73 square kilometers (and also includes a bingtuan administered area), while that in the city of Yining is 35 square kilometers big, and the one at the natural reserve of Qingshui River extends approximately for eight square kilometers.

During the Xinjiang Working Forum held in May 2010, the central government deliberately promoted the Urumqi Conference to be held at imminent China-Eurasia International Fair, organized every year from 1 to 5 September in Urumqi, the capital of Xinjiang. Similar investments, business efforts and undertakings were planned for Tibet, Inner Mongolia and Qinghai. The China-Eurasia International Fair replaced the Urumqi Foreign Economic Relations and Trade Conference, which took place in the regional capital from 1991 to 2010. In September 2011, amid deep security concerns and a tight policy enforcement, the China-Eurasia International Fair was launched, attracting delegations of businessmen from all over Central Asia and the Muslim countries. The second edition, in September 2012, saw a broader participation of international guests, with representatives of business communities from European countries, including an Italian delegation of businessmen organized by the National Institute for Foreign Trade (Istituto per il Commercio Estero—ICE).

A review and critical assessment of the officially released documents related to the launch and execution of the *Xibu Da Kaifa* highlights the more realistic scope of the project: Allegedly conceived as a means to attract investments to still underdeveloped regions of China, the scheme was promoted as comprehensive and organic, with the clearly stated goal of emulating the successful coastal SEZs. In reality, the whole plan comes out to be more a batch of measures not linked to each other, mainly responding to necessities linked to contingencies and on-the-spot situations. Even if official documents refer to a "strategy" (*celue* 策略), implying an organically structured plan, we are mainly in front of an outline of political intents which have the goal of resolving some of the most urgent issues in an area which was once considered "peripheral China", but that was gradually gaining a relevant place in connection with the needs of contemporary China. The necessity to find new investment channels for capitals under the state management and SOEs also represented a strong motivation to implement this long-term program.

2.7 The Project "Nineteen Provinces and Municipalities Support Xinjiang"—Year 2010 (19 个省市对口支援新疆 *Shijiu shengshi duikou zhiyuan Xinjiang*)

The concept of 支援新疆 ***zhiyuan Xinjiang***, "supporting Xinjiang", emphasized during the Xinjiang Working Forum in 2010, is not a new one in the history of the development projects targeting the border region. The basic idea behind the label is that, regardless of the region's natural resources, such as water and good agricultural and pasture land, the positive aspects of being located on China Northwestern border are often not so obvious. The transportation of resources is costly, thus competitive advantages decline, the exploitment of natural resources requires significant investments, and it becomes thus difficult not to recognize that the process of economic development entails remarkable difficulties and obstacles. Since the second half of the 1990s, different support measures started to be launched and implemented, with officials from other provinces conducting fieldworks in Xinjiang to assess the difficulties on the spot, getting prepared to organize the transfer of thousands of cadres to work in Xinjiang, and the implementation of a great quantity of dedicated projects with different impacts on the local situations, and, eventually, the investment of billions of RMB. The stated goal of the "supporting projects" has always been the improvement of people's life standards, "the prosperity and wealth of all ethnic groups in Xinjiang". The general framework and level of commitment related to this program were also consistent with those of the *Xi Bu Da Kaifa*.

The "19 provinces and municipalities support Xinjiang" project was officially approved in 2010, just after the eruption of popular discontent in the region, in the summer and autumn of 2009. Up to November 2012, 15 provinces and 4 municipalities had started to implement projects in different administrative units in Xinjiang, including divisions of the Xinjiang Production and Construction Corps. In the same way as the "Large-Scale Development of the West", the number of actors, beneficiaries and program entailed by this investment scheme was not fixed, with new provinces and cities willing to join it and starting to invest in Xinjiang, and other areas of the region asking for support progressively emerging. This means that the Table 2.2 shall be taken as an approximate reference.

Table 2.2 Projects related to the "Nineteen provinces and municipalities support Xinjiang"—year 2010 (19 个省市对口支援新疆 Shijiu shengshi duikou zhiyuan Xinjiang)

Municipalities and provinces	*Supported area*	*Projects*
Beijing	Khotan Prefecture: Khotan Municipality, Khotan County, Moyu County, Luopu County; 14th Agricultural Division of the XJPCC	5 large-scale pilot projects: (1) long-term engineering project to ameliorate Penghu district in Khotan Municipality; (2) an engineering construction project to develop new land for safe and earthquake-proof dwellings in Khotan County; (3) construction project for agricultural facilities in Moyu County; (4) construction works in the sickroom building of Luopu People's Hospital; (5) engineering works for red dates processing at the 14th Agricultural Division of the XJPCC
Guangdong	Kashgar Prefecture: Shule County, Jiashi County; Tumushuke Municipality (belonging to the 3rd Agricultural Division of the XJPCC)	In 5 years, Guangdong Province (including Shenzhen) allocated 9.600.000.000 RMB to support "2 cities and 3 counties" for special projects in Kashgar Prefecture; before the end of 2011, the authorization procedures for every collective project, public service, basic construction, production development, buildings in the countryside need to be completed
Shenzhen	Kashgar Prefecture, Tashkurgan County	Make an effort to solve the problems connected with people's livelihood in the supported areas, to improve people's lives, to invest people's properties into assets which will be useful for the entire life; solve the most urgent and basic problems connected with people's lives
Jiangsu	Artush Municipality (Kyzilsu Kyrghiz Autonomous sub-prefecture), Haheqi County, Wuqia County, 10 counties and municipalities in Ili Kazakh Autonomous sup-prefecture; 4th and 7th Agricultural Divisions of the XJPCC	Projects related to the improvement of people's standards of life

(continued)

Table 2.2 (continued)

Municipalities and provinces	*Supported area*	*Projects*
Shanghai	Kashgar Prefecture: Bachu County, Shache County, Zepu County, Yecheng County	To solve the most important issues related to people's lives and start a process of continuous development
Shandong	Kashgar Prefecture: Shule County, Yingjisha County, Maigaiti County, Yuepuhu County	To encourage projects aimed at guaranteeing a certain standard of life for the people; support the production fields of particularly interesting and typical local products; put emphasis on people's intellect, and strengthen the work of supporting Xinjiang through its local talents; promote the political awareness from the grassroots and the creation of grassroots organizations
Zhejiang	1 municipality and 8 counties of Aksu Prefecture; Alaer Municipality (belonging to the 1st Agricultural Division of the XJPCC)	Attach importance to people's standards of life, and to the support of cadres and local talents; special projects for particularly poor areas, and support for the production base and for handling and developing local natural resources
Liaoning	Tacheng Prefecture	Mainly support families and individuals who suffered from the earthquakes and build earthquake-proof houses
Henan	Hami Prefecture; 13th Agricultural Division of the XJPCC	Improve the employment chances for local people, focusing on the strong and advantageous conditions of the territory and the development of the local potentialities
Hebei	Bayinguoleng Mongol Autonomous sub-prefecture; 2nd Agricultural Division of the XJPCC	Work on the local talents and on the territory potentialities, making sure that all the population will take advantage of the outcomes of the support
Shanxi	Wujiaqu Municipality (belonging to the 6th Agricultural Division of the XJPCC); Fukang Municipality in Changji Autonomous sub-prefecture	Consider the enterprises as local backbone; work for the unity among nationalities and for the common advantage

(continued)

Table 2.2 (continued)

Municipalities and provinces	*Supported area*	*Projects*
Fujian	Changji Municipality, Manasi County, Hutubi County, Qitai County, Jimushaer County, Mulei County	Work in the fields of education, technology, production in order to improve all people's lives and ameliorate the social and natural environment
Hunan	Turpan Prefecture	Infrastructural projects and social projects aimed at improving life standards
Hubei	Bole Municipality in Bortala Autonomous sub-prefecture, Jinghe County, Wenxiang County; 5th Agricultural Division of the XJPCC	Social and economic development and attention to the satisfaction of the local population
Anhui	Pishan County in Khotan Prefecture	Work on the interaction between state and market, together with the improvement of health services
Tianjin	Minfen, Cele and Yutian Counties in Khotan Prefecture	10 infrastructural projects aimed at improving people's standards of life and the local industries
Heilongjiang	Fuhai, Fuyun and Qinghe Counties in Altai Prefecture; 10th Division of the XJPCC	Work on the agricultural and mining sectors, with emphasis on local talents and potentialities
Jiangxi	Aketao County in Kyzil Kyrgyz Autonomous sub-prefecture	Projects in hydroelectric and industry fields
Jilin	Altai Municipality, Abahe County, Buerjin County and Jimunai in Altai Prefecture	Projects aimed at solving the basic problems in peoples' lives, pointing at health, education and commercial services

2.8 Knowledge and Technology Transfer

Chinese authorities openly encourage and promote, with different measures, the immigration of Han professionals moving to XUAR with the aim of looking for job opportunities better-paid positions in both the public and private sectors, in a quickly developing business. With "knowledge transfer", we mean the transfer of knowledge from one place to another, mainly through professionals working in education, as well as through graduates and technicians working as trainers for the local workforce. "Technology transfer" is a broad concept indicating the process of transferring skills, knowledge, technologies, methods and samples of manufacturing, together with facilities, to ensure that scientific and technological developments are accessible to a wider range of users, who can eventually further develop and pump in the acquired technology into new products, processes and applications, materials or services. Han professionals and technicians, Uyghur workers with experience in factories and FIEs in Inner China, are among those who play the leading role in transferring technology to the region. According to the narrative popularized by Beijing, regional authorities welcome these new personnel as a richness for Xinjiang population and society.

While exhaustive statistical data about human resources and technology transfers to XUAR are not available, I still collected data useful to analyze the educational and business environment in specific areas of the region. The majority of the available studies and documents do not provide an exhaustive picture, nor data disaggregated in consideration of ethnic affiliation. Our selected case studies will help us to gain more clear a picture on these issues.[116]

The demographic explosion in the region is attested since the Communist takeover in 1949: According to official data, between 1964 and 1982 the population grew by 79.9%,[117] a much higher growth rate than the 45.2% registered for China as a whole in the same time span. The policy of transferring peoples to the Northwestern regions was supported by scholars such as the sociologist Fei Xiaotong, who, in 1984, writes:

[116] See the following chapters on Kashgar and Shihezi.

[117] Li (1989).

> Efforts are being made to change both the ecological imbalance and the population lack in the Northwest, preparing it to become an important socialist economic base in the next century. It is estimated that the natural conditions can be substantially improved within 20 years. This will require financial support from the central government, and additional manpower. The developed areas in the East will help the West achieve rapid economic and cultural development. The Northwest can absorb the population increase of the East, relieving the pressure of its high population density.[118]

As a result of state-orchestrated and self-initiated migrations, between 1949 and 2008, the proportion of Han in Xinjiang rose dramatically: from 6.7% (220,000) to 40% (8.4 million).[119] This represents the largest demographic change ever occurred in a major region of China since the founding of the People's Republic.[120] The increase rate of Han population in Xinjiang cannot be explained with a natural increase of the birth rate, but only if we take into consideration the policies aimed at sending migrants to regions considered backward and underdeveloped implemented since the 1980s.[121] According to Prof. Ma Rong's studies on labor force in Western China, the dominant indigenous ethnic groups of Xinjiang—Uyghurs, Kazakh and Kyrgyz—are mainly engaged in agriculture and animal husbandry, whereas the Han, the Hui and the Mongols have greater access to non-agricultural professions. The non-agricultural labor force in the region is chiefly absorbed by state-owned enterprises. The gap in educational achievements by Han and minority labor force within the region has been amply assessed.[122]

Since 1989, with arrangements made by the central government, more than eighty institutions from different parts of the country started to support Xinjiang. In order to train qualified and technically skilled minority personnel, a project called "221 Human Resource Project" has

[118]Quoted in Li (1989, p. 517).

[119]XJPCC and military personnel, migrants and temporary workers without *hukou* are not included in the official data.

[120]Iredale et al. (2001).

[121]Ibid.

[122]As assessed by Starr (2004, p. 12).

been introduced in the region.[123] The number of specialized technical personnel increased at an average of 5.8% annually and reached 632.900 at the end of the tenth FYP in 2005, and further increased at an average rate of 4.98% every year until 2015.[124]

As mentioned, case studies and scholarly works allow us to draw some data and valid inferences on Han professionals and technicians moving to Xinjiang. According to Starr (2004), "(...) the existing economy strongly favors Han Chinese, who fill approximately four fifths of all jobs in manufacturing, the oil and gas industries, transport, communications, and science and technology, and fully nine-tenths of jobs in burgeoning field of construction".[125] According to Qiang and Xin, in addition to joining the XJPCC, skilled Han migrants were relocated and strategically placed to develop Xinjiang's infrastructure and natural resource extraction industries, in particular the oil, gas and cotton industries. According to Sautman (1998), by the end of the 1990s, 95% of the technical workers in the Taklamakan Desert oil exploration program were Han Chinese, while Bachman argues that the history of migration into Xinjiang has been characterized by Han Chinese who joined the XJPCC or obtained government, administrative and managerial jobs in the public sector. In summary, scholars assessed that Han migrants to Xinjiang are still given priority over minorities in obtaining urban employment, a situation which represents a source of instability and persistent inequality between Han and minorities.[126] Focusing on both migration and ethnicity in Urumqi, Howell and Fan (2011) assume that the labor market and the migrants' profile are rapidly changing, the main transformation being the fact that Uyghur workers, since the 1980s, started to be competitive. At the same time, the authors found out that, against their original hypothesis based on previous literature, the labor market in Urumqi is sufficiently developed, and social networks and government sponsorship are not any more important to find a job.

[123] A number of training programs for peasant workers and women have been launched in the region since then, the latest being the establishment of ideological reeducation facilities.

[124] Data collected from different articles published in the *Xinjiang Daily*.

[125] Starr (2004, p. 18).

[126] Among the others, see Chaudhuri (2005), Iredale et al. (2001), Sun and Fan (2011), Gladney (2004), Wiemer (2004), Pannel and Schmidt (2006), and Li (2018).

The increasing number of self-initiated migrants, both among Hans and Uyghurs, is then emphasized. At the same time, the three richest cities in the region are still Urumqi, Shihezi and Karamay, where the majority of the Han population lives. In 1979, 75% of Xinjiang's population resided in the Southern part of the region, while in 1990 the population of Northern Xinjiang started to exceed than in the South. Chinese scholars[127] acknowledge disparities and provide a causal reading: (1) the development of the Chinese economy from a planned to a market-oriented one; (2) the reforms which led enterprises to be free to hire personnel and professionals, not respecting the quota previously imposed by central authorities; and (3) the necessity to be competitive on internal as well as international markets, naturally resulted in a more competitive labor market, which requires more and more Han professionals, educated in environments considered "modern", speak Mandarin as mother tongue and are hard workers. Han personnel is then supposed to be more apt to operate in internal and international business environments. On the contrary, minority workers and professionals often do not speak fluent Mandarin, they are educated in incompatible contexts by unsatisfactory teachers[128] and need to cope with several difficulties before finding a job. I could also assess that prejudice and resistance against Muslim Uyghurs, usually not trusted by Han employers, play a big role in a broader perspective. This said, what we can say is that unemployment among Uyghurs is still important. The resistance by part of Uyghur intellectuals and society to integrate into the Han Chinese environment and to engage in learning Mandarin, together with deficiencies in the national education system for minorities,[129] are regarded by Han Chinese scholars as the first causes of unbalance.

Though the Chinese government still encourages the transfer of Han labor force, both professional and unqualified, to XUAR, by offering advantageous career incentives and other facilitations, the current situation is significantly different from what we have seen in the past, with

[127] A reference work which represents the point of view of the scholarly community in China on the subject can be found in Ma Rong (2006), while a more recent book on the topic is Li (2018).

[128] See the chapter on social development in the region, in particular the section on education.

[129] See note 128.

voluntary migration allowed, easy and rather common.[130] Interviews made in the region clearly show that a young engineer moving from Inner China can obtain a salary in Xinjiang which is three times more than what he/she would be able to get in other parts of the country, live in a comfortable apartment paying a cheap rent, enjoying, at the same time, a convenient welfare system. Workers in constructions and agriculture can earn salaries which are double with respect to those normally available in China, especially in comparison with those offered in their regions of origin, mainly Gansu, Sichuan, Shanxi and Henan.[131] What they usually do is to work in the region for a few years, until when they take the decision of settling or either to return home and reinvest the accumulated earnings into new ventures.

In many cases, qualified jobs in Xinjiang are better payed than in the rich South-Eastern coastal areas, even if the professional level of those migrating to Northwestern China is lower than those who go to work in South-Eastern provinces. Investment and cooperation schemes such as the "Nineteen Provinces and Municipalities" project represent important career opportunities for cadres, professionals and technical personnel who are sent to the region to participate in meetings, train local people, give their contribution for the creation of a middle class and ready to grasp the chances offered by the improvements in Xinjiang's economic situation. These schemes are also working as bridges between students in Xinjiang and universities in Inner China: Special programs aimed at sending Uyghur students to universities in Inner China with good scholarships, and asking them to sign a pledge to return to Xinjiang after graduation and to work there, are also categorized as knowledge transfer. Another way of transferring technology is to send young Uyghur teenagers, mainly girls, from the countryside to textile companies in South-Eastern China: In this way, young peasant workers who did not receive any formal education, due to poor family conditions, have

[130] The recent developments in the region created a sense of fear among Han Chinese willing to move there, especially among those of older generations who are conscious of the developments in the region over time. As far as younger generations are concerned, there is a deep awareness about the degree of militarization in the region, which sees the presence of different security forces with a diverse range of aims, who patrol the territory and monitor the situation. The process is easier thanks to the more convenient mobility that Chinese people enjoy in their country, regardless of their *hukou*.

[131] Howell and Fan (2011, p. 129).

the chance to be trained as technical personnel or simple workers. After the completion of the program, they are supposed to return to XUAR and to start working at the newly established factories.[132] At the end of December 2008, 900.000 peasant workers were among those transferred from Xinjiang to Inner and coastal China, on a total of 1.870.000 workers. They moved to destinations such as Beijing, Tianjin, Guangdong and Fujian. According to the fieldwork conducted by Qarluq that year, peasant workers who are sent to Inner China are mainly non-married girls between 16 and 18 years old who move out of their villages for the first time in their life. They usually do not speak Mandarin Chinese as soon as they arrive, but they start learning in language trainings and easily adjust to the new Han environment in the new city and new jobs, starting wearing and behaving like Hans.[133] According to some assessments, they quickly lose their cultural and religious values.

While Chinese scholars see these programs as an opportunity to take young Uyghur workforce out of the countryside, out of poverty and backwardness, and train them in modern contexts in order to transfer skills which will be re-channeled into the regional economy, critics of these policies, among them Uyghur intellectuals in China[134] and abroad, together with Western scholars and experts focusing on Xinjiang, argue that the real aim of the government is to use these transfers as a form of strengthening the "internal colonialism" of the region, mainly to rebalance its demographic equilibrium, diluting the Muslim identity and sense of belonging, and eventually exploit its resources for the benefit of provinces and populations in Inner and coastal China. Some of the claims consist in assuming that in this way it would be very easy to dilute the ethnic evenness of some traditional areas in the region, modify its religious and traditional beliefs and customs, and create a context which is the most similar possible to the Han's one.[135] Another target of the central government could be turning the area into a relief valve for China as a whole, to solve problems such as unemployment, overpopulation and over-exploitment of land for construction or other types of

[132] Qarluq (2012).

[133] Ibid.

[134] Mainly before 2015, when the ideological reeducation facilities were established.

[135] This goal is being pursued through different channels, replacing trees, transforming squares and so on.

investments, all issues which are currently very common in coastal and Inner China. Beijing's interest in creating a dynamic Han-dominated business hub between China and Central Asia is often put forward as one of the main reasons for transferring Hans to Xinjiang.

Young female Uyghur peasant workers are unaware of the intents behind these projects: They do not sign any contract, nor have contractual power, and are often forced to leave their families at a very young age, the majority of times also against their family and their own will. In the framework of what is often seen as an attempt to weaken the ethnic awareness in these young girls, who are allegedly pushed to get in touch with Han culture and potentially marry a Han man (according to a government official interviewed in Beijing in July 2009, intermarriage between Hans and Uyghurs is an implicit aim of the central government, connected with stability and development in the region), some families force their girls to marry very soon in order to forbid them to leave. Girls who work for a temporary period in Inner China, and go afterward back to their rural villages in Xinjiang, often suffer from a kind of disorientation syndrome, not being able to feel at home anymore in their families and communities, and being at the same time seen with a suspicious eye within the Uyghur society, since they could have been "contaminated" by Han culture, food and society.[136] Some of them allegedly become prostitutes since they have difficulties in finding someone willing to marry them, after such experiences in Inner China. According to some scholars, when they cannot find a way to return to Inner China, these girls often end up living at the margins of Uyghur society. Of course the opposite interpretation is also possible, meaning that these programs represent an opportunity offered to these girls to get out of a macho-centered society and enjoy equal rights as men. This way of technology transfer is probably not working properly, since those girls who go back to Xinjiang usually do not find a proper business environment to sell their new skills, and if they do not manage to leave the region again, they end up having to face too many obstacles and problems in their hometowns.

[136]Which means they have probably eaten in not *qingzhen* (清真, Muslim) restaurant, where pork is served, or maybe they have probably got in touch with Han men and non-Muslim customs.

2.9 Conclusive Remarks

The sixth and seventh FYPs included Deng Xiaoping's policy for promoting growth in coastal regions, an overall concept based on the assumption that a process of technological transfer from the East–West axis would have generated a spillover effect in the interior and frontier areas.[137] Back in 1984 interior provinces received 49% of state investments, only 2% less than the coastal provinces, but by 1994 the gap widened, with coastal provinces getting 59% and the interior ones 41%. Outcomes of economic policies during the Reform period are exceptional,[138] but at the same time they generated a remarkable widening of the income gap between coastal and interior regions.[139] The difficulties which China was facing in 2009 to tackle with poverty reduction are well illustrated in the report by the WB—Poverty Reduction and Economic Management Department (2009). This notwithstanding, Xinjiang's performance was sustained, maintaining an average 8.9% annual growth between 1978 and 1990.[140] From data available in Statistical Yearbooks, we can notice that Xinjiang's GDP grew faster in the 1990s than in the previous decade. In the early 1990s and for the whole decade, the region received massive state subsidies and investments mainly targeted at infrastructural works, and this policy shift must have been the result of the acknowledgment, from the side of the central leadership, of the importance of Xinjiang as a resource-rich and strategically located region. In the year 2000, Xinjiang ranked twelfth among China's thirty-one provinces for per capita GDP, with the first eleven positions being mainly taken up by coastal regions.[141]

According to our analysis, Xinjiang's GDP increased at a fast pace up to the year 2000, when it started to grow at a slightly slower rate. Moreover, from 1999 to 2009, the GDP in the region increased at a slower rate if compared to the national figure. This notwithstanding, the efforts of the central and regional governments to relieve the local population from poverty and underdevelopment turned out to be successful:

[137] Renard (2002, p. 343).

[138] Poverty Reduction and Economic Management Department (2009).

[139] Smith (2000).

[140] Wiemer (2004, p. 164).

[141] Beijing, Tianjin, Hebei, Liaoning, Heilongjiang, Shanghai, Jiangsu, Zhejiang, Fujian, Shandong and Guangdong were ahead of Xinjiang.

Development plans and investments in infrastructures from different provinces and regions, as well as from the central government, noticeably improved the standards of life of the local population and triggered an urbanization process which is changing the XUAR's cities and countryside forever. An important characteristic of the economic development in the region is the still state-owned nature of the majority of Xinjiang assets, which shape an economic environment which has not been fully integrated into the socialist market system such as it came out from the Reform era.[142] At the same time, while there are authors who maintain that the economic policies implemented in Xinjiang following Beijing's directives until 2012 are nothing more than a continuation of developmental measures implemented during the 1990s,[143] we here assume that embryonic dynamics of market economy are appearing in the region. On this line, Chaudhuri (2005) assesses that back in 1996, 41% of Xinjiang labor force was employed in state-owned units, which decreased to about 34 and 30% in 2000 and 2001, respectively. Despite the fact that this percentage is still very high if compared to the national average, during the Reform period the ownership patterns changed considerably. Chaudhuri then underlines that the growth of private and other types of ownership in 2001 contributed up to 75% of the gross industrial output value in the region at current prices. A "tremendous success",[144] if compared with the performance of state-owned enterprises, which reached a mere share of 14%.[145]

Matched with still planned investment policies, this new economic environment is having an impact on the society, and playing a role in the distribution of resources and capital, making space for the gradual appearance of an emerging Uyghur bourgeoisie, a social class which is clearly distinguishing itself from the rest of Uyghur society, mainly rural and still conducting a traditional way of life.[146] As Chaudhuri argues,

[142] An interesting updating on the current debate on state-owned versus private ownership in Chinese economy can be read in Xie et al. (2012).

[143] Mainly Becquelin (2004, p. 360) and Wiemer (2004).

[144] Chaudhuri (2005, p. 15).

[145] I calculated percentages from data available in the XJSYs.

[146] These dynamics internal to Uyghur society are analyzed and discussed in the works by Ilham Tohti.

widening rural–urban income disparities became the main source of inequalities in Xinjiang during the Reform period. At the same time, I appraise that over the years, the share of urban households' living and food expenditure per capita decreased consistently, and this was not the case in the case for rural residents. This can be explained with the growing costs of life in Xinjiang's urban areas, where investments are changing the value of local resources and commodities.

A comprehensive but concise overview of policy measures and development projects launched in order to cope with growing disparities within the Chinese population can be found in the report by the WB's Poverty Reduction and Economic Management Department (2009), while a better understanding of the implemented development projects in Xinjiang can be grasped when placed in a broader perspective: While it is usually emphasized that the central government aim is to politically control and stabilize the region, we cannot forget that these development plans fall within the national-level political agenda of an overall interregional rebalancing. Since at least 15 years, Beijing efforts have been aimed at reaching a more even distribution of wealth, which means that the target of investments shifted from South-Eastern coastal China to the interior provinces (like Shaanxi) and peripheral regions. This rebalancing has a significant importance in the national equilibrium: Due to the shift in investments' directions, the reduction in purchases from Western countries caused by the financial crisis, the migration of workforce to China's developing areas and the increasing number of strikes and trade-union-led demonstrations aimed at claiming higher salaries and better conditions for workers, the rich South-Eastern coastal areas are currently undergoing deep structural socio-economic changes. If we take into consideration this broader context, it then becomes more clear how and why the still not developed areas of Western China, with their cheap labor, become a key asset in Beijing's agenda and a perfect place where investments and capitals can be directed to build up a manufacturing base and develop the market. Xinjiang's cheap labor and the developing neighboring countries of Central Asia are also an asset in Beijing's strategic agenda of finding new end markets and turning its export-oriented system in an economy which relies on internal markets and low-intensity highly skilled labor.[147]

[147] Cheap labor is needed because it fills the gap left empty by workers in the Eastern parts of China, who do not accept low payments anymore, and they match the requests of cheap labor by companies working in infrastructure and construction.

This renewed emphasis on Western regions is indeed testified by the *Xibu Da Kaifa*, which states in its own wording the target areas for investments, Xibu 西部. The project's geographical scope encompassed, in its first phase, nine provincial-level jurisdictions: Xinjiang Uyghur Autonomous Region, Tibetan Autonomous Region, Ningxia Hui Autonomous Region, Qinghai, Gansu, Shaanxi, Sichuan, Yunnan and Guizhou. Chongqing Municipality was added afterward, and from October 2000, the West came to be defined in terms of eleven provincial-level units, with the addition of Inner Mongolia and Guangxi Zhuang Autonomous Region. In September 2001, the Xiangxi Tujia Miao Autonomous Prefecture, Hubei, Jilin and the Yanbian Korean Autonomous Prefecture in the Chinese Far East were also added.[148] As a first remark, we can say that there is a fundamental ambiguity in the geographical scope of the project: While regions like Xinjiang, Tibet and Sichuan are actually located in Western China, Jilin and the Yanbian Prefecture are in the Chinese Far East. This inconsistency in terms of geographical scope of the project partly reflects a sort of lack of transparency as far as the main targets of the plan are concerned. While the official goal is narrated throughout the propaganda channels as "rebalancing development disparities between South-Eastern coastal provinces and Inner and Western areas of China", also by transferring migrants from overcrowded coastal cities to underpopulated areas at the Western border, some authors see an effort to undertake a huge social engineering operation aimed at finalizing a not-yet-completed state-building process.[149] This process as such has been going on essentially since the first military campaigns aimed at annexing border territories into the imperial core and continued throughout the Qing Dynasty when the Northwestern territories, as last conquests, were annexed (in the case of Xinjiang, in 1759 with Emperor Qianlong's campaigns westward). Due to a number of different factors, such as the vast geographical spaces, the distinctly multicultural environments, as well as the fluctuating governmental presence in these border areas, the state-building capacity and effectiveness of whatever central authorities, have been questioned through different means across the centuries. The debate in Beijing is partly focused on understanding which kind of modern country China

[148] Goodman (2004).

[149] When using these categories afferent to political and social studies, I mainly follow Millward (1998) and Goodman (2004).

wants to be, a "national" country, or either, as it uses to represent itself, a "multinational" country.[150] The whole debate among political scientists, anthropologists and sociologists is going in the direction of backing the idea of a "nation-state", with a population belonging to a general concept of "Chinese nation" (*zhonghua minzu* 中华民族[151]). The *Xibu Da Kaifa* is thus considered as a crucial state-building effort, also considering that it entails different levels of administrative units collaborating and interfacing among each other while joining the project. In this way, a transfer of best practices and socio-institutional path dependency are in some ways guaranteed. State building is thus closely interrelated with the nation-building process, which is currently understood by Beijing as one of the main answers to potential socio-political instabilities.

2.9.1 Investment Policies at the Local Level and Center-Periphery Relations

Considering stated and implicit goals of the whole investment scheme, an assessment shall be made on how investments were understood and policies implemented by regional authorities, as well as which kind of state-center relation came out of this process. The economic performance of Xinjiang from 2001 up to now registered an overall growing trend, which is not yet matched by an equivalent social stability. According to my fieldwork outcomes, the government top-down approach toward the local population, together with the rampant corruption among local authorities, shall be pointed out as the main causes of the enduring unrest and instability in the region, and of the low consensus of the *Xibu Da Kaifa* among the Uyghur population. As in every dynamic and highly unstable socio-political context, there are those who are losers and those who gain something: This situation has a negative impact on local communities, but can also be easily turned into an advantage for certain sections of the local society, mainly allowing them to preserve the status quo in terms of geography of power and to get something in return. What is important to underline is that the largest part of the local society is left behind in the whole process.

[150] Diversity in unity.

[151] The theses which are being followed the most by the government think tanks are mainly argued by the sociologist Ma Rong and the politologist Barry Sautman.

One of the main results of our fieldwork is that the central government does not seem to have a firm grip on corrupted local cadres. If we consider the kind of socio-political transformations that the implementation of this project entails, together with what can be considered as side effects at a local level in terms of redistribution of power, what comes out is that the reallocation of the generated wealth is still unequal. This assessment is backed by field observations and the collected data: Those companies which are winning the bids and joining the huge construction efforts are mainly state-owned enterprises (SOEs) managed by Han Chinese officials and businessmen connected to the Party, or wither by PLA high-ranking officers. These perceived and actual inequalities and creeping tension,[152] together with the total distrust in an entire political system by the Uyghur people, culminated in the events of July 2009, when hundreds of people took the streets of Urumqi in a protest against discrimination and in a quest for equal rights for Uyghurs and Hans.[153] In the way discrimination is understood in this context, it can be explained as both perceived and real.[154]

On the other side, official documents and reports on the Great Development of the West consist basically in a series of figures, which show growing trends and outstanding results, together with how the standards of living for all the peoples in Xinjiang increased. The import-export volume, local GDP growth rates, FDIs and other economic data are all considered and analyzed as key factors of economic and social development.[155] Simultaneously, a better environment for cooperation among administrative entities and a wealthier Northwest, open to every aspect of the outside world and markets, are being propagandized as outstanding outcomes.

Jia Qinglin, member of the CCP's Politburo Standing Committee, and Chairman of the Chinese People's Political Consultative Conference (CPPCC), conducted an inspection tour in Xinjiang in August 2011, where he stressed the need to accelerate development in the region, by "leaps and bounds" (跨越式 kuàyuèshì) in line with the goals of both the *Xibu Da Kaifa* program and the Xinjiang Working Forum. During visits

[152] Which can be compared to what happens in a steamer.

[153] Different narratives.

[154] It depends on the point of view, Han and Uyghurs.

[155] http://news.xinhuanet.com/ziliao/2005-11/02/content_3719691.htm.

to Urumqi, Khotan, Ghulja and Changji, and to the new Khorgas Free Trade Zone, Jia called for efforts to "turn Xinjiang into an important gateway and base for China's opening-up policy". Jia emphasized the need to implement "reconstruction" projects with the aim of "improving the livelihood of all ethnic groups". He inspected the "safe houses for a well-off population" (*anju fumin* 安居富民) in Khotan County, the "project sites for protecting and reconstructing old urban areas" in Nanshi district in Ghulja and the "Heijiashan shantytown reconstruction area" in Tian Shan district in Urumqi. Jia urged local authorities to implement the CCP policies toward ethnic minorities, including educational activities to promote the spirit of "loving the great motherland and constructing a beautiful homeland" and to reinforce ethnic solidarity. He mentioned bilingual education, government-directed religious management and the training of ethnic minority cadres as important political tools for maintaining stability in the border region.[156] Zhang Chunxian, the Xinjiang CCP secretary who replaced Wang Lequan in 2010 and was succeeded by Chen Quanguo in 2016, specifically linked the implementation of housing projects with the promotion of long-term stability in the region, referring to the development and improvement of people's livelihoods entailed in the region's 12th Five-Year Plan.[157]

At the same time, critics of the housing projects maintain that the destruction of the old city of Kashgar, carried on since 2001 in the framework of a "residents' resettlement project", is mainly provoked by the massive investments in real estate entailed by the Great Development of the West. Demolitions and evictions reached a climax in 2009 and 2010, with approximately 60.000 households involved in the Old City, and 900 million of RMB allocated for the "redevelopment plan". Human right advocates and some political analysts argue that the protests of 2008 in Tibet and 2009 in Xinjiang urged the government to adopt aggressive assimilative programs in Southern Xinjiang, programs which were categorized under the "umbrella" of governmental development and investment plans. At the same time, the still preserved small

[156] Xinhua, "Jia Qinglin Inspects Xinjiang, Calls for Advancing Leapfrog Development and Long-Term Stability" (贾庆林新疆调研: 推进新疆跨越式发展和长治久安 "Jia Qinglin Xinjiang diaoyan: tuijin Xinjiang kuayueshi fazhan he changzhi jiuan", 26 August 2010).

[157] Xinhua, "Leapfrog Development in Xinjiang Highlights the Concept of People's Livelihood" (新疆跨越式发展彰显民生理念 "Xinjiang kuayueshi fazhan zhangxian minsheng linian", 9 December 2010).

parts of the Old City have been put under the management and supervision of private touristic companies from Inner China. Resettlement of nomads and problems due to overpopulation—caused by the huge migration of Han peoples from Inner China—are also considered to be negative consequences of the Western Development Plan. Scholars and human rights advocates like Nicholas Becquelin affirm that economic and social developments are not the ultimate goals of the Western Development Plan, while the German scholar H. Holbig (2004) maintains that the main objective of the scheme is to quell unrest among non-Han people through concerted fast economic transformations of the region.[158]

The explosion of tensions occurred during the July 5 events, which have been regarded by a number of sources as a reaction of the local population to the failure of the plan to convey interethnic economic parity. Therefore, the main idea supported by analysts and scholars is that interregional economic balance as pursued through broad state investments did not "tackle the nationalities issue", but merely exacerbated Uyghur marginalization from the economy. Over ten years (2000–2009), Uyghurs' poverty rate increased, and job discrimination continued to be widespread. In separate surveys of jobs advertised on the Internet, CECC and UHRP reported that Uyghurs were frequently excluded from employment opportunities on the basis of their ethnicity and linguistic abilities. Becquelin writes: "(…) The socio-economic development of ethnic minorities continues to fall behind on all indicators: Southern Xinjiang (with a 95% non-Han population) has an average per capita income half the provincial average. In the more prosperous Eastern Yili Kazakh Autonomous Prefecture, at the border with Kazakhstan, 98% of the officially designated 'poor' population is non-Han. (…) The campaign to Open up the West, serving primarily as a vehicle for the interests of the state, gives no sign of altering this discriminative pattern".[159] The Work Forum on Xinjiang held in Beijing in May 2010 has been perceived by a number of analysts as a tacit admission of the plan failures by the Chinese central leadership, which convened it to assess the economic policies in the region and to adjust them accordingly. At the meeting, there were no Uyghur participants, not even

[158] Holbig (2004).

[159] Becquelin (2004, pp. 358–378).

those within the CCP ranks. At the Work Forum, the focus on natural resources industries had been largely reaffirmed, but also a few initiatives to move state investments from the Han-dominated Northern parts of Xinjiang were included.

If we take a look at the criticisms triggered by the "19 provinces and municipalities support Xinjiang" concept and implementation, we shall firstly focus on the original idea for the whole plan. As a first remark, we shall say that "support Xinjiang" can be interpreted with a political meaning, well before the operational one. In the framework of the national policy aimed at reaching a new equilibrium of economic and social development at the national level, and of the broader need to find new development areas to invest the surplus of capital owned by private and public enterprises, it is important to underline that the development of Western and Inner regions, and the shift of investments from the South-Eastern rich coastal areas to the less developed areas, is deeply embedded in Beijing's strategic plans. Another goal is to relieve the overcrowded coastal areas from the overpopulation problem and transfer migrants to different territories, maybe closer to the migrants' places of origin. In this way, the issue of social services to be provided to migrants and their families in overcrowded cities could also be partially solved.

What has been considered problematic by intellectual and academic circles in Xinjiang is the basic concept of "supporting Xinjiang", with its rather implicit unidirectionality. The first official challenge to this idea was represented by a conference organized in Urumqi's Kunlun Hotel from 24 to 26 June 2011. This meeting of academics and scholars, which attracted experts of Xinjiang and Islam from all over the country, was named "The leapfrog development and the construction of a harmonious society in Xinjiang" and was organized by Prof. Dilmurat Omar, of Kazakh ethnicity, director of the College of Anthropology at Xinjiang Normal University.[160]

[160]At the time, I was in Urumqi and invited by two professors to participate in the meeting, but when I asked Prof. Omar to be enrolled he said that "foreigners were not allowed to attend the meeting, and that, in case you would have joined them, the participants would consider it not convenient". These difficulties and ambiguities notwithstanding, which are actually not so rare in the region, did not prevent me from obtaining information about the talk: Under the official wording, the main issue in question was: "why always talking about supporting Xinjiang, and ever think of Xinjiang giving a contribute supporting something elsewhere"? Due to the nature of the conference, and to the organizers and participants, some of whom are well connected with the regional political leadership,

The officially accepted narrative had an opposite flavor: At China's Joint Provincial Pavilion at the Shanghai Expo 2010 (1 May–31 October), the Xinjiang wing was emphasizing the fact that "Xinjiang is a good place", which means that businessmen must be optimistic about the regional investment environment, that its land is exceptionally gifted with natural resources and high-quality farmland and pastures, and that Beijing payed a particular strategic attention to investments in Xinjiang. Thus, the official message puts still an emphasis on the necessity to support Xinjiang. This means that while Beijing admits that problems hindering the smooth investment process, at the same time it is showing to consider and take important measures to tackle with them and, thanks to a better understanding of the regional environment, to significant support and subsidies, and to a new entrepreneurial spirit, it will be possible to take advantage from the strategic location and the resource-rich territory, and to gain more than what could be imagined at the beginning. This is the basic argument underpinning the government propaganda on the 19 provinces and cities plan. Up to 2012, it seemed to have been rather convincing.

An effective synthesis of concerns and reservations raised by economists and the wider scholarly community has been published by the magazine *Outlook Weekly* on 4 May 2010, in a piece titled "While central authorities start the biggest plan to support Xinjiang, next year funding will probably exceed 10 billion Rmb" (中央启动最大规模对口新疆，明年资金可能超百亿 *Zhongyang qidong zuida guimo duikou Xinjiang, mingnian zijin keneng chao baiyi*). After a brief premise on the meaning of funding, talents and management, combined altogether to better support Xinjiang, and the assessment that in 2009 the average income of Xinjiang people was just 70% of the national average, the journalist quotes part of the interviews made during the Conference on the National Plan to Support Xinjiang (全国对口支援新疆工作会议 *Quanguo duikou zhiyuan Xinjiang gongzuo huiyi*), held the same year.

we shall say that the event was organized in an attempt to convey a message to Beijing, in relation to the 19 provinces and cities plan: "Inner China provinces are supporting us, but do not you think that we might also be willing to support other parts of China? Why the national policy is so focused on a XUAR which needs help, and never considers the help and support which can be provided by Xinjiang itself?" Due to the political sensitivity of the issue, foreigners, even foreign students affiliated to a Chinese university, were not allowed to attend. In general, when we come to issues related to Xinjiang, their meaning notwithstanding, international attention was not welcomed yet.

The Plan is considered as a great opportunity to solve once and for all the development problems in the region, and as an adjustment and attempt to reframe the previously implemented policies related to the Great Development of the West plan. Accordingly, the 19 provinces and cities plan is understood as a completion and an integration of the *Xibu Da Kaifa*. Tracing a brief history of the "supporting plans" implemented by the Chinese government in Xinjiang since the 50s, the final goal of this huge influx of investments, professionals and technology is assessed as being the reduction in the development gap between Western and Eastern China, and the setting-up of a relatively well-off society (小康社会 *xiaokang shehui*). Considering the thirteen years experience of the already implemented "supporting plans", including the rebuilding process after the devastating Wenchuan earthquake, three main adjustments are noticed in this last one: (1) The range of the support is vaster: new supported and supporting areas are included, broadening the scope of the plan. The emphasis is on the support to the Xinjiang Production and Construction Corps, which, for being the guarantors of stability in the region, deserved—in the mind of the central government—a strengthened help. (2) A better coordination between donors and beneficiaries: the two parts needed to feel engaged, and work together in order to overcome difficulties and obtain results. On this basis, a more rational matching of supporting and supported parts is required and shall take into consideration the geographical, economic and cultural common features of the two parts (for instance, provinces rich in carbon shall support similar areas in Western China). (3) The focus of the support is shifted to grassroots units, border areas and bingtuan farms, and particularly poor agricultural areas in Southern Xinjiang. The main aim of the central government has been to set up an effective development mechanism in Xingjian in order to obtain the best outcomes from the investment measures. Using a metaphor, a better integration between hardware and software would have been able to ameliorate the whole Xinjiang economic and political environment. We can reasonably say that a complete transformation and final integration of the region in the Han national core was expected.

Concerning the experience of the recovery measures after the Wenchuan earthquake, the article underlines that it entailed an overall plan to transfer not only funding, but also technology, qualified personnel and knowledge, and, most importantly, it supported local people in their self-development process. At the same time, the recovery plan represented a good opportunity for the government to map out an overall development, which included several important social aspects, like welfare improvement, and financial and pro-market measures. A third positive experience was considered to be the increased possibility to enhance the cooperation and mutual understanding between supporting and supported parts.

Support measures toward areas in extreme need include the strengthening of institutions, and previous experiences in supporting and recovering areas in difficult situations are like a "storage room" where all the tools and useful tips for bilateral development projects are accumulated and can be taken as background advantage to proceed with similar plans in the future.

At this point, we can say that:

- The legislative framework regulating this kind of bilateral support plans is not clear and defined. The technical and economic aspects are not well harmonized on a legal basis, and in the implementation of the project measures, too much is still left to personal discretion without clear regulations, often leaving room to abuse. Moreover, after the completion of the whole project, there is no way to guarantee that the beneficial outcomes will last. We can then say that the legislative framework within which the project measures have been implemented is particularly weak.
- Secondly, the implementation of the bilateral supporting plan, the managing system and the implementing mechanisms are not yet sound: Often the enthusiasm of helping enterprises and personnel is not evident, and there is no way to guarantee that the planned outcomes will be reached. Moreover, in some projects, there are preliminary opening procedures which are not standard, others that after the signature of the agreement are hard to carry out, and there are also other projects which die during their implementation process. All these problems certainly, on a certain degree, freeze the enthusiasm of the two parts.
- Furthermore, a real evaluation mechanism on the scientific nature and effectiveness of the whole program is lacking. For example, during the implementation of support-related measures, because of the shortcomings in the evaluation work, some policies which had already proved to be a failure were still being adopted. At the same

time, the span and depth of the supervision of the policies in force were not sufficiently effective, the focus of the supervision was not clear nor complete, and it lacked a supervision on the outcomes of the project phases and measures.

- As a fourth remark, the relationship between supporting and supported parts is often inadequate and, for certain aspects, lacks transparency. Guo Lihong, former leader at the Research Centre for Economic and Technological Development, now researcher at the Research Center on Development Issues at the Council of State, thinks that, in supporting the highly damaged areas in the past, because a systematic plan coordinating the local economic and social development was lacking, the result was that "the buildings hit by the natural adversities, were probably constructed on very good foundations, but could be never used for industrial purposes". When the supported part decides which supporting project is needed, it usually adopts a nearsighted perspective, considering just that funding, goods and materials, the most abundant possible, can be obtained, striving to receive free help just to resolve the immediate difficulties, simply looking for a big quantity of projects, since an issue of "honor" (面子 *mianzi*) is still there. At the same time, the supporting part has usually little knowledge in terms of development projects. The financing parts are normally opting for this or that project on the basis of the benefits which can be gained for itself, while at the very end the effectiveness of the allocated funding was not so high, and at the same time, the management of the later stages of project implementation was still weak.
- Another important assessment is that it is almost impossible to correctly handle the relationship between market and government during the implementation process of the supporting measures. Since several projects are government-directed, it becomes difficult to avoid the planned economy mind-set, and the efficiency of the deployment of resources remains low, thus it is not possible for the government to fully act as a guide, and in this way, the positive and lacking aspects of the government intervention become both clear.

Xiong Wenzhao, a renowned political scientist, considering the problems presented here, holds that the present univocal support plans lack systematization, and that the first necessary step to take is to speed up the path toward the accomplishment of an exhaustive legal system, which should stand out for systematization. In his works, he remarks that only through one system, one standard and one procedure, the legal framework can stabilize the dynamics of these unilateral development projects. There is also the need to distinguish the relation between free support and help from profits, to build a "harmonious system" following the tracking of these support projects in a market environment. This is the only guarantee for an effective long-term implementation of these unilateral support projects. A critical stance is adopted also by Li (2018), who argues that the swift changes brought about by these assistance programs have a negative impact on Uyghurs and Xinjiang society as a whole. For instance, the perception to depend on external assistance might not help Uyghurs to put forward a concept of development for their own territory, and the adopted model, perceived as top-down, should be adjusted to local conditions.

Bibliography

Anderson, Benedict (1983), *Imagined Communities: Reflections on the Origin and Spread of Nationalism*, Verso.

Barboza, David (15 August 2010), "China Passes Japan as Second-Largest Economy", in *The New York Times.*

Becquelin, Nicholas (2004), "Staged Development in Xinjiang", in *The China Quarterly*, vol. 178, pp. 358–378.

Beller-Hann, lldikò (2007), *Community Matters in Xinjiang 1880–1949—Towards a Historical Anthropology of the Uyghurs*, Brill.

Beller-Hann, Ildikò (2008), *Community Matters in Xinjiang 1880–1949: Towards a historical anthropology of the Uyghur*, Brill.

Benson, Linda (1998), "The *Begs* of Xinjiang: Between Two Worlds", in *Bulletin of the School of Oriental and African Studies*, Vol. 61, Issue 2, pp. 207–278.

Bhalla, A. S., Shufang Qiu (2006), *Poverty and Inequality Among Chinese Minorities* (Routledge Studies on Chinese Economy), Routledge Chapman & Hall.

Bloomberg (1 July 2002), "Exxon, Shell, Gazprom Buy 15% Each in China Pipeline".

Bovingdon, Gardner (2010), *The Uyghurs: Strangers in Their Own Land*, Columbia University Press.

Burke, Jason (2004), *Al-Qaeda: The True Story of Radical Islam*, I.B. Tauris.

Cappelletti, Alessandra (2014), "Social Change in Kashgar: From a Cultural and Religious Oasis Along the Silk Road to the 'Dubai of Central Asia'", in *Proceedings of the "Social Changes in China" Academic Workshop*, Catholic University of Milan, Aracne Editrice.

Chaudhuri, Debasish (2005), "A Survey of the Economic Situation in Xinjiang and its Role in the Twenty-First Century", in *China Report*, Vol. 41, Issue 1, pp. 1–38.

Clark, William (2011), "Ibrahim's Story", in *Asian Ethnicity*, Vol. 12, Issue 2, pp. 203–219.

Colacoglu, Selcuk (2012), "Turkey's East Asian Policy: From Security Concerns to Trade Partnerships", in *PERCEPTIONS*, Vol. XVII, Issue 4, pp. 129–158.

Dawut, Rahila, Rachel Harris (2002), "Mazar Festivals of the Uyghurs: Music, Islam and the Chinese State", in *British Journal of Ethnomusicology*, Vol. 11, Issue 1, pp. 101–118.

Dillon, Michael (2004), *Xinjiang—China's Muslim Far Northwest*, Routledge Curzon.

Fan, Shenggen, Ravi Kanbur, Zhang Xiaobo (2009), *Regional Inequality in China: Trends, Explanations and Policy Responses*, Routledge Chapman & Hall.

Fleming, Peter (1936), *News from Tartary: A Journey from Peking to Kashmir*, Tarcher.

Forbes, Andrew D. W. (2011), *Warlords and Muslims in Chinese Central Asia: A Political History of Republican Xinjiang, 1911–1949*, White Lotus (reprint—first edition 1986).

Fravel, Taylor (2008), *Strong Borders, Secure Nation*, Princeton University Press.

Gladney, Dru C. (1991), *Muslim Chinese: Ethnic Nationalism in the People's Republic*, Harvard University Press.

Gladney, Dru (2004), "Responses to Chinese rule: Patterns of cooperation and opposition", in S.F. Starr (ed.), *Xinjiang: China's Muslim Borderland*, pp. 375–396. Armonk (NY): M. E. Sharpe.

Goodman, David (2004), *China's Campaign to "Open Up the West": National, Provincial, and Local Perspectives*, Cambridge University Press.

He, Lan, Weiming Shi (1994), *'Mo nan qing': Portrait of the Production and Construction Corps. in Mongolia*, Law Press (何岚, 史卫民, 漠南情: 内蒙古生产建设兵团写真, 法律出版社, 北京 1994).

Holbig, Heike (2004), "The Emergence of the Campaign to Open Up the West: Ideological Formation, Central Decision-Making, and the Role of the Provinces", in *China Quarterly*, Special Issue "China's Campaign to 'Open Up the West': National, Provincial and Local Perspectives", No. 178 (June), pp. 335–357.

Hopkirk, Peter (1980), *Foreign Devils on the Silk Road*, University of Massachusetts Press.

Hopkirk, Peter (1992), *The Great Game: The Struggle for Empire*, Kodansha International.

Hoppe, Thomas (1995), *Die ethnischen Gruppen Xinjiangs: Kulturunterschiede und interethnische Beziehungen*, Mitteilunen des Instituts fur Asienkunde, Hamburg.

Howell, Anthony, Cindy Fan (2011), "Migration and Inequality in Xinjiang: A Survey of Han and Uyghur Migrants in Urumqi", in *Eurasian Geography and Economics*, Vol. 52, Issue 1, pp. 119–139.

Hsu, Immanuel (2000), *The Rise of Modern China*, Oxford University Press (6th edition).

Iredale et al. (2001), *Contemporary Minority Migration, Education, and Ethnicity in China*, Edward Elgar Publishing.

Jarring, Gunnar (1935), "The Ordam-Padishah-System of Eastern Turkistan Shrines", in *Geografiska Annaler*, Vol. 17 (Supplement: Hyllningsskrift Tillagnad Sven Hedin), pp. 348–354.

Khalid, Adeeb (1999), *The Politics of Muslim Cultural Reform: Jadidism in Central Asia*, University of California Press.

Khalid, Adeeb (2007), *Islam After Communism: Religion and Politics in Central Asia*, University of California Press.

Kim, Hodong (2004), *Holy War in China. The Muslim Rebellion and State in Chinese Central Asia, 1864–1877*, Stanford University Press.

Kuchins, Andrew, Frederick Starr (2010), "The Key to Success in Afghanistan—A Modern Silk Road Strategy", Silk Road Paper, Central Asia-Caucasus Institute, Silk Road Studies Program.

Kuo, Lily (7 May 2019), "Revealed: New Evidence of China's Mission to Raze He Mosques of Xinjiang", in *The Guardian*.

Li, Rose Maria (1989), "Migration to China's Northern Frontier, 1953–1982", in *Population and Development Review*, Vol. 15, Issue 3, pp. 502–538.

Li, Yuhui (2018), *China's Assistance Program in Xinjiang*, Lexington Books.

Lin, Christina (2011), "China's New Silk Road to the Mediterranean: The Eurasian Land Bridge and Return of Admiral Zheng He", ISPSW Strategy Series, Issue. 165.

Lin, Shaun, James D. Sidaway, Chih Yuan Woon (2019), "Reordering China, Respacing the World: Belt and Road Initiative (一带一路) as an Emergent Geopolitical Culture", in *The Professional Geographer*, Vol. 71, Issue 3, pp. 507–522.

MacKerras, Colin (1994), *China's Minorities: Integration and Modernization in the Twentieth Century*, Oxford University Press.

Martin, Terry (2001), *The Affirmative Action Empire: Nations and Nationalism in the Soviet Union 1923–1939*, Cornell University Press.

McMillen, Donald (1979), "Xinjiang and the Production and Construction Corps: A Han Organisation in a NonHan Region", in *The Australian Journal of Chinese Affairs*, No. 6 (July), pp. 65–91.

McMillen, Donald H. (1984), "Xinjiang and Wang Enmao: New Directions in Power, Policy and Integration?" in *The China Quarterly*, Cambridge University Press.

Millward, James (1998), *Beyond the Pass: Economy, Ethnicity and Empire in Qing Xinjiang, 1759–1864*, Stanford University Press.

Millward, James A. (2004), "Violent Separatism in Xinjiang: A Critical Assessment", East West Center.

Millward, James (2007), *Eurasian Crossroads: A History of Xinjiang*, Columbia University Press.

Millward, James (2009), "Does the 2009 Urumchi Violence Mark a Turning Point?" in *Central Asian Survey*, Vol. 28, Issue 4, pp. 347–360.

Orlik, Thomas (2011), *Understanding China's Economic Indicators: Translating the Data into Investment Opportunities*, FT Press.

Pannel, Clifton W., Philipp Schmidt (2006), "Structural Change and Regional Disparities in Xinjiang, China", in *Eurasian Geography and Economics*, Vol. 47, Issue 3, pp. 329–352.

Qarluq, Abduresit J. (7 November 2012), "Policy and Socio-Cultural Change Among Uyghurs in Contemporary China—The Transfer of Uyghur Peasant Workers from XUAR to the Chinese Coastal Areas", Presentation at Oriental University of Naples.

Rashid, Ahmed (2002), *Jihad: The Rise of Militant Islam in Central Asia*, Yale University Press.

Reed, J. Todd, Diana Raschke (2010), *The ETIM, China's Islamic Militants and the Global Terrorist Threat*, Greenwood Publishing Group.

Renard, Mary-Francoise (2002), "A Pessimistic View on the Impact of Regional Inequalities", in *China Economic Review*, Vol. 13, pp. 341–344.

Rong, Ma (14–15 April 2006), "Education of Ethnic Minorities in Contemporary China", Paper presented at the International Symposium on China's Positive Policies in Minority Education: Plural Perspectives, Dickinson College.

Rong, Ma (2011), *Population and Society in Contemporary Tibet*, Hong Kong University Press.

Rudelson, Justin Jon (1997), *Oasis Identities: Uyghur Nationalism along China's Silk Road*, Columbia University Press.

Sautman, Barry (1998), "Preferential policies for ethnic minorities in China: the case of Xinjiang", in *Nationalism & Ethnic Politics*, 4, 1 (Winter), pp. 86–118.

Sawada, Minoru (2001a), "The System of Ordam Padishah (the Oasis of Yangi Hisar)", in *Journal of the History of Sufism*, Vol. 3, pp. 89–111.

Sawada, Minoru (2001b), "Tarim Basin Mazars: A Fieldwork Report", in *Journal of the History of Sufism*, Vol. 3, pp. 39–61.

Schein, Louisa (2000), *Minority Rules: The Miao and the Feminine in China's Cultural Politics*, Duke University Press.

Shah, Angela, Stanley Reed (1 May 2012), "A Modern Silk Road Between Asia and the Middle East", in *The New York Times*.

Sheel, Kamal (1989), *Peasant Society and Marxist Intellectuals in China: Fang Zhimin and the Origin of a Revolutionary Movement in the Xinjiang Region*, Princeton University Press.

Schiek, Sebastian (2017), "Movement on the Silk Road: China's 'Belt and Road' Initiative as an Incentive for Intergovernmental Cooperation and Reforms at Central Asia's Borders". SWP Research Paper 2017/RP 12, 33 pages.

Smith, Christopher J. (2000), *China in the Post-utopian Age*, Westview Press.

Starr, Frederick S. (ed.) (2004), *Xinjiang. China's Muslim Borderland*, M. E. Sharpe.

Thum, Rian (2012), "Modular History: Identity Maintenance before Uyghur Nationalism", in *The Journal of Asian Studies*, Vol. 71, Issue 3, pp. 627–653.

Thum, Rian (2014), *The Sacred Routes of Uyghur History*, Harvard University Press.

TIME World (23 May 2011), "In China's Wild West, a 'Black Gold' Rush Takes Place".

Wan Weiping, Wang Hanlin (2008), *A Hundred Years of Wang Zhen*, Xinjiang Production and Construction Corps. Publishing House (万卫平, 王瀚林, 百年王震, 新疆生产建设兵团出版社, 五家渠 2008).

Wang Shuanqian (1999), *Xinjiang Towards the 21st Century*, Xinjiang People's Press (王拴乾 [1999], 走向21世纪的新疆, 新疆人民出版社, 乌鲁木齐).

Warikoo (ed.) (2016), *Xinjiang—China's Northwest Frontier*, Routledge.

Wen Jun and Hu Angang (2001), "The New Thinking in Accelerating the Development of National Minorities Areas", in Hu Angang (ed.), *The New Strategy of the Opening Up of the West*, table 8.17, p. 295, China Planning Press (胡鞍钢, 温军 [2001], 少数民族地区加快发展新思路, 西部大开发新战略, 中国计划出版社).

Wiemer, Calla (2004), "The Economy of Xinjiang", in Frederick Starr (ed.), *China's Muslim Borderland*, M. E. Sharpe.

Xie, Li, Li (2012), "Guojinmintui: A New Round of Debate in China on State Versus Private Ownership", in *Science & Society*, Vol. 76, Issue 3, pp. 291–318.

Xinhua News Agency (4 February 2002), "Xinjiang's 'Black and White' Strategy Boosts Economy, Living Standards".

Xinhua News Agency (2 January 2009), "Xinjiang Becomes China's Second Largest Crude Oil Producer".

Xinjiang Statistical Yearbook, China Statistical Publisher, Beijing 1990–2017 (新疆统计年鉴, 中国统计出版社, 北京 1999–2017).

Yang, Dali (1990), "Pattern of China's Regional Development Strategy", in *The China Quarterly*, Vol. 122, pp. 223–257.

Yitao, Tao, Zhiguo Lu (2018), *Special Economic Zones and China's Development Path*, Springer and Social Sciences Academic Press.

Yuan, Qing-li (1990), "Population Changes in the Xinjiang Uighur Autonomous Region (1949–84)", in *Central Asian Survey*, Vol. 9, Issue 1, pp. 49–73.
Zhang, Anfu, Alessandra Cappelletti (2012), "Study on the Development of the Tuntian System in Northern Xinjiang During the Qing Dynasty", in *MING QING Studies*, Aracne Editrice.

CHAPTER 3

Social Development in Xinjiang Uyghur Autonomous Region

3.1 Preliminary Notes on Sociological Research in China and Xinjiang

This analysis cannot be conducted without considering, even though in a preliminary manner, the stage of development of sociological research and methods in China.[1] While modern sociology is considered to be born in Europe in the eighteenth century, in China it became a prominent and respected discipline, in the way it has been articulated by Western scholars, only recently. Shortly after the 1949 Communist takeover, studies in the field of sociology have officially been banned from the official curricula as well as from scholarly research. Under the influence of Lenin's characterization of Auguste Comte's sociology as "bourgeois", the new government of Mao Zedong shut down all the related educational and research programs in 1952. Sociologists were labeled "guardians of the bourgeoisie" and became targets of censorship

[1] For an exhaustive outline of the history of sociological research in China, see Chen (2018). Bian (2003), Bian and Zhang (2008), and Cheng and So (1983) are useful readings to understand the various stages in the development of the discipline in China.

This chapter is a development of the idea expressed in the article "Developing the Land and the People: Social Development Issues in Xinjiang Uyghur Autonomous Region (1999–2009)", in *East Asia*, June 2015, Vol. 32, No. 2, Springer, pp. 137–171.

A. Cappelletti, *Socio-Economic Development in Xinjiang Uyghur Autonomous Region*,
https://doi.org/10.1007/978-981-15-1536-1_3

and torture during political campaigns, anti-rightist movements and the Cultural Revolution. After the Mao era, Deng Xiaoping started to acknowledge that sociology could play a role in the improvement of education, and mainly within the context of the modernization process that China started to uncritically embrace. The rehabilitation of the discipline as scholarly and academic knowledge in China can be traced back to 1979, when the Chinese Sociological Association was re-established. Due to previous historical events, at the time only a few sociologists were still in the country, and Fei Xiaotong (1910–2005) was called to be in charge of the restoration of the discipline. Educated both in China and abroad—mainly with Bronislaw Malinowski at the London School of Economics and with Robert Redfield at the University of Chicago—he was deeply influenced by the interpretations of sociology put forward by Northern American scholars. Reputed to be China's first and most influential social scientist, Fei Xiaotong was a pioneer in scholarly research related to Chinese minorities, and in particular to sociological and anthropological aspects of Chinese population.

Case study analyses and fieldworks started to be conducted only relatively recently. This said, research in territories such as Tibet and Xinjiang is still subject to a number of restrictions; therefore, fieldworks conducted in those areas can produce biased or difficult-to-interpret outcomes. Because of these limitations, researchers have been inclined to rely on official reports, data and figures; case study analyses and fieldworks are usually conducted on limited samples; an interdisciplinary approach is therefore requested to generate valid outcomes. Relying on hybrid sets of data and developing interdisciplinary analytical and interpretative tools is an essential aspect for delivering sophisticated studies and research works. At the same time, the debate on research methods and standards in minority areas is still ongoing.[2] As a consequence, researches conducted in minority areas which include survey outcomes started to be published only recently in Chinese scholarly journals specialized in sociology, and on a few scholarly publications in English language.[3] My choice has been to look at one of the politically and socially most controversial areas

[2] See Previato (2016).

[3] Scholars who have conducted such researches in Xinjiang Uyghur Autonomous Region are, among the others, Yang Shenming, Ma Rong, Abduresit Jelil Qarluq, Ilham Tohti, Zulhayiat Ismayil, Rahile Dawut, Yitzhak Shichor, Justin Rudelson, Micheal Dillon, Li Yuhui. The works of these scholars will be quoted across this chapter.

of China, Xinjiang, adopting a perspective "from inside",[4] to analyze socio-economic conditions and intraregional disparities, with an effort to identify the major determinants of inequality. During the research process, new research hints emerged thanks to the adopted methodology, which was flexible enough to be adjusted to the different circumstances encountered during the research.

3.2 Research Methodology and Fieldwork in Xinjiang

I conceived this part of the work by considering the structure of the United Nations Development Programme (UNDP) reports on social development, as well as a variety of secondary sources.[5] As far as specific issues with limited availability of data and information are concerned, for instance the analysis of phenomena such as alcoholism, family violence and HIV in Xinjiang—I made an effort to rely on the available case studies, fieldwork outcomes published by other authors, possible indirect proxies, as well as at existing debates on the generalization of micro-analyses.[6] Research outcomes emerged from this work can be considered as generalizable enough to be interpretable beyond the stringency of severely disciplinary approaches, allowing me to move forward toward a more dynamic and less formalized structuring of the analysis.[7]

In the Poverty Analysis report published by the Poverty Reduction and Economic Management Network of the World Bank in 2009, the importance of household surveys and fieldworks for studying poverty from a qualitative perspective is generally acknowledged. Budget and human capital necessary to conduct such studies are usually limited, and, when not available, analyses and publications released by international organizations tend to depend on official data provided by government agencies. The hybrid set of indicators utilized by Bhalla and Qiu (2006), whom mainly rely on household surveys conducted by foreign

[4]When I write about a perspective "from inside" means that an in-depth fieldwork, involving a particularly intense activity of "participant observation", has been conducted.

[5]For instance, Bhalla and Qiu (2006).

[6]Flyvbjerg (2006, 2011) and Stake (1995, 2006).

[7]Works which contest constraining disciplinary perspectives in conducting research are, among the others, Becher and Trowler (2001), Kuhn (1962), Flyvbjerg et al. (2012), Wenger (1999), and Gibbons (1994).

scholars and CASS researchers,[8] have been taken as reference here, as well as the kind of indirect proxies adopted in the field of micro-history,[9] and cross-sectional analyses conducted on limited samples in studies on education and labor in minority areas.[10] What the two authors do is to provide new insights on 8.41% of the Chinese population (the percentage which the fifty-five Chinese ethnic minorities represent), who also, at the time the authors conducted their research, represented the 40–50%[11] of the absolute poor. As mentioned, the work is based on a hybrid set of indicators and macro data related to a vast geographical area and to culturally and linguistically different peoples.[12] Their analysis has been widely discussed mainly for its originality, new informative material and solid effort to disaggregate data and figures by ethnic affiliation, but it has also been criticized for the considered-too-broad range of peoples it encompasses and attempts to analyze. While Ding Sai states "Minorities living in the Northwest and the Southwest have different socioeconomic characteristics, and hence the patterns of poverty and inequality differ markedly between the two Western regions",[13] Morris Rossabi (2004) appreciates the adoption of Amartya Sen's capability approach and the possible policy direction of this work, which identifies the roots of inequality among Chinese minorities in economic rather than cultural factors. Björn Anders Gustafsson and Sai Ding (2008) challenges some data[14] contained in the work, by highlighting the difference in the living standards among specific minorities.

Off-limits topics such as alcoholism and domestic violence in Xinjiang offer the scientific community a number of research hints which could be considered as suggestions for future enquiries. In some cases, observation, interviews and research intuitions, if cross-matched and cross-referenced, lead to exhaustiveness and rigor.[15]

[8] p. 21.

[9] Levi (1985), Ginzburg (1976), and Bloch (1984).

[10] Hannum and Xie (1998), Hannum (2002), Qarluq (2011a), and Leibold and Chen (2014).

[11] Bhalla and Qiu (2006).

[12] For instance, Uyghurs have a Turkic origin while the Mosuo in Yunnan, for example, have Sino-Tibetan roots.

[13] Ding Sai (2007).

[14] Gustaffson and Zhong (2000).

[15] As far as the theoretical understanding of the adopted methodological framework is concerned, please consider Feyeraband (1984, 1993).

Due to factors such as the characteristics of sociological research in China, and sociocultural and political variations across localities, while it is still possible to find official figures about HIV in Xinjiang over certain spans of time, topics such as alcohol abuse, prostitution and domestic violence are underresearched and collecting data can be a challenge. In some cases, a limited number of case study analyses based on small samplings have been conducted, research results are published in Chinese language, and some topics started to be debated in public opinion circles, mainly blogs and internet forums, normally until censorship make them not available anymore. For these more sensitive issues,[16] I mainly rely on studies conducted by Uyghur scholars such as Abduresit Jelil Qarluq, Zullayat Ismayil and Ilham Tohti, as well as by Han Chinese sociologists such as Ma Rong and Yang Shengmin. In studying alcoholism, I mainly looked at the proxy of pancreatitis and liver-related sicknesses: their spread among Uyghurs can be considered a sign of the diffusion of alcoholism among the Uyghur male population. These authors argue that HIV, alcoholism and family violence are on the rise in the region. All the countries in the world are affected by these issues, but an increasing trend in XUAR takes on a special meaning: some authors questionably blame the diffusion of social and health problems among Uyghurs to a somewhat intentional policy carried on by the central government, which purportedly would have an interest in causing socio-economic damages among Uyghurs, but on the other side they would also contribute to weakening the capacity of autonomous management on the territory by local Uyghur authorities.[17] Some authors strongly assume that the spreading of these problems, like the overall increasing inequality, follows an ethnic trajectory. In summary, we can say that data for this chapter have been collected from the existing articles by Uyghur and Western authors[18]; reports by area experts[19]; Chinese journal articles downloaded from the database China National Knowledge Infrastructure (CNKI); and Chinese national and local government documents.[20]

[16] In this specific case, the wording "sensitive" does not mean political sensitivity, but implies a certain cultural, ethnic and religious stigma which creates problems to free expression and a neutral understanding of issues.

[17] Something which is against Beijing's interests.

[18] Primarily Qarluq and Hayes (2011) and Gill and Gang (2006).

[19] Rudelson (1997) and Renwick (2002).

[20] Mainly provided by the Xinjiang Centre for Disease Control and the Xinjiang AIDS Working Committee Office.

3.3 Xinjiang and Its Development Processes

According to official data published in Xinjiang Statistical Yearbooks, exceptional progresses have been made in Xinjiang society from 1999 to 2016. Just to mention a few figures, the per capita annual expenditure of rural households has more than duplicated: While in 1999 it was 3652 RMB, in 2016 it reached 8277 RMB. The same can be said as far as the per capita annual expenditure of urban households is concerned, which from 18.927 RMB in 1999 got to 75.877 RMB in 2016. Looking at education, students' enrollment in regular institutions of higher education jumped from 74.063 (31.989 of them from minorities) in 2000 to 339.089 (154.404 from minorities) in 2016, registering an increase of almost five times. The number of health institutions (village clinics excluded) increased from 7650 in 2000 to 8330 in 2016, while hospital beds increased from 65.916 in 1999 to 144.535 in 2016. The engagement in infrastructural works from the side of the government can be inferred by looking at the length of paved roads in the region, which increased from 31.059 km in 2000 to 123.929 km in 2016. In terms of environmental protection, investments in pollution treatment projects increased from 223.110.000 to 24.937.180.000 RMB (roughly 112 times more) in the same span of time. This kind rising trend can be assessed in all the items related to social development which can be found in Xinjiang Statistical Yearbooks. The interpretation of these achievements requires an analytical and critical perspective, which can be adopted by selecting a hybrid set of indicators and looking at them from different angles and a qualitative mind-set.

3.3.1 Urbanization

Due to its special role in Xinjiang contemporary society, to its centrality and the unique transformations which is generating in the structure and deep dynamics of Uyghur society, urbanization is considered, in the framework of this book, a breakthrough process in contemporary Xinjiang (Fig. 3.1).

In considering "urbanization" as a sociological concept which can produce inequalities, we mainly rely on the work written by Kenneth Little (2004)[21] on urbanization in the African countries. In the history

[21] Little (2004).

Fig. 3.1 Newspaper board in a village (DSCN 5291. Picture taken by the author)

of Xinjiang, Han settlements close to Uyghur oases and villages were called Han cities (Hancheng 汉城) or *yengi sheher/Hitay bazari*, and represented the first urban settlement in a predominantly rural environment. Their establishment was basically meant at boosting economic development and cultural exchange, increasing fiscal revenues, matching the needs of the entrepreneurial class and spreading the Han system and culture all over the national territory. Classical sociology, modernization theories and the diffusionist and structural schools all consider urbanization as an important contribution to nation building and stabilizing processes,[22] a concept which informed the strategy adopted by central authorities in China.[23] Among the Han settlements in Xinjiang, the most important actors involved in the urbanization process are the

[22] An exhaustive review on the theories of urbanization can be found in Kasarda and Crenshaw (1991).

[23] Millward (2007) and Pannel and Ma (1997).

agricultural-military colonies supported by the central government: Efficient in both military and agricultural tasks, the peoples of these settlements became slowly accustomed to the new environment and developed in parallel with the growth of Uyghur oasis towns. The agricultural-military settlements, once called *tuntian* 屯田 and now *bingtuan* 兵团,[24] shall be considered as one of the main tools in the hands of the authorities to implement their plans of integrating the far-Western border region into the national economy and culture.[25] A comprehensive and detailed study of the process of national integration into the national core of what is now called Xinjiang during the Qing Dynasty is Millward (1998).

When the People's Republic of China was established, the agricultural sector contributed for over 50% of the GDP composition, while in 1979, with the implementation of the free-market reforms, the government started to support the urbanization process. According to the figures dated back to the November 2010 national census, more than 50.3% of the Chinese people (in total 1.34 billion) still lived in the countryside, and only in 2012, the urban population surpassed the rural one for the first time.[26] The comparison of today's data with those related to the first national census in 1953 shows that the urban population is now 43% bigger than then. For the first time, the 2010 census included migrant workers as they were registered in their living place, rather than where their official residence (*hukou* 户口) was, normally in remote countryside villages. China's industrial zones and factories are the main magnet within the cities job market and attract a huge number of urban residents and immigrants. According to the census results, in 2010 more than 220 million Chinese had worked far from home for over six months, almost doubling the 2000s figure. In fact, the census figures announced by the Chinese government show a trend which had already been identified long ago.

[24] For an overview of the history of the bingtuan, see the historical introduction; for getting an understanding of today's bingtuan, see the chapter on Kaṣhgar and Shihezi.

[25] Shichor (2006), Cliff (2009), and Borei (1992).

[26] "China's Urban Population Exceeds Countryside for First Time", in *Bloomberg News*, 17 January 2012.

In addition, the census data show some of the challenges and issues that the Chinese government will have to cope with in the coming decades. For example, Chinese society is aging: The growing amount of pensioners is looked after by fewer workers. China's One-Child Policy can be considered one of the causes of this situation. Moreover, as mentioned, migrant workers are 50% more than ten years ago. The so-called floating population (*liudong renkou* 流动人口) is mainly composed of farmers who move to the country's booming towns and cities to look for a job. They face several problems: Access to services (for instance, health care and education for their children) in the new urban environment is limited; forced evictions and financial speculation in the real estate sector generate social problems which can impact on the overall socio-economic stability of the country; and figures show an imbalance in the proportion female–male population (since nearly six boys to every five girls are born, the situation can turn into a social problem in the future).

According to *The Economist*,[27] in 2005 in order to reach 80% of China's middle class a company needed to be present in at least 60 cities. The projections show that, to reach the same share in 2020, a company will need to set up venues in 212 cities. This means that the Chinese middle class is growing at a significantly fast pace.

What it clearly comes out is that, while a high-powered and well-off middle class can afford a life among skyscrapers offices, shopping malls, expensive cars and brand-new apartments, there is still a vast part of the population, which has to cope with everyday problems mainly due to low wages and weak welfare conditions, ranging from access to adequate housing (the majority of them is living in *danwei* 单位—provided overcrowded dormitories, with public toilets and without kitchen services) to access to educational and healthcare services for themselves and their family members. Furthermore, having a *hukou* from a rural area restricts the possibilities to apply for social services and, for instance, the passport, to access municipal subsidies and bank loans; therefore, the transient status of this floating population creates a general sense of frustration, insecurity and social weakness. In addition, frequent strikes and protests in Chinese industrial cities make authorities worry about the rise of inflation and the related increase in the costs of living, a situation which might be precursor of a divided society divided into a leisure class and a worse off one.

[27] *The Economist*, 16 September 2010.

It is thus evident that China is undergoing one of the greatest demographic shifts in history. Shanghai reached 23.019.148 residents in 2010, Beijing, Chongqing, Tianjin and Guangzhou became megalopolis. The official statements issued by the Chinese government declare that the promotion of rapid urbanization improves living standards and productivity, while millions of peasant laborers are moving to urban centers attracted by the boom in the construction sector and by high wages. As a natural consequence, the pressure on space and resources is increasingly manifest, with traffic growth rates and housing prices rising at a worrying level. But the central plan to transform armies of peasants into citizens and taxpayers is a priority in the government agenda, and the interests at stake behind the real estate sector and automotive industry are too much lucrative and politically relevant to be questioned on a political and social level.

3.3.1.1 Urbanization Processes in Xinjiang After 1949

The logic behind the economic and socio-political measures implemented for pushing ahead the urbanization process in Xinjiang after the "liberation"[28] needs to be understood in the broader context presented here above. The narrative spread by the Chinese central government emphasizes the main two and interconnected targets in the national agenda for Xinjiang: development and stabilization of the region. We assume here that more complex dynamics, involving factors such as the relation between the center and its periphery, are involved, and are at the basis of deep transformations which changed, and still are changing, the region's rural and urban environments. Particularly after the riots started on 5 July 2009, which continued during the whole autumn in different parts of the region,[29] new understandings of the impact of fast urbanization and development emerged: The surplus of rural labor force in the region has generated massive transfers of rural population to urban areas in and outside the region. This "floating population" became known as that part of the society which sells its workforce for cheap. According to

[28] "Liberation" is a term adopted by the Maoist propaganda to name the victory of the CCP over the Nationalist armies in the different regions of China, implying that the Maoists liberated China's peoples from socio-political feudal conditions.

[29] The 2009 riots in Urumqi and other parts of Xinjiang are still a topic of speculation among scholars, due to the lack of verified accounts of the facts. They will be mentioned and partially explained in different parts of this book.

the research fieldworks conducted by Prof. Abduresit Jelil Qarluq in the factories of coastal China, forced transfers of Uyghur peasant workers have been planned and implemented by the central government, with a deep impact on Uyghur communities in Xinjiang. To maintain the situation under control, the Chinese government is adopting a mixture of modernization and diffusionist measures,[30] transferring consistent capitals to Xinjiang and launching massive development projects. At the moment (July 2019), an unprecedented effort to carry on ideological re-education across different sections of the Uyghur society—intellectuals, academics, artists, businessmen, students and so on—is underway.[31]

While statistical figures show that the rate of enrollment in compulsory education, the health system and the standards of living in general are all of benefitting from the rapid urbanization and economic growth in the region, social problems such as alcoholism, HIV diffusion and the disruption of traditional social networks still represent a problem to be managed. The long-term political aim is to urbanize the countryside to facilitate not only economic, but also political development, in order to set the conditions which could eventually favor a long-term growth as well as ultimate national integration. Policies on the use of Uyghur language and regulations on Islam, as well as the diffusion of "modern" dressing codes and ways of life, are pushing toward a sort of full assimilation of the Uyghur regional majority into the national Han core.

Urban development becomes then the central narrative and the alleged focus of the efforts made by central and regional authorities to boost economic growth and improve the people's living standards.

Tuning in Xinjiang Television was already a first step, back in 2010, to understand the plans of the central government for Xinjiang development and to foresee probable consequences. The audience is "bombed" by images of ancient oases like Kashgar and Turfan, emerged from the fragile ecosystem of the Taklamakan Desert, turned into bustling cities with high skyscrapers, new apartment blocks, highways and overpasses, an impressing night illumination and an overall feeling of expectations and vibrancy. In the visual narrative, Uyghurs and Hans live together

[30]On development, modernization and diffusionism, see Dibua (2013).

[31]This is related to the 2014 political campaign "Strike Hard Campaign Against Violent Terrorism", which implied the establishment of ideological reeducation facilities all over the region. The campaign is still ongoing (August 2019).

happily and proactively collaborate for the realization of a modern and harmonious Xinjiang. This is a symbolic dimension of what Beijing and the Xinjiang CCP secretary Zhang Chunxian maintain as their overt intentions: Xinjiang is deemed to be quickly turned into an economic and commercial hub in Central Asia, and its population will have the honor to be living in the new "Dubai of Central Asia".[32] Enormous investments in infrastructures and services, an invasive emphasis on ethnic unity and dialogue in a modern environment, and the long-stated dream to transform the desert into a green and fertile land are rapidly changing the nature and the aspect of those historical human settlements which, in the South of the region, were ancient Silk Road oases. The urbanization model which has been followed is pretty much the same—with no particular adjustments due to local specificities and characteristics—which turned South-Eastern China into the most developed area in the country.[33]

3.3.2 Population

In light of the situation presented here, there is enough evidence to say that Xinjiang has gone through a considerable urban growth in the past seventy years, especially since the implementation of the reforms[34] which started in 1978. The main factors which can explain the outlay of urbanization patterns in the region are geographical, such as topography and the water system; institutional, such as urban policies; economic, such as per capita GDP; and social, such as the level of education among the population and migration issues. In 1955, when the autonomous region was established, only three cities reached a population of 870 thousand people, while, in 2008, 21 cities already had a total urban population of over 8.45 million residents, a trend which continued up to now. Before focusing on the specific analysis, we would like to briefly illustrate the overall situation in XUAR through the main statistical indicators.[35]

[32] Jacobs, Andrew, "Aid Fuels Change of Fortunes on Silk Road", in *The New York Times*, 14 November 2010.

[33] Li and Liu (2009).

[34] For a historical understanding of the Reform Era, see the related chapters in Hsu (2000).

[35] Data from *Xinjiang Statistical Yearbook 2010–2017*.

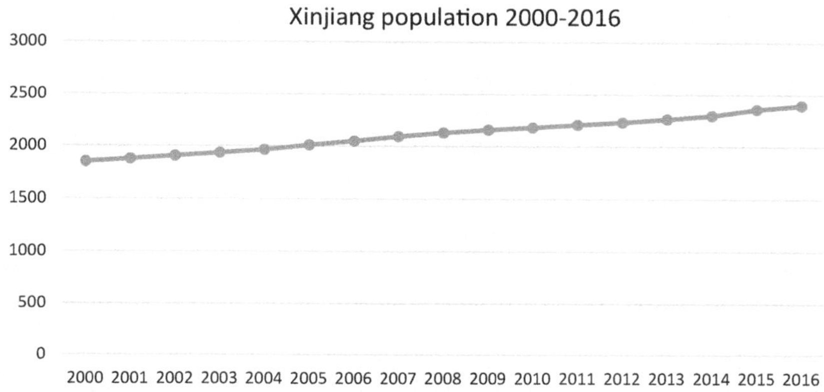

Fig. 3.2 Xinjiang population from 2000 to 2016

In the year 2000, the total population in the region amounted to 18 million and 500 thousand people,[36] with an increase of 1.3% over the previous year, registering a dramatic change from 1955, when the total population only amounted to slightly more than five million people. With a population of almost 24 million, Xinjiang registered a sustained growth in its population and economic base. In 2009, 13.169.433 people of the registered population belonged to ethnic minorities (*shaoshu minzu* 少数民族), the main national minority being the Uyghur with 10.019.758 people, accounting for 46.42% of the total population, while the second largest ethnic group, the Han, accounted for 38.99% (8.416.867 people).[37] An interesting figure is the increase of the Han population in the region, which in 1949 accounted for not more than 6% of the total (Fig. 3.2).

In 2009, 60.15% of Xinjiang's total population was still living in the countryside. According to scholars of Xinjiang and field research data,[38]

[36] Migrant workers, bingtuan residents and members of the armed forces are not included in these figures. In the case of the bingtuan, which have a registered population of almost three million, data are available in Statistical Yearbook of Xinjiang Production and Construction Corps.

[37] For more recent data on the population in the region, see the related section in this chapter.

[38] See below in this chapter.

the phenomenon of a rapid urban expansion enhanced geographic inequality between the two major areas in Xinjiang[39] and generated a selective distribution of wealth along ethnic lines.

State authorities played an important role in encouraging and arranging the immigration. A special frontier migration project and its attached institutions, the Xinjiang Production and Construction Corps (XJPCC), had been the major vehicle of immigration since 1949 up to now. Together with XJPCC immigrants, spontaneous migrants moving both to rural and to urban areas also need to be reckoned. By 1982, about 2.3 million of the region's overall population was XJPCC residents. As a paramilitary organization, structured in a series of state-owned farming-industry-commerce enterprises, its development developed with the history of the military troops in the region. The troops of the People's Liberation Army (PLA) entered Xinjiang in 1949, in close collaboration with the People's Army of the Three Districts administration[40] and the surrendered Guomindang troops. As a multinational army, it counted around 200.000 soldiers which settled in the region to defend and develop the border frontier. The XJPCC were institutionalized in 1953, when a great deal of work on farming, building an irrigation system, mining, construction and light industry had already been carried out. According to the Statistical Division of the XJPCC, the number of formal employees whom in 1953 engaged in non-military jobs reached 93.000, including about 8.000 non-Han. During the '50s and '60s, about 100.000 youths mainly from Shanghai[41] and other large cities in the Eastern coastal areas joined the organization, together with peasants from Shandong, Henan, Jiangxi, Hebei, Shaanxi and Sichuan. Different waves of spontaneous migration also enriched the Corps. By 1974, the population under the XJPCC reached 2.26 million. It was 1/5 of the total regional population, two-fifth of the Han. The XJPCC were dissolved for about seven years between 1974 and 1981 and reestablished after 1981. During this period, some of its industrial enterprises were separated from the XJPCC, and the number of its members declined rapidly to 1.77 million in 1975. In 1983, its population reached

[39] See the related section on XUAR geography in Chapter 2.

[40] An administrative division in pre-1949 Xinjiang.

[41] Large numbers of educated youth moved from Shanghai to Xinjiang, encouraged by the Party units. This flow of migrants is called in Chinese 上海知青 *Shanghai zhiqing*.

2.26 million, accounting for 16.9% of the total, and for the 42% of the Han in the region. The XJPCC played a crucial role in the social and economic development of the region, in terms of frontier migration of Han people to Xinjiang since 1949, and in framing ethnic relations among different nationality groups, that its importance cannot be underestimated. With their own territory, agricultural venues, industries, commerce enterprises, courts and police, they administer two national-level universities, Shihezi University and Tarim University, and at least ten cities (Shihezi, Wujiaqu, Kuitun, Tumushuke, Alaer, Beitun, Tienmenguan, Shuanghe, Kokdala and Kunyu). These cities' residents are mainly Han. The development of the mainly Uyghur cities has followed different paths, since once important Uyghur cities like Yarkent, Karghalik and Kuchar have now a lower administrative level than before, and did not grow like the others in terms of size and services.

3.3.3 Statistical Figures on Urban and Rural Population

In 2009, the urban population in Xinjiang was 39.5% of the total, up by 1.8% from the previous year, while 60.15% of the population was still living in the countryside, 1.0% more than the previous year. The urbanization rate in 2009 was 39.9%. In 2016, the urban population was 11.594.900, 48.35% of the total, while the rural population was 12.386.100, 51.65% of the total. This trend, with the proportion of urban population increasing every year, and, from 2000 to 2016, at an average rate of 4%, is slowly but progressively aligning with the values recorded at the national level (in 2016, 57.35% of the Chinese population lived in urban areas, 42.65% lived in the countryside) (Fig. 3.3).

Interestingly enough, the rural population and its percentage over the total remained stable over the years (see Fig. 3.4). This means that the increase of the urban population is attributable to migrants coming from other parts of China. There has even been a slight increase in the rural population in Xinjiang, in some ways against the national trend of the last decades, and it was caused by the boost of the agricultural sector generated by growth and agribusiness activities of the XJPCC, as well as by the new waves of migrants attracted and absorbed by new enterprises and job opportunities in the large-scale agricultural ventures.

At the end of 2009, the per capita disposable income of urban residents in the region was 12.258 RMB, an increase of 7.2% in comparison with the previous year, while that of rural residents was 3.883 RMB,

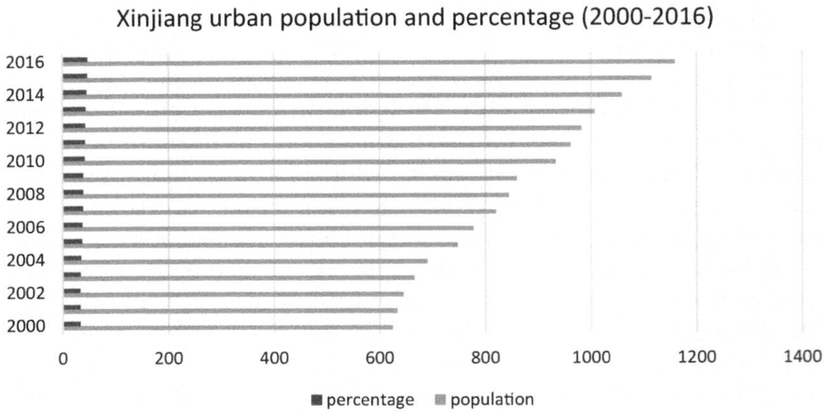

Fig. 3.3 Increase in the urban population in Xinjiang and related percentage (2000–2016)

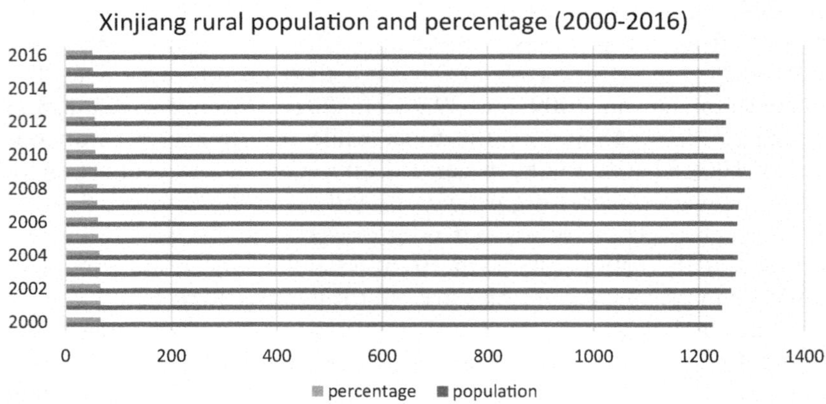

Fig. 3.4 Urban population in Xinjiang and related percentage (2000–2016)

10.8% more than the 2008 value. In 2016, the per capita disposable income of urban residents was 28.463 RMB, and that of rural residents 10.183 RMB. Both values increased substantially over the selected year span, but the rural–urban divide remained unvaried.

In 2009, 64.72% of the total workforce in XUAR was still employed in agricultural activities, while 35.28% was working in non-agricultural

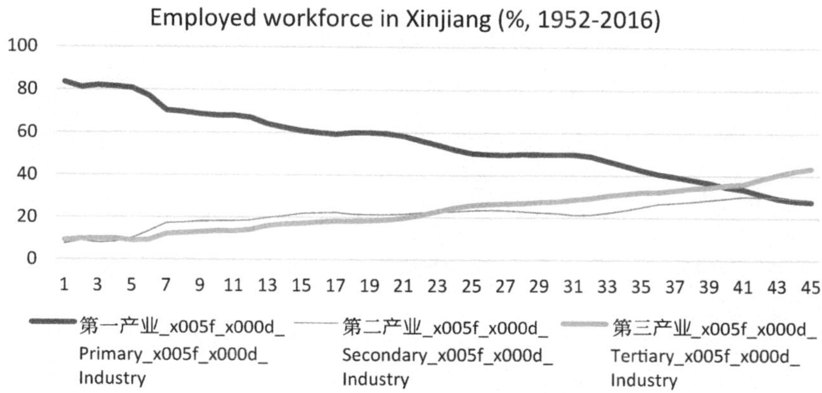

Fig. 3.5 Employed persons in Xinjiang by industry in percentage (1952–2016)

activities. This figure also can be explained with the success of the agricultural sector, highlighting at the same time the poor performance of the industry and service sector. In 2016, 27.2% of the economically active population in the region was employed in the agricultural sector, while 28.8 and 43.5% were employed in the secondary and tertiary sectors, respectively (Fig. 3.5).

In 1978, when the total population in XUAR was merely 12.330.100 people, 26.7% of it was living in cities and 73.93% in rural areas. Data related to the following years show that the general trend has always been toward an urbanized society. Disaggregated figures, taking into account prefectures, cities and autonomous administrative divisions, show that between 80 and 90% of the Uyghur population lived, and still lives, in the countryside.[42] Moreover, only 1/5 of the Uyghurs in Xinjiang lives in the Northern part of the region, and since the ancient times the Tarim Basin, with its underground waters and fertile oases in the South of the region, has been hosting human settlements and Uyghur warriors from the Orkhon Valley in Mongolia. Nowadays, Southern Xinjiang only hosts 33.3% of XUAR's urban areas and 35% of its total urban population. Uyghurs predominantly live in rural areas, thus the increase in the urban population is mainly attributable

[42] Data collected during field researches conducted by Prof. Ilham Tohti and Yang Shengmin when they were teaching at Minzu University of China.

Fig. 3.6 Barbers in a village—barbieri

to migration waves from Inner China (*neidi*), Han population mainly employed in urban activities and therefore contributing to the speedup of the overall urbanization process.

The unequal development in Xinjiang is the object of scholarly research since the 1990s, but extensive analyses and in-depth surveys still need to be realized.[43] In this work, my point consists in arguing that, despite the efforts made so far by central authorities to create a more equal and harmonious urban society, obvious intraregional disparities between the Han and Uyghur population living in today's Xinjiang cities still exist. Uyghurs mainly live in rural areas; they are mainly employed in rural jobs and enjoy a lower degree of welfare in comparison with the Han population in the region. Lower income, a limited access to services and to developed urban contexts, restricted work opportunities and possibilities of social progresses all characterize today's Uyghur society.

[43] Among the others, see Cao (2010) and Ping (1990).

The adopted model of urban development can thus be challenged as far as it does not benefit the whole of the Chinese citizens. The internal colonial model has been taken as an interpretative framework by part of the scholarly community: Is it appropriate to describe and interpret the current situation in Xinjiang? Gladney (1998) and Moneyhon (2002) endorse the internal colonialism hypothesis, while Sautman (2000) puts it under a problematic light. A number of factors included in the model can be considered for the interpretation of the Xinjiang's situation, while others need to be reconsidered according to the specific historical, political and socio-economic characteristics of the local environment.

Huge immigration and a variety of new opportunities created by industrialization and urbanization, including the development of education and public health care, simultaneously encourage acculturation and structural assimilation, but this does not necessarily lead to the absence of prejudice, value and power conflicts. Value and power conflicts can be defined as the struggle among different nationalities over values or claims to status, power and scarce resources, as well as to economic opportunities. As a consequence of this situation, conflicts may break out over the distribution of a great variety of values and goods, such as income, status, power, control over the territory or ecological position (Fig. 3.6).

3.4 Notes on Disparities in Xinjiang

According to the examined material, I summarize here below some of the most interesting issues which could be discussed and researched in the future. On the basis of the fieldworks conducted in August and September 2012 in the Kashgar Prefecture, it is clear that a new phenomenon is emerging in the poor rural areas of Southern Xinjiang: Small Uyghur villages enjoying the coolness of the local white poplars[44] are being demolished and re-built as towns with a Han Chinese-style. While Uyghur villages have usually a central square with trees and a mosque, and several lanes with one-story houses on both sides,

[44]Called *baiyang shu* 白扬树 in Mandarin, and *turghun* in Uyghur. These trees are particularly respected by the local Uyghur population for the coolness they provide during Xinjiang's dry but very hot summers, as well as for being efficacious barriers against sandstorms. The importance of poplar trees for Uyghurs is underlined in many occasion, also in documentaries such as "Loulan Mysterious Ancient City", a tourist video on Xinjiang, Duration: 15 minutes, Date: 2006, Production: XUAR Government.

the rebuilt settlements usually consist of a central square which is a wide cement platform, with a big staircase and a tribune at the top end surrounded by red flags, and Han Chinese-style red lanterns as illumination system for the night. Han dances and music are performed in the evenings. ***While the "modern-style" built-up area which develops from the new central square is mainly populated by Han Chinese newcomers, the local Uyghur population tends to be marginalized in the poor rural areas at the outskirts of the villages, which barely enjoy the newly-built facilities and infrastructures which pop up together with the new waves of migrants.*** This new phenomenon which characterizes urbanization in Xinjiang has been documented by the author in the counties of Yopurgha, Peyzawat, Shufu, Shule and Akto.

Urbanization in Xinjiang can be considered as integral part, and sharing the same intents and aims, of the wider process on national construction which is going on everywhere in China, where authorities work hard to build a national unity and identity. The applied model is the same for the whole Chinese national territory. Policies, directives, funding, political and economic regulations are defined by the central government, which leaves little space to local and private initiatives.

However, Xinjiang presents some peculiarities which need to be taken into consideration: The majority of the population is of Uyghur nationality (different language, religion, physiognomy, historical and cultural influences, memories from the Han one); the geographical position is strategic and sensitive; the natural resources are abundant; the government emphasizes a terrorist threat mainly linked and connected to the groups of Uyghur émigrés in the United States and Germany (mostly affiliated to the World Uyghur Congress).[45]

Since Xinjiang is considered a political problem, the plan of the central government is to assimilate the Uyghur population into the Han cultural core mainly through a process of acculturation and intermarriage.[46] In the intents of the authorities, the urbanization process is meant to play an important role in the enactment of this idea. Evidences emerging from statistical data and fieldwork outcomes, as well as from secondary sources, show that urbanization is moving forward by following both ethnic and socio-economic lines. It seems thus that the Han

[45] Zhang (2009) and Millward (2004).

[46] Personal communication by a Han senior Party official, November 2011, Beijing.

population—and a limited part of Uyghur élite society—is gaining the main benefits from the urbanization policies and process, also because it has the right cultural and socio-economic tools to seize this kind of opportunities.

The vast majority of the Uyghur population is still living in the countryside. Despite the government-claimed successes in building infrastructures, expanding the electricity network, guaranteeing tap water, enhancing the health and education systems in rural contexts, including the minority population in the implementation of the new social model is still a challenge, since part of it perceives the process as having a top-down direction. The main outcome is that the vast majority of the population is excluded from the benefits of urbanization, which is naturally connected with industrialization and modernization. The central authorities, back in 2012, still had problems in devising an integration strategy for Uyghurs, mainly in the economic, political and cultural realms. This situation can create tensions which sporadically result into episodes of violence.[47]

Thus, ***urbanization in Xinjiang seems to follow mainly ethnic lines***, with the Han population receiving almost all the benefits of a booming development. The difficulties and discriminations suffered by Uyghurs in the cities of *neidi* have been researched by Qarluq (2011b), while the social situation of Uyghur residents in Xinjiang cities still needs to be researched.[48]

At the same time, there is a ***rising emigration trend among Uyghurs from rural to urban areas.*** Uyghur workers are more and more present in underpaid jobs in the construction and service sectors (restaurants, hotels, transportations and so on). A conversation I had with Professor Ilham Tohti in November 2011 showed that his opinion is that by entering the urban job market and mobility dynamics, and being hired in urban underground jobs, even if these situations can be humiliating and hard to bear, young Uyghurs from the countryside were starting to get an awareness about their conditions. According to this critique from the left, this process would eventually allow Uyghurs, in the future, to ask

[47] See, for instance, the events of July and September 2009 in Urumqi and in several other cities in the region.

[48] Some preliminary researches have been conducted by Rahile Dawut and her research team at Xinjiang University.

for better and more paid jobs, and gradually take advantage of educational and service opportunities offered by the new urban environments. Better educational opportunities and job mobility would have allowed part of the urban Uyghurs to improve their life conditions, eventually entitling them to gradually participate in the decision-making processes in modern urban contexts. These thoughts, though interesting, did not find the right ground in the Xinjiang's situation, especially if we consider the current policies in the region.

On the other hand, ***within Uyghur society there is not a univocal voice and a generalized consensus over a strategy to be followed in order to obtain more political representation within Chinese society.*** Therefore, Uyghur society is split between acceptation of the acculturation process (normally in exchange of s economic and social benefits) and resistance (by different sections of the society and in diverse ways). The lack of cultural references and political representatives for Uyghurs is mainly due to central policies preventing publishers to publish in Uyghur language, and Uyghur intellectuals to freely express their views. As a result, the lack of actual political representatives is the main problem now affecting Uyghur society. As in internally colonized societies,[49] this generates an amount of social problems such as corruption, alcoholism and depression, all factors which discourage a process of building self-consciousness and political awareness. In Xinjiang's booming cities, it is becoming more and more evident the gap in the standards of living between an emerging Uyghur bourgeoisie normally linked to the CCP and government circles, and the population relegated to the lower strata of society: While this process can help acculturation, it can be conducive to worst social tensions. As we read in Ping (1990), urban realities are possibly more prone to give birth to an assimilationist process.

3.5 Social Problems and Ethnic Divide

3.5.1 HIV

Since China's first officially reported indigenous case was identified in Ruili County, in the Southwestern province of Yunnan, in 1989, HIV diffusion has been geographically and numerically impressive over the whole

[49] See Hechter (1987).

national territory. Today, the virus reached all the thirty-one provinces, regions and municipalities of China. On the spread of HIV on a national level, both first- and second-hand material is available.[50] In Xinjiang Statistical Yearbook 2017, it is reported that more than eight people on 100 thousand are HIV infected in Xinjiang, with a mortality rate of 2.83%, which is rather high, considering the widespread use of antiretroviral drugs. In 1998, Xinjiang accounted for 37% of all reported HIV infections in China.[51] These cases were found mainly within the Uyghur population, representing over 85% of HIV infections in the region: Over 94% of them have been recorded in the two cities of Urumqi and Ghulja, with a particularly high injection drug use (IDU)-related infection rate. Liu et al. (2017) write "Xinjiang region has been reported with the highest of HIV-1 prevalence in China", and, going back to the 1990s, 85% of the cases were reported in Yining in 1999 (over twice the percentage of those documented in Urumqi). Always in 1999, XUAR had the second highest number of patients with HIV/AIDS and the highest increase rate in China, after Yunnan Province.[52] Since 2000, the HIV yearly increase rate in the region has been recorded at around 0.13%, a remarkably high figure if we consider the national data, 0.05%. The areas which come out as the most interested by the epidemic are the cities of Ghulja, Urumqi and Kashgar,[53] even if scholars warn that this could be simply the result of increased medical checks in those urban areas.[54] According to the data reported by Gill and Gang (2006),[55] in 2005 around 60.000 people were HIV infected in the region, while by the end of September 2014, 501.000 people were reported to be living with HIV/AIDS in China, and by the end of June

[50] As reference works, among the others, we shall mention Tucker and Poston (2009), Jun and Worth (2010), and Liu (2010).

[51] For figures and data about HIV/AIDS in Xinjiang, we mainly rely on Gill et al. (2007), on the report on the issue by the Australian Agency for International Development in the framework of the *Prevention and Care Project* (2000), and on the WHO Report (2005). More recent publications are Shu et al. (2018), Liu et al. (2017), Maimaiti et al. (2017), and Tian et al. (2017).

[52] Reference works in Chinese language are, among the others, the Report of the CASS (2010), Zhang (2005), Xu (2005), together with MA thesis discussed in different universities in Xinjiang, mainly consisting in fieldworks on limited samples.

[53] Qarluq and Hayes (2011, p. 3).

[54] Gilles and Gang (2006, p. 36).

[55] Ibid., p. 43.

2016, 386.873 was the number of people reported to be living with HIV in Xinjiang.[56] This figure is consistent with what has been reported by the news: In an article appeared on China News on 1 December 2011,[57] the journalist writes that the number of HIV infections exceeded 60,000. These figures show that, on a per capita basis, Xinjiang is the heaviest-hit province among the Chinese provinces and regions by a large margin. In fact, while accounting for around 1% of the Chinese total population, it represents 10% of its estimated HIV-infected part. At the same time, it is still a problem to obtain reliable data on infections, since HIV is still considered a serious stigma in Chinese society, and even a more serious one in the traditional Islamic Uyghur environment. The main problem related to this disease is that part of HIV carriers is not aware of their condition, mainly in rural areas, where health facilities and checks have been introduced as a normal practice only recently. Simultaneously, part of those who are aware to be infected often do not disclose the situation to family members and friends, mainly for fear of exclusion within their community and retaliation in their work environment.

At the end of 2005, the Ministry of Health estimated that approximately 650.000 persons (tentative range: 540.000–760.000) could be HIV-positive in China, with about three quarters of them living in five Chinese provinces and regions: Yunnan, Henan, Xinjiang, Guangxi and Guangdong. Always at the end of 2005, in some provinces and regions such as Yunnan, Henan and Xinjiang, HIV prevalence rates exceeded 1% among pregnant women and among persons who receive premarital and clinical HIV testing. This figure meets the criteria of the UN Joint Program on HIV/AIDS (UNAIDS) for a "generalized epidemic" (China HIV Demography). According to the document "China HIV Demography", in Xinjiang, where the epidemic was actually concentrated among Uyghurs Injection Drug Users (IDUs),[58] HIV spreading was soon going to affect commercial sex workers (CSWs) and the larger population. The high rate of mother-to-child transmission[59] cases was seen as the most worrisome phenomenon related to HIV diffusion within Uyghur society (Map 3.1).

[56] Shu et al. (2018).

[57] "HIV Infections Exceed 60,000 in Xinjiang. 4777 Persons Died", in *China News*, 1 December 2011.

[58] UNAIDS (2002).

[59] Ibid.

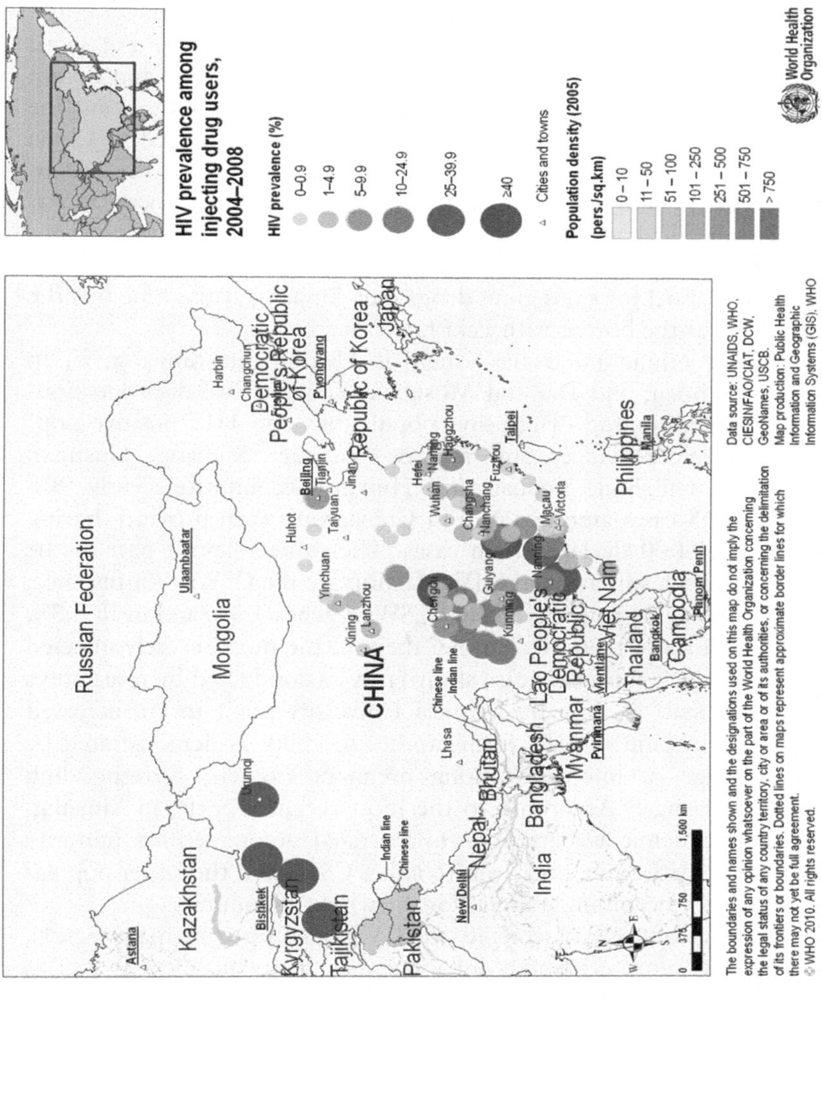

Map 3.1 HIV prevalence among IDUs in East Asia (*Source* WHO)

As mentioned, the biggest part of HIV-positive population in Xinjiang was represented by IDUs, also considering that back in the 1980s, heroin and opium abuse were a serious social problem in China. The opening of borders, rising incomes and the increasing personal mobility all contributed to a growing epidemic of drug abuse in the country. In other cases, the mounting social problems of joblessness and social alienation led more and more persons to drug use. Heroin and opium were first available in the Southwestern border areas, mainly along the Yunnan and Myanmar borders. Much of the heroin imported to China was produced in Myanmar and was easily smuggled across the mountainous border. Smuggled into Yunnan and Guangxi provinces, it was ultimately destined to Xinjiang, or to cities along China's prosperous East Coast, where it was either consumed or smuggled abroad. Another important channel for smuggling drugs into Xinjiang at the time was the Gwadar Pass at the border with Pakistan.[60]

In China, ethnic minorities—such as Uyghurs in Xinjiang; Yi in Southern Sichuan; and Dai and Mosuo in Yunnan—are disproportionally represented among drug-using populations and HIV-positive populations. Seven provinces and regions—Yunnan, Xinjiang, Guangxi, Guangdong, Guizhou, Sichuan and Hunan—account for nearly 90% of HIV/AIDS cases among IDUs in China, with each province having more than 10.000 declared such cases. The other relevant part of the population which suffers from HIV infection are the CSWs. For instance, in Turpan the percentage of infected CSWs reaches 4.3%, and in Ili 3.3%, with peaks of more than 10% among them in the most severely infected areas. Data which appear on case study analyses conducted by researchers and medical staff at Xinjiang Medical University point to an increased vertical transmission of HIV from mother to child, as demonstrated by the percentage of infection among pregnant women, corresponding to 5.3% in Kashgar. According to the most recent reports, in Xinjiang, where the epidemic is currently concentrated among ethnic minority IDUs, it will, with time, break out to affect CSWs and the larger population, eventually becoming a threat for the whole community.

In Xinjiang context, vulnerability to HIV is aggravated by many factors, including migration, economic disparities, gender inequalities, as well as industrial development policies that attract workers from all over China. Vulnerable groups, those who are more likely to engage in behaviors that

[60] Haider (2005).

put them at risk of sexual and blood-borne infection, include CSWs, workers in bars and entertainment centers, IDUs, workers in beauty salons, and long-distance truck drivers. Many of these are part of the migratory and floating population, which is primarily adults of sexually active age, who often lack access to appropriate services, have disrupted social norms, and face discriminatory policies. Male-to-male sex practitioners and street children are also categories at high risk of HIV infection.

The several support projects on HIV awareness and treatment, for instance those launched by AusAid and UNAID, represent an effort to address the causes of this situation. Those which have been identified are basically three: (1) cultural and religious environment, which is Islamic and male-centered, and does not allow women to expect men to use AIDS-preventive contraceptives like condoms; (2) a lack of state and local authorities response to the situation, and the implementation of measures which are not effective and not targeting the whole of the HIV-positive population; (3) increased personal mobility and migration of millions of peoples from Inner China to Xinjiang, together with the effects of the opening of and increased exchanges at the Western borders, especially with Pakistan.

In their article published in 2011 in the *Australian Journal of International Affairs*, Qarluq and Hayes argue that the spreading of HIV, together with ineffective measures implemented by the authorities, could eventually end up to represent a threat not only for the social cohesion within the Uyghur society, but also for the political and social stability of the nation as a whole, with possible negative effects beyond the Central Asian region. The resentment of Xinjiang locals against the government for not being able to solve the issue is seen as a potential threat for China overall stability. While HIV epidemic in Xinjiang is identified as one of the most serious threats in the region, its spread disproportionately interests national minorities. According to the data provided by Qarluq and Hayes, Xinjiang accounts for almost 40% of all HIV infections in China, with 85% of those infected in Xinjiang are Uyghurs.[61] The age range of HIV-infected Uyghurs seems to reflect the patterns of positivity recorded in sub-Saharan Africa.[62] According to the fieldwork conducted by the two authors, the Han population, including sex workers, have a

[61] Qarluq and Hayes (2011, p. 3), quoting Renwick (2002).

[62] Ibid., quoting the Xinjiang Centre for Disease Control 2007.

higher knowledge of HIV and its ways of transmission, and it seems that the planned measures to tackle with the problem are benefitting more the Han population. An important part of Uyghur sex workers does not know Chinese language and does not have access to the material distributed by the HIV prevention centers, and this is why cultural and ethnic reasons are also indicated as the source of the ethnic impact of HIV.

There are authors[63] blaming the unstable ethnic and political environment in the region, which allegedly nullifies the effectiveness of the political measures implemented to deal with HIV positivity. What is sure is that infection in the region follows ethnic lines and could eventually have an impact on the national situation as a whole, at the economic, political and social level. According to Rudelson (1997), nationalistic Uyghurs assume that the spread of HIV among Uyghurs in Xinjiang is part of a political plan to eliminate Uyghurs and adjust the demographic balance in the region, a sort of genocide.

The positive outcomes of the measures taken by the authorities are summarized in what Juret Kerim, Deputy Director of the Xinjiang AIDS Working Committee Office, reported to Qarluq and Hayes (2011). Among the more important measures, the officer said that since at least 2003, the Chinese Minister of Health started to allocate substantial funding for the implementation of programs aimed at coping with the increasing rate of HIV infections in the whole of China and Xinjiang. Moreover, international projects and funding started to be accepted by China since the same year,[64] in order to get international health organizations and NGOs to cooperate with the Chinese government on this sensitive issue. A brief overview of these programs actions, measures and funding can be found at p. 44 in Gilles and Gang (2006).

3.5.2 *Alcohol Abuse*

While studies on the relation between alcohol abuse and minorities are plenty,[65] as well as works on alcoholism in China (indicating that there has been a striking increase of alcoholics, and the related problems,

[63] Gill and Gang (2006).

[64] Mainly programs by the UN, World Bank, Global Fund, AusAid, United States Centre for Disease Control and Prevention, Clinton Foundation.

[65] A rich bibliographical survey can be found in Galvan and Caetano (2003).

over the recent decades[66]), comprehensive studies on the same issue in Xinjiang, and in particular among Uyghurs, are still missing. In this context, I needed to adopt proxies like alcohol abuse-related sicknesses—for instance, acute pancreatitis and liver disorders—in order to obtain a reliable insight into the actual situation. Case studies conducted by research teams and doctors, published in journals of medical sciences, are particularly useful to draw some interesting, even if only partial, information. In the breakdown of the outcomes of these case studies, we shall pay a particular attention on the bias entailed by the fact that the percentage of the Uyghur population who turns to hospitalization is still very low, mainly because of the high costs of health care, but also due to the still strong attachment to popular beliefs and traditional practices. With 80% of Xinjiang's healthcare services located in urban areas——mainly populated by Han Chinese—rural Uyghurs do not enjoy an efficient healthcare assistance. The result is that many people residing in rural areas seek out the services of unregistered medical clinics that are often below standards, staffed by practitioners lacking professional training. Wang and Zhang (2012) consider a sample of 1148 patients affected by acute pancreatitis in Hospital No. 1 in the regional capital Urumqi, and found out that the large majority of the patients affected by pancreatitis caused by alcohol abuse are Uyghurs.[67] In the same article, authors draw the conclusion that these outcomes must reflect a particular inclination toward a high consumption of alcohol among Uyghurs. On the other hand, but again keeping in mind the mentioned structural bias of these outcomes and the consequent underestimation of actual numbers, Wang and Zhang (2012) analyze a sample of 4023 patients from Hospital No. 2 in Urumqi who are affected by serious liver problems and find out that 14.8% of them are Uyghurs and 76.4% are Hans. The major source of these liver diseases among the hospitalized Uyghurs has been identified in "alcohol abuse".[68] Another outcome bias could derive from the fact that Urumqi is a predominantly Han city, and that Uyghurs living there might prefer to turn to hospitals adopting Uyghur traditional medicine, and in this sense, an underestimation of data can be even more serious. According to one study realized among 396 undergraduates at Xinjiang Medical

[66] Among the others: Wu (1996), Hao et al. (2004, 2005), and Zhang et al. (2008).

[67] Wang and Zhang (2012, p. 285).

[68] Ibid., p. 812.

University,[69] the proportion of minority students, mainly Uyghurs, with a lifestyle which would easily affect personal health in the future, is much higher than that of Han students. Among the indicators used by the researchers, alcohol abuse and smoking were the most important.[70]

According to part of foreign Xinjiang scholars and experts,[71] a deep impact on alcohol abuse and on the diffusion of prostitution needs to be ascribed to the growing numbers of Han Chinese migrants moving to Xinjiang, and to the fact that the majority of them are male between 25 and 45 years old, single, and apparently consider the regions as a temporary destination, where they can spend some years, have a well-paid job, save money and at a certain point go back to their hometown. In this context, there is no sense of belonging, and Xinjiang can be simply considered as a place to be exploited and eventually left. In these conditions, these migrants are not willing to claim a better society for Xinjiang, but they simply pursue the short-term fulfillment of their personal needs. The importance of alcohol for the Hans is also considered a fundamental factor: The history of the Chinese brewing industry can be traced back to 4.000 years, and alcohol has a high status in traditional Chinese culture, being as well a frequent theme in Chinese classical poetry. During official and representative dinners, alcohol has a ritual meaning, its consumption following a strict hierarchical plot. If a superior in level offers a shot, it is impossible to refuse drinking, since this act can be easily seen as a sign of disrespect and, among friends, disaffection. Taken into this loop of bilateral and coral toasts, usually proposed by the highest in the hierarchy at the table, the most common conclusion of this kind of official dinings is that everybody needs to get heavily drunk. Another problem is that alcohol is consumed in a very chaotic way, without respecting any alcohol gradation order, such as starting with drinking lower gradation beverages and proceeding with those with higher gradation. When this drinking culture is exported to Xinjiang, the local Uyghur population absorbs it, mainly within those in the government and official environments where it is almost compulsory to adjust to this habit, if an official wants to be respected in the job environment and eventually promoted. This habit also applies to women, but with a certain degree of flexibility which does not include men.

[69] Yang et al. (2008).

[70] Ibid., p. 1662.

[71] Dillon (2004), Millward (2007), and Becquelin (2000, 2004).

As a conclusive assumption, we can say that alcoholism represents a social problem among the Uyghur male population ranging from 16 to 55 years old living in Xinjiang. The traditionally mild form of Islam that Uyghurs follow, mainly attached to the Hanafi school or to branches of Central Asian Sufism, can also be considered a factor which does not prevent Uyghur society to adopt habits usually strictly forbidden by Islam, like alcohol abuse and prostitution. In order to get a deeper understanding of the situation, we can also take a look at historical analyses where Xinjiang's cultural and customary background is outlined. For instance, referring to 1830, Laura Newby (1998) states: "Reports by travelers of the almost decadent life-style of the local Muslims, the prevalence of prostitution, the drinking of alcohol and smoking of hashish, should not be interpreted as a sign of 'sinification', but rather as a reflection of the lack of a strong Islamic authority".

The same suggestion of a "soft" and liberal Islamic identity and culture related to Uyghurs is made by Ahmed Rashid (2002). Uyghur militants are described as willing to get trained in camps in Pakistan and Uzbekistan, but as often not taken seriously by Islamic leaders due to their alleged ignorance of the ethics and principles of Islam.

It is important to add historical elements to the picture in order to add knowledge on the cultural and customary background which characterizes Xinjiang and its peoples, beyond the current local hybrid Islamic faith.

3.5.3 Gender Issues

Uyghur women who live in very traditional rural environments[72] are grown and educated in a rigorously religious environment where they are supposed to take care of the house and look after the family. They typically get married relatively early between 15 and 18 years old, and also after the marriage, they are not expected to work, but to commit themselves to household-related activities, children and elders, and the family well-being in general in terms of hygiene, food and education. Women can be respected religious teachers, Sufi leaders or wise figures,

[72] Uyghur oases and villages in the Southern part of Xinjiang, on the Southern edge of the Taklimakan desert, normally are defined as very traditional rural environments where subsistence agriculture, goats and government subsidies are the basis of the local economy. Islam and religious authorities are normally still the recognized leaders and define the social customs, economy and politics, regardless of the CCP's increasing power.

with a charisma which becomes stronger when they grow older.[73] Before the Xi Jinping administration's campaigns in the region, it was not unusual to see, in Uyghur rural houses, children from the neighborhood going from one house to the other at certain times in the day to listen to Islamic teachings delivered by an influential Uyghur woman in the host family, where they could learn local Islamic ethic and the Quran.[74] When the family conditions are too poor, women still need to support the family economy and go farming. Marriages usually take place within members of the community or the larger family: The main idea is that the accumulated wealth and properties shall stay within the familial line.

Uyghur communities living in these traditional environments have an idealized concept of "woman", such as a shy creature whom is good at singing and dancing, chosen to transmit moral and religious values to the next generations. Women are thus considered examples of morality and pureness by the community.

3.5.3.1 Beijing's Policies

Reference works on the life of Uyghur women are mainly MA and PhD theses, the majority of which written by students at Minzu University of China, together with articles published on Chinese scholarly journals.[75]

Fieldwork data and the available literature show that the position and roles for which Uyghur women are respected in their traditional communities normally cannot match with accomplishing the duties, fulfilling the requirements and expectations that the contemporary Chinese society implies for women. Chinese women's role in the society, as it has been redefined after Mao, entails that they are individuals who independently build their future, in a condition of quasi-parity with the male counterparts.

In order to make Uyghur women familiarize with standards and requirements of Chinese contemporary society, the central government started to launch campaigns and implement policies aimed at weakening their religious, ethnic and cultural identity, diluting their sense of belonging and supporting them in the process of adjusting to new

[73] Outstanding researches on Uyghur women who are recognized Sufi leaders and wise figures for the community have been realized in the Turpan area by Rahile Dawut, Professor of Uyghur Folklore at Xinjiang University.

[74] This practice is considered illegal by the Chinese government, and those to engage in it are arrested.

[75] A good bibliographical survey can be found in the PhD dissertation by Wei Baihan (2007).

socio-political conditions. For instance, Beijing facilitates intermarriage by encouraging encounters between Uyghurs and Hans and guaranteeing fiscal facilitations for young mixed couples,[76] and at a certain point, this became an important goal in the central government's political agenda toward the Uyghur minority in China.[77] On the other side, intermarriage is not easily accepted, both socially and ethically, among Uyghurs, especially if a Uyghur woman is involved. In some cases, it is accepted that a Uyghur woman marries a foreign Muslim, or who converts to Islam, but if a Uyghur woman marries a Han man she can be easily rejected by her family and the community. Up to now, intermarriage between Hans and Uyghurs has been a rare phenomenon, noted only in big cities like Shanghai and Beijing, and mainly among rich and wealthy élites, often in artists and musicians' communities. The new policies—including ideological reeducation—notwithstanding, Beijing still has a long way to go before seeing Uyghurs and Hans eventually mixed.

Another policy implemented by the Chinese government at least since 2005 has been to launch programs aimed at relocating groups of unmarried Uyghur girls from 16 to 22 years old from their rural villages in Southern Xinjiang to big cities in Inner and South-Eastern coastal China, where they get a temporary employment, normally in textile factories.[78] The nature and impact of these measures of social engineering on Uyghur society are still an object of debate: While part of the Han Chinese scholarly community sees Uyghur girls moving from poor villages in the countryside—where their destiny would be to get married and have children at a very early age—to big cities—where after the expiry of their temporary contract they might find new job opportunities and start a new life—as an opportunity, concerns have been raised among the Uyghur community, since claims of forced relocations have been advanced. Moreover, female peasant workers move from Xinjiang without signing any labor contract, which has instead the form of an agreement signed by local authorities and the new employers. In order

[76] Such as mortgage waivers and free education for children.

[77] According to an interview I conducted with a Central Government official working in the office of Prof. Yu Keping, in Beijing (June 2009), the authorities plan to make Hans–Uyghurs intermarriage more and more frequent.

[78] An overview of these policies has been presented by Prof. Qarluq during his lecture at Università "L'Orientale" di Napoli on 7 November 2012. Documents on this issues can also be found among those published by human rights groups and by the World Uyghur Congress headed by Rebiya Kadeer (2011).

to guarantee the proper implementation of these policies, a specific mechanism has been created: One Uyghur local cadre goes together with the group of Uyghurs by train to the new destination in Inner China and gets indeed relocated to the factory where Uyghur workers are transferred with the task of supervising them. This is conceived to avoid direct contacts, and potential problems, between Han bosses and Uyghur workers, which could lead to tensions and make latent conflicts outbreak.[79] The Uyghur supervisor is de facto in charge of all aspects related to the private and working life of the relocated workers. Cases of very early marriages imposed by Uyghur parents on their daughters to prevent them to be forcibly relocated from their home villages have been recorded. Extensive field researches about these women's conditions have been carried out by Prof. Abduresit Jelil Qarluq in different contexts in Inner China. According to these works' outcomes, the government plans of relocating Uyghur women to Chinese big cities are highly disruptive for Uyghur communities and the society as a whole. Qarluq makes a clear distinction between women who move voluntarily and those who are forced: While the former are willing to learn Chinese and to start a new life in a modern urban environment, the latter develop a form of disorientation and negative symptoms which have deep impacts on their future life. According to Qarluq, their destiny is more or less predetermined: If they do not return to their villages, they become low-paid workers, or, in the worst situation, prostitutes, in big cities of Inner and coastal China. Those who go back to Xinjiang suffer from exclusion and prejudices by their communities, since they are believed to having been "contaminated" by a hostile and non-Muslim society. A number of them do not find any change to be re-employed in Xinjiang urban areas, and they stay in their home villages where they cannot find a husband because considered "impure", do not adjust to the conditions and often end up being prostitutes.[80] Several reports and analysis on the issue have been released by the organizations of Uyghurs abroad like Uyghur

[79] The 2009 riots were apparently generated by such an episode in Guangdong, where in a factory a Uyghur worker had been accused, in an online post on Weibo, to have harassed a Chinese female worker. The authenticity of the accusation has never been confirmed.

[80] During the fieldwork I conducted together with Professor Qarluq in a poor Uyghur village, we noticed a girl was standing at the poorhouse door with very short yellow skirt and a heavy makeup, and parents complained that she was in Guangzhou, went back to the village and did not want to help the mother anymore. Both parents were extremely worried for the change in attitude of their daughter, as well as for her future within the community.

Human Rights Project (UHRP) and Uyghur American Association, the reliability of which still needs to be tested.

A custom which is considered problematic by Chinese authorities is the fact that Uyghur women wear headscarves. While in public institutions such as schools, universities and public offices it is already forbidden, campaigns have been launched by local authorities to dissuade women not to wear them also in the country's most remote rural areas. The efforts to spread these measures among the broader Uyghur women population are evident in the posters attached to household doors in rural villages, with contain pictures reproducing which kind of headscarf is allowed to wear for women, and how men should cut their beards.[81] In fact, headscarves and long beards are considered as marks of illegal religious behaviors.

Campaigns aimed at discouraging Uyghur women to wear headscarves are enforced regularly in the most traditional Uyghur areas of Khotan and Kashgar and occasionally lead to outbreaks of violence, like in the summer 2011 in Khotan, when deadly clashes between Uyghur demonstrators and police erupted. The tones of these political and social campaigns, which stress the "beautiful women's hair" and the "right to make them wave in the wind", are particularly adverse to the Muslim concept of woman, even if it should not be completely alien to the traditionally soft Uyghur Islamic religion.[82]

What is needed to be noted is that the condition of women is changing rapidly: According to the first region-wide survey on women's social status carried out by the regional Women's Federation and Statistics Bureau in April 2012, in 2010, 41.5% of women in Xinjiang had a job, up from the 10 years—before percentage of 14.4%. This figure includes both Uyghur and Han women, and data disaggregated by ethnicity have not been issued. The same can be said as far as Uyghur sex workers are concerned, a topic on which sociological research has not been conducted yet. At the same time, scholarly articles appeared in medical journals concern sex workers' related diseases, and the measures to prevent and treat them,[83] but no comprehensive disaggregated data according to ethnicity have never been released.

[81] Figure 3.7 show which headscarves women should wear and how the beard should be cut.

[82] An exhaustive and detailed report on the facts on July 2011 can be read in *The Economist*, "Let Them Shoot Hoops", 30 July 2011.

[83] Zhao et al. (2011) and Gao et al. (2006).

Fig. 3.7 Poster indicating the length of beards and accepted kinds of clothes

3.5.4 Domestic Violence and Divorce Rate

Domestic violence is a social issue in Uyghur families and is mainly related to alcohol abuse, as well as to divorce rate. According to the Uyghur scholar Zulhayat Ismayil, Associate Professor at the Department of Sociology at Xinjiang University in Urumqi,[84] during a series of fieldworks in the region the diffusion of severe phenomena of domestic violence within Uyghur families has been assessed. The problem emerged as more serious, and with a deeper social impact, than what the original hypothesis advanced by Zulhayat team envisaged. For five years from 2005 to 2010, Zulhayat and her research team conducted fieldworks in different areas in Xinjiang, the results of which have not been published and are still considered *neibu*. One outcome which is worth noting is

[84]The following information have been collected during an interview I conducted with Prof. Ismayil, a student of the sociologist Ma Rong, on 30 April 2011, in the campus of Xinjiang University.

that, among Islamic minorities living in Xinjiang,[85] the problem has been demonstrated as more severe among Uyghurs, while for instance among Kazaks and Kyrgyzs the percentage of women who suffer from episodes of domestic violence perpetrated by their husbands came out as remarkably lower than that of Uyghur women.[86] Another outcome worth of mention is that domestic violence among Uyghurs has been recorded across all social classes, from farmers to academics, from rural to urban areas.[87] As we already mentioned above, only fieldworks and case studies, often conducted by Uyghur and Chinese researchers on limited samples, are available on this issue up to now.

The seriousness of the problem in Xinjiang is proved by regulations issued at the end of 2000s: An article published in *Xinjiang Daily* on 9 December 2008 reports the full text of the "Regulations to stop and control domestic violence in Xinjiang Uyghur Autonomous Region", issued by the People's Standing Committee of Xinjiang. The document introduces a new legal framework according to which domestic violence is officially illegal and must be punished by law, at the same time identifying and putting government departments and social establishments institutionally in charge and responsible of enforcing the new rules. Responsibilities and punishments reserved for the violent husband are outlined in details, and a range of bureaus are put in charge and became officially responsible for rescue and punishment measures. The issue of domestic violence on Uyghur women is also discussed in Chinese microblogs, like Weibo and Hexun.[88] At the same time, Li Huigen, in her Master thesis discussed at Lanzhou University in May 2012,[89] argues that the traditional forms of mutual help and cooperation among women in Uyghur society are strong and effective nets for protecting and supporting weak social groups.

[85] Six major ethnic groups in Xinjiang are Muslim: Uyghur, Kazak, Hui, Kyrgyz, Tajik and Uzbek.

[86] This outcome seems not to be in line with the more general studies on Islamic societies where, if very traditional, violence on women can be, for some aspects, accepted (see Salhi 2013). This difference recorded by Zullayat is a controversial finding and still object of research.

[87] Zullayat reported that it was not unusual seeing Uyghur female academics at the university with black eyes.

[88] See the following discussions on Weibo: http://www.weibo.com/zt/s?k=9673&hasori=1, and this chat on Douban: http://www.douban.com/group/topic/30716097/.

[89] Zhihuan Li (2009).

In an article by Wang, an in-depth discussion on the origin and causes of the high rate of divorce in the countryside of Southern Xinjiang is disclosed: I assume that social mobility generated by economic development helped the creation of a new social group, peasant women left aside by husbands who go to work in Inner China or Central Asian countries. These different life directions of husband and wife are considered in the study with a sort of Manichean perspective: Women stay in backward and poor environments to look after children and elders, while men have the opportunity to benefit from the modernity of urban environments. When the separation lasts for too long, and the couple cannot reach an agreement (normally on often conflicting ideas on life), problems arise and divorce is seen as the easiest way to solve the issue.

3.5.5 Health Disparities

During the Reform era, more precisely between the 1980s and the 1990s, the healthcare system in China has gone through structural transformations and a fundamental reorganization. The restructuring of this sector changed the meaning of health care as such in China, converting it from a service dispensed for free into a commodity delivered under payment. The state started not providing free treatments nor full reimbursements to work units and individuals for health expenses anymore. During the 1980s, the health system went through large-scale structural reforms, becoming very similar to the healthcare system in the United States: the blossoming of private health insurance companies, pharmaceutical industries and compulsory medical insurances for those who are not affiliated to any work unit, triggered new business opportunities. Nowadays, patients get treated in hospitals only if they can afford it and pay the fees in advance on a daily basis. For instance, in Turpan People's Hospital (*Tulufan Renmin Yiyuan* 吐鲁番人民医院), every early morning nurses knock at the patients' doors to collect the daily fee from each patient, an amount of money which differs according to the entity of the diseases and to the provision of drugs.[90] In 2009 in Turpan

[90] Shi et al. (2010) on the interaction between pharmaceutical companies and hospitals, and the corruption dynamics which underlie agreements and provisions. Moreover, since hospitals pay the medical personnel through the payments of patients, as a consequence prices of health services are high, especially for that part of the population which does not belong to any work unit.

People's Hospital, 500 RMB (around 65 euros) was the daily fee which a patient needed to pay to treat a simple flu.[91] Patients working for a *danwei* (单位, work unit) have part of their medical expenses refunded (from small to more substantial percentages, which can reach 90%, depending on the richness of the *danwei* and on the type of contract), while those who do not depend on any work unit, like individual farmers, need to turn to their personal fundings. In the contemporary Chinese medical system, hospitals pay doctors, nurses and the hospital's staff with the money they get from patients. On this basis, *danweis*' workers can have their expenses reimbursed, while the others usually do not dare to go to hospitals, and prefer to choose self-treatment and turn to pharmacies. As already mentioned, they might address themselves to non-qualified and often non-authorized structures, with untrained medical personnel.

As a result, farmers and those who belong to the weakest levels of society are penalized, and the healthcare system in the Chinese countryside continues to represent a problematic issue and a tough challenge for Beijing.[92]

Uyghur farmers, especially in particularly poor areas (where the annual income can amount to 700 RMB a year for a four members family[93]), are deeply affected by this economic and social transformations. Since the majority of them cannot afford to go to hospitals, it became a common practice to turn to pharmacies and choose self-treatment. These problems in basic healthcare services in Xinjiang have a deep impact on the regional economic and social development, since people's spending capacity is low due to the necessity of save money for health insurances as well as for the children's education expenses. Life expectancy in Xinjiang, attested at 65.98 for men and 69.14 for women in 2000,[94] the fifth worst in China following Tibet, Guizhou, Qinghai and Yunnan. In 2010, it was 72.35 as an average, against a national average of 79.43 years old.[95] Back in 1982, infant mortality among Uyghurs was as high as 45.9%, while in 2008 it has been attested to 161 deaths per 100,000 live births, the second highest registered in China[96] (Fig. 3.8).

[91] Personal observation during fieldwork in October 2011.

[92] See Liu (2015).

[93] Personal observation during fieldworks in August and September 2011 and 2012.

[94] China Statistical Yearbook 2005. The most recent data available for Xinjiang are those of 2000, while for the whole country data have been released for the year 2004.

[95] The last available data are those collected during the 2010 census.

[96] Schuster (2009, p. 434).

Fig. 3.8 "Sending children to school is glorious, not sending them is illegal" (DSCN 4074)

A major measure which has been implemented by the authorities is the introduction of the *dibao* 低保, a "minimum insurance" of a few hundred RMB per month which is distributed to poor families in the countryside.[97] Apparently, this subsidy mentality is not helping much. At the same time, for the central government it is the easiest way to start coping with the problem, since *dibao* is a measure which does not constitute a permanent expenditure for the State finances, and can be revoked once it starts to become a financial burden. Eventually, there is an agreement among Uyghur scholars on the fact that it does not represent a solution to the whole problem because it provides a too small financial support and can be considered as a temporary measure since the government did not implement it as a permanent policy.[98]

[97] Liu and Weng (2011).

[98] Statement by a Uyghur sociologist during a conversation.

The seriousness of the health problems in Xinjiang is represented by the recurrent outbreaks of poliomyelitis, the most recent occurred in the summer of 2019. It usually happens that the virus enters the region via Pakistan, hitting only the Uyghur population in Southern Xinjiang. This could be due to bad hygiene conditions in the area, as well as to the fact that vaccination, for different reasons, does not cover the whole population. As a response to the last outbreak in 2011, the local government implemented measures like medical education campaigns and compulsory vaccination for both children and adults in the areas interested by the pandemic.

Brenda Schuster (2009) argues that major health indicators outline severe differences between Hans and Uyghurs, health disparities that clearly follow ethnic lines. I here examine different factors: residency, infant mortality rate, education, unemployment and life expectancy. Her conclusion is that, for all these indicators, Uyghurs are in a much penalized situation than Hans. In an attempt to identify the causes underlying these conditions, she realizes that different socio-economic, cultural and historical factors, related to ethnicity, can be considered responsible. The health gap thus depends on the lack of education, low income, cultural attitudes about gender, group-specific psychological stress, and the socio-economic and demographic changes of the past 60 years as major factors. While the findings of Schuster analysis are clear, she acknowledges the fact that different research methodologies, an unavoidable bias, and the choice of variables could have led to a different picture.[99]

Moreover, the region has several natural and endemic problems which affect, in particular, drinking water. According to data provided by Erika Scull (2009), written for the China Environmental Health Project, the low levels of iodine caused a high rate of iodine deficiency disorders among the local population. The author writes that in 1995 goiter was endemic, with an occurrence of 43.29% rate among children between the 8 and 10 years old. When UNICEF-China collaboration started in 2000, and the use of iodized salt increased, infant goiter rate dropped to below 15%. As a matter of fact, Xinjiang's poorest residents still suffer from this disorder, mainly because iodized salt remains not affordable for them. To cope with this problem, and to make an effort to meet the Universal Salt Iodination goal set by the UN in 1990 (which fix at 90% the percentage

[99] Schuster (2009, pp. 438–439).

of households which have to consume iodized salt), the government started to distribute iodine-releasing devices for cooking water.[100]

The presence of arsenic and high levels of fluoride are also both causing serious health problems,[101] including skin anomalies, fatigue, heart problems and cancer. Xinjiang is ranked among the first five provinces with the highest proportions of excessive arsenic, caused by natural geological conditions, in village wells. The substance was first discovered in 1983 in the village of Kuitun in the Zungar Basin. In the mid-1980s, water with low levels of arsenic was provided for the villagers, but the mortality rates for cancer and health problems were abnormally high. Arsenic, as a poisonous substance, has also been linked to reduced intellectual functions in exposed children. Moreover, while the maximum level of fluoride allowed in China is 1 mg per liter, in Kuitun and other areas it can reach 21.5 milligrams per liter. High levels of fluoride can cause arthritis and tooth decay and can impact children's physical and mental growth. In addition, it has been found that fluoride can have detrimental health defects when combined with low iodine levels. A study[102] conducted on children in areas of Xinjiang with low iodine levels and high fluoride levels revealed that fluoride can exacerbate neurological disorders caused by iodine deficiency, including mental retardation, hearing loss and degenerative effects on the central nervous system. The issue of nuclear testing, and the extraction of strategic resources such as uranium, connected to human health, and specifically interesting Uyghurs, is discussed in the paragraph here below.

3.5.6 Environmental Degradation

Xinjiang is a unique arid ecosystem with an independent and self-balanced hydrological cycle, which means that the total volume of water in the region is basically stable, and at the same time, it is particularly fragile and vulnerable to human impact. The region is surrounded entirely by mountains, with the Tian Shan range dividing the province into two basins: the Zungar Basin in the North and the Tarim in the South. The larger and more populated of the two, the Tarim Basin, is one of the

[100] *People's Daily* (2004) and Wen (2004).

[101] Scull (2009, pp. 4–5).

[102] Lu et al. (2000).

driest places on earth. Its only water sources are the melting glaciers of the surrounding mountains: snow from the Tian Shan Mountains melts to form China's longest inland river, the Tarim. In the last decades, the region became one of the unhealthiest areas in China: the growing negative impact of air and water pollution, desertification, the overall ecological damage caused by nuclear experiments conducted until 1996, and by a rapid highly polluting industrialization process, all constitute important factors endangering health and affecting the development of Xinjiang as a social system. A comprehensive study conducted by scholars and scientists of the Chinese Academy of Social Sciences,[103] based on indicators such as population growth, health status, education, natural conditions, environmental pollution, economics and health care, shows how the region became the fifth with worst environment and health indices on a national scale. Interesting reports on environmental problems in the region can be downloaded from the Web site China Dialogue (www.chinadialogue.net), an online platform created and run by the Chinese environmentalist Ma Jun.

Since the 1950s, transfers of pioneers from Inner China and large-scale land reclamation schemes started to be implemented: Between 1950 and 1970, the population of the XJPCC increased from less than 20.000 to 420.000, while today they became almost 3 million. The region experienced substantial environmental pressure when the demographic increase led to a fast growth of cultivated land, which led to an almost doubled area between 1950 and 2000. As a consequence, the Tarim River's downstream zones started to receive a lower quality and quantity of water. By the 1980s, this large-scale agricultural ventures shortened the Tarim by 320 km, severely degrading land and water in its lower reaches, with a serious impact on human health. This has been one of the factors causing an overall migration of the local population in the 1990s.

Before 1980, grain production, including rice, constituted 60–80% of the cultivated land in the Tarim. By the 1990s, cash crop production replaced grain, amounting to more than 70%. Economic incentives and water scarcity were the main two reasons for the switch to cash crops. At the same time, when China became one of the global leaders in textile production and export during the 1990s, Xinjiang experienced a boom

[103]Wang et al. (2004), quoted in Scull (2009).

in cotton production. The historically high cotton prices led most of the land cultivators in the Tarim Basin to switch to this labor-intensive activity, which in turn led to population growth, bad land degradation and increased water scarcity. Large sections of unused land were then converted into cotton fields, which often entailed a land reclamation and leaching process, due to the high alkalinity of previously considered unusable plots. The leaching process implied that large volumes of water were drawn from the river, and then re-directed back into it, thereby reducing the quantity and quality of water reaching downstream. In response to water-scarcity problems, China plans to divert up to 10% of the water volume of the Irtysh and Ili rivers, on which the Central Asia neighbors, particularly Kazakhstan, heavily rely upon. Projects financed by the World Bank have also been realized to cope with the problem of water scarcity.

In the *Annual Nationwide Urban Environmental Management and Regulation Report* released by China's Ministry of Environmental Protection for the year 2007, and in a 2008 central government report, Urumqi, the capital of the region, was listed as one of the most polluted cities in China with severe air contamination and low-quality water. A 2008 report published by the UN Environment Program (UNEP) and the World Health Organization (WHO) highlighted how Urumqi's severe air pollution was contributing to a high mortality rate from respiratory and cardiovascular diseases and malignant tumors. A Sino-Italian Cooperation Program for Environmental Protection allocated 500.000 Euros to monitor the level of air pollution in the city.[104] Urumqi heavy air pollution is not surprising when we consider that the city is number one for coal consumption in China, without taking into account the fact that Xinjiang provides 40.6% of the national coal supply. This abundance as a natural resource makes coal to represent 67% of Urumqi energy use, with a per capita coal consumption in the city which is four times higher than the national average, the highest in the whole country. With the increasing number of coal-fired power plants in the city—its coal use increased by 47.8% between 2001 and 2006—the overall air quality has been rated as grade III, the worst in the national scale of air quality standards. In 2016, Urumqi alone counted for almost 10% of the total consumption of coal in Xinjiang.

[104] http://cleanairinitiative.org/portal/node/396 (accessed on 8 August 2019).

Shihezi, the second largest city in Xinjiang, has three large chemical plants in its immediate outskirts, and the air quality is heavily impacted, as well as the health of the population. Chinese environmental scientists and scholars are looking at factors impacting the air quality in the city and mainly point out to coal and sand storms, and to Shihezi chemical plants.

The rapid increase in population over the past three decades represents a more and more heavy burden for the limited resources in the region (only in 2001, around 500 Han Chinese moved to Xinjiang each week looking for a job). Even if data on migration are sensitive, it is believed that the scale of migration waves was, from 2008 to 2012, in the order of the hundreds of thousand people a week, while today it probably stabilized on a hundred people a week. This demographic pressure makes health services and natural resources such as water become a social and economic issue, for this reason Chinese scholars started to be concerned about environment in Xinjiang, with more and more studies and alarming analyses being published on the topic.[105] The history of the Lop Nor Desert started to be covered by international media: the Lop lake, in the middle of the homonymous desert and once surrounded by a flourishing oasis, source of nourishment and business activities for the bordering villages centered on fishing and agriculture, now disappeared. Desertification due to intensive agriculture in the surroundings is deemed as the main factor causing the death of the oasis and the subsequent migration of all the villagers to other parts of Xinjiang. A more recent environmental problem concerns lake Aibi in Northern Xinjiang: According to the reports of Xinhua News Agency, the lake has been shrinking at more than 15 square miles a year because of encroaching sands. Unrestrained land reclamation and flood irrigation make the situation worse, and according to local officials, growing desertification and sandstorm problems have disrupted local people's lives, their agricultural and business activities. Experts assessed that about 5.5 million tons of sand and salt are blown away each year, reaching as far as Beijing. Transmission lines are often interrupted for salt dust, and cattle deaths tripled in recent years.[106]

[105] Zhang et al. (2007) and Pan et al. (2010); an updated bibliography can be read in Scull (2009).

[106] "Ecosystem Worsens Despite Efforts in China", in *Xinhua News Agency*, 5 November 2012.

Water scarcity has historically been one of the biggest problems in Xinjiang. Between the 1950s and 1980s, the region experienced a huge decrease in the total surface area of its lakes, from 9700 to 4953 square kilometers. Climate-related drought and human activities are the two main causes for the shrinking of Xinjiang lakes. In the late 1950s, 13 dams were built on the upper reaches of the Kongque River for irrigation purposes. By 1964, Lake Lop Nor, which was fed by the homonymous river and its tributaries, completely dried up. Since the whole region has natural salty water, it has serious problems of water salinization. There are only three freshwater lakes in Xinjiang—out of a total of the national number of one hundred and thirty-nine. Over the past few decades, the salinity of the region's lakes has increased as many lakes have begun to dry up.[107] As lake water depths decreased, the proportion of salt in the water, and alkalinity, increased. As an effect of climate change, the melting glaciers will increase the amount of available water in the region's cities, a factor which may encourage further development, especially for water-intensive industries. The increase in water flow is expected to last for about 40 years, after which the region's economy will need to be re-adjusted to new conditions. Ultimately, if nothing is done to counter climate change, within one century the glaciers in the region may disappear. Since Xinjiang's reliance on glacial water is one of the highest in Asia, the disappearance of these glaciers would be catastrophic for the almost 24 million people living in the region. Landslides and floods are also a threat in the region.

3.5.6.1 Desertification

With almost 45% of its total land area occupied by deserts, Xinjiang is currently severely affected by desertification.[108] In 2004, Xinjiang's deserts were estimated to be expanding at a rate of 10.700 hectares per year, an improvement over previous years, when an expansion of 38.400 hectares a year was registered. The central and local governments invested huge capitals to cope with this problem. Between 2000 and 2004, 1.43 million hectares of trees were planted, while forest increased from 1.92 to 2.1% of the total land area. In 2004, a government campaign channeled 27 million dollars of investments into methane gas

[107] Guo and Liu (2012).

[108] Hu et al. (2004).

facilities, using animal and human waste as cooking and heating fuel, measures which reduced the habit of the communities to cut trees for firewood.

In 2009, about 10% of Xinjiang's rural population was using methane,[109] while also being encouraged to plant trees through government campaigns to control desertification. In 2007,[110] China's central government announced plans to reduce desert areas of 7.6 million hectares by 2015, through investments aimed at planting trees, training professional forestry staff, setting up monitoring stations and improving irrigation systems. The central government covered 80% of the planned 2.46 billion dollars in investments, while the remaining 20% were covered by local governments. Over the past years, Xinjiang received funding also from foreign governments, including Japan and South Korea, to reduce desertification. Most of Xinjiang's desertification is caused by excessive farming and over-grazing. Local people's use of wood for fuel also contributes to desertification, as trees act as a windbreak, retain moisture and prevent erosion. Before the campaign to encourage the use of methane, the average rural family used to burn 500 kilograms of wood per year. Experts consider impacts of climate change—particularly reduced rainfall—as another challenge to the halt of desertification. Ecological consequences of desertification are cropland infertility, drinking water shortages and sandstorms. Desertification can also affect human health by increasing respiratory diseases and eye irritations. In Khotan, there are over 300 days per year of sand-filled wind, which are leading to a marked increase in respiratory problems. Furthermore, due to desertification and encroaching sand, Qira County residents had to relocate three times.

3.5.6.2 Nuclear Tests

In a recent article, Becky (2019) refers to Beijing's nuclear activities in Xinjiang and argues that "Uyghur experience of environmental racism is extensive and extreme",[111] and that "the Uyghur people were originally witnessed to the destruction of their life-worlds during the nuclear imperialism of the PRC's Cold War nuclear weapon tests, yet have had their demands for recognition of their lands and their claims for

[109] Xinjiang Statistical Yearbook 2011.

[110] Cheng (2007).

[111] p. 3.

restitution of damage ignored".[112] Between 1964 and 1996, the Chinese government used to carry out nuclear testing in the Lop Nor area in Eastern Xinjiang. The *Christian Science Monitor* reported that 45 official nuclear tests led to radiation poisoning which caused 210.000 estimated deaths. However, it has been assessed that secret nuclear testing has also been going on, with serious effects on the health of the people in the surrounding areas.[113] An investigative work by the London daily *The Independent* revealed that in the areas surrounding the Lop Nor nuclear test site the cancer rate that is 35% higher than in the rest of China: leukemia, tumors and birth defects such as cleft palates hit people at a higher rate than the average in the country. An anonymous doctor claimed that during the testing period, 80% of children he was visiting had cleft palates. The effects of the site radioactivity on people living around the lake have been reported by the Uyghur doctor Enver Tohti, who participated in a *Channel Four* documentary on the issue, collaborated to the editing of a book on the topic,[114] and is now living in London from where he goes around the world to speak about his experience as a doctor in the Cancer Department of the First Hospital in Urumqi. When he was still working there during the 1990s, he found out that cancer rated in the region was 30–35% higher than the national average. As the head of the London section of the World Uyghur Congress, Tohti is currently dealing with topics such as organ transplanting from living convicts, something which he has been allegedly forced to perform when he was still working as a doctor in Xinjiang.

Concerning the Chinese nuclear experiments sites in Xinjiang, after the establishment of new theme parks in Dunhuang, Kaifeng and other parts of China, Beijing authorities started to give access to the public to the deserted nuclear experiment sites where scientists developed the country's first atomic bomb in 1964, the remote Malan atomic base in Lop Nor. The costs of this "requalification project" amounted to six million RMB, around 732.000 EURO.[115] According to Chaudhuri (2005), the emphasis on the importance of resource-based development and cultivation of cotton in Xinjiang is a glaring example of a mentality which is not attentive to environment. The author argues that without a systematic plan for controlling environmental degradation, the twin strategy of

[112] p. 18.

[113] Merali (2009).

[114] Takada (2009).

[115] BBC: http://www.bbc.co.uk/news/world-asia-china-19958011.

oil and cotton may create a disaster. Moreover, this author argues that the approach to the Western Development Program allowed unbridled market forces to seek profit from the region, with the government not being able to develop Xinjiang according to local conditions.

3.5.7 Education

The Chinese national education policy basic requirement is that minority children learn their mother tongue at school, and all children have to learn the national language: Mandarin. Until the late 1990s in Uyghur primary schools, the teaching language was Uyghur, and Mandarin was taught as the second language. At the beginning of the twenty-first century, a complex system of bilingual education has been established in all autonomous regions in China. In 2002, a new education policy on bilingualism has been introduced by the Xinjiang Regional Education Bureau: Mandarin replaced Uyghur as language of instruction, and the mother tongue started to be taught as second language. The official narrative and declared goal of this policy shift was the improvement of Mandarin skills among minority students, who could in this way build profiles allegedly more competitive for the job market, Arienne M. Dwyer (2005) offers a critical assessment of these new measures, underlying the political aims of Beijing in encouraging education in Mandarin. The author argues that monolingual education, the covert middle-term aim of the Chinese Ministry of Education, is perceived as a "cultural attack" by Uyghurs and can indeed be understood as an effective measure for a quick assimilation. These positions are endorsed in Leibold and Chen (2014) (Fig. 3.9).

The implementation of the policy was initially slow. In 2002, in most rural areas and in many cities apart from Urumqi, just a few minority teachers had good Mandarin skills, thus the mother tongue continued to be the main language of instruction. Mandarin was adopted as language of instruction in urban minority schools, where it was easier to find qualified teachers. To accelerate the implementation of the policy, the government started implementing learning programs aimed at improving the Mandarin level of established teachers, and started sending minority teachers with a good level of Mandarin to rural schools. In 2005, Mandarin became the official language of instruction all over the region, according to the Regional Education Bureau's new requirements. Since then, the pace of policy implementation continued to vary, depending on the capacity to teach Mandarin effectively by existing teachers, or on the interpretation of the policy by local government officials.

Fig. 3.9 Uyghur children in a bilingual school in a village (DSCN 4134)

In today's Xinjiang, there are three kinds of primary school: the "Han school", with the majority of children being Han, and a small but increasing number of students belonging to minorities, with all subjects taught in Mandarin by Han teachers; the "combined school", attended by Han and minority children who can study in minority languages just some optional subjects, with all the other classes taught in Mandarin; and the "ethnic school", the so-called Uyghur schools, where 100% of students belong to minorities, the mother tongue is learned as a subject, and the language of instruction for all the other classes is Mandarin.

The "Han schools" registered a rapid increase of enrollments in the past few years. This is mainly due to the increase of Han people living in Xinjiang and to the choice of a growing number of Uyghur families, mainly belonging to the emerging Uyghur bourgeoisie and middle class, to send their children to Han schools. They assume that a fluent level of Mandarin and an education in Mandarin would help children to access good universities, find suitable jobs and achieve better positions in Chinese society. The second type of schools is mainly attended by minority nationals who want to study their mother tongue but also be fluent in Mandarin. The Uyghur schools are mainly attended by Uyghurs who do not have any other choice because this kind of school is the only one available in the surroundings, or by a minority of Uyghurs who believe that an education in Uyghur is more appropriate. According to the majority of Uyghurs, we have been talking to on the issue, Han schools are much better than Uyghur schools in terms of teaching quality, since the latter are permeated with propaganda activities and educational standards are lower. This is due to a number of different factors, including the fact that Uyghur schools are located in remote countryside areas, where only young and non-experienced teachers and educators are willing to work.

The link between human capital, economic growth and development is underlined by Wang Jinbo (2009), who argues that investment in an education which is competitive on the job market is a fundamental factor of growth and development. The author assumes that the gap between Xinjiang and the Eastern part of China does not only concerns economy, but also education, which should be able to train, attract and retain talents. In this framework, in the year 2000 the Xinjiang Class, *Xinjiang Neidi Gaozhong Ban* 新疆内地高中班, has been launched. This special program consists in selecting the best Uyghur middle school students, reserve a place for them in prestigious high schools in Inner and coastal

China, eventually allow them to attend the best universities in China and at the end employ them in different professional realms in Xinjiang.[116]

Until 2015, policies on education in minority areas were still not consolidated and under discussion: In fact, they were constantly reframed and adjusted on the basis of the specific situation, with pilot experimental projects being implemented all over the region. For instance, since September 2007 all minority children in the city of Ghulja/Yining are required to learn Mandarin from grade one, and do not receive any teaching in their mother tongue. In Ghulja, children continue to learn in Mandarin as they progress through primary school, and get some rudiments of their mother tongue only from grade four. Since 2009, in other areas of Xinjiang, including Urumqi, primary teachers use Mandarin as the language of instruction, and minority children will follow between two and four hours per week of mother tongue taught as a subject. According to Strawbridge (2009), education authorities in Xinjiang intend "bilingual" education a school system where Mandarin is adopted as the language of instruction. In other words, "bilingual" teachers are minority teachers who teach subjects in Mandarin and are required not to use the mother tongue during their lessons. The widespread implementation of this kind of bilingual policy has increased pressure on children, meaning that they need to have a basic understanding of Mandarin from the time they start primary school. This led to Mandarin being widely taught in pre-schools and even kindergartens, to prepare children for school life in a second language environment.

From 2007, education authorities have sought to further improve the standard of Mandarin in primary schools by stepping up language training for teachers. This included programs for minority teachers with good Mandarin skills to attend courses to improve their skills in spoken and written Mandarin for up to two years. Temporarily, these teachers were replaced by young graduates from Mandarin language institutions who have good language skills but no experience in teaching. At the same time, minority teachers in ethnic and combined schools with limited Mandarin were replaced by graduates with good Mandarin but no teaching skills[117] (Fig. 3.10).

[116]An exhaustive overview of this programme, including its outcomes, is provided by Grose (2010).

[117]Educational enrollment and attainment disparities in China following ethnic lines are analyzed by Hannum (2002).

Fig. 3.10 Training room in a government facility with Lei Feng and Confucius (DSCN 3363)

3.5.7.1 Impact on Minority Schools

The pragmatic approach toward education for minorities adopted by Ma Rong (2006), which advocates the combination of the interests of ethnic minorities for their cultural heritage and the interest of the government for national development and integration, has guided the work of the central authorities on the issue. The implementation of the bilingual language policy throughout the region had a deep impact on the composition and status of the different types of schools in Xinjiang. The trend is that parents are moving their children from classes in combined schools that provide mother tongue lessons into classes entirely taught in Mandarin. The status of Mandarin as language of instruction has been boosted by the many Uyghur government officials who are enrolling their children in Han schools. According to the authorities of the Regional Bureau of Education, the quality of teaching, particularly in ethnic schools, gradually declined, because experienced teachers in minority schools were replaced by unqualified graduates with good

Mandarin skills. This has contributed to the transfer of minority children into classes where Mandarin is the sole language of instruction. The outcome of these policies is that there are now declining numbers of children attending ethnic schools, and fewer minority children studying their mother tongue in combined schools. It is likely that, within a few years, Mandarin will be the only language of instruction for minority children in many combined schools, if the trend in urban schools is of any indication. As the number of classes providing mother tongue instruction reduces and more Mandarin is used in schools, mother tongue teachers are being retired or transferred to other roles. According to the survey made by Strawbridge (2009) for Save the Children, already 21% of minority children are no longer learning their mother tongue. This is likely to increase to 40% or more in the next years.

3.6 Conclusive Remarks: Uneven Regional Development

Referring to the dimensions set by the UNDP for the calculation of the Human Development Index (HDI—health, education, living standards), its related indicators (life expectancy at birth, average years of schooling, expected years of schooling, gross national income per capita) and a hybrid set of criteria which we consider "place-specific" (like alcohol abuse, domestic violence and women conditions), the available literature, together with my fieldwork outcomes,[118] highlight a situation of neat disparities between the Han and the Uyghur population living in today's Xinjiang Uyghur Autonomous Region. This trend, over a time span from 1999 to 2016, is stable, with part of the Uyghur population (mainly an emerging tiny middle class connected to the Party and the government) enjoying the new opportunities, and another part seeing its life standards gradually worsening (mainly farmers and migrant workers).[119] Ethnic affiliation of groups and individuals, originally a socio-political construction,[120] turned to be a commonly accepted de facto inflexible classification for individual and group identities, a consolidated label with

[118] See the following chapters.

[119] For an in-depth elaboration on this socio-economic divide, see the conclusive chapter in this book.

[120] Buttino (2007), Carter and Fenton (2009), Fabietti (2007), and Rughinis (2011).

a specific meaning within the society. Access to resources and services is strictly associated with it.

It has already been assessed that Xinjiang is a fast-growing region, where job opportunities are increasing and wealth is more and more widespread, reaching the remotest areas, and where substantial investments from the central government and SOEs are allegedly aimed at improving people's life standards, by leveraging on environmental conditions and infrastructures. According to Kuznets theory of the U-shaped relationship between development and inequality,[121] this fast growth and developmental drive shall produce a "spillover effect" in the long term, and should lead to the inclusion of all social actors in the new developed environment, entailing an equally distributed access to resources and wealth. Up to now, remarkable inequalities still exist, with the Southern part of the region, mainly rural and populated for the 80% by Uyghurs, suffering from severe economic and social problems, and the Han-dominated and mainly urban Northern part apparently almost exclusively benefitting from the incoming new wealth. The still very complex situation in the poorest areas of Southern Xinjiang, matched with socio-economic measures which are unpopular and often contested,[122] is leaving room to the feeling that this development model is imposed from the top, a distant and alien center mainly concerned about its own interests and too much engaged in matching requests and claims by a more compliant Han population. This sense of "having been left behind" is common and widespread across the broader Uyghur population. A major problem which has almost always been mentioned in interviews during our fieldworks is the lack of "capacitations", which means that Uyghurs have the neat perception of being unable to climb the social ladder, no matter how much effort they put in their studies and works. Obstacles are always perceived as too tough. Among those who have been interviewed, a frequent reason of complaint is the impossibility to move forward in professional and educational contexts, due to the presence of Han counterparts who are unfair competitors, mainly due to language and educational factors.

The increasing local discontent, together with the perception of being considered as "second-class citizens", erupted in large demonstrations

121 Acemoglu and Robinson (2002).

122 Such as the dibao, measures to cope with religious belief, education and unemployment are just a few of the contested measures implemented in Southern Xinjiang.

of Uyghur students, migrant workers and common people in July 2009, covering with blood the streets of Urumqi. The clashes which followed left almost 200 people dead and hundreds of causalities. These data have been officially released by the central and regional authorities, and they highlighted that the majority of those killed were of Han ethnicity. For the whole autumn 2009 tensions continued, with frequent violent outbreaks in different parts of the region, making the international community question how much the area is really stable.[123] President Hu Jintao was forced to return to China from Italy, where he was on an official visit for a tour which included several European countries in occasion of the G8.[124]

The interpretations which followed the riots range from an alleged involvement of terrorist groups—the existence and the extent of whom are difficult to assess[125]—to the more "traditional" narrative proposed by Chinese central authorities. This argues that Xinjiang is a harmoniously developing area, where peoples of all the nationalities are cooperating for the construction of a better society, and the problems of terrorism, religious extremism and separatism depend on foreign forces, like the US government and the US-financed WUC (World Uyghur Congress). The 2009 riots are thus ascribed to those forces, supported by Uyghurs émigrés who oppose the central government often for power dynamics.[126] According to a US diplomat[127] who prefers to remain anonymous, the Chinese government is insisting with a certain strength that a terrorist threat really exists on its territory and is allegedly looking for support from foreign countries which, like the US and Germany,[128] are particularly sensitive to the same problem. This notwithstanding, the "view from inside" provided by the local population, mainly consists in the perception of being left behind, which means not having been consulted, nor included, in the decision-making process and the

[123] Millward (2009).

[124] "Troops Flood Urumqi as Chinese President Quits G8 Summit", in *The Guardian*, 8 July 2009.

[125] An informative but controversial work on the issue is Reed and Raschke (2010).

[126] This is the narrative provided by Prof Yang Shenming during one of his classes at Minzu University of China in March 2012.

[127] Interviewed in August 2012 in Beijing.

[128] Personal observation while at Stiftung Wissenschaft und Politik (The German Centre for International and Security Affairs) as guest fellow.

Fig. 3.11 Board on the political work in a village (DSCN 3861)

new developmental push interesting the region. For instance, the thesis of some Uyghur intellectuals is that the outbreak of the 2009 riots has mainly been triggered by contrasts concerning the transfers of Uyghur peasant workers, planned and managed by Beijing, from the poor areas of Southern Xinjiang to the factories of Inner and coastal China.[129] The interpretation proposed by Prof. Ilham Tohti is that the constant discrimination of the Uyghur population by the central government and the Hans is the reason why Uyghurs took to the streets (Fig. 3.11).

A valid interpretative approach is provided by Micheal Hechter and by his theory of internal colonialism and cultural division of labor.[130] In his work, Hechter assumes that in internally colonized societies class

[129] Prof. Qarluq illustrated his thesis in a lecture he gave at Università di Napoli "L'Orientale" on 7 November 2012.

[130] Hechter (1987).

struggle has been replaced, and in a way disguised, by ethnic struggle and discrimination. This situation can be assessed in Xinjiang, where a clear link between ethnicity and life standards exists: The rich, powerful and wealthy are Hans, while the worse off are the Uyghurs. At the same time, these class/ethnic dynamics reproduce themselves within the Uyghur community, whereas, for instance, corrupted officials exploit poor Uyghur farmers.[131]

To summarize, the "human geography" of intraregional inequality highlights a pattern where a certain socio-economic status is associated with a certain ethnicity. Ethnic categories assume a kind of "solidity", they are written on identity cards and personal documents, different laws and regulations entail diverse ethnicities, and what emerges is an over-ethicized society.[132]

The question now is how current developments are going to impact the peoples of Xinjiang. We need to understand whether, within a more urbanized and industrial society, it will not be possible that Uyghurs will necessarily be involved in the decision-making process. Up to now, dynamics underlying disparities are still engrained and rooted in social interactions and political implementation. These questions cannot be answered by only looking at official data and scholarly texts, but only by being part of Xinjiang society it is possible to get a better understanding of the situation. The outcomes of the long and often complex fieldwork in the two areas chosen as representative, Kashgar and Shihezi, are illustrated in the following chapter.

Bibliography

Acemoglu, Daron, and Robinson, James A. (2002), "The Political Economy of the Kuznets Curve", in *Review of Development Economics*, Vol. 6, No. 2, pp. 183–203.

Alexis-Martin, Becky (2019), "The Nuclear Imperialism-Necropolitics Nexus: Contextualizing Chinese-Uyghur Oppression in Our Nuclear Age", in *Eurasian Geography and Economics*, https://doi.org/10.1080/15387216.2019.1645611.

[131] See the related chapter in this book.

[132] Carter and Fenton (2009), and the conclusive chapter of this book.

Baihan, Wei (2007), "Empirical Research on Uygur Women's Socioeconomic Characteristics Influences on the Number of Family Children", Supervisor: Feng Shiping, PhD Dissertation Discussed at Lanzhou University. 维吾尔族妇女的社会经济特征对其家庭子女数影响的实证研究,闻伯汉,指导教师:冯世平,兰州大学, 2007年.

Becher, Tony, and Trowler, Paul (2001), *Academic Tribes and Territories: Intellectual Enquiry and the Culture of Disciplines*, Society for Research into Higher Education & Open University Press.

Becquelin, Nicholas (2000), "Xinjiang in the Nineties", in *The China Journal*, No. 44, pp. 65–90.

Becquelin, Nicholas (2004), "Staged Development in Xinjiang", in *The China Quarterly*, No. 178, pp. 358–378.

Bhalla, A.S., and Qiu, Shufang (2006), *Poverty and Inequality Among Chinese Minorities* (Routledge Studies on Chinese Economy), Routledge Chapman & Hall.

Bian, Yanjie (2003), "Sociological Research on Reform-Era China", in *Issues & Studies*, Vol. 38/39, pp. 139–174.

Bian, Yanjie, and Zhang, Lei (2008), "Sociology in China", in *Contexts Magazine*, Vol. 7, No. 3, pp. 20–25.

Bloch, Marc (1984), *La società feudale*, Einaudi.

Borei, Dorothy V. (1992), "Beyond the Great Wall: Agricultural Development in Northern Xinjiang, 1760–1820," in Jane Kate Leonard and John R. Watt (eds.), *To Achieve Security and Wealth: The Qing Imperial State and the Economy 1644–1911*, Ithaca.

Buttino, Marco (1997), *L'URSS a pezzi. Nazionalismi e conflitto etnico nel crollo del regime sovietico*, Paravia, Torino.

Buttino, Marco (2003), *La Rivoluzione Capovolta. L'Asia Centrale tra il crollo dell'impero zarista e la formazione dell'Urss*, L'Ancora del Mediterraneo.

Buttino, Marco (2007), "Tra l'Urss e le colonie. L'uso di categorie collettive, appunti di ricerca", Research Paper Published in the Website of the Italian Society for the Study of Contemporary History.

Buttino, Marco, Ercolessi, C., and Triulzi, A. (2000), *Uomini in armi. Costruzione etnica e violenza politica*, L'ancora del Mediterraneo.

Cao, Huhua (2010), "Urban-Rural Income Disparity and Urbanisation: What Is the Role of Spatial Distribution of Ethnic Groups? A Case Study of Xinjiang Uyghur Autonomous Region in Western China", in *Regional Studies*, Vol. 44, No. 8, pp. 965–982.

Carter, Bob, and Fenton, Steve (2009), "Not Thinking Ethnicity: A Critique of the Ethnicity Paradigm in an Over-Ethnicised Society", in *Journal for the Theory of Social Behavior*, Vol. 40, p. 1.

CASS Report on the Situation of AIDS in Xinjiang, Xinjiang Academy of Social Sciences, 2010. 2010 年新疆艾滋病研究报告, 新疆哲学社会科学网.

Chaudhuri, Kausik, and Dasgupta, Sugato (2005), "The political determinants of central governments' economic policies in India: an empirical investigation", in *Journal of International Development*.

Chen, Hon Fai (2018), *Chinese Sociology: State-Building and the Institutionalization of Globally Circulated Knowledge*, Palgrave Macmillan.

Cheng, Zhiliang (2007), "Tree by Tree, China Rolls Back Deserts", in *China Features*, Vol. 26.

Cheng, Lucie, and So, Alvin (1983), "The Reestablishing of Sociology in the PRC: Toward the Signification of Marxian Sociology", in *Annual Review of Sociology*, No. 9, pp. 471–498.

Cliff, Thomas (2009), "Neo-Oasis: The Xinjiang Bingtuan in the Twenty-First Century", in *Asian Studies Review*, Vol. 33, March, pp. 83–106.

Dibua, I. Jeremiah (2013), *Development and Diffusionism: Looking Beyond Neopatrimonialism in Nigeria, 1962–1985*, Palgrave Macmillan.

Dillon, Michael (2004), *Xinjiang—China's Muslim Far Northwest*, RoutledgeCurzon.

Dwyer, Arianne M. (2005), "The Xinjiang Conflict: Uyghur Identity, Language Policy, and Political Discourse", in *East-West Center*, Washington.

Fabietti, Ugo (2001), *Storia dell'antropologia*, Zannichelli, Bologna.

Fabietti, Ugo (2007), *L'identità etnica, storia e critica di un concetto equivoco*, Carocci.

Feyeraband, Paul (1984), *La scienza come arte*, Laterza.

Feyerabend, Paul (1993), *Dialogo sul metodo*, Laterza.

Flyvbjerg, Bent (2006), "Five Misunderstanding About Case Study Research", in *Qualitative Inquiry*, Vol. 12, No. 2, pp. 219–245.

Flyvbjerg, Bent (2011), "Case Study", in Norman K. Denzin and Yvonna S. Lincoln (eds.), *The Sage Handbook of Qualitative Research*, 4th edition, Sage, Thousand Oaks, pp. 301–316.

Flyvbjerg, Bent, Todd, Landman, and Sanford, Schram (2012), *Real Social Science: Applied Phronesis*, Cambridge University Press.

Galvan, Frank H., and Caetano, Raul (2003), "Alcohol Use and Related Problems Among Ethnic Minorities in the United States", in *The Journal of the National Institute on Alcohol Abuse and Alcoholism*, Vol. 27, No. 1, pp. 87–94.

Gao, Xuelian, Ma, Yan, and Lei, Zhigang (2006), "Analysis of the Situation of Medical Cares and Venereal Infections Among CSWs in Urumqi", in *Dermatology and Venereology*, Vol. 28, p. 3. 高雷莲,马燕,雷志刚,乌鲁木齐市娱乐场所性工作者梅毒感染及治疗状况分析,皮肤病与性病,2006年第28卷第3期.

Gibbons, Michael (1994), *The New Production of Knowledge: The Dynamics of Science and Research in Contemporary Societies*, Sage.

Gill, Bates, and Gang, Song (2006), "HIV/AIDS in Xinjiang: A Growing Regional Challenge", in *China and Eurasia Forum Quarterly*, Vol. 4, No. 3, pp. 35–50.

Gill, Bates, Huang, Yanzhong, and Lu, Xiaoqing (2007), *Demography of HIV/AIDS in China. A Report of the Task Force on HIV/AIDS*, Center for Strategic and International Studies.

Ginzburg, Carlo (1976), *Il formaggio e i vermi. Il cosmo di un mugnaio del Cinquecento*, Einaudi.

Gladney, Dru C. (1998), "Internal Colonialism and the Uyghur Nationality: Chinese Nationalism and its Subaltern Subjects", in *Cahiers d'Etudes sur la Méditerranée Orientale et le monde Turco-Iranien*, Vol. 25.

Grose, Timothy (2010), "The Xinjiang Class: Education, Integration and the Uyghurs", in *Journal of Muslim Minority Affairs*, Vol. 30, No. 1, pp. 97–109.

Guo, Liu, and Liu, Meng-li (2012), "Assessment on Ecological Environmental Quality of the Tarim River: Important Ecological Function Zones", in *Arid Environmental Monitoring*, Vol. 1.

Gustaffson, Bjorn, and Zhong, Wei (2000), "How and Why Has Poverty in China Changed? A Study Based on Microdata from 1988 and 1995" (Research Note), in *The China Quarterly*, No. 164, pp. 983–1006.

Gustafsson, Björn Anders, and Ding, Sai (2008), "Temporary and Persistent Poverty among Ethnic Minorities and the Majority in Rural China", IZA Discussion Papers 3791, Institute of Labor Economics (IZA).

Haider, Ziad (2005), "Sino-Pakistan Relations and Xinjiang's Uighurs: Politics, Trade and Islam Along the Karakoram Highway", in *Asian Survey*, Vol. 45, No. 4, pp. 522–545.

Hannum, E. (2002), "Educational Stratification by Ethnicity in China: Enrollment and Attainment in the Early Reform Years", in *Demography*, Vol. 39, No. 1, pp. 95–117.

Hannum, E., and Xie, Y. (1998), "Ethnic Stratification in Northwest China: Occupational Differences Between Han Chinese and National Minorities in Xinjiang", in *Demography*, Vol. 35, No. 3, pp. 323–333.

Hao, Wei, Su, Zhonghua, Liu, Binglun et al. (2004), "Drinking and Drinking Patterns and Health Status in the General Population of Five Areas of China", in *Alcohol and Alcoholism*, Vol. 39, No. 1, pp. 43–52.

Hao, Wei, Chen, Hanhui, and Su, Zhonghua (2005), "China: Alcohol Today", in *Addiction*, Vol. 100, No. 6, June, pp. 737–741.

Hechter, Michael (1987), *Internal Colonialism: the Celtic Fringe in British National Development*, University of California Press.

Hsu, Immanuel (2000), *The Rise of Modern China*, 6th edition, Oxford University Press.

Hu, Li, Xiaofeng, Wang, and Yaqi, Gao (2004), "Analysis and Assessment of Land Desertification in Xinjiang, Based on RS and GIS", in *Journal of Geographical Sciences*, Vol. 14, No. 2, pp. 159–166.

Human Rights Council, Uyghur Women and Human Rights, report by Rebyia Kadeer, President of the WUC, at the Forum on Minority Issues, Fourth Session, 29–30 Nov, 2011.

Jinbo, Wang (2009), "A Study of Education Investment and Xinjiang Economic Development", in *International Journal of Business and Management*, Vol. 4, No. 5.

Jun, Jing, and Worth, Heather (2010), *HIV IN CHINA. Understanding the Social Aspects of the Epidemic*, UNSW Press.

Kasarda, John D., and Crenshaw, Edward M. (1991), "Third World Urbanization: Dimensions, Theories, and Determinants", in *Annual Review of Sociology*, Vol. 17, pp. 467–501.

Khun, S. Thomas (1962), *The Structure of Scientific Revolutions*, University of Chicago Press.

Leibold, James, and Chen, Yangbin (2014), *Minority Education in China: Balancing Unity and Diversity in an Era of Critical Pluralism*, Hong Kong University Press.

Levi, Giovanni (1985), *L'eredità immateriale. Carriera di un esorcista nel Piemonte del seicento*, Einaudi.

Li, Zhihuan (2009), "Uyghur Women in Economic Organizations", Supervisor: Xu Lili, PhD Dissertation Discussed at Lanzhou University. 经济组织中的维吾尔族妇女, 李智环,指导教师,兰州大学, 2009年.

Li, Meirong, and Liu, Wenjing (2009), "Research Report on the Development of the Urbanization in Xinjiang", in *Ethnic Economy*, No. 3.

Little, Kenneth (2004), *Urbanization as a Social Process: An Essay on Movement and Change in Contemporary Africa*, Routledge (first ed. 1974).

Liu, Shaohua (2010), *Passage to Manhood: Youth Migration, Heroin and AIDS in Southwest China*, Stanford University Press.

Liu, Xiaoyun (2015), "The Development of Rural Primary Health Care in China's Health System Reform", in *Journal of Asian Public Policy*, Vol. 8, No. 1, p. 88.

Liu, Qingrui, and Weng, Qianwei (2011), "Urban Minimum Living Security Line: The Analysis and the Strategy Discussion of the Gap Between Actual Payment and Theoretical Criterion", in *Population & Economics*, No. 4.

Liu, Zhenqiu, Fang, Qiwen, Zhou, Sujuan, Minhas, Veenu, Wood, Charles, He, Na, and Zhang, Tiejun (2017), "Seroprevalence of Kaposi's Sarcoma-Associated Herpesvirus Among HIV-Infected Uygurs in Xinjiang, China", in *Journal of Medical Virology*, Vol. 89, No. 9, Wiley.

Lu, Sun et al. (2000), "Effect of High-Fluoride Water on Intelligence in Children", in *Fluoride*, Vol. 33, No. 2, pp. 74–78.

Maimaiti, Rena, Yuexin, Zhang, Kejun, Pan, Wubili, Maimaitaili, Lalanne, Christophe, Duracinsky, Martin, and Andersson, Rune (2017), "Assessment of Health-Related Quality of Life among People Living with HIV in Xinjiang, West China", in *Journal of the International Association of Providers of AIDS Care*, Vol. 16, No. 6, pp. 588–594.

Merali, Zeeya (2009), "Did China's Nuclear Tests Kill Thousands and Doom Future Generations?", in *Scientific American Magazine*, Vol. 8.

Millward, James (1998), *Beyond the Pass: Economy, Ethnicity and Empire in Qing Xinjiang, 1759–1864*, Stanford University Press.

Millward, James (2004), *Violent Separatism in Xinjiang: A Critical Assessment*, No. 6, East-West Center Washington, Washington, DC.

Millward, James (2007), *Eurasian Crossroads: A History of Xinjiang*, Columbia University Press.

Millward, James (2009), "Does the 2009 Urumchi Violence Mark a Turning Point?", in *Central Asian Survey*, Vol. 28, No. 4, pp. 347–360.

Moneyhon, Matthew (2002), "Controlling Xinjiang: Autonomy on China's 'New Frontier'", in *Asian Pacific Law and Policy Journal*, Vol. 3, No. 1.

Newby, Laura (1998), "The Begs of Xinjiang: Between Two Worlds", in *Bulletin of the School of Oriental and African Studies*, Vol. 61, No. 2, pp. 278–297.

Pan, Cheng et al. (2010), "Research Progress and Developing Trends on Micro-Organisms of Xinjiang Specific Environments", in *Journal of Arid Land*, Vol. 2, No. 1, pp. 51–56.

Pannel, Clifton W., and Ma, Laurence J.C. (1997), "Urban Transition and Interstate Relations in a Dynamic Post-Soviet Borderland: The Xinjiang Uygur Autonomous Region of China", in *Post-Soviet Geography and Economics*, Vol. 38, No. 4, pp. 206–229.

Ping, Ji (1990), "Frontier Migration and Ethnic Assimilation: A Case of Xinjiang Uyghur Autonomous Region of China", PhD Thesis, Brown University.

Previato, Tommaso (ed., 2016), *Moving Across Borders in China: Interdisciplinary Approaches to the Study of Cultural Diversity in Marginal Areas*, Aracne Editrice.

Qarluq, Abduresit (2011a), "Fieldwork on the Conditions of Uyghur Peasant Workers in Beijing and Tianjin", in *Journal of Beifang University of Nationalities*, No. 2.

Qarluq, Abduresit (2011b), "Research on the Conditions of Uyghur Farmers Working in Beijing and Tianjin", in *Journal of Northern Minzu University* (Philosophy and Sociology Series), Vol. 98, No. 2. 阿布都热西提· 基力力(c), 维吾尔族农民工在京、津两地生活适应的调查, 北方民族大学学报(哲学社会科学 版), 2011 年第2 期, 总第98 期.

Qarluq, Abduresit, and Hayes, Anna (2011), "Securitising HIV/AIDS in the Xinjiang Uyghur Autonomous Region", in *Australian Journal of International Affairs*, Vol. 65, No. 2, pp. 203–219.

Rashid, Ahmed (2002), *Jihad: The Rise of Militant Islam in Central Asia*, Yale University Press.

Reed, J. Todd, and Raschke, Diana (2010), *THE ETIM, China's Islamic Militants and the Global Terrorist Threat*, Greenwood Publishing Group.

Renwick, N. (2002), "The 'nameless fever'. The HIV/AIDS pandemic and China's women", in *Third World Quarterly*, Vol. 23, No. 2, 337–393.

Rong, Ma (2006), "Education of Ethnic Minorities in Contemporary China", Paper Presented at the International Symposium on China's Positive Policies in *Minority Education: Plural Perspectives*, Dickinson College, USA (April 14–15, 2006).

Rossabi, Morris (ed., 2004), *Governing China's Multiethnic Frontiers*, University of Washington Press.
Rudelson, Justin (1997), *Oasis Identities: Uyghur Nationalism Along China's Silk Road*, Columbia University Press.
Rughinis, Cosima (2011), "Quantitative Tales of Ethnic Differentiation: Measuring and Using Roma/Gypsy Ethnicity in Statistical Analyses", in *Ethnic and Racial Studies,* Vol. 34, No. 4, pp. 594–619.
Sai, Ding (2007), "Poverty and Inequality Among Chinese Minorities" (Book Review), in *Asian-Pacific Economic Literature*, Vol. 21, No. 1, pp. 83–84.
Salhi, Zahia Smail (ed., 2013), *Gender and Violence in Islamic Societies: Patriarchy, Islamism and Politics in the Middle East and North Africa*, I.B. Tauris.
Sautman, Barry (2000), "Is Xinjiang an Internal Colony?", in *Inner Asia*, Vol. 2, No. 2, pp. 239–271.
Schuster, Brenda L. (2009), "Gaps in the Silk Road: An Analysis of Population Health Disparities in the Xinjiang Uyghur Autonomous Region of China", in *The China Quarterly*, Vol. 198, pp. 433–441.
Scull, Erika (2009), "Environmental Health Challenges in Xinjiang", a China Environmental Health Project Research Brief, Issued as Part of the China Environment Forum's partnership with Western Kentucky University on the USAID-Supported China Environmental Health Project.
Shi, Wuxiang, Brombal, Daniele et al. (2010), "The Influence of the Rural Health Security Schemes on Health Utilization and Household Impoverishment in Rural China: Data from a Household Survey of Western and Central China", in *International Journal for Equity in Health*, Vol. 9, p. 7.
Shichor, Yitzhak (2006), "Company Province, Civil-Military Relations in Xinjiang", in Nan Li (ed.), *Chinese Civil-Military Relations: The Transformation of the People's Liberation Army*, Routledge, pp. 135–150.
Shu, Z., Abudureyimu, A., Ma, J., Ma, X., Chen, Y., Li, T., Yuan, T., Yang, R., Li, X., Jang, C., Bao, G., and Sun, B. (2018), "Surveillance of HIV-1 Drug Resistance in Xinjiang: High Prevalence of K103N in Treatment-Naïve Individuals", in *Archives of Virology*, Vol. 163, No. 8, pp. 2111–2119, Springer.
Stake, Robert (1995), *The Art of Case Study Research*, Sage.
Stake, Robert (2006), *Multiple Case Study Analysis*, Guilford Press.
Strawbridge, David (2009), "The Challenges of Bilingual Education in the Xinjiang Uyghur Autonomous Region—People's Republic of China", Save the Children.
Takada, Jun (2009), *Chinese Nuclear Tests*, Iryokagakusha.
The People's Daily (2004), "Pain in the neck" is a thing of the past in Xinjiang, 12.02.2004.
Tian, Tian, Mijiti, Peierdun, Bingxue, Huang, Fadong, Zhang, Ainiwaer, Abidan, Guoyao, Sang, Zhanlin, Zhang, Mahan, Yeledan, Xiaoqin, Tuo, Zheng, Gong, and Jianghong, Dai (2017), "Prevalence and Risk Factors of Anal Human Papillomavirus Infection Among HIV-Negative Men Who Have

Sex with Men in Urumqi City of Xinjiang Uyghur Autonomous Region, China", in *PLoS One*, Vol. 12, No. 11.

Tucker, Joseph, and Poston, L. Dudley (eds., 2009), *Gender Policy and HIV in China*, Catalyzing Policy Change, Springer Science+Business Media B.V.

UNAIDS (2002), *Report on the Global HIV/AIDS epidemic*, July.

Wang, Juan, and Zhang, Jie (2012), "Analysis of the Causes of Acute Pancreatitis Among Hans and Uyghurs in Xinjiang", in *Journal of Clinical Emergency*, Vol. 13, No. 4. 汪娟, 张杰, 乌鲁木齐市汉族与维吾尔族急性俟腺炎致病多因素分析, 2012年13卷4期.

Wen, Chihua (2004), "Device Helps Free Uygurs with Goiter", in *China Features*, 20.01.2004.

Wenger, Etienne (1999), *Communities of Practice: Learning, Meaning, and Identity*, Cambridge University Press.

WHO Report on HIV/AIDS in China: Summary Country Profile for HIV/AIDS Treatment Scale-Up, December 2005.

Wu, Yanrui (1996), "Changing Patterns of Alcohol Consumption in Rural China: Implications for the Grain Section", Chinese Economies Research Centre (CERC) Working Papers, No. 7.

Xu, Xifa (2005), "Sociological Consideration on the AIDS Problem in Xinjiang", in *Social Sciences in Xinjiang*, No. 6. 新疆艾滋病问题的社会学思考,新疆社会科学,2005年,第6期.

Yang, Xiang, Saidula, Youdusi, and Xia, Zhu (2008), "The Survey Analysis of University Students' Lifestyle", in *Journal of Xinjiang Medical University*, Vol. 31, No. 12, December.

Zhang, Yuping (2005), "HIV/AIDS Prevention Among Chinese Minorities", in *Journal of Guangxi University for Nationalities*, Vol. 27, No. 2. 张玉萍, 少数民族防治艾滋病的思考,广西民族学院学报(哲学社会科学版),第27卷第2期,2005年3月.

Zhang, Xiuming (2009), *Theory and Practice of the Work for the Fight of Separatism and the Stabilization of Xinjiang*, Xinjiang People's Press, Urumqi. 张秀明, 新疆反分裂斗争和稳定工作的实践与思考,新疆人民出版社, 乌鲁木齐2009.

Zhang, Chen, and Rui, Lihong (2007), "Coal's City: Measures to Control Urumqi Health-Threatening Air Pollution", in *China Environment Series*, Vol. 9, pp. 161–163.

Zhang, J., Casswell, S., and Cai, H. (2008), "Increased Drinking in a Metropolitan City in China: A Study of Alcohol Consumption Patterns and Changes", in *Addiction*, Vol. 103, No. 3, pp. 416–423.

Zhao, Sun et al. (2011), "Acceptability of Pre-exposure Prophylaxis Among Female Sex Workers in Xinjiang", in *Journal of Zhejiang University (Medical Sciences)*, Vol. 40, No. 3. 赵,孙,等,新疆女性性工作者艾滋病暴露前预防用药使用意愿调查,浙江大学学抱(医学版),第40卷,第3期2011年.

CHAPTER 4

Walking in Two Worlds: Kashgar and Shihezi

4.1 Kashgar and Shihezi: Main Statistical Indicators (2011 and 2016)

See Table 4.1.

Table 4.1 Selected statistical indicators of Shihezi and Kashgar (2011 and 2016)

Indicator	*Kashgar prefecture*	*Shihezi sub-prefectural-level city*
Population	4.515 million (3.775.300 in 2011)	573.800 (631.600 in 2011)
Major ethnic groups	92% Uyghurs (90.2% in 2011) 6% Han (7.2% in 2011)	94% Han (92% in 2011) 1% Uyghurs (2.5% in 2011)
Area	137.579 square kilometers	460 square kilometers
GDP	75.986 billion RMB (2.776 million RMB in 2011)	30.647 billion RMB (108.36 million RMB in 2011)
GDP composition	34,2:25,2:40,6 (40,6:17,2:42,2 in 2011)	21,9:45,3:32,8[a] (6,6:51,1:42,3 in 2011)
GDP per capita	16.860 RMB (7.085 in 2011)	78.200 RMB (42.728 in 2011)

(continued)

A. Cappelletti, *Socio-Economic Development in Xinjiang Uyghur Autonomous Region*,
https://doi.org/10.1007/978-981-15-1536-1_4

Table 4.1 (continued)

Indicator	*Kashgar prefecture*	*Shihezi sub-prefectural-level city*
GDP as percentage of provincial GDP	1.2% (0.06% in 2011)	5.7% (2.53% in 2011)
State-owned enterprises	56 (11 in 2011)	42 (36 in 2011)
Urban population	1.020 million (1.398 million in 2011)	573.800[b] (631.600 in 2011)
Rural population	3.5 million (2.474 million in 2011)	//
Birth rate	23.5% (27.02% in 2011)	4.36% (5.72% in 2011)
Unemployment rate	3.03% (3.95% in 2011)	1.02% (2.02% in 2011)
No. of employed persons in state-owned units	378.765 (146.895 in 2011)	67.093 (49.239 in 2011)
No. of employed persons in units with a different kind of ownership	67.730 (30.396 in 2011)	59.395 (40.046 in 2011)

[a]Heavy industry counts for 62.2% and light industry for 37.8%
[b]Shihezi residents, regardless of their activity, have an urban *hukou*

4.2 Commonalities and Differences Between Kashgar and Shihezi

See Table 4.2.

Table 4.2 Cross-sectional comparative table on differences and commonalities between Kashgar and Shihezi

	Commonalities	*Differences*
Geographical position	Both areas are located in Xinjiang Uyghur Autonomous Region	Shihezi is located in Northern Xinjiang (***beijiang*** 北疆) and Kashgar in Southern Xinjiang (***nanjiang*** 南疆). Kashgar is an oasis city on the fringe of the Taklamakan Desert; Shihezi is located in a lowland area in between steppes and mountains
Administrative classification and governance	The two areas are located in the same country (***guojia*** 国家) and the same autonomous region (***zizhi qu*** 自治区)	Kashgar (***kashi diqu*** 喀什地区) is a regional prefecture (***difangqu*** 地方区) which depends from regional authorities, while Shihezi (***shihezi shi*** 石河子市) is a sub-prefectural-level city (***zizhiqu zhixia shengji shi*** 自治区直辖甚级市) which belongs to the bingtuan 兵团 organization and depends only on the Corps' administration and the central government. As a bingtuan city, Shihezi enjoys a high degree of autonomy: It has its own judicial system, health, educational and welfare system, welfare measures and other autonomous bodies/benefits. In some cases, for example, in official statistical publications, the XJPCC are considered as a state within the state. In the Kashgar Prefecture, there are some areas closed to both foreigners and Chinese non-residents, and in Shihezi and surroundings no similar situation has been found
Population rights and duties, ethnicity	Kashgar and Shihezi residents are citizens of the same country. They are all subject to the national law	Kashgar Prefecture residents are 92% Uyghurs and 6% Hans. They are subject to the rules and regulations enforced by the authorities of Xinjiang Uyghur Autonomous Region 94% of Shihezi residents are Han, and 1% is Uyghur. They are subject to the rules and regulations of the Xinjiang Production and Construction Corps In both areas, members of the Uyghur ethnic group enjoy the preferential policies they are entitled by law,[a] as the region enjoys a certain degree of formal autonomy
Economic situation	Both areas have Special Economic Zones 经济特区. Kashgar is a national-level ***teshu jingji kaifaqu*** 特殊经济开发区, "zone of special economic development", since 2010, while Shihezi is a 经济技术开发区 ***jingji jishu kaifaqu***, "a zone of economic and technologic development" at the national level since 1992	Shihezi is mainly an industrial city, while the Kashgar economy is essentially based on the tertiary and the agricultural sector

(continued)

Table 4.2 (continued)

	Commonalities	*Differences*
Central investments and development	When this research was conducted, from 2007 to 2012, Kashgar was in the Chinese government agenda as a target area of the developing scheme One Belt One Road, later called Belt and Road Initiative (BRI). At the time, Kashgar was considered one of the most important gateway to markets and natural resources—mainly natural gas and oil—of Central Asia. The potential of connectivity projects in Central Asian countries was well understood by Chinese leaders since the years 2000s, who had in mind a broader project reaching Europe, which was later officialized and became the BRI. Shihezi is a core area for the exploitation of natural resources in Northern Xinjiang, mainly oil and coal, but also for a number of other minerals. Due to their strategic positions, the two areas are receiving funding and taking advantage of several special investment projects conceived and implemented by the central and regional governments since at least 2008	Shihezi experienced a booming urban development, becoming the 2nd largest city in Xinjiang after the capital Urumqi already in the 1990s. Kashgar urban development has been much slower also because, after 1949, the prefecture came to include historical important cities like Yarkand and Yenghissar, major Central Asian oases before the '50s. Urbanities in Southern Xinjiang came to include a number of oasis towns. The efforts of the Chinese central government, in partnership with authorities at the regional and local level, are going in the direction of developing Kashgar as a touristic city, and also through development schemes, targeting architectural and cultural heritage such as the controversial Kashgar Dangerous House Reform Program (KDHRP), launched in 2009 and now still in progress, aimed at rebuilding the century-old walled heart of Kashgar according to earthquake-proof criteria. The citadel, located on a hill, was already under the control of a Beijing's touristic company, which turned it into a tourist site where a ticket is needed
History	Both Kashgar and Shihezi are important for their agricultural output, and are target areas, at the national level, for investments aimed at the construction of an agribusiness sector (developed at different levels in the two areas)	Kashgar has more than 3000 years of history, and it belongs to the historical, cultural and political realm of the Fergana Valley and Central Asia. Its history, since the seventeenth century, is strictly connected with the diffusion of Islam and Sufism in China. Kashgar developed as a major cultural and religious center both for the Uyghur Muslim ethnic minority in China and for part of the Central Asian populations, especially for Sufis. In Kashgar, there is a history of opposition and conflict with the imperial court first and the CCP later. Shihezi was established in the '50s as a garrison and bingtuan settlement, and only in 1974, it became a full-fledged city. It lies in the steppe area of Northern Xinjiang, in the Southern part of the Zungar Basin, where, in the eighteenth century, the Qing troops defeated the Zungar Empire armies. It developed as a major industrial and agricultural center in Xinjiang and China, and it has a history of acquiescence with the CCP

	Commonalities	*Differences*
Higher education and research	Both areas enjoy a strong demand for higher education and research activities/opportunities from potential students, researchers and academics, due to the scarce supply of higher education programs/opportunities and the limited chance, for professionals and academics in Xinjiang, of finding and employment in universities and research centers. In both Kashgar and Shihezi, there is the necessity to liaise with international higher education institutions, due to the high demand from the side of students, professionals and academics to conduct study/academic activities abroad and to the need of the two areas to become more international in terms of student, professional and academic population. Moreover, due to similar development goals, defined at the national level, both areas' demand for R&D institutions and investments in research is high	While the Kashgar area is traditionally connected with Islamic and Sufi education in Uyghur and Arabic performed both in madrasas and at familial educational venues (often inside homes) since centuries, Shihezi education history is linked to the CCP and therefore has more recent secular educational traditions Shihezi University, established in 1996, is one of the two largest universities in Xinjiang (together with Xinjiang University), with 41.832 students. With a broad range of international partnerships especially in the field of medicine and hard sciences, one-fourth of its students is from foreign countries, mainly from Africa, India, Pakistan and Bangladesh. The university can boast a large number of laboratories and research centers, which are competitive at the international level. There are also public and private research centers active in the city and independent from the university (i.e., affiliated to different kinds of private and public companies). Kashgar University was established in 2015, and it is modeled on all the other universities in China. Until then, a Kashgar Teachers' College (Kashi Shifan Xueyuan 喀什师范学院), established in 1962, modeled as well on the other Teachers' Colleges in Inner China, was the only comprehensive, at least in terms of vocational training, higher education institution present in the Kashgar area and in Southern Xinjiang in general. Kashgar University is now the only university in Southern Xinjiang, with approximately 12 thousand students Investments in education vary across the two areas, with Shihezi receiving significantly larger investments from Beijing, making the case for a situation of "selective development". Uyghurs, as all the other members of ethnic minorities, enjoy preferential policies in terms of education. For instance, they obtain 10 additional points at the *gaokao* and are therefore facilitated when entering the university.[b] Moreover, if they are outstanding students, they can apply to join special programs and attend the best high schools and universities in Inner China (e.g., the "Xinjiang ban" at the high school level)[c]

(continued)

Table 4.2 (continued)

	Commonalities	*Differences*
Relations with Beijing and with the Party-State	Both areas have close ties with Beijing since they are subjected to the same national policies and under the same autocratic political regime. At the political, fiscal, bureaucratic and administrative level, they depend on the Chinese central authorities	In terms of political, social and economic culture, Shihezi looks at and depends on Beijing, while Kashgar looks at the Fergana Valley in Central Asia, its *stans*, as well as in Turkey. There is thus a profound difference in the kind of authorities recognized in the two territories. This means that the work of local authorities in Kashgar consists in mediating between the CCP and the local population and in keeping a difficult balance between political reality and local perceptions and expectations. The role of Islam is central in this situation. This kind of work is not necessary in Shihezi, where authorities administer a population already compliant with the CCP rule While Shihezi is in good terms with the central government which strongly supports the development and growth of the city, Kashgar has always experienced a conflictual interaction with central authorities. This is due to historical, political and cultural reasons. Beijing sees Shihezi and the XJPCC as a bulwark of Han culture and values in a predominantly Muslim region. Moreover, due to historical and political reason, Beijing's agenda consists in pursuing a complete assimilation of the region within the Han system, and Shihezi acts as a tool in the central government's hands. Kashgar has been considered at the outskirts of modernity for centuries, a landlocked area reputed not worth of any kind of investment by Beijing. It attracted the attention of the central government only recently for its strategic location and for its natural resources (minerals, oil and natural gas) and as a territory worth to invest in for the sake of the resource-hungry Inner China and for improving the connectivity in Central Asia in the framework of the BRI. As a consequence, prices are rising and hundreds of thousand Han are moving to the city to invest in the real estate sector or to look for career opportunities, tightening, in an incremental but steady way, Kashgar's ties with Beijing

	Commonalities	*Differences*
Type of society	In Kashgar's society, there is a deeply rooted prejudice against Hans, whom are seen as invaders, occupiers and exploiters of local resources. In some cases, where very religious people are involved, they are seen as infidels. In Shihezi, Uyghurs are usually seen as lazy and backward, not good at work. The way of depicting each other in both areas is similar, biased by deep-rooted preconceptions and a superficial understanding of each other's cultures and values. In both cases, the narrative consists in the creation of an enemy, often for political reasons, an unknown entity, the Other, different and alien. In Shihezi University, there is a very limited number of Uyghur students while in Kashgar University there is a balanced percentage of Han and Uyghur students (this situation changed only recently, with a growing number of Han students enrolling at Kashgar University). Both Kashgar and Shihezi have a faith (meaning something superior to look at): Islam and the CCP ideology, respectively	Kashgar society is a traditional one, characterized by norms and values that ascribe a definite place to each individual within that society. Basically, there is a horizontal but not vertical mobility, no concept for changing these traditional structures since norms and values of this archaic society support the status quo Shihezi in sociological terms can be considered a modern society; its social relations are determined by interpersonal actions motivated by the desire to attain rational goals. In this kind of environment, status is not ascribed but rather is achieved through personal effort and skills. Norms and values tend to be oriented toward change, progress, innovation and maximum benefits at minimum costs While Shihezi is a migrant city (移民城市) because it accepts migrants but does not generate them, Kashgar is not, but is gradually becoming a migration context, as Uyghurs migrate to other cities in Xinjiang or Inner China, and Hans continue to flow in the city. This means that while Kashgar is increasingly becoming a Han Chinese city, Shihezi is preserving its main characteristic of being a predominantly Han city. Social conditions (hygiene, access to services, schooling, public transportation and so on) are in a much better shape in Shihezi than in Kashgar. Access to education as well as students' performance is lower in Kashgar and high in Shihezi, also due to the fact that Uyghurs do not speak Chinese as Hans do, since their mother tongue is Uyghur, but the official language in universities is Chinese. Only in some elementary and middle schools in the rural areas of the Kashgar Prefecture, a bilingual system is offered

[a]Preferential access to government positions in the autonomous region; higher marks at the *gaokao*; possibility to have more children; facilitated access to credit in some situations and so on

[b]The *gaokao* is the very competitive national exam that every Chinese student with a high school degree, willing to access the university, needs to pass

[c]At the time of the fieldwork, the Xinjiang Jiaoyu Nianjian 新疆教育年鉴 was still neibu, only "for internal circulation", probably because data about enrollment and education levels, back in 2012, were still considered sensitive. For the Xinjiang ban, see Leibold and Chen (2014, Chapter 9)

4.3 Historical Background

4.3.1 Kashgar

The earliest written reference about Kashgar appears in Persian documents referring to an alliance of Tushlan tribes, which established their capital in the oasis area. Always referring to the Persian epic, Kashgar—Shule in the Chinese sources—was the capital of a kingdom founded by a Tushlan (also Tulan) warrior, Afulabuseyav. There is no archeological evidence of this first settlement, since the ruins of the old walls surrounding the oasis date as early as the second century B.C. The name Kashgar might be connected with the Khasa population, Indo-Aryan peoples who were once dominant in the region.

The history of places which are quickly changing cannot be easily frozen into such a historical background. Walking on the streets of Kashgar or Urumqi today means getting the unusual feeling of stepping on layers of hidden and forgotten histories, and the main understanding a visitor gets is that what is seen on the surface seems to be a coarse replacement of what it had been there before.

Geographically, Kashgar lies on a plateau at 1300 meters on the sea level, between the Pamir mountains on the West and the Taklamakan Desert on the East, a favorable geographic location where it is possible to enjoy a dry and salubrious climate. The altitude makes the air in Kashgar rarefied and light, giving people the impression of living a particularly healthy environment. Today the largest oasis city in Chinese Central Asia, it has a remarkable importance for its strategic position, mainly for its facilitated access to the glacial passes of the Silk Road routes toward Central Asia, Pakistan, India and Iran. A major center of trade and politics, its history spans over 3000 years. Quite surprisingly, a comprehensive work on the history of Kashgar has not been written yet, even if the oasis played such an important role in history and has been mentioned since the first travelers and monks left from Europe and Africa and, across the Eurasian continent, eventually reached China.[1] The Greek geographer Ptolemy writes of "Kasia Chora" in its *Geography*, a place which some modern historians identify with current Kashgar. While the most detailed and in-depth work on the oasis has been written

[1]Some of them leaving written reports, such as Marco Polo's *Il Milione* and Ibn Battuta's *The Adventures of Ibn Battuta*.

by the Russian General Kuropatkin in 1882,[2] containing useful information on daily life, business activities and religion, comprehensive historical records and accounts are missing. The full history of the oasis has not been written yet since political and historical issues pose questions to this process of knowledge accumulation. The Chinese government would not consider acceptable a history of Kashgar where the historian does not accept the official line, by assuming that the whole of Xinjiang is under Han Chinese rule since the Han Dynasty in 221 B.C. At the same time, plenty of material written by local historians has been destroyed or secretly stored in private houses during the Cultural Revolution. Looking for and collecting the still available firsthand material is indeed possible, but arduous. Moreover, firsthand material written by local historians is normally written in Uyghur language in different alphabets (Latin, Farsi or Cyrillic, depending on the publication time[3]). Archive research is problematic because of the limitations in force, especially for foreign researchers, as well as because of the still unintelligible filing system and the need to be able to read the several ancient languages, now dead, of the region.[4] Travel accounts and reports by Russian and British diplomats of the eighteenth and nineteenth centuries mainly focus on the political situation and the Great Game historical plots.[5]

Archaeological remains, mainly preserved under the desert sands, speak of a territory inhabited by Indo-European and Mongolian peoples since at least 3000 B.C., who moved Westward under the pressure of Mongol and Turkic tribes escaping from local conflicts and in search of fertile territories. Kashgar was geographically, historically and culturally distant from the sphere of influence of the Chinese Empire, and more connected instead with the religious, political and social environment of the Fergana Valley, and the Sufi centers of Samarkand and Bukhara in today's Uzbekistan.

Indo-European and Altaic populations met with Tibetan and Chinese peoples in the area over the millennia: Languages and faiths such as Zoroastrianism, Animism, Manichaeism, Nestorian Christianity,

[2] Kuropatkin (2008).

[3] See Dwyer (2005).

[4] Among the others, Tocharian, Avestan, Khotanese Sogdian, Baktrian, Saka, Chagatai Uyghur and Pamiri languages.

[5] The works by Hopkirk present, through the stories of archaeologists and diplomats who were active in the region, the geopolitical aspects of such a key area of Central Asia.

Buddhism and Islam flourished in Kashgar and in the whole of Southern Xinjiang, generating a highly diverse and dynamic environment. Being the region located at the Eastern edge of Central Asia—identified in the historical sources as Turkistan[6]—a vast area inhabited by Turkish-speaking populations—in the Arabic and Persian medieval sources today's Xinjiang appears as Eastern Turkistan/*Sharqi Turkestan* (uig.), while its Southwestern section is usually referred to as "Kashgaria" or Altisheher.[7] Closed by the Pamir and Kunlun mountain ranges on the West and South, respectively, Kashgar North-Eastern frontier has always been open to the influx of nomadic populations from the Mongolian steppes, moving Southward and South-Westward in search of fertile lands and agricultural products. These populations of Mongolian origins started to push the Indo-European inhabitants of the area Westwards and mixed with them, giving birth to an extremely diverse demographic environment[8] in Kashgar, who have Mongolian, Indo-European (even Mediterranean), Persian and Indian characters (Fig. 4.1).

Kashgar is reported to be the first Buddhist kingdom in the Tarim Basin.[9] In the second century A.D., Buddhism started to be influential in the oasis, and remained dominant until the ninth and tenth centuries, when rulers and peoples started to convert to Islam in large numbers. During the Buddhist period, the Indian and Persian cultural influences were remarkable. The Chinese Buddhist monk Xuanzang noted that Kashgarians had green eyes and "for their writing they take their model from India…".[10]

During the first century A.D., the Chinese imperial court lost its power over the Tarim Basin. In order to regain control over the area, general Ban Chao was sent to fight local armies, which formed an alliance with the Xiongnu—a confederation of nomadic tribes representing

[6] As the area is referred to in Arabic sources of the medieval times.

[7] Kuropaktin (2008) and Dillon (2004).

[8] *AFP*, "Genetic Testing Reveals Awkward Truth About Xinjiang's Famous (Red-Headed) Mummies", 19 April 2005.

[9] Heirman and Bumbacher (2007, p. 97). The history of the diffusion of Buddhism in Central Asia can be read in Ch. 3 of the same work. One of the first archeological evidences showing the importance of Buddhism in the history of Kashgar is represented by the Mor Pagoda, on the South-Eastern edge of the Taklamakan Desert, close to the village of Bashkiram, once a rich trading hub and flourishing village near Kashgar.

[10] Michell (2008, p. 153).

Fig. 4.1 Kirghiz nomads on the Karakorum Highway (DSCN 1767. Picture taken by the author)

a source of constant concern for the court—against the imperial power. Ban Chao succeeded in conquering the kingdoms of Kashgar, Khotan and Kroran, by both force and strategy, gave support to pro-Chinese rulers and reopened the Southern Silk Road to trade. The general remained in Chinese Central Asia for 31 years, in charge of coping with and crushing rebellions, as well as of establishing diplomatic relations with states in the Western regions (xiyu 西域). Ban Chao and his armies reached Merv and established contacts with Parthia, Babylonia and Syria, and overall he managed to create a network of diplomatic friendships with approximately 50 kingdoms of Central Asia.

Up to the seventh century, when the Tang Dynasty re-garrisoned the city, the oasis experienced waves of raids and conquests led by both Western Turkish Khanates and the Tibetan Empire to its South. Following the opportunistic approach of "being ally with the strongest ones", in the early seventh century Kashgar accepted the rule of the Tang Dynasty court. With the temporary stability guaranteed and imposed by Emperor Taizong, traders and monks traveling on the Silk Roads started to settle in Kashgar, where each population lived in separate residential quarters. Between 670 and 694 A.D., the imperial armies were forced to withdraw under the pressure of the Tibetan Kingdom, which was expanding its territories throughout the Southern oases of the Tarim Basin. In 840 A.D., the oasis was occupied by Uyghurs, a nomadic population fleeing from the Orkhon Valley in today's Mongolia, where a war with the Kyrgyz tribes was underway. The incorporation of other Turkic tribes made Kashgar the capital of the Kharakhanid Uyghur Khanate. When Satuk Bughra Khan, the first of the Kharakhanid kings, converted to Islam in 934, the Kharakhanids became the first Islamic Dynasty in today's China territory. Between the tenth and the twelfth centuries, the Khanate controlled the whole area between Bokhara and Khotan. Satuk Bughra Khan and his successors engaged in wars against the Buddhist kingdoms of Yarkand and Khotan. The political instability which followed, together with the struggles internal to the Kharakhanid kinship, badly impacted the East–West caravan trade, with sea routes increasingly regaining importance.[11]

In 1219, Kashgar and the surrounding territories fell under the rule of Genghis Khan, who promoted the so-called Pax Mongolica and made the Silk Road trade re-flourish. In the thirteenth century, Marco Polo wrote that Kashgarians "have very fine orchards and vineyards, and flourishing estates…(but) are very close-fisted and live very poorly…There are some Nestorian Christians in this country, having their own churches and observing their own religion".

After the death of Chagatai, who inherited the control of the region from his father Genghis Khan, numerous succession wars followed. By the time that the Muslim Turkish warrior Tamerlane conquered the city in the fourteenth century, almost the whole of the population in Kashgar and in the greater Eastern Turkistan Region had already adhered to Islam. In the sixteenth century, the oasis became the main residence of the influential yet divided Khoja clans, the religious leaders whose counterparts were powerful political rulers in Bukhara and Samarkand. A theological split saw the formation of two opposite sects, the Black and the White Hats, which started a bloody seesaw in power struggles between Kashgar and Khotan, which ended only with the Qing conquest two

[11] Kauz (2010).

centuries later. The Khojas attempted to return to power in Kashgar no fewer than six times, frequently backed by the Kokand Khanate and aided by Kirghiz nomadic horsemen, performing fearful reprisals on local peoples. An unfortunate observer of the Khoja's last attempt in 1857 was a German, Adolphus Schlagintweit, whose throat was cut because of his arrogant comment that the three-month siege to conquer Kashgar would have been reduced to a mere three days if his countrymen were in charge. This family of religious leaders from Bukhara built Id Gah mosque in the center of Kashgar and erected the Afaq Khoja Mausoleum, an important pilgrimage site at the outskirts of the city. Id Gah Mosque and its surrounding Koranic schools (*madrasas*) turned the city into a regional center for religious education.

Since resistance to the Qing Dynasty occupation of the city in 1755 was organized in Kashgar, the city started to be viewed as a center of Islamic rebellion. The brief reign of the Kokand ruler Yaqub Beg, who led the revolts against the Qing imperial armies from 1866 to 1877, brought considerable development in the city. In 1869, a visiting Englishman, Robert Shaw, described Yaqub Beg's strongly controlled city as follows: "Entering the gateway, we passed through several large quadrangles whose sides were lined with rank of brilliantly attired guards, all sitting in solemn silence so that they seemed to form part of the architecture of the building… Entire rows of these men (were) clad in silken robes and many seemed to be of high rank judging from the richness of their equipment".[12] Yaqub Beg fortified the city walls and built an additional Great Mosque at the Afaq Khoja Mausoleum. By the end of the Qing Dynasty, in 1911, the city had a mosque in each street, 126 in total, as well as seventeen *madrasas.* After a three-year advance toward the Chinese Turkestan, the 60.000-strong Chinese army of Zuo Zongtang suppressed the Muslim rebellions in Gansu and then moved South-Westwards to the oasis towns, eventually ending Yaqub Beg rule in 1877. The Uzbek ruler died in Kashgar, rumored to have either had a stroke or poisoned himself.

In 1877, the Chinese imperial court ultimately annexed the area called Eastern Turkestan, renaming it "Xinjiang", "New Frontier Territory", and provoking rebellions among the majority of Uygur, Kazak and Kyrgyz Turkic populations. The distinct ethnic and cultural identity of the people in Xinjiang continued to be a factor of tension between local

[12] Shaw (1871, p. 260).

leaders and the Chinese government. The annexation meant not only the definitive expansion of imperial China into the Northwestern territories, and its first step toward Central Asian resources, but also the emergence of a distinct region, which, within the political borders of China, continued to retain its local political and sociocultural characteristics. Until the 1990s, Xinjiang was considered by the Chinese as a faraway periphery. Implicitly and explicitly, the area has been considered by many scholars and experts as a cultural backwater of the great Central Asian centers of Islamic civilization and perhaps, by extension, of the Islamic world.

Gunnar Jarring, a Swedish diplomat and scholar who spent some months in the oasis in 1929, wrote: "The city of Kashgar was surrounded by a massive wall about ten meters high and built of sun-dried brick with mud filling in the spaces between. On top it was wide enough for a two-wheeled cart. Communication with the outside world was through four great gates which were closed at dusk and reopened at sunrise. Inside the walls were bazaars, large mosques, and dwellings for both rich and poor. The Chinese authorities were outside the walls, as were the British and Russian consulates, and the Swedish mission with its hospital and other welfare establishments. Outside there was green nature, sunshine and light; inside it was always half dark".[13] A major rebellion led by Ma Zhongying from 1928 to 1937 established an Independent Muslim Republic of Eastern Turkestan in the Kashgar region, supported by a pan Turkish Islamic movement which had as its symbol a flag emblazoned with a crescent moon and a star. In 1933, the flag was weaving over the walled city for two months. Chinese troops from Urumqi, supported by the Soviets, moved South to reach Ma Zhongying and his army. It was the provincial warlord Sheng Shicai that in 1943, in coalition with the USSR, made Ma flee to the Yenghisheher fortress for 6 months, before mysteriously disappearing across the Soviet border in a truck he requisitioned from the Swedish explorer, Sven Hedin. In 1955, the province was renamed Xinjiang Uygur Autonomous Region. As an effect of the rapid demographic changes, Uyghurs are no longer the majority outside of the southern Tarim area, while Kashgar and Khotan remain the settlements with the highest concentration of Uyghur population. Currently, Xinjiang local population is predominantly Muslim, officially Sunni of the Hanafi school, but de facto strongly influenced by Sufi and Shia streams.

[13] Jarring (1986).

4.3.2 *Shihezi*

The history of Shihezi shall be understood in the context of the military past of Xinjiang and of China as a whole, in particular of the events preceding and following the Communist takeover in the Northern part of the region. Before the 1950s, the place where the city lies today was an alluvial plain with a human presence concentrated in military and agricultural settlements. These consolidated only when the Communist brigades reached the area after the power shift occurred in Beijing in October 1949. These settlements, in the 1950s, under the auspice of the new Communist leadership, became the Xinjiang Production and Construction Corps (XJPCC). Shihezi is the main city built by the XJPCC, born out of the so-called *bingtuan*, the old settlements believed to be the development of Han Dynasty's *tuntian*. It was during the rule of emperors Qianlong and Jiaqing (1735–1820) of the Qing Dynasty (1644–1911) that Northern Xinjiang experienced the greatest expansion of the *tuntian* settlements. This expansionist strategy continued during Emperor Qianlong, his reign being characterized by a special attention to Western territories. According to the official discourse, the *tuntian* system in the region not only satisfied the needs of the stationed garrisons and promoted local economy, but also gave an important contribution to the consolidation of the border defense system and to the stabilization of the local socio-political environment. What we can reasonably say is that the military-agricultural settlements called *tuntian* gave an important contribution to the imperial court for the establishment of a long-term control over the Northwestern frontier regions. The Qing court, with the strategy of "developing the North and ignoring the South"[14]—originated by the difficulty of managing Southern Xinjiang where local religious leaders were extremely influential and by the presence of oases populated mainly by Uyghurs—actively promoted the stationing of troops in the Northern belt of the Tian Shan with the aim of opening up wasteland. This favorable context has been the perfect background to make the economy of the area North of the Tian Shan mountain range, with Shihezi at its center, develop quickly. The Qing Dynasty strategies and policies in fact represent the origin of the current achievements of the economy in the Tian Shan Northern belt, including the areas of Urumqi and Ili, and already prepared the ground for

[14] Zhang and Cappelletti (2012).

subsequent patterns of economic development for the whole region. In this case, past policies and their genealogies can help identifying contemporary achievements and political determinants.

Following this logic, we can reasonably argue that the beginning of the success of today's XJPCC can be traced back to the support and investments provided by the imperial authority back in the eighteenth and nineteenth centuries. Migrants from Inner China, and, to a much lesser extent, Southern Xinjiang, started to move to the area of the Northern Tian Shan belt, attracted by new opportunities generated by the rapid development of the industrial and agricultural sectors. The Northern Tian Shan belt became in this way the economic center of the whole region, leaving Southern Xinjiang behind. The implementation of reclamation measures and establishment of different forms of settlements during the Qing Dynasty made a broad range of people, including militaries, prisoners, exiled, poor families, temporary personnel and peddles, all reach the same goal of improving their life standards. They moved to Xinjiang together with their families, settled there and gradually built villages and small towns. For instance, Ili was originally a "spacious place, where not even city walls could be found".[15] Migrants from different parts of China contributed to shaping Shihezi's multicultural society, with Hans being the dominant group.[16] This social texture made of a variety of languages, customs and habits, cultures and faiths,[17] helped Shihezi's society to develop and reach the standards which we can see today, after the unification of small and big settlements and the creation of Shihezi as a city.

Since 1949, the new Communist leadership has been paying a particular attention to Shihezi, by encouraging and supporting its growth as well as the overall development of the Xinjiang Production and Construction Corps as an organization. Amy Kardos Pozza, in her PhD work published in 2009 by UMI, collected the oral histories of former "pioneers", who moved to the Northwestern frontier, reclaimed the land and built the city, undergoing enormous difficulties and hardships.

[15] *Records from the Travels to the Western Territories* (西域闻见录 *Xiyu wenjian lu*), 1777, Ch. 1.

[16] The fact that the majority of the population in Shihezi is Han does not mean that the society is not multicultural, since the Han ethnic group is a construction and a mixture of different identities and ethnicities.

[17] See Kardos (2009).

The author argues that the first phases of Shihezi development did not respect the original CCP plan of creating a New China in Xinjiang, and they had little to do with the grand ideological directives of Moscow or Beijing either. The originality and autonomy of Shihezi as a multicultural settlement on China's Western frontier is a unique finding in Kardos' work.

The following inflow of capital and the stream of migrants contributed to the fast development of Shihezi, resulting in the original steppe environment transformed via large-scale projects of land reclamation, infrastructural plans and massive real estate schemes. Today, Shihezi looks like a flourishing, fertile and well-irrigated territory, also thanks to advanced technology and the cooperation with Israeli and Australian companies famous for the production of irrigation equipment specifically designed for arid and desert territories. Shihezi is now the core economic center of the whole of Xinjiang, with industrial groups renown at the national level establishing their headquarters or either branches there, and a growing influx of foreign capitals. As a strategic settlement, it became the second largest city in the region after the capital city Urumqi, hosting national-level research centers and educational institutions, as well as advanced healthcare premises. Quasi-military farms surrounding the city fueled its development. In 1974, Shihezi became a sub-prefectural-level municipality, while during the 1980s and 1990s different areas under its administration have been granted fiscal and economic incentives similar to those guaranteed to the Special Economic Zones (SEZs), with the aim of attracting investments from other parts of China and abroad.

4.4 Endowments and Administrative Framework

4.4.1 Kashgar

The Kashgar Prefecture is located on the Northwestern border of China, approximately 4.400 kilometers far from Beijing. Called "little Kabul", the oasis was a key halt on one of the main thoroughfare along the Silk Roads, over six months of journey were necessary to reach it by camel from today's Beijing. Osh and Bishkek (in Kyrgyzstan), Almaty and Astana (in Kazakhstan) and Kabul (Afghanistan) are all closer. Trade relations with Central Asian kingdoms and khanates have always been a favorite option for Uyghur merchants and traders in the oasis, and, also today, Uyghur businessmen are active in these countries and beyond. The prefecture has international frontiers with Tajikistan, Afghanistan (Wakhan Corridor) and Pakistan on its West, while domestically it borders with Kizilsu Kyrgyz Autonomous Prefecture (North), Aksu Prefecture (East) and Khotan Prefecture (South-East) in XUAR. Situated on the Westernmost edge of the Tarim Basin and the Taklamakan Desert, the prefecture is surrounded by mountains on three sides: The Southern ridge of the Tian Shan range lies on its North, the Pamir mountains on the West the Kunlun mountains on its South and on the East, only the vast shifting sand dunes of the Taklamakan Desert. Due to its strategic position on the main thoroughfares of ancient Silk Roads, to its favorable climate and to the three main rivers originating from the surrounding mountain ranges—Kashgar River, Yarkand River and Tizinapu River—and flowing across its territory, Kashgar has always been an important oasis settlement. Flowing downward from mountain springs, these rivers' waters are fed by plenty of smaller streams. Besides some well-irrigated lands, the rest of the soil is hit by chronic water scarcity which depends on the desert environment. The increasing number of water-consuming industrial activities in the area, together with the fast increase of the population, makes water scarcity a major concern for farmers and public officials in today's Kashgar. In some rural villages, farmers need to excavate wells as deep as 160 meters in order to reach groundwater.[18] The prefecture lies on a plateau with an average altitude of 1300 meters above the sea level; thus, the climate can be defined as continental, with hot dry summers and cold dry winters, with a broad night-day and summer-winter temperature leap. Kashgar is one of the driest cities on the planet, averaging only 64 mm. of precipitation per year.[19] The city wettest month, July, only sees an average of 9,1 mm. of rain. Because of the extremely arid climate, snowfall is rare, despite the cold winters. Records have been as low as minus 24.4 °C in January and up to 40.1 °C in July. The frost-free period averages 215 days a year. The population in Kashgar city is for the 85% Uyghur, with a 10% Han and the rest from other minorities. In the whole prefecture, Uyghurs represent more than 90% of the population.

[18] Assessment by a Uyghur professor coming from a village close to Kashgar, during an interview with the author at Xinjiang University, Urumqi 1 April 2011.

[19] These and the following data are taken from the XJSY 2010–2017.

Today, rail, road and air connections are available to and from Kashgar. A rail link built in 1999 covers the 1.600 kilometers distance from Kashgar to Urumqi, the capital of Xinjiang. In December 2010, the freight train activity on a new extension of this line, which connects the oasis city to the rest of Southern Xinjiang up to Khotan, started to be operational. Since June 2011, the passenger connection is also available. A project which in 2011 was still under evaluation implied a further extension of this line up to the Pakistani port of Gwadar.[20] In November 2009, China and Pakistan agreed to set up a joint venture in order to carry on a feasibility study on the proposed rail link, which was supposed to cross the Khunjerab Pass at an altitude of 4,700 meters. A rail connection to the city of Osh in Kyrgyzstan[21] is under discussion at various levels since 1996. Investments in transnational rail networks and infrastructures are promoted and sponsored by the Chinese government, which appears to be a major investor in finalized, as well as under discussion, bilateral agreements.[22]

The city is located on the China National Highway G314 (Urumqi—Khunjerab Pass—1,948 kilometers) and on the G315 (Xining, Qinghai—Kashgar—3,048 kilometers). A major transnational link is the Karakorum Highway, which connects Kashgar with Islamabad through the Khunjerab Pass, with bus routes for passengers traveling South into Pakistan. Kashgar is also connected with Kyrgyzstan via the Torugart and Irkeshtam passes, while since the summer of 2007 a daily bus service is available between Kashgar and Bishkek, the capital of Kyrgyzstan. Due to frequent bad weather conditions and to high maintenance costs, it often happens that rail and road connections are damaged, and even closed, in certain periods of the year.

Kashgar has an airport with routine flights to Urumqi and other cities in the region, while a direct flight to and from Beijing started to be operated by Air China in 2010. Up to now, no international flights are

[20] Syed Fazl-e-Haider (2009).

[21] The project is illustrated in the Web site of the Intergovernmental Commission TRACECA (http://www.traceca-org.org/en/home/, http://www.traceca-org.org/en/technical-assistance/pre-feasibility-study-of-a-new-rail-link-between-the-ferghana-valley-bishkek-and-kashgar-china/documents/), funded by the European Commission.

[22] *China Daily*, 2 September 2011.

available; therefore, going abroad means essentially to make a stopover in Beijing or in some cases in Urumqi.[23]

On an administrative level, Kashgar is one of the prefectures in Xinjiang Uyghur Autonomous Region, while Shihezi is under the administration of the XJPCC. The prefecture includes eleven counties with over three million people in total:

- Shufu County (Uy. Konasheher Nahisiyi);
- Shule County (Yengisheher Nahisiyi);
- Yingjisha County (Yengisar Nahiyisi);
- Zepu County (Poskam Nahiyisi);
- Shache County (Yarkand Nahiyisi);
- Yecheng County (Kharghalik);
- Maigaiti County (Mekit Nahiyisi);
- Yuepuhu County (Yopurgha Nahiyisi);
- Jiashi County (Peyzawat Nahiyisi);
- Bachu County (Maralbeshi Nahiyisi); and
- Taxkorgan Tajik Autonomous County (Tashqurqan Tajik Aptonom Nahiyisi).

The Trans-Karakoram Tract, stretching across 5,800 square kilometers approximately over both sides of the Shaksgam River, today part of Yecheng County and Tashikuergan Taxkorgan Tajik Autonomous County, is still claimed by India as part of the state of Jammu and Kashmir.

Because of its location at the Eastern edge of Central Eurasia and its strategic borders, the Kashgar Prefecture is a natural political and economic hub, a gateway to resources and markets of Central Asia. The proximity of Afghanistan and Pakistan to the Kashgar Prefecture is a source of constant concern for the Chinese government, which understands the political and religious conflicts in the two countries as potential destabilizing factors for both China's national and transnational order, basically because of the potential contacts between Islamic militants and Uyghurs in China and abroad.[24] A strategic partnership aimed at tackling with transnational terrorism is the Shanghai Cooperation

[23]At the moment, flights to Almaty, Teheran and Istanbul are available from Urumqi.

[24]Uyghurs are linked with Islamic transnational networks following both a political and religious rationale.

Organization[25] (SCO), established on 15 June 2001 with the following political agenda: settlement of border issues, control of drug trafficking and smuggling, signing of mutual agreements about energy resources exploitation and other related factors of interest in the area, control of the territory and cooperation on counter-terrorism activities. The member states are eight: India, Kazakhstan, China, Kyrgyzstan, Pakistan, Russia, Tajikistan and Uzbekistan. Afghanistan, Belarus, Iran and Mongolia have the status of observer states, while Azerbaijan, Armenia, Cambodia, Nepal, Turkey and Sri Lanka are "dialogue partners". Back in 2011, the member states were China, Russia, Uzbekistan, Kazakhstan, Kyrgyzstan and Tajikistan; India, Iran, Mongolia, Pakistan and Afghanistan were observers, while Belarus and Sri Lanka "dialogue partners". We can reasonably argue that changes occurred during those eight years reflect the shifting power dynamics between members and other countries in other positions, as well as modifications in the international position and standing of countries involved in the SCO. China and Russia are leading the organization; their political and strategic decisions exert a particularly significant influence on the other SCO members. There are also scholars who argue that SCO's hidden goal is to control and limit US interests in Central Asia, to the extent of interpreting SCO as a strategic enemy of NATO. On the other side, the US government has often the perception of being left behind in this geopolitical and geostrategic setting.

The main interests behind the strategies of these world powers in Central Asia consist in gaining a more significant role in an increasingly important resource-rich area, a pivotal region in terms of natural resources and new markets. It is within this framework that we should understand the economic and development programs that the Chinese central government launched and is in the process of finalizing in Xinjiang. For instance, the establishment of a Special Economic Zone in the Kashgar Prefecture in 2010; the "Nineteen provinces and cities support Xinjiang" plan (*shijiu sheng shi yuanzhu Xinjiang* 十九省市援助新疆)[26]; the Grand Development Scheme for the Western Territories (*xibu da kaifa* 西部大开发); and the Project for the Adjustment and Extension of Kashgar Airport to be turned into Kashgar International Airport

[25] *Shanghai hezuo zuzhi* 上海合作组织: http://www.sectsco.org/EN/.

[26] See Chapter 3.

(*Xinjiang Kashi shi Guoji jichang gaikuojian xiangmu* 新疆喀什市国际机场改扩建项目). The goal of the Chinese government is to prepare the ground for the accumulation of capitals in the whole area, a process which should lead to the transformation of the prefecture into a developed and advanced area able to match—in terms of both infrastructures and human capital—the needs generated by future potential volumes of businesses arising from possibly increasing economic interactions with neighboring countries.

The prefecture boasts a flourishing agriculture—the output consists mainly in cotton, rice, wheat, corn, beans and fruit—and important quarries of building materials, while a newborn industrial area is in the process of being extended and funded by the central as well as by the regional government. Uranium ore deposits started to be discovered in the Kashgar and Khotan areas in the '50s.[27] On the other hand, a serious, endemic problem in the Kashgar Prefecture is water scarcity. Nevertheless, it is not rare to read in local media that deposits of drinkable water are discovered, as the *People's Daily* reported on 20 September 2011 in a news announcing that, according to the Xinjiang Bureau of Geology and Mineral Exploration, a deposit of drinkable water 1300 square kilometers. large had been found and that investments in new advanced technological water-saving equipment were supposedly going to alleviate the water supply problem.[28] A number of poverty alleviation projects aimed at coping with water scarcity have been funded at a national level, while the international presence in these humanitarian projects is still scarce mainly because the whole area is politically off-limits for international actors.[29] The problem is worsening, and the

[27] Shichor in Starr 2004. The reason why a number of rural villages in the Kashgar and Khotan areas is closed to Chinese non-residents and foreigners is allegedly the presence of uranium ore deposits. Interview with a student at the Minzu University of China's campus, April 2011.

[28] *People's Daily Online*, 20 September 2011.

[29] This notwithstanding, a Sino-German project aimed at raising the life standards of farmers by installing water-saving equipment in the poorest rural villages of the Kashgar Prefecture was implemented from 2004 to 2014. The project was launched and carried on by a consortium of development agencies from the German side and by the Kashgar and Urumqi Water Bureau Administrations from the Chinese side. The financing agencies were the Chinese Ministry of Finance and the German bank KFW. I was member of the Land Allocation Monitoring Mission led by Professor Abduresit Jelil Qarluq, at the time my PhD supervisor, as consultant for land allocation affairs.

increasing demographic unbalances are considered as one of the most important causes of this deprivation.[30]

In May 2010, the Chinese central government designated Kashgar "Special Economic Zone", the first nomination in more than 15 years. Special Economic Zones (SEZs) are normally selected areas which, as such, enjoy policies related to trade and investments which are more liberal than those in place in the rest of the country. SEZs can be designated at the national, regional/provincial and local level according to a variety of factors. The model is Shenzhen, China's most famous SEZ, which has proved to be an enormous success. Not all cities have responded or have been able to respond equally to the challenges of the reform era, including the creation of SEZs. Shanghai and Guangzhou, each in its own and different way, have responded extremely positively, but size, location and political connections—that may not be universally available—are obvious factors of advantage for the success of those two cities.

Kashgar as a SEZ can be considered a challenge: Whereas Shenzhen gained great advantages from its proximity to Hong Kong and access to the sea, the oasis city is landlocked and separated from the prosperous Eastern provinces by the vast deserts and steppes. Another challenge is the potential conflict arising from swift social changes: With the designation of Kashgar as a SEZ, investments and businesses from Eastern China inevitably pose a threat to the preservation of the local language and culture of the Uyghur majority. In a broader perspective and according to the official narrative, the government aims at bringing the oasis city back to the once prominent position it had as a strategic trading location between Eastern China and Central Asia, supporting Chinese companies in entering markets and catching business opportunities in Central Asian countries.

4.4.2 Shihezi

Shihezi is a sub-prefectural-level city 136 kilometers. North of the regional capital Urumqi. With a total area of 460 square kilometers, the municipality borders with Changji Hui Autonomous Prefecture on the East, West and North. On the South, a chain of mountain ranges

[30] Unofficial reports mentioned an inflow of approximately three million Han people from Inner China to different areas of Xinjiang only in 2012.

separates it from the Taklamakan Desert. The proximity of the desert and the distance from the sea makes Shihezi climate continental, with extremely dry hot summers and cold winters. Located in the fertile territory of North-Eastern Xinjiang, Shihezi has the Tian Shan mountain range on its South, the green Zungar Basin on its Western and Northern sides and the Guerbantonggute Desert on its Eastern side. Water reserves in the city are replenished by rivers coming down from the Tian Shan range and by the waters of the Manas River on the Eastern side of Shihezi. While water scarcity is still an issue in the city, nevertheless the soil, both in and around Shihezi, is well irrigated, mainly thanks to the collaboration of local companies with Israeli and Australian ones in the field of irrigation of arid regions. Advanced technologies and irrigation equipment, specific for soils in arid areas, are on exhibition at the Bingtuan Museum, Beisan Road No. 59, in Shihezi.

A daily bus service across the Lianhuo Expressway (stretching from Lianyungang in Jiangsu Province to Khorgas in Northern Xinjiang, at the border with Kazakhstan) connects, in two hours and a half, Shihezi with Urumqi. The National Highway 312, from Shanghai to Yining (4967 kilometers), passes through the municipality. The regional road S204 connects Shihezi with Northern Xinjiang, with a final stop at the Corps' farm No. 150. The Northern Xinjiang Railway (Urumqi-Alashankou), connected to the Lanzhou-Xinjiang Railway on the East and the Turkestan-Siberia Railway on the West, has a stop in Shihezi, as well as the Second Urumqi-Jinghe Railway. The construction works for a new passenger and freight airport—the Shihezi Huayuan Airport—started in 2012 and were completed in 2015. They implied the rebuilding and relocation of the old military airport 15 kilometers. Southwest of the city center. Close to the regional capital Urumqi, Shihezi is an important industrial center, with a flourishing agricultural sector, an immigrant city with a total population of 640.000, 98% Hans and the remaining 2% Uyghurs, Huis and other ethnic groups. This is due to the history of the Municipality, to its environment as well as to the policies implemented at the national and local level.

The Shihezi Economic and Technological Development Zone (ETDZ), the core area of the Northern Foothills Economic Belt of the Tian Shan Mountains, as well as the center of the consumption market in Northern Xinjiang, has been established in 1992 by the regional government. In the year 2000, in consideration of the economic achievements obtained so far, the State Council promoted it to a State-level

Economic and Technological Development Zone. In 1996, a Hi-Tech Industrial Park was established in the ETDZ, while in 2006 the Scientific Committee of the Autonomous Region created the Northern Shihezi Industrial Park. With an area of 31,2 square kilometers, its construction, management and development have been entrusted to the Xinjiang bingtuan's Administrative Committee of the Shihezi Development Unit of the 8th Division.[31] "Green", "ecology", "environmental protection", "people-oriented", together with the concept of a "green ecological industrial park", are the leitmotiv of the Shihezi ETDZ's branding strategy, which hosts four main industries: textile, food processing, chemical engineering and agricultural equipment, while other supporting industries are developing, such as energy-saving equipment, new type construction materials, mechanical and electrical factories, packaging, pharmaceutical companies and a growing third sector. According to the central government strategic plans, Shihezi, as the most prominent Xinjiang SEZ, is deemed to rapidly become the Westernmost state-level development zone on the Euro-Asia Continental Bridge,[32] and the Shihezi ETDZ to be integrated into the regional industrialization processing base, as an export-oriented and export processing zone (EPZ) focusing on countries along the Euro-Asia Continental Bridge.

Shihezi is a sub-prefectural municipality under the administration of the XJPCC, including county-level cities as Kuitun, Aral, Wujiaqu, Tumushuke and Beitun. On the administrative, political and economic level, it acts as a core area of the Corps and has the functions of a capital city. The actual status of the XJPCC is nevertheless still not clear. Once under the administration of the XUAR, in the 1990s they have been upgraded to a provincial-level organization under the direct control of the State Council. While in the 1980s they were considered as a tool for the stabilization and consolidation of the state power in a socio-political environment which was not yet integrated into the Han core, with the structural reforms of the 1990s, the State Council deliberated to turn them into an "autonomous planning unit" (*jihua danlie* 计划单列), entitled to launch its own five-year plan, independently from that of the XUAR. With their own courts, health and educational systems, and autonomous administrative setting, the Corps resemble a "state within

[31] Goodman (2004, p. 54). Information about the Shihezi SEZ can be found in http://cnbusinessnews.com/investment-environment-of-shihezi-etdz/.

[32] Yeung and Sheng (2004, pp. 202–204).

the state",[33] raising doubts and criticism among Western scholars about the legal framework and related justification.[34] It is not possible to read, in the Chinese Constitution or other fundamental laws, any political and administrative item which could in any way justify the existence of the organization as such within the Chinese territory. An explanation to this could be that the Corps belong to that sort of off-limits entities pertaining to the "national security apparatus", which are regulated by undisclosed norms. With 86% of their residents being of Han ethnicity, and the 6% Uyghurs, the size of the territory occupied by the XJPCC is contested: While Becquelin (2000) writes that 40% of the regional territory is occupied by the XJPCC, according to the author calculations, made on the basis of the XJSY and to data provided by Chinese authors,[35] a more realistic figure would be a little more than 5%. While their economic and political power in Xinjiang is outstanding, the real extent and strength of the organization remain to be assessed, and it could be object of future enquiry.

4.5 Cultural Background

4.5.1 Kashgar

Kashgar is an oasis settlement, an important religious and trading center along one of the segments of the ancient Silk Roads. Rich of archeological remains testifying a variety of cultural influences, in the ancient times Kashgar used to be a reference oasis town for the whole of Central Asia, mainly due to the presence of some of the most important Muslim mosques and Sufi shrines. Called "little Kabul" for the similarity with the architecture of the Afghan capital, 90% of its population is Uyghur, and the oasis is considered an important cultural and religious center for all Uyghurs, both in China and in the world.

As already mentioned, Kashgar has a history stretching back for more than 2000 years. The "weight of history" is visible for anyone strolling around the narrow lanes of the ancient walled citadel, it shapes and frames the identity of the oasis architecture as well as of its dwellers, whose habits, features and customs come out as the result of centuries

[33] Shichor (2006).

[34] Mainly Becquelin.

[35] Bao (2010).

of interaction and exchange among cultures. The first cultural influence that archeology passed down to us is that of Kashgar's Indo-European heritage. The first oasis dwellers were Indo-Europeans, presumably Tocharians, speaking Indo-Iranian languages. Shamanism, Zoroastrism, Christianity and Manichaeism were coexisting and common in the oasis before the spread of Buddhism from India and Tibet. The facial characteristics of Kashgarians reflect a deep diversity of cultural influences: The mixture of Indo-European, Caucasian and Mongoloid features is evident in faces' shapes and colors. The tests allowed by the Chinese government in 2006, on the up to 3000-year-old mummies buried in the Taklamakan Desert and discovered by Chinese and Western archaeologists, show that European and Mediterranean elements are present in the DNA of the Uyghurs. These evidences are considered by part of the scholarly community as a sign that the origins of Indo-Europeans are in Chinese Central Asia.[36]

Buddhism spread in Kashgar from Afghanistan in the second century and third century A.D.: Remains of old Buddhist settlements and temples are barely visible today; nevertheless, 50 kilometers North-East of today's Kashgar, close to the village of Bashkiram, it is possible to see the Mor pagoda, the main archaeological remain of Buddhist Kashgar, and believed to be the first Buddhist temple in China. Buddhist Kashgar is described by the monk Xuanzang in the seventh century A.D. as being a highly devoted oasis with giant Buddha statues. Islam spread in the region during the Kharakanid Dynasty in the eighth century, and from Kashgar, it moved to the Yarkand and Khotan kingdoms. Evidences of the turbulent period when Islamic and Buddhist armies were fighting for supremacy, and fierce struggles between the Islamic Kashgar and the Buddhist Khotan and Yarkand destabilized the area, can be found in *mazar*, tombs of saints, scattered in the desert on the South-East of the oasis. The most important one is called Ordam Mazar, and it lies close to the village of Sahan and hosts the body of Ali Arslan Khan (his head is buried in another *mazar* in the city). The *mazar* complex, consisting in a mosque, the lodge of the sheik, ritual buildings, some tombs and houses for pilgrims, lies where the Islamic warrior is believed to have been beheaded by the Khotanese Buddhist armies while preying Allah. Other evidences of those initial implacable struggles between Islamic and Buddhist armies are the statues and frescoes of Buddha without

[36] See Mair and Mallory (2000).

heads. While Muslims believe that human figures cannot be represented and beheaded the Buddha's representations, according to local superstitions human eyes in paintings and on stone or wood bring bad luck,[37] for this reason local villagers used to erase the eyes in statues and frescoes. Buddha representations without heads are thus either clear remains of Islamic iconoclasm or of popular beliefs. After centuries of religious conflicts for power, Islam replaced Buddhism as the dominant faith in the Kashgar area and spread across the oases in the Altisheher region in the form of Central Asian Sufism from the Fergana Valley, mainly influenced by the Naqshbandi[38] and Hanafi schools. Islam is a fundamental characteristic of Uyghur society and permeates it at both the social level and the political level. It is mainly a syncretic form of Islam: From Shamanism/Animism to Manicheism, from Zoroastrianism to Buddhism, faiths are visible in the different layers of pieces of art and religious representations, as well as in the diversity of practices and customs claimed to be Islamic by locals, but in reality being heterodox and syncretic, referring to a variety of rituals and beliefs, if we compare them with Sunni Islam. According to sources, the old town area of Kashgar is home to the world's largest earthen architectural complex. After a major "restoration" plan started in 2010 and in the process of being finalized, people in Kashgar old city still live in one-story houses made of mud and brick. The number of Kashgarians living in these traditional dwellings is decreasing and will be limited, since these are gradually being replaced by "modern" newly built, allegedly earthquake resistant constructions, multi-story apartments realized with funding provided through development projects and invested from different sources, mainly from the central and regional government. Ancient craftsmanship like carpet and silk production, together with iron and wood workmanship, is still practiced and developed across generations, as well as traditional music and dance (*muqam*), mainly performed during festivities and ceremonies. The *madrasas* are the Koranic schools which were very popular before the Communist takeover, and a reformed Islam, inspired by Jadidism in Turkey and Central Asia, influenced the teaching in local *madrasas*, until it had been opposed by the warlord Yang Zengxin at the beginning of the twentieth century.[39]

[37] Belief explained during the interviews in the Kashgar rural areas by local farmers.

[38] Dillon (2004, pp. 11–17).

[39] See Clark (2011).

4.5.2 *Shihezi*

Shihezi is a city with approximately seventy years of history. The events which led to its creation, expansion and consequent development are linked with the emergence of Communist China and the new policies on frontier regions. While there are many continuities between the Qing Dynasty and Republican China, the Communist takeover represented the turn of the screw, since the project of integrating XUAR into the Han Chinese national identity raised to the first positions in the agenda of the Chinese leaderships, and policies envisioned to reach this aim became more sophisticated. Shihezi as such has been one of the main instruments of this assimilationist and acculturation drive.

The hundreds of thousand immigrants sent by the CCP as "pioneers" who went to the city in the 1950s, and those who voluntarily moved there as economic migrants looking for job opportunities and a better life from the 1980s onward, are the backbone of Shihezi's society. The population has a deep connection with the ideology and politics of the new Communist China, and periodical political campaigns on the history and meaning of their city and of the Corps take place there. Residents perceive the urban environment they live in as something they themselves built up, something special, an asset and a leverage in front of Beijing, which considers the stability of the region as a priority. The old generations of Shihezi's residents are all Party members, and, as part of former agricultural-military settlements, still retain some practices such as participating in regular military and political training. Their hybrid status of "civilians with weapons" makes them self-confident and responsible for being "defenders of the motherland", as well as for being first class Chinese and citizens in an underdeveloped land with backward peoples. This is how they are taught to think, and this awareness permeates all their attitudes, perspectives and actions. This is particularly evident when they deal with Chinese people belonging to other ethnic groups: Shihezi residents know and show that power is on their side. This feeling is backed by a number of benefits which they enjoy just as Shihezi's residents. For instance, the welfare system for those who are Corps' members is particularly advantageous and includes financial incentives to buy houses and invest in Corps-owned companies. Moreover, salaries in Shihezi are higher than in the rest of Xinjiang, and social services like health, education and public transportations boast international standards. This range of advantages makes Shihezi residents particularly aware of their importance vis-à-vis Beijing.

92% of Han ethnicity, the population of Shihezi has origins mainly in the provinces of Gansu, Sichuan, Shanghai and Henan. The proportion of Han peoples is the same as the national level one, making Shihezi an ideal microcosm for understanding China's major ethnic group and composition. These immigrants retain a number of characteristics which belong to their culture of origin, from cuisine to beliefs, from dialects to facial features, replacing and adjusting their identities in the distant XJPCC city. These local "centripetal identities" are gradually disappearing, with the XJPCC and the national government plan the city as a canonized Han political and cultural system. The national and local governments have been implementing actual measures to carry on this operation of leveling identities, something which can be reasonably defined as a clear project of social engineering. To fulfill this goal, actual measures have been implemented, ranging from the planting of trees common in Inner China to building compounds and parks according to the architectural style and canons of Chinese architecture and landscape design. At the same time, it will take some time to make the broad variety of Sichuan and Gansu local cuisine which can be found in the streets of the city, as well as the local accents from all over China, fade into oblivion.

4.6 Higher Education

4.6.1 Kashgar Teachers' College (喀什师范学院 Kashi Shifan Xueyuan) and Kashgar University (喀什大学 Kashi Daxue)

With a population of over 350.000, and almost four million residents at the prefectural level, the only institute of higher education available for the whole of the Kashgar Prefecture until 2015 was the Kashgar Teachers' College, established in 1962 and located in the central part of the city. In China, Teachers' Colleges have been created in peripheral (in a geographical—at both the national level and the local level—and metaphorical sense) and not strategic areas, offering programs aimed at obtaining the qualification to teach at elementary and middle schools. Teachers' Colleges are non-university-level higher education institutions, they are considered as institutes for vocational training, and the teaching quality is not comparable to a university-level education. For this reason, students who enroll at Teachers' Colleges are usually those who have difficulties in passing the national examination for university admission called *gaokao*. The study curriculum is more limited than the one usually offered by universities, and the main job position a College graduate can apply for is teacher at elementary and middle schools. In 2012, Kashgar Teachers' College counted around 12.000 students, the majority of whom Uyghurs who followed modules in the official teaching language for higher education at the national level, Mandarin. Up to 2009, foreign students were admitted at the College to study Uyghur language and culture, with Xinjiang University and Xinjiang Normal University in Urumqi being the more common destinations. From 2009, only students and staff with an ID could enter the campus, and while foreign students were still officially admitted to enroll, de facto they were not welcome anymore. Moreover, from 2009 to 2015, the Web site of the College could not be opened anymore. Kashgar residents used to complain about the scarce educational offer in the city, allegedly not matching the needs of the people in the prefecture, on both a quantitative level and a qualitative level. In order to cope with these issues, as well as to match the needs of Kashgar as a new SEZ and an international city deemed to be revived in its role as major commercial and logistic hub between China and Central Asia, the central government planned to make investments for the development of the College, in order to establish a "Kashgar University" by 2020.

This original plan was considered of a particular strategic value by Chinese authorities at the national and local level, and this official attention led to an acceleration of the project implementation. Kashgar Teachers' College was thus turned into Kashgar University in 2015. The university homepage can be opened from China both with and without a commercial VPN. It is entirely in Chinese and shows a number of Xi Jinping's quotes and pictures, as well as photos and slogans about the unity of nationalities and national education under the New Era. Almost 15.000 students are enrolled in BA, MA and PhD programs, both in the traditional programs related to education and in a number of other different fields: mathematical sciences, engineering, literature, arts, law, economics and management. Of the 1098 members of staff, 660 have a teaching role. With two campuses, the university has both a physical library (1.315.500 volumes) and a digital library (600.000 volumes and documents). Overall, Kashgar University has the characteristics of a small standard Chinese university based in Inner China. The degree of control is probably much higher due to the socio-political problems which interest the area. Two research centers, one for the development of education in Xinjiang and one on socio-economic development in Southern Xinjiang, have been created and are meant to support the territory in facing opportunities and challenges brought about by the New Era. In the presentation of the university, the role of Kashgar as an important hub for connecting China and Central Asia is highlighted. The information available on the university Web site is scarce, since some sections cannot be accessed, including those on enrollment, research centers and activities. Information, data and figures about students, including their place of origin and ethnicity, are not provided.

4.6.2 *Shihezi University (石河子大学 Shihezi Daxue)*

As the second biggest institute of higher education in the region after Xinjiang University in Urumqi, by both importance and numbers, Shihezi University was founded in April 1996 as a Teachers' College (a fusion of the Shihezi Agricultural School established by the Ministry of Agriculture, Shihezi Medical College, the Bingtuan Normal Polytechnic and the Shihezi Economic Polytechnic) and turned into a national-level university in 2006. Its student population of almost 50 thousand can enjoy a large and modern campus which boasts advanced research facilities and hi-tech laboratories, a rich library, a large gymnasium, a multi-functional stadium, and modern and functional teaching buildings. It is a well-funded university not only for being at the heart of the bingtuan system and considered a highly strategic institute at both the national level and the regional level, but mainly for having been selected as part of national programs aimed at increasing the quality and international standing of Chinese universities such as Project 211[40]; the Double First Class University Plan[41]; the State Program for building one high-level

[40] Project 211 is a project of National Key Universities and colleges initiated in 1995 by the Ministry of Education of the People's Republic of China, with the intent of raising the research standards of high-level universities and cultivating strategies for socio-economic development.

[41] The *Double First Class University Plan* or *Double Top University Plan* (双一流, *shuāngyīliú*) is a Chinese government plan conceived in 2015 to comprehensively develop a group of élite Chinese universities and individual university departments into world class universities and disciplines by the end of 2050.

university in each of the provinces in the Mid-Western Regions[42]; Program 973[43]; and Program 863.[44] Besides the campus, the university has offices and laboratories scattered all over the city and boasts 11 faculties (economics, law, education, literature, history, sciences, engineering, agriculture, medicine, management and arts), 92 bachelors, 42 masters, 16 PhDs and four post-doctoral degrees. The most important research institutes are active in the fields of medicine and chemistry. Students are mainly of Han ethnicity, while a small population of foreign students is represented by Russians, Kazakhstanis, Pakistanis, Kyrgyzstanis and South Koreans, whom enroll in full university programs or either join exchange agreements. When I conducted interviews at Shihezi University in the summer of 2011, she was prevented from speaking with students and researchers from ethnic minorities. When asked about the reasons for this limitation, which could have impacted the research outcomes, my contacts within the university argued that, due to their small numbers, ethnic minority students were not representative of Shihezi educational environment. I insisted by arguing that, according to the research design, it was important to collect the broadest sample of respondents possible, regardless of their importance and relative "weight" within a certain social group, but it was still forbidden to get in touch with minority students.

In less than a decade, Shihezi University became the second largest university in the whole of Xinjiang after Xinjiang University in the capital city Urumqi and, thanks to its broad network of international

[42] Both Xinjiang University, located in the capital city Urumqi, and Shihezi University are included in this program, and this is indeed telling in consideration of the fact that this scheme is designed to appoint one university per province (e.g., Qinghai University in Qinghai, Ningxia University in Ningxia and Yunnan University in Yunnan). As in many other cases, for example, in Statistical Yearbooks and in other province-wise rankings, the XJPCC are treated as an independent province, and, as some scholars argue, a "state within the state".

[43] Program 973 (973计划 *jihua*), also known as National Basic Research Program, is a research program initiated by the People's Republic of China to achieve technology and strategic edge in various scientific fields and especially the development of the rare earth minerals industry.

[44] Program 863 (863计划) or State High-Tech Development Plan (国家高技术研究发展计划 *guojia gaojishu yanjiu fazhan jihua*) is a national scheme funded and administered by the Chinese government, intended to stimulate the development of advanced technologies in a wide range of fields for the purpose of rendering China independent of financial obligations for purchasing foreign technologies.

partnerships and exchange schemes, is quickly becoming one of the best universities at a national level as well as raising in the rankings. Shihezi University receives major investments and is part of generous funding schemes provided by the Chinese Ministry of Education and the Corps' administration. This is mainly due to its strategically important status as an institution aimed at training the future political and economic establishment of the powerful Corps, as well as the regional government and Party, both of them developing at a fast pace and experiencing an increasing demand for professionals and "talents". Because its graduates gain the much needed scientific and technical curricula, Shihezi University quickly became the major recruitment basin for enterprises and state bureaus, for those leading companies and institutions which are enjoying the fiscal advantages and the new dynamic business environment in the region. This rapid rise did not occur by mere chance: A political choice has been made by the Chinese leadership to provide a strong support to higher education in Shihezi, regardless of the ethnic composition of its students and staff (90% Han). While being not easily accessible—for a different range of reasons, including quota of minority students imposed on the university—by Uyghurs and other minority students, large groups of Uyghur teachers from all over the region are still recruited for intensive advanced courses of Chinese language, for improving their teaching, in their home towns and villages, is conducted in good Mandarin.

4.7 Water Resources

Water scarcity is a major problem in the whole of Xinjiang. Authorities in Beijing are willing to solve, or at least alleviate the problem, and large investments are envisioned to build large-scale dams on the rivers flowing from the mountain ranges surrounding Kashgar. Feasibility studies on a number of projects are currently being conducted by the Kashgar Water Resource Bureau. The fast development which is dramatically transforming the city is visible in the large construction sites and development areas dotting the city skyline, generating a high level of water consumption which exceeds by far the capacity of the current water infrastructures. While endemic water scarcity is a major issue in Kashgar, in some areas of the prefecture underground waters can still be used thanks to technologically advanced irrigation and water-saving systems, provided by projects funded by both foreign and Chinese investments in the framework of either development or poverty alleviation programs. One of the objectives of these international projects consists in raising awareness among farmers and water users in general about the need to rationalize water consumption and in more general terms save water, in terms of both agricultural irrigation and personal use. Water is such a key resource in the area that the WRB has a very high status as an institution. The Han farmers I interviewed mainly cultivate plots under the administration of the XJPCC (those in charge of the main farming businesses in the region) and argued that Uyghur farmers were used to cultivate the best irrigated land, while they argue that the Corps needed to invest huge capitals back in the 1950s and 1960s in order to reclaim desert arid lands.

On the other hand, even if also Shihezi lies in an area with relatively scarce water resources, financial abundance allowed the municipality to employ Israeli and Australian irrigation technologies: Shihezi intensive agriculture is mainly characterized by greenhouses, and the whole city is covered by colorful well-irrigated flowerbeds. While the huge amount of water resources necessary to support the rapid development of the region is a source of concern for scholars and environmentalists in China, the political establishment seems not to share the same concern, and this optimism probably derives from the significant amount of capitals and technology employed for the solution of these problems. Xinjiang desert and steppes are thus being irrigated by Israelis and Australians technology, and it would be interesting to see whether the urban and rural development, which was planned to be reached, in its full potential, by 2020, is at all sustainable and whether a resources consumption scheme is envisaged and implemented.

4.8 Xinjiang Production and Construction Corps (XJPCC): "State Within the State" and "Region Within the Region"

The Xinjiang Production and Construction Corps, *Xinjiang Shengchan Jianshe Bingtuan* 新疆生产建设兵团 (commonly known as *bingtuan* 兵团), are a paramilitary organization established in the 1950s in China's border regions to protect the frontiers, coherently with the historical tradition of the *tuntian* 屯田, and dismantled at the end of the 1970s. At the beginning of the 1980s, these agricultural-military settlements have been reestablished and revitalized only in Xinjiang, while in other border regions like Heilongjiang and Yunnan they disappeared for good or either turned into economic entities and companies. Established in the 1950s following the orders of General Wang Zhen[45] and the directions of President Mao Zedong,[46] the Corps represented, and still represent today, the development of an historical strategy devised and implemented by the central authorities toward the Northwestern frontier, up to the point that all Chinese authors, as well as some foreign scholars, draw a direct line between the Han Dynasty *tuntian* 屯田, the agricultural-military colonies, and nowadays bingtuan.[47] Anyway, as Peter Perdue points out: "In its relations with the Western Regions, or modern Xinjiang, in particular, [China's imperial past] carries on in modern guise some of the policies of the Qing Dynasty, but never exactly repeats them"[48] (Fig. 4.2).

A number of Chinese authors and scholars have dealt with the topic of the bingtuan by writing on a broad range of aspects: Bao (2010) can be considered the most complete and up-to-date scholarly work on today's *bingtuan*, providing interesting points of view from outside the Corps. Li, Fang (1997) is one of the most extensive works which adopt a historical perspective, exploring the development of the organization from its establishment in the '50s up to now. Zhang (2010) looks at the pre-"liberation" *tuntian*, providing archeological and documentary evidences on the *bingtuan* precursors, as well as an accurate analysis of the managing and reclamation system in the Western regions, from the Han Dynasty to the so-called liberation. The Han migration to Xinjiang, a phenomenon which is strictly linked to the Corps, is analyzed through archive material and interviews in the essay by Yao Yong (1999, 2011), as well as in White (1979). The debate about urbanization and the related "civil-military integration" processes in the *bingtuan* is taken into account by Zhang Fengyan and Gao Gangcang (2007), who provide a rich analysis and sharp insider's perspective.[49] For a broader idea on the current

[45] Wan and Wang (2008).

[46] Wang and Wang (1998).

[47] Becquelin (2000, 2004), Borei (1992), Cliff (2009), Millward (2007, 2009), and Seymour (1998, Unpublished).

[48] Perdue (2002, p. 81), quoted in Becquelin (2004)

[49] They are both professors at Shihezi University.

Fig. 4.2 XJPCC pioneers with Wang Zhen in the 1950s (Picture taken by the author in the Bingtuan Museum in Shihezi)

debate on the topic, Li and Liu (2009) has an extensive bibliography (Fig. 4.3).

The current debates about the status, criticalities and uncertainties related to the organization take place and are mainly collected in scholarly works published in a range of periodicals, including those listed here below:

兵团教育学院学报 ***Bingtuan Jiaoyu Xueyuan Xuebao***
"Periodicals of the Education Institute of the XJPCC"
兵团职工大学学报 ***Bingtuan Zhigong Daxue Xuebao***
"Periodical of the Education Institute for the bingtuan staff members"
兵团建设部 ***Bingtuan Jianshe bu***
"Bingtuan construction"
兵团党校学报 ***Bingtuan Dangxiao Xuebao***
"Periodical of the Bingtuan Party School"

Fig. 4.3 XJPCC pioneers in Shihezi in the 1950s (Picture taken by the author in the Bingtuan Museum in Shihezi)

石河子大学学报 *Shihezi Daxue Xuebao*
"Shihezi University periodical"
新疆农垦经济 *Xinjiang Nongken Jingji*
"Xinjiang State Farm Economy"
新疆财经学院学报 *Xinjiang Caijing Xueyuan Xuebao*
"Periodical of the Xinjiang Finance and Economics Institute"
新疆石油教育学院学报 *Xinjiang Shiyou Jiaoyu Xueyuan Xuebao*
"Periodical of the Xinjiang Oil Studies Institute"
新疆社会科学院学报 *Xinjiang Shehui Kexueyuan Xuebao*
"Periodical of the Xinjiang Academy of Social Sciences"
中国农业经济 *Zhongguo Nongye Jingji*
"Agricultural economy in China"
中国农垦经济 *Zhongguo Nongken Jingji*
"Reclamation economy in China"

According to the majority of Chinese authors, the Corps had been, and still are today, fundamental actors for the stability and development of the XUAR, its economy, political environment and society. During the years 2000s, there have been intense debates on how to reform the *bingtuan* system, mainly focused on how to make its economy more profitable and the integration into the local environment more effective. These debates are still ongoing, and the reforms are in progress. A number of scholars involved in the debate[50] underline the necessity to provide more investments and financial support from the center, in order to strengthen the power of the organization, while others[51] claim that changes are needed in the political and economic realms, reforms which should eventually channel the *bingtuan* economic might into the process of transformation of the organization into an active and prominent economic actor of the Chinese socialist market economy at a national and international level. There are authors[52] whom express doubts and concerns on the legal framework that allows the *bingtuan* to exist as such, since they argue that the organization is not contemplated by any existing legal and constitutional framework, but justified only through special and ad hoc regulations. The response to these concerns by government officials[53] and other authors[54] tends to highlight the special nature of the organization, which has a peculiar history and a unique status in the XUAR and in the whole of China.

Western authors who conducted research on the *bingtuan* mainly adopted a historical perspective: Donald McMillen focused on the Maoist times and on the issues and factions of the Cultural Revolution, while Millward (1998, 2007) and Dillon (2004) dealt with more recent historical events.

Shichor (2006), and Seymour and Anderson (1998), focuses on the structure and on the military and security aspects of the Corps, while Wiemer (2004) and Becquelin (2000) analyze the economic situation in Xinjiang and the Corps' contribution. The socio-political aspects of the bingtuan presence in the region, especially as a main destination for Han migrants, have been analyzed in Kardos (2008) and Li (1989).

[50] Reported in Bao (2010).

[51] Mainly young scholars of Shihezi University, whose papers can be found in 石河子大学学报 "Shihezi University periodical".

[52] Wang (2009); Ilham Tohti, lecture at Minzu University, 3 December 2010.

[53] Fan (2007).

[54] Such as Zhang, Gao, and Shi (2007). For a more specific approach linking the terrorist threat and the bingtuan, see Millward (2004).

Western authors pay a special attention to the political and social role of the *bingtuan* in the area, assuming that the organization is actually serving the purposes of Beijing, namely the necessity to control and exploit the XUAR. As the military and economic functions of the organization are assessed as marginal (Shichor, Wiemer), the emphasis is put on the political and social impact that the Corps are exercising on the territory and the local population (Bequelin, Cliff, Dillon) and on the fundamental contribute to creating a sinicised, corrupted and discriminatory environment in Xinjiang.[55] As policies considered to be the main responsible of this situation, worth mentioning are the migration of Han peoples, the nature of the *bingtuan* (built and organized by the Han for the Han) and the exploitation of water, fertile fields and the local economic potential by the Corps' residents and companies (mainly works by Millward, Shichor and Seymour).

The first *bingtuan* were garrisons in distant frontier regions, and in Xinjiang, they were established mainly by infantrymen, soldiers and officials who took part in the, according to the narrative, occupation, liberation, invasion or conquest of the region by the CCP, as well as by former Guomindang personnel who surrendered to the People's Liberation Army (PLA) and joined it over different stages of the civil war. A lot of changes occurred from the 1950s to nowadays: First of all, the Corps were established in different border regions in China. Seymour (unpublished) assumes they existed in twelve regions, while He and Shi (1994) write about fourteen regions. At the end of the 1970s, they were all dismantled or converted to other activities, and in 1982, Deng Xiaoping decided to reestablish them, but only in Xinjiang Uyghur Autonomous Region.[56] This decision, which turned out to be a watershed in the history of the region, can be traced back to a number of political and economic evaluations, and it is still object of debate among Chinese historians and scholars.[57] From the 1980s, the *bingtuan* experienced a

[55] HRIC Report (2007) and Kjell (2006). On language policies, see Dwyer (2005).

[56] For an extensive and detailed history of the Corps, see the works by Donald H. McMillen, Wang (2009), as well as the official papers published by the Committee for the compilation of historical works of Xinjiang and China.

[57] Some recent contributions on the topic are Chen (2007), He (2005), and Yue (2007).

deep and extensive process of reform which completely transformed and represented a challenge for the very nature as well as image of the organization. Characterized by a planned economic system and a military structure, with residents who are farmers enjoying the "iron rice bowl" (*tiefan wan* 铁饭碗), trained to become soldiers when necessary, the reforms of the 1990s aimed at opening the *bingtuan* economy to the broader national and international context. The Maoist welfare system, with its social benefits, was discussed and revised in the direction of a more flexible and market-oriented system.[58] These reforms were unpopular and bingtuan residents and workers opposed them.[59] An agreement between the central government and the bingtuan authorities has been reached, and today the area administered by the bingtuan covers 74.600 square kilometers[60] (5% of the regional area, only partly habitable, twice Taiwan) with 2.573.077 residents, 1.900 state enterprises with independent accountancy (commerce, industry and transportations), 13 companies listed on the stock exchange, 11 key agricultural companies at the national level, 50 at the bingtuan level, a press company, radio and tv channels, two universities and several higher education institutes and research departments.[61] These are only a few official figures showing the transformation of the organization from an archipelago of military-agricultural settlements to a contemporary, fully developed, economic power. More substantial and manifest evidences make the case and help us understanding the importance of state support and political choices at the highest level of the decision-making spectrum.

In terms of governance and administration, until the 1990s the Corps have been under the responsibility of both the central and XUAR governments, and afterward promoted to the status of a full-fledged province, under the direct control of the State Council, and listed as such among the beneficiaries of the investments envisaged by the Great Development Plan of the Western Regions of 2001.[62]

[58] Bao (2010).

[59] Mozur (2007) and Sommerville (2005).

[60] There are different data on this figure: Becquelin (2000) argues that the bingtuan cover 45% of the whole area of Xinjiang, but this figure needs to be confirmed.

[61] Bao (2010), 新疆生产建设兵团统计年鉴 (2009); Guo and Liu (2001).

[62] In the plan, the Corps were listed as special organization together with the provinces of Xinjiang, Tibet, Gansu, Qinghai and so on. See Cliff (2009) and Goodman (2004).

4.9 Conclusions

While Shihezi can be considered a stable and continuously developing socio-political context, Kashgar continues to generate security concerns among Han elites and Party officials.[63] The perception of insecurity and risk is deep among them, as well as among the Han general public, and this situation is continuously impacting the business environment, as well as the overall stability, in the Kashgar Prefecture.

On 30 and 31 August 2011, Kashgar has been hit by two deadly "terrorist"[64] attacks, which were covered by international media and mainly reported through statements issued by the central government. These facts have therefore been interpreted according to the official line.[65]

According to media reports and witnesses' accounts,[66] the first raid was carried on by a small truck which run at a very high speed. The vehicle run into a pedestrian area in the commercial district of the Han area of Kashgar, in the city center. Targets of the assault were Han Chinese residents and shop owners located in and around the area. After having run over a few pedestrians, the attackers (apparently two) got down from the truck and stubbed several people with a knife. The raid left fifteen people dead, attackers included, the latter being shot down by the security forces.

The following day, a Uyghur restaurant owned and run by a Han Chinese resident was attacked with grenades and knives. Twenty people died, attackers included.

In both cases, the ethnicity of the victims of the raid remained unspecified (considering the area where the facts occurred, they were probably mainly Han Chinese), while the attackers were said to be all Uyghurs. Soon after the attack, vindication documents were published on different Web sites: One was posted on a Web site run by the so-called Turkestan Islamic Party (TIP) and another one on a Web site run by a Kurdish Party (Fig. 4.4).

[63] For understanding the security concerns and related government measures in Kashgar, see Steenberg and Rippa (2019).

[64] On the concept of "terrorist" attack in the Xinjiang context, see Millward (2004).

[65] From 31 August on, the news was reported by international media such as the New York Times and the Financial Times. For an overview of the attacks in Xinjiang in the last 20 years, see Steenberg and Rippa (2019) and Millward (2009).

[66] I met witnesses in Kashgar between 10 and 15 September 2011.

Fig. 4.4 Uyghurs selling jade stones to Han buyers near Khotan (DSCN 7758. Picture: Michelangelo Cocco)

According to sources, twelve people were involved in the organization of the two raids: Between 18 and 25 years old, the young boys were from the countryside of the Kashgar Prefecture, in particular, from Kargalik, Yarkand and Peizawat counties. Two of them had been still wanted for years, with their pictures distributed to all taxi drivers of the area, with the promise of a 100.000 RMB for those who would be able to provide information about them. Since they have not been caught, the two boys are reputed to be missing or even dead. By 28 September 2012, four people had been condemned to the death penalty for being involved in the organization of the attacks.

Just eleven days before these events, 500 kilometers. away from Kashgar in the Khotan Prefecture, where at the time the population was 98% Uyghur, fifteen Uyghurs had been shot by police forces. Accounts differ on the basis of the source: World Uyghur Congress representatives issued pro-Uyghur statements, declaring that security forces opened fire on a pacific demonstration in front of a government building, while Chinese media reports depict aggressive attackers with knives gathering in front of a local shopping mall.

This kind of events cannot be considered accidents, since, up to 2014, they were very frequent, especially after the 5 July events in Urumqi, mentioned by some scholars and journalists as a "small Tiananmen". According to Kashgar and Urumqi residents, riots and fatal events were, until 2014 when drastic security measures were implemented, much more frequent than what media report.

A new phenomenon was that of fights among gangs in the streets of Kashgar during the night time. From internal sources, they are Han and Uyghur gangs fighting against each other. In 2011 and 2012, the streets of Kashgar and the whole prefecture were constantly patrolled by several police and army forces, equipped to cope with riots and terror attacks (mainly SWAT special forces). Checkpoints with militaries and sand-made barriers were arranged in key places inside and outside the city. Uyghurs were subjected to regular checks, while whole counties, like Jiashi/Peizawat and Akto (where in 1990 a violent riot occurred in Baren), were closed to Chinese non-residents and foreigners.

Foreigners staying in the city were checked by regular as well as secret police upon their arrival, except for those traveling with touristic agencies and a clear announced itinerary. Authorities were trying to prevent that Uyghurs could find a way to communicate with foreigners.

As a general consideration, we can say that the attacks were generated by the desperate conditions of the local people and did not imply any political strategy. Hans, considered as unfamiliar occupiers with whom it is impossible to communicate, are not welcome by Kashgar's Uyghurs. On one side, there is a huge population looking for a better life and job opportunities in a distant and foreign land (the plan of the government at the time was to bring 3 more million Han to Xinjiang in the year 2012), supported by a powerful government making all the necessary arrangements in order to make their lives comfortable (from a better environment to convenient housing and social services), and on the other a poor population mainly living in the countryside (85%), witnessing a radical transformation of its environment, living standards and culture (conditions questioned and reframed by the way of life and culture of alien newcomers) neatly created two worlds, with one encroaching upon the other. In this context, we can say that the whole geography and culture of the area are undergoing a process of deep political, social and economic transformation, mainly through a top-down process. New actors are emerging and power is being redistributed, while this is not the case for Shihezi, which, as already mentioned, is stable and continuously growing. Needless to say, the social development in the Uyghur world is heavily impacted by these security concerns and measures which represent limitations to their free movement and expression.

Bibliography

Bao, Yajun (2010), *Research on the Structure of the Xinjiang Production and Construction Corps*, Central Translation Press, Beijing.

包雅钧, 新疆生产建设兵团体制研究, 中央编译出版社, 北京, 2010.

Becquelin, Nicholas (2000), "Xinjiang in the Nineties", in *The China Journal*, No. 44 (July), pp. 65–90.

Becquelin, Nicholas (2004), "Staged Development in Xinjiang", in *The China Quarterly*, No. 178 (June), pp. 358–378.

Beller-Hann, lldikò (2007), *Community Matters in Xinjiang 1880–1949—Towards a Historical Anthropology of the Uyghurs*, Brill, Leiden.

Borei, Dorothy V. (1992), "Beyond the Great Wall: Agricultural Development in Northern Xinjiang, 1760–1820," in Jane Kate Leonard and John R. Watt (eds.), *To Achieve Security and Wealth: The Qing Imperial State and the Economy 1644–1911*, Ithaca, New York.

Chen, Ping (2007), "Brief Analysis of the Causes Which Brought to the Repeal of the Xinjiang Production and Construction Corps", in *Local histories of Xinjiang*, No. 3.

陈平, 新疆生产建设兵团被撤销的原因及教训浅析, 新疆地方志, 2007, 3.

Clark, William (2011), "Ibrahim's story", in Asian Ethnicity, Vol. 12, No. 2, pp. 203–219.

Cliff, Thomas (2009), "Neo-Oasis: The Xinjiang Bingtuan in the Twenty-First Century", in *Asian Studies Review*, Vol. 33, pp. 83–106.

Dillon, Michael (2004), *Xinjiang—China's Muslim Far Northwest*, RoutledgeCurzon.

Dwyer, Arienne (2005), "The Xinjiang Conflict: Uyghur Identity, Language Policy, and Political Discourse (Policy Studies)", East-West Center Washington.

Fan Genyao, Wu Lei, Jiang Li (2007), "Empirical Study on the Industrial Structure and the Economic Development of the Bingtuan", *Periodical of Shihezi University—Philosophy and Social Sciences Series*, 1/2007.

樊根耀, 吴磊, 蒋莉, 新疆兵团产业结构与经济增长实证分析, 石河子大学学报(哲学社会科学版), 2007年01期.

Fisher, F. James (1978), *Himalayan Anthropology: The Indo-Tibetan Interface*, Mouton.

Goodman, David (2004), *China's Campaign to "Open Up the West": National, Provincial, and Local Perspectives*, Cambridge University Press.

Guo, Liu (2001), "Assessment on Ecological Environmental Quality of the Tarim River: Important Ecological Function Zones", in *Arid Environmental Monitoring*, 2012–01.

Haider, Ziad (2005), "Sino-Pakistan Relations and Xinjiang's Uighurs: Politics, Trade and Islam along the Karakoram Highway", in *Asian Survey*, Vol. 45, No. 4, pp. 522–545.

He Lan, Shi Weiming (1994), *Mo Nan Qing: Portrait of the Production and Construction Corps. in Mongolia*, Law Press.

何岚, 史卫民, 漠南情: 内蒙古生产建设兵团写真, 法律出版社, 北京 1994.

He, Libo (2005), "The Production and Construction Corps. in the High Spheres of History", in *Readings on the History of the Chinese CCP*, (10).

何立波, 历史风云中的新疆生产建设兵团, 党史博览, 2005 (10).

Heirman, Bumbacher (eds.) (2007), *The Spread of Buddhism*, Brill.

Hopkirk, Peter (2011), *Foreign Devils on the Silk Road*, University of Massachusetts.

Hopkirk, Peter (1992), *The Great Game: The Struggle for Empire in Central Asia*, Kodansha International.

HRIC Report (2007), "China: Minority Exclusion, Marginalization and Rising Tensions", Minority Rights Group International (2007).

Jarring, Gunnar (1986), *Return to Kashgar: Central Asian Memoirs in the Present*, Duke University Press.

Kardos, Amy Pozza (2008), Transformation in China's Northwest Borderland: The Making of an "Immigrant City", 1949–1958, Supervisor: Prof. Sherman Cochran, PhD Dissertation Discussed at Cornell University, UMI.

Kardos, Amy Pozza (2009), "Transformation in China's Northwest Borderland: The Making of an "Immigrant City", 1949–1958", Supervisor: Prof. Sherman Cochran, Dissertation Discussed at Cornell University, UMI.

Kauz, Ralph (2010), *Aspects of the Maritime Silk Road: From the Persian Gulf to the East China Sea*, Otto Harrassowitz Verlag.

Kjell, Sigurd Roisli (2006), "Development or Marginalisation? Xinjiang Bingtuan and State-Run Development in China's Wild West", in *Internasjonal Politikk*, Vol. 64, No. 4, p. 509.

Kuropatkin, N. Alexei (2008), *Kashgaria, [Eastern or Chinese Turkistan]: Historical and Geographical Sketch of the Country, Its Military Strength, Industries and Trade*, Read Books.

Leibold James, Chen Yangbin (2014), *Minority Education in China: Balancing Unity and Diversity in an Era of Critical Pluralism*, Hong Kong University Press.

Li Fusheng, Fang Yingkai (1997), *A History of the Xinjiang Production and Construction Corps. Reclaiming Land and Protecting the Borders*, Xinjiang Technology Press.

李福生, 方英凯: 《新疆兵团屯垦戍边史》, 新疆科技卫生出版社 1997 年版.

Li Meirong, Liu Wenjing (2009), "Research Report on the Development of the Urbanization in Xinjiang", in *Ethnic Economy*, 3.2009.

Li, Rose Maria (1989), "Migration to China's Northern Frontier, 1953–82", in *Population and Development Review*, Vol. 15, No. 3, pp. 503–538.

李美荣, 刘文静, 新疆城镇化发展研究综述, 民族经济, 2009 第 3 期.

Mair Victor, Mallory J. P. (2000), *The Tarim Mummies: Ancient China and the Mystery of the Earliest People from the West*, Thames and Hudson.

Michell, G., et al. (2008), *Kashgar: Oasis City on China's Old Silk Road*, Frances Lincoln.

Millward, James (1998), *Beyond the Pass: Economy, Ethnicity and Empire in Qing Xinjiang, 1759–1864*, Stanford University Press.

Millward, James (2004), Violent Separatism in Xinjiang: A Critical Assessment, in "Policy Studies", No. 6, East-West Center, Washington, DC.

Millward, James (2009), "Does the 2009 Urumchi Violence Mark a Turning Point?", in *Central Asian Survey*, Vol. 28, No. 4, pp. 347–360.

Millward, James (2007), *Eurasian Crossroads: A History of Xinjiang*, Columbia University Press.

Mozur, Paul (2007), "Retaining the Loyalty of Xinjiang's Hans", *Far Eastern Economic Review*, pp. 27–30.

Perdue, P. (2002), "Bringing Xinjiang into the Fold: The Ming-Qing Era", in Francois Godement, *China and its Western Frontier*, Ifri.

Puri, Baij Nath (1987), *Buddhism in Central Asia*, Motilal Banarsidass Publications.

Records from the Travels to the Western Territories (西域闻见录 *Xiyu wenjian lu*), 1777.

Seymour, James, "Making China's Northwest Safe for the Han: The Role of the Production and Construction Corps" (to be published).

Seymour James, Anderson Michael R. (1998), *New Ghosts, Old Ghosts: Prisons and Labor Reform Camps in China*, Routledge.

Shaw, Robert (1871), *Visits to High Tartary, Yarkand and Kashgar (Formerly Chinese Tartary) and Return Journey Over the Karakorum Pass*, Murray.

Shichor, Yitzhak (2006), "Company Province, Civil-Military Relations in Xinjiang", in Nan Li (ed.), *Chinese Civil-Military Relations: The Transformation of the People's Liberation Army*, Routledge, pp. 135–150.

Sommerville, Quentin (2005, November 29), "China's Grip on Xinjiang Muslims", BBC Online.

Steenberg Rune, Rippa Alessandro (2019), "Development for All? State Schemes, Security, and Marginalization in Kashgar, Xinjiang", in *Critical Asian Studies*, Vol. 51.

Syed Fazl-e-Haider (2009), "Gwadar: An Emerging Centre of the New Great Game", ISPI Policy Brief, No. 162

Wan Weiping, Wang Hanlin (2008), *One Hundred Years of Wang Zhen*, Xinjiang Production and Construction Corps. Publishing House.
万卫平, 王瀚林, 百年王震, 新疆生产建设兵团出版社, 五家渠 2008.
Wang, Jinbo (2009), "A Study of Education Investment and Xinjiang Economic Development", in *International Journal of Business and Management*, Vol. 4, No. 5.
Wang Yunhua, Wang Mingji (1998), *Thought and Practice of Mao Zedong on Land Reclamation Works*, Xinjiang University Press.
王运华, 王明基, 毛泽东屯垦思想与实践, 新疆大学出版社, 乌鲁木齐 1998.
White III, Lynn T. (1979), "The Road to Urumchi: Approved Institutions in Search of Attainable Goals During Pre-1968 Rustication from Shanghai", *China Quarterly*, Vol. 79 (September), pp. 481–510.
Wiemer, Calla. (2004), "The Economy of Xinjiang", in Starr Frederick, *China's Muslim Borderland*, M. E. Sharpe.
Yao, Yong (2011), "The Arrival of Female Soldier and Stability Maintenance in Xinjiang in the 1950s", in *Social Sciences in Xinjiang*, Vol. 4, pp. 148–151.
Yao, Yong (1999), "The History of Shanghai Educated Youths' Construction in Xinjiang", in *Journal of Xinjiang University*, Vol. 27, No. 2, pp. 42–47.
Yeung Y. M., Shen Jianfa (2004), *Developing China's West: A Critical Path to Balanced National Development*, Chinese University Press.
Yue, Tingjun (2007), *Brief History of the Xinjiang Production and Construction Corps.*, Xinjiang University Press.
岳廷俊, 新疆生产建设兵团简史, 新疆大学出版社, 2007, 乌鲁木齐.
Zhang, Anfu (2010), *Research on the Development of the System and Management of the Reclamation Economy in Xinjiang During the Past Dynasties*, China Agricultural Press.
张安福, 历代新疆屯垦管理制度发展研究, 中国农业出版社, 石河子 2010.
Zhang Anfu, Cappelletti Alessandra (2012), "Study on the Development of the Tuntian System in Northern Xinjiang During the Qing Dynasty", in *MING QING Studies*, Aracne Editore.
Zhang Fengyan, Gao Gangcang, Shi Xiaoying (2007), "Analysis of Quickening the Social Administration of XPCC Towns", in *Journal of Bingtuan Education Institute*, 2007-01.

CHAPTER 5

Land Use and Acquisition Dynamics in Kashgar: Power Struggles and Social Change in a Contemporary Oasis

5.1 Land in China

Starting from the years 2000, the whole of China has been experiencing a relatively new phenomenon: the increasing economic value of land and the consequent spiraling of leasing prices. Agricultural land started to be turned—following the dynamics of the market—into a commercial asset, managed by local authorities who have the power to lease it to investors and developers, with the guarantee of high profit margins. As a state-owned asset, land in China is categorized by law as a collectively owned resource, and Chinese local authorities—normally the Land Administration Bureau (LAB) at the prefecture or county level, the Village Committee (VC) and Township Government (TG)—are in charge of processes and negotiations related to land management and lease.[1]

The fast economic development China has been going through for the last 40 years gradually turned "land" into a contested concept and a source of profit as well as of political and social tensions, a disputed idea and a contentious issue.[2] "Land" as such has therefore become a central

[1] See the works by Peter Ho (2018) and Lin and Wu (2014).

[2] Ethnopedology, as a field of study, can support authorities in the process of redefining the concept and value of "land" within their community, as well as in the redistribution of land resources. Because it is a discipline which helps acquiring knowledge on how people understand, view and manage land at different spatial scales in specific localities, it

A. Cappelletti, *Socio-Economic Development in Xinjiang Uyghur Autonomous Region*,
https://doi.org/10.1007/978-981-15-1536-1_5

topic of debate: A political concept connected to the "survival space" for Uyghurs as a nation,[3] as well as a legal concern for farmers and other actors involved, especially experts in affairs related to land use and land rights. The reason for this can be found by looking at the new status of land in the market, at collective perceptions, as well as at the overall economic and socio-political understanding of urban and rural localities in contemporary Chinese politics. Local authorities realized that land could easily be a key asset in their efforts to replenish the rapidly extinguishing local coffers.[4] Simultaneously, guaranteeing food security (and biodiversity) and enhancing productivity in the agricultural sector have been indicated as top priorities in the current agenda of the Chinese national leadership[5]: The aggressive market dynamics of profit-seeking corporations, together with the growing request—by a wealthier and more demanding population—of an increasingly diversified range of agricultural products, brought the development of the sector to the attention of

encourages the inclusion of local farmers in the evaluation of soil properties and therefore in the decision-making processes related to land use, redistribution and lease at different levels, therefore with the potential of avoiding tensions and conflicts. The knowledge of local soil is extensive and complex and therefore a prerogative of local people, since it can encompass spiritual, cognitive and practical aspects, as is documented since ancient times. For a discussion of these issues, see Briggs (2005).

[3]The Uyghur nation as a political concept has been explored by Bovingdon (2010) and, until a certain extent, it led to the politicization of every aspect of Uyghur life and Xinjiang society. Just to provide an example, the mummies which have been discovered in the Taklamakan Desert and date back to 2500 years ago have been identified as the ancestors of contemporary Uyghurs in order to claim that Xinjiang has always been Uyghur land. This is a historical bias since the contemporary Uyghur population is a mixture of Indo-European/Iranian and Mongolian peoples which started to live together and interact in the ninth century B.C., after the Turkic tribes of the Uyghurs fled from the Orkhon Valley in today's Mongolia to the Tarim Basin in today's Xinjiang, because of an internal conflict with the Kyrgyz tribes.

[4]For an analysis of fiscal decentralization in China, see Liu et al. (2017), while for the problem of the increasing local government debt, see Pan et al. (2017).

[5]China's 13th Five-Year Plan (2016–2020) calls for "agriculture to be the foundation for building a moderately prosperous society in all aspects and to achieve modernization, by restructuring China's agriculture sector, introducing improved technology innovation as well as service systems for an effective agricultural socialization", making of the development of the agricultural sector and its productivity a national priority. See Aglietta and Bai (2016).

authorities in Beijing. The combination and interrelation of these major factors made them reconsider their strategies and policies for agricultural development: Their first concern became delivering results to Beijing, namely getting the profit and loss account (P&L) back on an even keel and increase productivity. These changing needs implied an effort, back in the years 2000s, to reconsider rules and regulations of land governance at the local level, in order to adjust them and take advantage of the new foreseeable scenarios.[6]

In consideration of these priorities spurring from the socio-economic and political circles, local authorities in different parts of China, relying on a mutable degree of local consensus and a broad range of operational practices (formal and informal), started to put on the ground policy steps aimed at seizing the opportunities that agricultural land had to offer. As a broader dynamic, they started to recollect small plots of land from farmers, rented them out in big parcels to external actors—normally investors and developers coming from Inner China—with the intention to establish agribusiness ventures by taking advantage of fiscal facilitations such as tax reductions and benefits, or either to engage in other public and private infrastructural projects; operationalize policies that, especially by renting out the land, proved to be highly profitable for local authorities; started to upgrade agricultural production through the establishment of large-scale; mechanized agricultural ventures; characterized by a low-intensity employment of labor and the heavy use of chemicals.

5.1.1 The Farmers' Position

Within this broader context, farmers found themselves in a challenging condition: As they (1) cultivate small plots which could be more profitable if collected in larger parcels and leased out to investors willing to engage in construction and infrastructural works and (2) have a low status, weak voice and almost no agency in the socio-political and economic environment of contemporary Xinjiang,[7] it happens that they occupy

[6] Especially in view of the yet-to-be-launched BRI.

[7] See the fieldwork outcomes here below.

the weakest gears in the social ladder. Regardless of the specific situation of Xinjiang, it is important to recognize that farmers' status and voice in local societies across China vary sensibly, especially their negotiation capacity, which is defined by their level of social and collective awareness, as well as by the contribution of their work to the local GDP. This means that areas where small-plot farming, which is less productive and profitable, is the norm, have a relatively weaker farmers' voice.

5.2 "Results Delivering" as a Defining Trait of Local Officials' Identity in Xinjiang

5.2.1 A New Situation

At the time of the fieldwork, in 2011 and 2012, Xinjiang was in the middle of a government campaign aimed at promoting the region as a crossroad in the framework of the new initiative of foreign policy which Xi Jinping was about to launch the following year, in 2013, during a speech at Nazarbayev University in Kazakhstan. The Belt and Road Initiative (BRI) was just an empty concept at the time, and nothing specific was put forward yet, but Kashgar was already supposed to become "the Dubai of Central Asia", and slogans such as "If you have not seen Kashgar you have not seen the Silk Road" could be found everywhere at the airport and on buses in town. At the same time, the price of land in Southern Xinjiang was increasing rapidly also because of massive investments and related development projects like the "Large-scale Development of the Western Regions" (*xibu da kaifa* 西部大开发) and the "19 Municipalities and Provinces Support Xinjiang" (*shijiu shi sheng yuanzhu xinjiang* 十九市省援助新疆), as well as thanks to the new Special Economic Zone established in Kashgar in 2010. Investors and developers from Inner China and abroad were eager to rent agricultural and urban land, with the aim of establishing new businesses or re-selling the land after the expected, further increase in the prices or either for construction purposes. The mechanism implied that developers negotiated the land price directly with local authorities, and if contracts in farmers' hands had a short validity, authorities were more unrestricted in dispossessing them and renting out the land, gaining major profits and in an easy position to offer minor compensations. According to interviews' outcomes, farmers were often forced, in a variety of ways, to agree in selling out their plots. The main result of this dynamic is that farmers lose their land, gain insufficient compensations or either are provided with a new apartment under questionable conditions[8] (Fig. 5.1).

In this context, since the expectation of local authorities was to collect massive investments and funding from a range of actors in the near future, the price of land increased fast and the rush to seize land resources became a priority for local authorities. The national government's efforts to protect farmers and to restrict the authorities' grip on agricultural land contracts were not in place yet at the time and that was the moment when unaware farmers were at the mercy of unscrupulous local authorities, and when investors—from both Inner China and abroad[9]—were full of expectations and willing to engage in financial speculative operations.

Real estate was one of the most impacted sectors. The Chinese new rich, around 200,000 people only in the capital Beijing,[10] accumulated reserves of capitals without having the possibility of reinvesting them in the international financial market, mainly due to the restrictions implied by Chinese regulations on financial investments in foreign capital markets. Turning to the booming internal real estate sector was then one of the easiest solutions to make capitals profitable. It has been since the middle of the 1980s that the sector started to grow in China, and since the beginning of the twenty-first century this phenomenon has reached such a tremendous dimension that analysts often ventilate the possibility of a financial bubble, triggered by spasmodic investments in real estate projects. "Ghost cities" became tangible evidences of these dramatic dynamics.[11]

The agricultural sector, which used to be strictly under state control and not particularly attractive as a business for those in power, almost abruptly turned into a sector with a high economic potential.

[8]Professor Rahile Dawut conducted in-depth fieldworks, together with her students, to investigate the conditions of dislocated Uyghur farmers in compounds at the outskirts of Kashgar. The outcomes of this work have not been published yet, but after a conversation I had with Rahile, it was clear that the lack of any community life, the high maintenance costs, unemployment die to lack of skills and a sense of general disorientation in the new rural environment emerged as key issues among dislocated Uyghurs.

[9]See a bit further in this paragraph.

[10]August 2012 data.

[11]See Wade (2015).

Fig. 5.1 Poster informing farmers on the necessity to sign a labor contract when they go to work in urban areas. Interestingly enough, the new represented worker in the poster is a kebab seller (Picture taken by the author)

Therefore, farmers found themselves sitting on a new gold: land. Rahile Dawut, professor of Uyghur Folklore at Xinjiang University in Urumqi, told the author in March 2011 that buses of Han Chinese—as well as Koreans—were heading to Kashgar to buy whole compound buildings, foreseeing a fast price increase in the property market. In the summer of 2012, prices of apartments in Kashgar reached 2000 RMB per square meter. According to residents' opinions, this was an incredible increase which even, due to skyrocketing prices, prevented local people to buy a property. When asked about the possibility that the Return on Investment (ROI) could eventually not be so good due to the uncertainties in the region, the Han and Korean buyers used to reply that prices were at the time so low that, in case the deal would not have been profitable, the lost capital would have not been so significant anyway.

5.2.2 Under Special Conditions

For these and other reasons, the Kashgar Prefecture is considered as being under "special conditions" (特殊情况*teshu qingkuang*) at least since 2008, the year of the Beijing Olympics. It was then the time when huge transformations swept across China due to Beijing's ambition to show the world the degree of development the country had reached, and the good job the CCP leadership had been doing over the past sixty decades. These special conditions, talking about administrative units in China as the Kashgar Prefecture, can mean a whole range of different things: First of all, local authorities in charge of those areas are entitled to interpret central and regional policies according to local specificities, adjusting laws, regulations and directives to local socio-political, economic and cultural peculiarities. Moreover, local cadres and officials are entitled to conceive and implement policies and regulations which skew from those which normally apply to rural and urban areas in other Chinese provinces and autonomous regions, since they can act with a certain degree of arbitrariness in the socio-economic governance at the local level. On the other side, the CCP is the only actor entitled to shape politics at every level of governance by being in charge of the political agenda setting and the long-term goals in any realm of the society. The room for manoeuver to achieve the political objectives set and propagandized by Beijing in ways and through measures deliberated locally, with an ample degree of arbitrariness, has been extensively explained to the author by a local official in Shule County, Kashgar Prefecture, referring to directives issued topically and empowering local officials to issue land documents with a validity much shorter than the standard 30 years.[12]

5.2.3 Delivering Results

As a general dynamic we can say that, while authorities in Beijing set long-term political goals for the whole country, dictating the political line and defining targets in terms of economic and social development, local authorities are in charge of working out solutions to deliver results topically. This process starts in formal and austere meeting rooms of central bureaus and Ministries in Beijing, where general political directions, mid- and long-term goals, are conceived, defined and approved; quotas are set and a top-down process is put into place. This means that what is decided at the center is then transmitted to provincial and regional administrators and cadres, who are in charge of formulating local directives and disseminating them to authorities at the local level. The latter receive directions, need to understand them according to the political climate of the moment, discuss across different local bureaus, and conceive strategies to operationalize policies into viable regulations according to local conditions. "Delivering results" becomes then the key final step in the overall policy-making process, when local authorities adjust their strategies on the ground to the broader directives and make any possible effort to reach the set targets. This often happens regardless of the actual local peoples' needs and consensus, but sticking—sometimes merely mechanically without too much thinking—to Beijing's goals. Local officials' identity and self-awareness are both defined in terms of how much they are able to do in terms of delivering results, and their performance and eventual promotion are also evaluated against how much close to Beijing's targets they have got.[13] Given the nature of the agricultural sector in Xinjiang, as well as the traditionally strong hierarchical relations

[12] Interview conducted by the author in August 2011.

[13] The current situation of ideological re-education facilities in Xinjiang can be understood in terms of local officials conceiving strategies on the ground which are aimed at delivering results. In this specific case, the regional CCP secretary, Chen Quanguo and President Xi Jinping are those who define the strategies, and local authorities implement them on the ground with a certain degree of arbitrariness, while the most important point is that results are delivered to higher authorities.

between farmers and authorities in the region, local farmers' agency is limited as they have no power to negotiate with authorities, oppose their decisions and propose alternatives. They merely have the obligation to comply with what authorities implement as local regulations. Their consensus is obtained by different means, legal and sometimes in non-transparent ways.[14]

5.3 Xinjiang as "Internal Other": Farmers, Authorities and New Rules and Regulations in the Management of Agricultural Land

The status of "internal other" poses the issue of "space" as central in the understanding of the political situation in Kashgar. In a conflict-driven context, the most powerful actors tend to grab space, therefore territory, from the "other". In the broader context, where a process of construction of a national identity is ongoing, the "other" needs to be nullified and neutralized in its identity and diversity.

In 2011 and 2012, the clash between the Kashgar authorities' necessity to deliver results and the need of farmers to be guaranteed against abuses of power became more evident than ever. The requests from Beijing to regional authorities had become sophisticated and pressing, also due to the imminent launch of the BRI,[15] and included: (1) secularize Uyghur society by downscaling the role of religion in Xinjiang society and politics, and strengthen the role of the CCP; (2) open the doors to private developers and investors both in urban and in rural areas; and (3) increase the productivity and the profitability of the agricultural sector. These directives were received by Uyghur local authorities with a sense of urgency and with the hope to gain profits out of new processes they would have needed to put in place to reach the targets. The room for manoeuver for Xinjiang local authorities is broader than what is normally allowed to local authorities in other parts of China: Xinjiang is approximately 6000 km far from Beijing; it is a region with a special

[14] See the fieldwork outcomes here below, which highlight how farmers are often forced to sign and to comply with authorities' wishes, regardless of their own specific interests.

[15] Launched in 2013 by the Chinese President Xi Jinping the BRI is a major foreign policy scheme aimed at connecting China and Europe via Central Asia, both on an economic and social level.

status and a high degree of formal autonomy; local Uyghur peoples are of Central Asian origin, distant from the Han culture, they are Muslim, this is why national authorities rely on local mediators and middlemen to govern the region; the integration of the area into the "Han core" occurred gradually and only in the eighteenth century after a military campaign launched by the Qing Emperor Qianlong and a consequent military conquest; the region has a history characterized by conflict and resistance to the imperial, Han and CCP rules.[16]

Xinjiang has always been characterized by small-plot farming, with a prevalence of oasis agriculture in the South and grazing systems in the North of the region. Due to the low profitability of these agricultural activities, farmers have a relatively weak voice on local issues, and they are mainly subjected to the authorities' directives, traditional powers—normally religious leaders—or either government officials and CCP cadres. Because farmers' status in this society is low and weak, laws and regulations related to land are very important for protecting this part of Uyghur society.[17]

In today's rapidly changing socio-economic and political context, passive receivers of government actions are usually the weakest actors within a community, and in the Kashgar Prefecture, this is the case of farmers. The large majority of them in Kashgar is practicing subsistence small farming; do not have a formal education; do not speak Chinese; do not have professional and technical skills; live in a traditional society relying on Islamic principles where nothing can be defined as secular; they are not used to a contemporary urban environment as they have a strong sense of belonging and village identity.[18] They are thus left at the mercy of local authorities (the majority of them of Uyghur ethnicity), sometimes actors with a predatory and profit-seeking mind-set. For these and other related reasons, farmers do not have the tools to take advantage from the new conditions which emerged within their environment.

As a general point, we can say that the dynamics triggered by newly enforced rules and regulations—in our case reflected in the agricultural land documents—exert a deep and overall impact on the local population, and contribute dramatically to shaping new balances of power at

[16] In some periods in history, actually Uyghurs were allies of the imperial powers. For a history of the region, see Millward (2007).

[17] 85% of Uyghurs in the whole of Xinjiang still live in rural areas.

[18] On Uyghur identity, see Rudelson (1997) and Beller-Hann (2007).

the local and regional level, in a context of profound transformation of the socio-political and economic environment. This is exactly what the author realized in Kashgar, where adjustments in the legal framework related to the management of agricultural land were conceived as a way to accelerate the "delivering of results" to the higher authorities in Beijing. These adjustments were mainly aimed at persuading farmers to leave plots in order to attract investors and developers in the area, as well as at complying with other general directions dictated by Beijing.

5.4 Fieldwork Design

5.4.1 Background

With almost 90% of the population living in rural areas and located at the fringes of the Taklamakan Desert, the Kashgar Prefecture suffers from an endemic problem: water. This has attracted both national and international attention. Projects such as the Sino-German Poverty Alleviation Programme Xinjiang meant to last for 10 years—from 2004 to 2014—were aimed at relieving poverty-hit families from subsistence-level life standards in some of the poorest counties of the prefecture, and at adding value to their plots, occupation and identity as farmers. The project, financed by the Chinese and German governments, entailed the installation of water-saving and irrigation equipment in ten project sites of the rural areas of the Kashgar Prefecture: A properly irrigated land increases the agricultural output, but at the same time better crops and a land with a high value can attract investors from Inner China ready to pay plots at higher prices than the actual market value, in consideration of the future economic potential of land, considered as an asset. The poverty alleviation program was in fact aimed at protecting farmers from these overarching dynamics and helps them increasing their life standards. The material collected for this research is part of what the author collected while she was consultant in the land allocation monitoring missions for the Sino-German Poverty Alleviation Programme Xinjiang and is covered by KFW's[19] authorization for its use as research material. I was part of the research team led by Professor Abduresit Jelil Qarluq, who led the work and whose support has been vital. What follows is the critical

[19] Kreditanstalt Fuer Wiederaufbau, the German financing agency for the project.

analysis of the collected land contracts and documents, of interviews as well as of the outcomes of participant observation conducted mainly during two land allocation monitoring missions.

5.4.2 *The Fieldwork*

The agricultural land contracts and documents analyzed here have all been collected by the author and members of the research team in the Kashgar Prefecture and in Kizilsu Kyrgyz Autonomous Prefecture, Xinjiang Uyghur Autonomous Region, from 2010 to 2012. The analysis of these documents serves the purpose of getting an understanding about (1) the mechanisms of land allocation processes; (2) the value of land; (3) the relation between Beijing and localities; (4) local and regional power dynamics; (5) the role of new actors in Xinjiang's rural areas, such as private investors and developers; (6) processes informing the shift from small-plot farming to large-scale agribusiness ventures and related consequences; (7) the concepts of agency and power in the fieldwork sites; and (8) the renewed political attention to "land" in China.

The research and fieldwork design have been conceived adopting both qualitative and quantitative approaches, especially relying on the literature on sociological enquiry, fieldwork methods in social sciences, qualitative research strategies with a focus on poverty-stricken areas.[20] Interviews with farmers, local authorities and the KFW project-related officers, as well as the collection and analysis of government reports and firsthand material, are the basis of this work. KFW project-related officers and agencies, such as TAT, PIA and CPOs, have been an essential support for my daily work. Without their assistance and cooperation my understanding of the situation on the ground would have been severely limited. Without farmers, it would have been impossible.

The first part of the fieldwork was conducted from 20 August to 10 September 2011. It consisted in collecting documents, conducting in-depth semi-structured interviews and participant observation activities in the following six sites of the Kashgar Prefecture:

[20] Banik (2014) and Cheema et al. (2018).

1. Yingwusitan/Yengiösteng Township (英吾斯坦乡, يېڭئۆستەڭ يېزىسى), Village 7 and 11, in Shufu/Konasheher County (疏附县, قەشقەر كونا شەھەر ناھىيىسى). Interviewed families: 28
2. Aiximan/Eshme Township (艾西曼乡, ئەشمە يېزىسى), Village 8 and 9, in Yuepuhu/Yopurgha County (岳普湖县, يوپۇرغا ناھىيىسى). Interviewed families: 25
3. Seyeke/Siyek Township (色也克乡, سىيەك يېزىسى), Village 1 and 2, in Yuepuhu/Yopurgha County (岳普湖县, يوپۇرغا ناھىيىسى). Interviewed families: 15
4. Qiaolepan/Qolpan Township (乔勒潘乡, چولپان يېزىسى), Village 7, in Yingjisha/Yengihisar County (英吉沙县, يېڭىسار ناھىيىسى). Interviewed families: 10
5. Xiaputule/Shaptul Township (夏普吐勒乡, شاپتۇل يېزىسى), Village 13, 14 and 15, in Jiashi/Peyzawat County (伽师县, پەيزاۋات ناھىيىسى). Interviewed families: 25
6. Alali/Aral Township (阿拉力乡, ئارال يېزىسى), Village 1 and 2, in Shule/Yengisheher County (疏勒县, قەشقەر يېڭىشەھەر ناھىيىسى). Interviewed families: 22

From 20 August 2012 to 6 September 2012, I conducted the second part of fieldwork in the following eight sites of the Kashgar Prefecture and Kizilsu Kirgyz Autonomous Prefecture:

1. Yingwusitan/Yengiösteng Township (英吾斯坦乡, ڭەتسۆئىڭېي يېزىسى), Village 7 and 11, in Shufu/Konasheher County (疏附县, قەشقەر كونا شەھەر ناھىيىسى), Kashgar Prefecture. Interviewed families: 35
2. Qiaolepan/Qolpan Township (乔勒潘乡, ناپلوچ يېزىسى), Village 7, in Yingjisha/Yengihisar County (英吉沙县, راسىڭېي ناھىيىسى), Kashgar Prefecture. Interviewed families: 8
3. Seyeke/Siyek Township (色也克乡, كەيىس يېزىسى), Village 1 and 2, in Yuepuhu/Yopurgha County (岳普湖县, اغرۇپوي ناھىيىسى), Kashgar Prefecture. Interviewed families: 23
4. Tielimu/Terim Township (铁力木乡, مىرېت يېزىسى), Village 6, 8 and 12, in Yuepuhu/Yopurgha County (岳普湖县, اغرۇپوي ناھىيىسى), Kashgar Prefecture. Interviewed families: 17

5. Xiaputule/Shaptul Township (夏普吐勒乡, لۇتپاش ىسىزيي), Village 13, 14 and 15, in Jiashi/Peyzawat County (伽师县, تاۋازيەپ ىسىيىهان), Kashgar Prefecture. Interviewed families: A random sample of farmers has been chosen for informal interviews, since contracts had not been distributed yet
6. Alali/Aral Township (阿拉力乡, لارائ ىسىزيي), Village 1 and 2, in Shule/Yengisheher County (疏勒县, رەھەشىڭېي رەقشەق ىسىيىهان), Kashgar Prefecture. Interviewed families: 18
7. Yangdaman/Yandurma Township (洋大曼乡, امۇدناي ىسىزيي), Village 11 and 12, in Shule/Yengisheher County (疏勒县, رەقشەق رەھەشىڭېي ىسىيىهان), Kashgar Prefecture. Interviewed families: 20
8. Baren/Barin Township (巴仁乡,نىراب ىسىزيي), Village 13, in Akto County (阿克陶县, وتقائ ىسىيىهان), Kizilsu Kyrgyz Autonomous Prefecture. Interviewed families: 21

Some families have been interviewed twice, thus the total number of the interview sample is 237 families.

In Shaptul Township, farmers had not yet received their land contracts, and since this situation and farmers' conditions did not see any significant change between the two fieldworks, in 2012 the research team decided to choose a random sample of farmers for informal interviews, even if their contracts had not been distributed yet.

The main steps undertaken during the fieldwork are outlined here below:

At first, the research team met the PIA and TAT personnel to listen to their reports and suggestions about the fieldwork plan. After the meetings, the team identified the legal documents to be collected in the field, material needed to assess the validity and fairness of the land allocation process: contracts and certificates of land use, official documents related to land distribution, cadastral maps and farmers' information tables.

Secondly, following a top-down process, the team met the CPOs, TG, VC and WUAs responsibles (where existing) and the Land Resources Department staff; the county, township and village leaders and administrative personnel; the Water Resources Departments and Land Resources Departments' leaders at the local level. These meetings took place for each project site.

After having studied the collected material (reports, cadastral maps, farmers' information lists, commitment letters, contracts and certificates of land use), and listened to briefings and explanations, we moved forward by interviewing farmers in the selected villages.

The in-depth semi-structured interviews were conducted on the basis of the following criteria: The sample represented more than 10% of the total number of farmers' households in each project site, and the families were selected according to the FIT[21] provided by local authorities. Interviews have been conducted mainly with the householder, who is also the legal responsible for the allocated plot/s and the person whose signatures appear on Land Use Certificates (LUC), Land Leasing Contract (LLC) and other land-related documents. As an outline, I followed a questionnaire[22] which included some standard questions, but interviews were basically semi-structured and sometimes not structured, since during the conversations interesting issues emerged, thus the team tried, at the best of its capacity, to help farmers express their points of views and opinions without interrupting them. The interviews often took unexpected directions, thus we mainly listened and focused on reporting farmers' words. We did not record interviews but took notes. This was done in order not to make the respondent feel uncomfortable.

During the interviews, the team mainly focused on the analysis of documents like the FIT and the CMs; the procedures followed during the land allocation process; the awareness of farmers about their current conditions in terms of legal protection of their rights; the importance of the CL, of land documents like LLCs, LUCs, and the role of agencies such as the WUA, where existent.

Each of the selected villages has its own peculiarities and unique characteristics, so our fieldwork notes include an assessment for each village. For better conducting the analysis of the collected data and information, fieldwork outcomes have been organized and structured into a report-like document for the research purposes, aimed at providing a consistent overall research assessment.

[21] See the Appendix B at the end of the book for acronyms.

[22] See the Appendix A.

5.5 "Regular" and "Additional" Agricultural Land in Xinjiang

5.5.1 Regular Agricultural Land

Cropland in Xinjiang is divided into two types: "regular agricultural land" and "additional agricultural land". Regular agricultural land is managed by the Land Administration Bureau (LAB) at the regional level. The LAB is in charge of issuing the LUC, a document with a validity of at least 30 years which guarantees farmers the rights to use the plots, in line with national laws and regulations on agricultural land. "Regular" land has been reclaimed by farmers themselves—or by their ancestors—in the past and has been cultivated by the same family across decades, or even across centuries. It is not "new developed land", a kind of land reclaimed in the recent past. Plots of regular agricultural land have been officially and formally distributed to farmers in 1979, and in 1997 the first LUCs with a validity of 30 years have been eventually issued to each farmer household by prefectural or county authorities. Regular land does not imply any recent allocation process, since farmers hold and cultivate plots which have been reclaimed by themselves. This kind of cropland represents a strong guarantee against risks of eviction or expropriation, since it is covered by documents, namely LUCs, issued at the prefectural level. Moreover, the LUC does not imply any land fee, thus there is no risk for farmers to see increases in renting prices, which are common for other types of land, also in consideration of market fluctuations. On the other hand, farmers who hold a LUC can be called by local authorities—TGs or VCs—for compulsory labor at any time. If not in presence of evidence-based mitigating factors, they are supposed to respond positively to the call.

5.5.2 Additional Agricultural Land

VCs and TGs manage the additional agricultural land and have the power to issue the **LLC**, a document which guarantees the use of land to farmers for short time periods, and which entails a yearly renting cost, duly indicated in the contract, both for land and water usage. Additional land is distributed by authorities to farmers through an allocation process which needs to comply with a number of standards which make the process fair. The value of this kind of land is not stable but increases constantly according to market dynamics, up to the point that in official documents is often categorized as "commercial land" (商品土地, ***shangpin tudi***). LLCs are signed by farmers and authorities at the local level (TGs or VCs) and normally provide a weaker legal guarantee than LUCs, since expropriation can occur at any time and does not need to be backed by a strong reason of public interest, since local authorities exercise a full power over this kind of land and thus do not need to report to the higher levels. The yearly land fee, in poor areas of Southern Xinjiang, ranges from 40 to 150 Yuan/mu,[23] while in richer areas the fee increases. Local authorities can redefine and raise the renting price every year or even several time in a year by using the argument of fluctuating market prices, without the need of considering the fact that the contract is not yet expired. The limited validity of contracts—normally from 1 to 10 years—and their price volatility do not encourage farmers to commit to long or mid-term investments in farming.

As long as institutions issuing LLCs are government bodies at the local level positioned at the lowest levels of the national hierarchy of power and often involved in informal practices, farmers as well as authorities at the higher levels are concerned that the contracts' terms are set arbitrarily and without the consensus of farmers. For this reason, a notarization of the LLC at the provincial court is requested, in order to provide farmers with a stronger legal grounding and guarantee against arbitrary actions eventually leading to land dispossession. Due to the increasingly high intensity of land-related conflicts, protests and petitions, these transformations and the issue of land, raised to prominence at the national level, became a key item in the agenda of the central government. In this broader context, current regulations and laws on agricultural land are being redefined nationwide in order to reinforce guarantees for farmers and to make local authorities accountable, as well as progressively restrain their power and interference, in land-related issues.[24]

[23]One *mu* corresponds to 1/15 of a hectare (0.0648 hectares), 648 square meters and 0.16 acres.

[24]See Jun et al. (2019).

5.6 Agricultural Land Contracts and Documents

During the fieldwork process, the team followed a series of different but interrelated steps. After having checked whether documents and informative materials about the land allocation process were available for each project site, the team collected them and examined their legal validity together with a team of two local lawyers.[25]

5.6.1 Land Use Certificate

The **LUC** is issued to farmers who cultivate regular land. 国有土地使用证 *Guoyou tudi shiyongzheng* (literally: Certificate for the use of state-owned land) in Chinese, it is signed by the institution in charge of regular land, and the householder who is going to acquire the land use rights. According to Chinese laws and regulations on agricultural land, this type of contract needs to have a minimum validity of 30 years. In Xinjiang, the LAB at the regional level, with headquarters in Urumqi, has the authority to issue the LUC. As long as this document complies with the law and is officially recognized at the regional level, it does not require any kind of notarization process and is automatically valid at the national level. A copy of the document is released to the household head, another copy is retained at the TG or VC premises, while the original document is stored at the LAB premises in Urumqi.

5.6.2 Land Leasing Contract

The **LLC**, in Chinese 农村土地承包经营权证 *Nongcun tudi chengbao jingying quanzheng* (literally: Agricultural Land Contract for the Management of Land Rights), is issued to farmers who cultivate additional agricultural land. The document is signed by the institution in charge and the householder who is going to acquire the land use rights. This kind of contract has a validity which can vary on the basis of local conditions and circumstances. When the contract validity is less than 20 years, farmers might feel discouraged to invest time, energy and economic resources to develop orchards, a kind of cultivation which requires a long-term planning, and is very popular in Xinjiang. The LLC is issued either by the TG or by the VC. After this document has been legally

[25] See the below section with the lawyers' statements.

issued and recognized at the local level, it still needs to be notarized at the Prefectural Court, in our case in the city of Kashgar, the Prefectural capital, in order to be validated and recognized at the national level. The legal validity of the LLC is subdued to the notarization. The law requires that a copy of the contract is given to the householder and that the original document is kept at the TG or VC premises.

5.6.3 *Cadastral Map*

China never had a national cadastre system for rural land, and only in 2013 the Ministry of Agriculture of the PRC started a process to create it. The **Cadastral Map** (**CM**, 户籍图 *hù jí tú*) is the document where the location of plots in the farming area, the household name and family members, the borders and neighbors are represented in a visual way and through codes. In the CM, a numeric code is assigned to each plot: It corresponds to a certain farmer's household and contract. All this information is available across different land documents, for instance in the FIT, which reports the codes of each plot and connects them to the household data. Information such as size (number of mu), shape, sources of water and position of each plot is all indicated in the CM, on the basis of the actual allocation of agricultural land to households. Plots and households are thus connected through numeric codes, and the information contained in the CMs have to be consistent with the data written in the land documents issued to farmers. This consistency represents one of the evidences that a transparent land allocation process was conducted and that farmers' rights are protected by land documents which comply with the law.

Even if the following documents are related to the Sino-German Poverty Alleviation Programme Xinjiang and, as such, project-specific, they have been analyzed by the team and considered by the author as useful sources also for the purposes of this research.

5.6.4 *Commitment Letter*

The **Commitment Letter** (**CL**) consists in a statement, by the authorities in charge, about how the land allocation process was conducted, including the various steps undertaken during the procedure, and in a declaration, signed by the same authorities, attesting that the consent of the involved farmers has been legally requested and obtained. The CL is signed by all the involved parties, as it is required by the "Transparent Land Allocation Monitoring Outline"[26] of the program. TGs, CPOs, VCs and WUA directors all have to sign the document, and a copy of it needs to be available at the WUA and CPOs offices, in a place which needs to be easy to find for farmers. Each household head shall be provided with a copy of it, while the original document shall be kept at the TG or VC premises.

5.6.5 *Program Commitment Letter*

In the **Program Commitment Letter** (**PCL**), the institution in charge of managing land use rights—normally the TG or the VC—commits itself not to lease the allocated plots (where the Program engineers installed water-saving equipment) to third parties for the whole duration of the contract validity, which has to be at least 20 years. The local authorities in charge have to sign it, and a copy shall be available at the WUAs and CPOs premises, and easy to find for farmers. Household heads shall receive copy of it, while the original document shall be kept at the TG or VC premises.

5.6.6 *Report on Land Allocation Provided by Local Authorities*

The **Report on Land Allocation** (**RLA**) is a document provided by local authorities in charge of land distribution, namely TG or VC, to the monitoring team. Its content consists in an explanation of the criteria which informed the allocation process. In the second part of the fieldwork, in some cases the report contained a description of the steps undertaken by local CPOs to address the shortcomings which had been found during the previous mission. This report is considered as informative material.

5.6.7 *Farmers Information Table*

The **Farmers Information Table** is also to be considered as informative material, it contains the farmers' names in Chinese and Uyghur language (based on the IDs' data); village and working group each farmer belongs

[26] Document related to the poverty alleviation scheme's arrangements.

to; farmers' income (most recent available data); the numeric code of the plot or plots as it is indicated in the cadastral map; and the farmers' signatures.[27]

5.6.8 Commitment Document

At the end of the debriefing meeting held with all the parties involved at the end of each mission, the monitoring team asked every county government and CPOs to provide a **Commitment Document** indicating a deadline for the pending work to be accomplished.

5.7 Within Kashgar's Rural Villages: Participant Observation and Engagement with Local Communities; Formal and Informal Interviews with Farmers and Local Officials

Besides collecting and analyzing land contracts and documents, a key part of our research consisted in conducting interviews with farmers, local authorities and other actors involved in the land allocation and land acquisition processes. Some interviews were conducted by the author individually, with other members of the research team, or either by others and then translated into English.[28] A major limitation was represented by the constant presence of TG CPOs, VC and WRB officials. During each interview, at least five officials were "assisting" and monitoring the team, and farmers were worried about potential interferences by local authorities, about possible impediments and political consequences in case an account of critical facts, perceptions, narratives and ideas was voiced. During the interviews, local officials were listening, taking pictures and sometimes even suggesting answers to farmers. In some

[27] In many cases, fingerprints due to farmers' illiteracy.

[28] Because one of the my responsibilities in the framework of the KFW mission consisted in writing the final report in English language addressed to the Natural Resource Division Asia of KfW Entwicklungsbank in Frankfurt, and to the Chinese Ministry of Finance in Beijing, I had access to the whole corpus of material emerged from interviews and participant observation outcomes of other research team members, and, after having received the authorization by KFW, I could use this material for research purposes. Moreover, I was in charge of translating materials and interviews from Chinese into English for the communications with the German part and the compilation of the report.

cases, they video-recorded the interview. It was thus evident that farmers needed, due to circumstances beyond the research team's control, to restrain themselves from presenting the situation as they really perceived it, in case that was too critical. It also often happened that authorities felt the urgency to express their opinions and points of view and did not mind interrupting interviewers and farmers. This notwithstanding, the majority of farmers managed to explain its perspective about local authorities being reluctant to issue legal land documents: They argued that a long-term use of plots would have represented more stringent legal restrictions if land evictions, land conversion and land lease would have happened. In order to avoid a substantial impact on research outcomes, we needed to resort to informal research methods, such as making an effort to talk with farmers when local authorities were distracted, talking to each other, or temporarily somewhere else, so that they would feel more comfortable to speak. In those situations, I could often sense that sincere answers emerged. Moreover, we managed to meet and talk with farmers after the local authorities' working time: I was invited at their homes to eat or drink tea, I used to meet them in the bazaar, in the buses, village eateries, in parks or close to mosques. Chinese officials, colleagues who are experts on different aspects of Xinjiang society, economy and politics, as well as members of the Uyghur diaspora in Turkey, Kazakhstan, Great Britain and Germany, were also interviewed, in order to double-check and integrate the farmers' answers. My Ph.D. tutors were fundamental across the whole process and extremely supportive, since they put me in contact with local intellectuals and encouraged me to talk with their own families, friends and acquaintances. I thus made an effort to avoid potential biases deriving from interviews by conducting participant observation and trying to find ways to give farmers the possibility to speak in a safe environment. In doing this, we complied with the basic ethical standards of academic research, mainly not to generate any kind of negative consequence for interviewees, their families and friends.

5.7.1 Participant Observation as a Fieldwork Approach to Double-Check Collected Information and Data

Participant observation as a research fieldwork approach implies techniques which are normally adopted in ethnographic research in social sciences. There is still a debate among scholars who have different understandings of how this approach shall and can be operationalized, about its advantages and challenges, as well as about which kind of research outcomes it can generate and support. The flexibility of this research method allows researchers to adapt it easily to a variety of research questions and purposes. In the specific case of this work, participant observation was adopted within the broader perspective of the Grounded Theory Approach (GTA).[29] In the field, I was normally seen by villagers and authorities as an external observer, but in some cases she would have been easily taken as an internal actor.[30] It is also reasonable to say that working for a rather long time period in the field leads to a situation where the researcher's identity and borders between external and internal observers lose meaning. As a matter of fact, it can happen that the researchers get involved in the fieldwork environment to such an extent that he/she can end up being considered as an integral part of the living context he/she is conducting research in. Therefore, after the research it is important to take some distance from the field and the collected material, and proceed gradually with the analysis and interpretation of data. In this specific case, a number of years were necessary to gain that distance, and to understand how to better analyze and interpret the gathered information and data.

5.7.2 Participant Observation Implied the Following Major Activities

1. Living with ***farmers***: moving with them from rural to urban areas for shopping, administrative duties, health issues and so forth; observing daily house activities; living in their houses and assisting women in their housework, including raising children and cooking, reading religious texts and praying; participating in social and religious activities both within and outside families, including marriages, Friday prayers, religious festivals, birthdays and funerals; going to nearby archaeological and religious sites together; accompanying them to venues such as hospitals, administrative offices, schools, bazaar; going to the fields and assisting their agricultural work; observing the way they understand agricultural production and its cycles; observing them in their relation with religious

[29] Glaser and Strauss (2006).

[30] Since Europeans can look like Uyghurs, I was usually taken as Uyghur when she was not involved in the research team and stayed in villages alone or with Uyghur friends.

and political authorities, including trainings, meetings and events; observing them in any kind of activity related to traditions and beliefs; listening to narrations of their past and present life, as well as to detailed narrations of their past experiences and future expectations; listening to their complaints and claims; observing the behavior of Uyghur farmers among themselves and vis-à-vis Han farmers, Uyghur officials and Han officials among and between themselves respectively; and observing socio-political dynamics of alliances and enmities in the processes of coping with major community problems and daily issues at different levels, as well as expressions of authority and power.

2. Living with ***local officials***: observing them in their daily work in offices, during missions within and outside of China, and in contact with other actors and the population in more general terms; participating in meetings, political sessions, trainings; participating in social and leisure activities, including working dinners, outdoor walks, and visiting families and friends; following them in their free time and during trips back home for the Spring Festival holidays; observing their way to deal with superiors and farmers; observing their way to live their house life, as well as urban and rural spaces, to experience local culture; observing the way they deal with stressing situations where problem-solving skills are needed; observing their relation with land issues and their way to deal with land-related actors; observing their way to manage their relation with higher-level authorities and with Beijing; observing behavior and attitudes of Uyghur and Han officials, both among and between themselves, as well as with external actors; and observing socio-political dynamics of alliances and enmities in the processes of unraveling of major community problems and daily issues at different levels, as well as manifestations of authority and power.
3. Living the ***village***: observing the village, as a place and space of socio-political and economic interactions, a microcosm where representations of identity and self-awareness are staged, where power and influence are asserted: the village as a place where conflicts unravel, and find a resolution; a place of alliances and enmities, of continuous renegotiations of identitarian, social, political and economic space; the village as a multidimensional space: a

metaphorical, symbolic, emotional, interactive, virtual, representational[31] and informal space; observing the village as a key religious space, with its mosques, mazars[32] and shrines as places connoted with a highly symbolic religious identity.

4. Living with **Uyghur** ***artists, intellectuals, academics, religious and spiritual leaders***: following performances, lectures and any kind of public event; observing their way of working in their daily life; observing dynamics of power, authority and credibility; following them in their leisure and family activities; seeking their assistance for fieldwork research; communicating with them in private venues and engaging in long and challenging conversations; working in their private household libraries; observing their interactions with the territory and the broader society; observing their relation with power and authority; and assessing their critical perspective on Xinjiang affairs with a focus on rural areas, if any.
5. Living and understanding the ***broader socio-political-religious context and environment***: observing the ecology, morphology, climate, border interactions, cultural influences, affiliations and sense of belonging of people living in the fieldwork areas; observing and experiencing key places which define the spiritual geography and the locals' sense of belonging to the local space, such as mazars,[33] pilgrimage sites and religious venues; experiencing unexpressed conflicts and living the hidden agenda; and understanding the knowledge of soil that local people have and the contribution they can give to a better use of land.[34]

Participant observation represented one of the main techniques I adopted to address biases potentially arising from significant limitations to fieldwork. In addition, a broad range of methods of informal research has been adopted. I also conducted many unstructured random interviews without the possibility to take notes on the spot, nor record answers, in different circumstances and times of the day and the night; talked occasionally with people in the villages (drivers, street sellers and

[31] Lefebvre (1974).

[32] Harris and Dawut (2002) and Dawut (2016).

[33] For instance, Ordam Mazar close to Kashgar.

[34] Ethnopedology is the discipline which studies the knowledge and understanding of soil by local people.

workers, women in their house activities, families, friends and friends of friends) and included focused questions in random conversations; relied on contacts who asked to remain anonymous and accepted to talk only under the condition of switching off mobile phones and extracting the battery; and adopted also other ways of collecting information in a not organized and systematic way.

5.8 Legal Validity of Land Documents

The legal validity of the collected documents could not be assessed without resorting to the collaboration of two Uyghur lawyers from local law firms, professionals with a certain degree of familiarity with land policies in the Kashgar Prefecture, as well as with dynamics and consequences generated by the fast transformation of the legal framework related to the management of agricultural land, and by evictions. The meaning of law and legal documents in contexts as rural China, and in this case as rural Kashgar, is widely debated across different disciplines and in particular in anthropology. In some contexts, it does not make too much sense to look at legal frameworks and at the degree of respect of the law as such. Traditional and customary practices shape the economy and politics of everyday life and are deeply entrenched in the society, regulating disputes, disagreements, economic transactions, as well as influencing decision-making processes at the individual and community level.[35] The analyzed rural areas of the Kashgar Prefecture are places where customary practices articulate the very nature of daily interactions and provide a meaning to social, economic and political life. This said, evaluating the legal validity of the collected documents together with two Uyghur lawyers can be understood as another method to double-check information and to add another perspective into the study.

5.8.1 The Lawyers' Tasks

The two professionals needed to assess the legal validity of the provided documents on the basis of recognized standards, of ethics and constituent documents and their compliance with the law, in respect of the principles of independence, objectivity and impartiality, according to

[35] Steinmüller (2013).

the provided data and facts and Chinese laws, regulations and normative documents in force at the time. Their assessment has been given against the: (1) "Law of the People's Republic of China on Rural Land Contracts" (中华人民共和国农村土地承包法 *Zhonghua renmin gongheguo nongcun tudi chengbao fa*); (2) "Interpretation of the Supreme People's Court of Applicable Law Issues in the Trial of Cases Concerning Rural Land Contract Disputes" (最高人民法院关于审理涉及农村土地承包纠纷案件适用法律问题的解释 *Zuigao renmin fayuan guanyu shenli sheji nongcun tudi chengbao jiufen anjian shiyong falu wenti de jieshi*); and (3) "Measures for the Administration in charge of transferring Rural Land's Contractual Management Rights". The lawyers needed to check whether the institution issuing contracts was qualified; whether the contracts' content was legal and effective; the declaration of intention valid; the legitimate rights and interests of the parties involved fully protected; and the form of the documents legal and complete. The basic principles of the assessments were legitimacy, authenticity, completeness, normativity and equity.

The major problems that the lawyers' report underlines can be summarized as it follows:

1. The most serious problem is that the majority of farmers are still without contract, and this could impact heavily on farmers' rights to use the land.
2. The main body of the contracts does not conform to the normative requirements of the law.
3. The details of the contracted land are not clearly specified (in many contracts the name, location, area and quality characteristics of the contracted land are missing).
4. The agreement on the contract period does not conform to the provisions of the law.[36]

[36]According to Article 20 of the "Rural Land Contracting Law" of the People's Republic of China, "The contracting period of cultivated land is 30 years. The contract period of grassland varies from 30 to 50 years. The contracting period for forest land ranges from 30 to 70 years, and the contracting period of land with special trees may be extended with the approval of the Forestry Administrative Department under the State Council". The contracting period specified in the majority of the analyzed contracts is not in accordance with the law.

5. The purpose of contracted land is not clear (the kind of agricultural production is not specified).
6. The contractor's rights are not duly clarified.[37]
7. Mode and method for transferring the contracted land are not clarified.
8. The contract cannot be terminated unilaterally by the issuing party and such acts cannot be performed without clear explanation.
9. The contract-issuing party's agreement to bear the liability in case of breach of contract is unclear.
10. The majority of contracts have some parts which are translated from Chinese into Uyghur incorrectly. The lawyer found inconsistencies, from the side of local authorities, to translate the requirements of the Sino-German project into effectively protective local policies. Cases of misunderstandings due to the translation from Chinese into Uyghur were found, for instance as far as water usage is concerned.
11. Transparency about the land distribution process is requested but the lawyers had difficulties in finding evidences of this transparency in the provided documents.
12. In the documents, it is not specified when Chinese law does not allow land transfer.
13. Across the documents, the lawyers found inconsistencies and unclarities about water usage and water fees.
14. In some cases, in documents related to the land distribution process the *mu* distributed to each farmer is not clarified.

[37]According to Article 16 of the "Rural Land Contracting Law" of the People's Republic of China, "Contractors shall enjoy the following rights: (1) they shall enjoy the rights of contracted use, income and the transfer of contracted land management rights according to law, and they shall have the right to organize production, operation and disposal of products independently; (2) if the contracted land is requisitioned or occupied according to law, the right shall be compensated accordingly according to law; (3) other rights prescribed by laws and administrative regulations". The majority of the analyzed contracts only stipulates that the contractor can engage in production and operation activities and dispose of products by himself. It does not specify that the contractor can transfer the right of contractual management of land in accordance with the law during the contracting period. It does not clarify either that the contractor has the right to obtain a corresponding compensation in case the contracted land is legally expropriated or occupied.

15. Uyghur farmers cannot be protected in case of dispute because the majority of contracts do not comply with the "Law of the People's Republic of China on Rural Land Contracts".
16. The lawyers highlight that, in case of land dispute, the time necessary to go through the legal case can be very long and harmful to farmers' interests.
17. The importance of lawyers in the land allocation processes is highlighted, especially having a lawyer following the whole process from the beginning and supporting farmers in the protection of their rights.
18. The two lawyers suggest that the issued contracts should be revised and perfected and provided a recommended format for rural land contracting suitable for household contracting.

5.9 Power Struggle and Displacement in a Transitional Environment: Interpretation and Reflection Over Fieldwork Outcomes

5.9.1 Land Acquisition as a Factor of Destabilization and Disorientation

"Land acquisition", or either—depending on the level of emphasis put on the degree of enforcement entailed in the process—"land grabbing" or "land seizure".[38]—is one of the most controversial and debatable phenomenon in contemporary China. Human Development Reports, compiled by the United Nations, contain dedicated analyses and insights due to the alarming level of social unrest connected with this.[39] Over the last decade, reports of public petitions, tensions, protests and disorders associated with land acquisition have been hot topics—on a daily basis—in the Chinese local and national news, as well as in the international media. When there are no reports of violence, it normally makes the news the story of a farmer, or of a group of farmers, dispossessed of land and provided with miserable compensations by profit-making local authorities. The latter argue that procedures and regulations were followed, but farmers still contend that they got tricked and were

[38] I use here "land acquisition" as a less political connoted expression.

[39] Among the others, see Ho (2005, 2009) and Deng (2011).

subject to mean and brutal persuasion techniques, violating their legitimate rights.[40] Narrowing the focus on the rural areas of the Kashgar Prefecture, my assessment is that farmers complain about officers' arrogant behaviors, and about being exploited and exhausted for the interests of other actors, in a context of significant changes framed in the official discourse under the label of "economic and social development". These quick developments interesting the regional economy, which made Xinjiang one of target areas for investments at the national level, triggered a price/investments dynamic generating a strong impact on the local economy, political struggles and social patterns.

5.9.2 Power Struggle

The fieldwork brought to light a story of abuse of power, powerlessness and instrumentalization of poverty and identity in the rural villages of the Kashgar Prefecture and Kizilsu Kyrgyz Autonomous Prefecture, the locations chosen for the fieldwork. The ongoing power struggles in the area have two main protagonists: the local traditional religious authorities—such as the imam and the sheik[41]—with a huge load of socio-political and cultural capital, and the new encroaching power of the CPP, consisting of cadres and local officials with a substantial economic capital. While the former is ethnically connoted (they are all Uyghurs), speaks the same language of local farmers, has the same culture and a strong leverage and influence over the population in the area, the latter is trans-ethnic and has significant economic power as well as a new development model to propagandize via slogans and campaigns, which might exert some appeal on younger generations of Uyghurs by relying on Uyghur capable middlemen and skillful mediators. This is a new power with means and leverage to co-opt both Uyghur and Han authorities and actors; it complies with Beijing's agenda and is thus backed by central authorities. The land, a recently, newly recognized source of profit and power, is under its supervision, and it represents, with its issues, a valid leverage to influence central authorities, and eventually gain profits and

[40]The literature on the topic or urban development and citizens' rights is extensive. Among the others, see Rowe et al. (2016), Gu and Wu (2010), and Hsing (2010).

[41]The imam is the Islamic priest, and the Sheik is the guardian of the mazar.

obtain promotions from Beijing. Following on this, the main concern of these new actors is to deliver results and negotiate better salaries and positions with authorities at higher levels, regardless of the needs and requests coming from local peoples. The narrative of the Han invaders and oppressors—as it is spread by Uyghur diaspora members and critics of Beijing—and of the passive and victimized Uyghurs represents a strong persuasion technique for divested traditional authorities, who can still exert some influence among communities living within a very traditional familial and clan-based social setting. This narrative generates tensions between Uyghurs and Hans, as well as among Uyghurs and among Hans, and the discontent it spurs potentially represented a destabilizing factor for Xinjiang society as a whole, with possible spillover effects at the national level. Under these circumstances, Uyghurs with roles such as local authorities, Party cadres, academics and members of the Xinjiang Production and Construction Corps act as stabilizers, bridges between the two populations and defibrillators against potentially explosive tensions. As part of this "social pact", these Uyghurs guarantee that the status quo is maintained on behalf of Beijing, in exchange of promotions and higher statuses in the social ladder.

5.9.3 Displacement

The analysis, assessment and interpretation of agricultural land documents conducted during and after the fieldwork with the support of two lawyers, led to the conclusion that 87% of the collected documents is outside of a legal framework. While in some cases farmers were aware of the situation, in general terms they were all worried and concerned about the possibility of being easily dispossessed of their land and displaced in unknown, unfamiliar and even hostile rural or urban areas. They felt that their future is uncertain, and this sense of precariousness and state of persistent insecurity for what it concerns employment, income, health and living conditions, combined with the perception of being powerless and of experiencing abuse. At certain points during the interview process, the whole situation became tense and, at different levels, emotionally loaded.[42]

[42] This combines as well with the sense of living in a territory occupied by invaders and of being B-series citizens.

5.9.4 A Transitional Environment

The creation of a new power which cuts across ethnicities and has mainly an economic capital; the dispossession and migration of Uyghur peasant workers from the countryside to "new rural villages" or urban areas—where they become unskilled labor and enter the grey economy—together with a dramatic transformation of urban and rural spaces in terms of socio-political and economic environment—as well in their landscape[43]—are the main dynamics generated by these new situations (Fig. 5.2).

Rural villages in Kashgar become then metaphorical spaces of place dispossession, symbols of displacement and alienation. Uyghur peasant workers, with a double identity of active and passive actors, are in the majority of cases unwillingly, contributing to the transformation of Xinjiang's rural and urban areas. By forcibly or voluntarily moving, they become major players in the development dilemma: Investments in infrastructures and industry, as well as political mechanisms related to urbanization imperatives, transform the countryside, while massive migration waves of peasant workers reshape the identity of urban areas, in a combination and renegotiation of concepts such as "poverty", "conflict" and "opportunity". The main narrative proposed by the central government consists in asserting that a widespread consensus exists, from the different social actors, toward Beijing's plans and policies, a narrative which disguises the deep sense of discontent and frustration among part of the Uyghur population.

One of the reasons of this discontent can be identified in the sense of loss, loss of identity, "traditional" way of living, and while part of the younger generations welcomes this change, older generations (approximately from 35 to 80 years old) are negatively affected. Loss of cultural roots; historical understanding; sense of belonging; community life; connection with the environment; as well as loss of understanding and control of a place are all major causes of discontent among Uyghurs.

[43]The replacement of trees in rural areas is a practice adopted by the Chinese government as well as by the Israeli government in the occupied territories of Palestine.

Fig. 5.2 New square, in a Han Chinese style and with trees common in Inner China, in a Uyghur rural village (Picture taken by the author)

5.10 Conclusions: Farmers Are Discouraged to Cultivate the Land and a New Xinjiang Is Being Built

A trend which emerged during the fieldwork is the replacement of LUCs with LLCs, the new three- to five-year validity land contracts issued by the VC or either by the TG. While local authorities were not willing to notarize LLCs, and blamed farmers by arguing that they did not want to pay the 200 RMB of notarization costs, according to the interviews' results farmers were keen to pay the notarization of their short-term contracts, since they were well aware of the stronger guarantee this could represent for them. The problem was that they simply did not know about this necessity. Local authorities, from their side, were discouraging this notarization process, and the replacement of LUCs with LLCs was occurring via non-transparent procedures. The loose legal framework, and a tacit consent from higher-level authorities, allowed local officials to put forward a wide range of different justifications, protests notwithstanding.

This new political, legal and social framework is having a deep impact on small-plot farming, as well as on farmers' behavior and future life. When they become aware that land documents and contracts provided to them do not represent a real guarantee against abuses of power perpetrated by local authorities and developers, farmers are discouraged from investing capitals and energy in their plots. Farmers know that they can be forced to give up their only means of survival from one day to another, and in some cases, especially when plots are farmed by the same family since generations, there can be outbreaks of social conflicts.[44] When Uyghur farmers lose their land, usually the only possibility left to them is moving to large cities and sell their labor for a cheap salary, becoming in this way part of that "floating population" with a rural *hukou* who cannot enjoy social services nor any aspect of the welfare system, and who gets easily involved in the black market or in underground activities. Another prospect is to work as daily-wage farmers in large-scale agricultural estates established by Han Chinese investors who have obtained the rights to rent and collect small plots. Authorities "persuade" farmers to sell out their plots by promising high compensations, or in some cases just threatening them of future retaliations, and in the majority of cases granting them a reward of about 500 RMB per month. After having received—in a different range of ways—the approval by farmers, they rent the land to investors at very high prices, and in this way a high profit is guaranteed. Farmers' signatures allowing local authorities to sell out the land are obtained thanks to tricks and threats, but at the very end in front of higher-level authorities the whole process of obtaining farmers' consensus appears perfectly regular, due to the fact that the legal process is respected on paper, the steps followed are not duly monitored, and a certain degree of informality is accepted by local authorities. Ignorance, socio-political and economic weakness and fear make farmers the first victims of this situation. In some counties of the Kashgar Prefecture, there are farmers dispossessed of their land, receiving

[44]This kind of situation has been observed in Peyzawat/Jiashi County, in the Kashgar Prefecture, in August–September 2011, and in August–September 2012.

500 RMB a month for a four-member family, without the possibility neither to find other jobs nor to move to the city, due to language and cultural issues. In the best of the cases, the whole household moves to a newly built apartment in twenty- or thirty-storey compounds at the outskirts of the urban centers: These families cannot afford to pay electricity, water, bills and maintenance costs, and they often end up living in miserable conditions, without any possibility to improve their life standards.

The situation of Han farmers, both in Xinjiang and in the whole country, is different: Hans know that the government is by their side, that they belong to the main culture and ethnicity in China. They do not have a strong voice in the Chinese society either, but those Han farmers have a deeper awareness of their conditions, and dare to raise claims and to organize themselves spontaneously to ask respect for their rights. They have an easier access to credit and can organize themselves to invest in their land and to accumulate capitals. They speak Mandarin, they belong to the same culture of their leaders and they know how to speak the language of power and to negotiate for being respected. The Han society they belong to is considered to be the most condescending and supportive toward central politics, trained and educated to comply and support the development model conceived and implemented by the CCP leadership. If they manage to raise their voices, through petitions or other channels, it can happen that their claims reach official desks.

Uyghur farmers are experiencing a different situation: They do not speak Mandarin, they suffer from a long-lasting discrimination, the majority lives in miserable conditions and do not know how to deal with a leadership which they feel distant and unable to listen, nor able to understand, their claims. Lack of self-confidence and fear completes the whole picture, for these reasons the only contact persons they have are those Uyghurs who occupy official positions in the government and act as middlemen. As I already assessed, Uyghur officials are usually corrupted, work for their own interests and for those of their Han leaders, so farmers do not have any channel to make their claims reach higher-level authorities. The lack of an efficient legal framework, of responsible local authorities and consistent information and advertisement on farmers' rights in Uyghur language, creates a particularly complex environment, and a situation which is still evolving and worth to be observed, also in connection with the national level policies aimed at coping with the increase of internal demand of food, and with the five-year plan on agricultural output.

Bibliography

Aglietta, Michel, and Bai, Guo (2016), "China's 13th Five-Year Plan: In Pursuit of a 'Moderately Prosperous Society'", CEPII Policy Brief No. 12.

Banik, Dan (2014), "Fieldwork Amidst Extreme Poverty and Deprivation: Ethical Dilemmas and Policy Impact", *Indian Anthropologist*, 44(1): 53–68.

Beller-Hann, lldikò (2007), *Community Matters in Xinjiang 1880–1949: Towards a Historical Anthropology of the Uyghurs*, Brill.

Bovingdon, Gardner (2010), *The Uyghurs: Strangers in Their Own Land*, Columbia University Press.

Briggs, J. (2005), "The Use of Indigenous Knowledge in Development: Problems and Challenges", *Progress in Development Studies*, 5(2): 99–114.

Cheema, Abdur Rehman, Mehmood, Abid, and Khan, Fazal Ali (2018), "Challenges of Research in Rural Poverty: Lessons from Large Field Surveys", *Development in Practice*, 28(5): 714–719.

Dawut, Rahile (2016), "Ordam Mazar. A Meeting Place for Different Practices and Belief Systems in Culturally Diverse Xinjiang", in Ildikó Bellér-Hann, Birgit N. Schlyter, and Jun Sugawara (eds.), *Kashgar Revisited: Uyghur Studies in Memory of Ambassador Gunnar Jarring*, Brill.

Deng, Annie (2011), "Dousing the Flames: The Tang Fu Zhen Self-Immolation Incident and Urban Land Takings Reform in the People's Republic of China", *Southern California Interdisciplinary Law Journal*, 20(3): 585–613.

Glaser, Barney, and Strauss, Anselm L. (2006), *The Discovery of Grounded Theory: Strategies for Qualitative Research*, Aldine Transaction.

Gu, Chaolin, and Wu, Fulong (2010), "Urbanization in China: Processes and Policies", *China Review*, 10(1): 1–9.

Harris, Rachel, and Dawut, Rahila (2002), "Mazar Festivals of the Uyghurs: Music, Islam and the Chinese State", *British Journal of Ethnomusicology*, 11(1): 101–118.

Ho, Peter (2005), *Institutions in Transition: Land Ownership, Property Rights and Social Conflict in China*, Oxford University Press.

Ho, Peter (ed.) (2009), *Developmental Dilemmas: Land Reform and Institutional Change in China*, Routledge.

Ho, Peter (2018), "Institutional Function Versus Form: The Evolutionary Credibility of Land, Housing and Natural Resources", *Land Use Policy*, 75(6): 642–650.

Hsing, You-Tien (2010), *The Great Urban Transformation: Politics of Land and Property in China*, Oxford University Press.

Lefebvre, Henri (1974), *La production de l'espace*, Anthropos.

Lin, Ye, and Wu, Alfred M. (2014), "Urbanization, Land Development, and Land Financing: Evidence from Chinese Cities", *Journal of Urban Affairs*, 36(supp. 1): 354–368.

Liu, Yongzheng, Martinez-Vazquez, Jorge, and Wu, Alfred M. (2017), "Fiscal Decentralization, Equalization, and Intra-Provincial Inequality in China", *International Tax and Public Finance*, 24(2): 248–281.

Millward, James (2007), *Eurasian Crossroads: A History of Xinjiang*, Columbia University Press.

Pan, Fenghua, Zhang, Fengmei, Zhu, Shengjun, and Wojcik, Dariusz (2017), "Developing by Borrowing? Inter-Jurisdictional Competition, Land Finance and Local Debt Accumulation in China", *Urban Studies*, 54(4): 897–916.

Rowe, Peter G., Forsyth, Ann, and Kan, Har Ye (2016), *China's Urban Communities: Concepts, Contexts and Well-Being*, Birkhauser.

Rudelson, Justin Jon (1997), *Oasis Identities: Uyghur Nationalism along China's Silk Road*, Columbia University Press.

Steinmüller, Hans (2013), *Communities of Complicity: Everyday Ethics in Rural China*, Berghahn Books.

Yang, Jun, Li, Yi, Hay, Iain, and Xianjin, Huang (2019), "Decoding National New Area Development in China: Toward New Land Development and Politics", *Cities*, 87: 114–120.

Wade, Shepard (2015), *Ghost Cities of China the Story of Cities Without People in the World's Most Populated Country*, Zed Books.

CHAPTER 6

Uyghurs vs. Uyghurs: Fragmented Identities in Contemporary Xinjiang

6.1 From a Multinational to a Nation-State: The Current Debate Over Ethnicity

In the anthropological, sociological and political science literatures, there has been much debate over the nature of ethnic groups (for an overview, see Gil-White 1999). The central question behind the whole debate relates to whether ethnic groups are primarily instrumental associations of rational political actors, or do such human agglomerations result from primordial sentiments which are relatively independent from "rational" considerations, in some ways inborn in human beings. According to fieldworks conducted by anthropologists, part of respondents tends to consider ethnic affiliation as a matter of biological descent rather than enculturation or "rational" choice. These findings open the way to other research questions which explore the nature of ethnicity, with implications for an understanding of (1) the brain's processing of social categories and (2) the evolutionary emergence of ethnic groups (including the functions they arose to serve).

Anthropologists once considered ethnic groups or "cultures" to be "peoples" in a unitary sense, along various dimensions: "ascriptive" (labeling), "moral" (normative) and "cultural" (linguistic and artifactual). An ethnic group therefore understood itself as such, was labeled by "others" as such, had a particular and distinctive culture (including a language/dialect), and its members preferred each other to non-members

A. Cappelletti, *Socio-Economic Development in Xinjiang Uyghur Autonomous Region*,
https://doi.org/10.1007/978-981-15-1536-1_6

(through endogamy, discrimination, in-group solidarity and so on). This simplification of the diverse anthropological positions allows us to capture the "culture area" perspective of ethnic groups, predominant under the influence of British functionalism, according to which societies are well-bounded and functionally integrated organisms, following the adoption of Malinowski's model of ethnographic work. The first reactions to this position can be found in Edmund Leach's Political Systems of Highland Burma (1973) and in Moerman's work among the Lue peoples in Thailand. These authors argue that ethnic identities do not coincide neatly with the distribution of the cultural material on the field, and proposed to move away from "objective" indicators of groupness, such as measurable discontinuities in the distribution of artifactual or ideational culture, toward a more "subjective" focus, mainly taking into account the labeling perception and processes of ethnic actors themselves. The most important essay on the subject has been published in 1969: Fredrik Barth's famous introduction to Ethnic Groups and Boundaries. In this work, the author maintains that in order to have a social identity a person must meet the conditions for being referred to by the linguistic expression, which means the label, naming that identity. Thus, the labeling processes of local ethnic actors themselves are considered as the only guides to the limits of the group, since "the cultural features that are taken into account are not the sum of 'objective' differences, but only those which actors themselves regard as significant". On the basis of these assumptions, any cultural aspect which is not recognized by local ethnic actors as significant would not necessarily correspond to different ethnic labels. Since then, society as a "thing", a bounded whole, is a concept which started to be questioned. The impact of Barth's theories was outstanding because his theoretical sophistication went well beyond an elaboration of the subjectivist approach. In the communities that Barth studied, some individuals born within a certain ethnic group were, later in life, labeling themselves with another ethnic name, as circumstances made this advantageous. Barth argued that an ethnic status implies a particular "kind" of actor, who will therefore easily coordinate with others "of the kind" for reciprocal exchanges. Thus, if I am an A, but it is better for me to interface and network with B, I shall acquire a B identity together with B's ways of being, so as to comply with the B network. In substance, ethnic actors are considered rational actors who make choices about their ethnic statuses, as (ecological/economic/political) circumstances make this instrumental. With this argument, the circumstantialist—instrumentalist—school of ethnicity was born.

Most scholars today would agree that Barth changed our views forever. Following the publication of *Ethnic Groups and Boundaries*, the idea that ethnicities are in the first instance collections of individuals sharing a common self-ascription, but with no necessary relation to any particular cultural content, became accepted by all.

The following question became the central in anthropological studies: Are ethnic groups rational associations of self-interested actors, as Barth claims, or are they irrational "primordial" groupings governed by emotional attachments, as others maintain?

The essentialist tradition, also called primordialist, begins with Shils (1957) and Geertz (1963), while its later elaborations can be found in Isaacs (1975), Stack (1986), and Grosby (1994). The basic idea is that "primordial" feelings are felt toward co-ethnics (usually, co-biological descendants from a primary group), and not necessarily as a result of interaction with them. In this framework, patterns of interaction follow the categorical borders, in a reversed mechanism if compared to the circumstantialist approach. Ethnic affiliation is not determined by a rational choice rather by an alleged commonly perceived tradition, and by emotions evoked by perceptions of a common ancestry. Thus, the behavior of ethnic actors is not a calculation of interests, but is rather motivated by a common history which binds them, as they themselves perceive this history. Except for the work by Nagata (1981), essentialist positions lacked theoretical sophistication. Shils (1957) observed that "the attachment to another member of one's kinship group is not just a function of interaction ... It is because a certain ineffable significance is attributed to the tie of blood". Geertz (1963) went a step further by adding to primary kinship groups those which rallied around: (1) perceived common biological descent, (2) race, (3) language, (4) region, and (5) religion.

6.1.1 *Ethnicity in China*

The current debate about ethnicity and nationality in China is headed by Ma Rong, Professor of Sociology at Beijing University and Senior Advisor at the State Ethnic Affairs Commission (国家民族事务委员会 Guojia minzu shiwu weiyuanhui). His main idea is that the Chinese multinational state shall turn into a nation-state, because only in this way a long-lasting prosperity can be guaranteed to the population. In Ma Rong opinion, the nation-state is the only political form that a modern state must aim at as final goal. In order to reach this aim, the concept of ethnicity needs to be downscaled. Ma Rong lists the steps he thinks are needed to transform the Chinese multinational state into a nation-state, such as:

1. delete the ethnicity from personal documents (including ID cards);
2. gradually abolish the preferential policies for minorities (minorities can have more children than Hans, can access universities with lower scores, have access to special subsidies for housing and education, have a preferential access to government positions in minority areas);
3. take the necessary actions of social engineering at the local and national level from the side of the authorities to downsize ethnicity to a marginal aspect of a person's identity;
4. in the government rhetoric and policy, downplaying the concept of "unity of nationalities" (民族团结 *minzu tuanjie*) and gradually introduce that of a national unity (国家民族 *guojia minzu*).

One of the most discussed and controversial steps taken in this sense, following Professor Ma ideas, has been to change the English translation of "Zhongyang Minzu Daxue 中央民族大学" from "Central University for Nationalities" into "Minzu University of China", a decision which was officialized, after a long internal debate, in 2009. This was due to the fact that the English term "nationality" could have been considered misleading since, according to Western categories, it might have involved the concepts of the right of a people to self-determination and "legitimate separatism".

While national minority cultures are still seen as a powerful touristic attraction and source of revenues—both within China and internationally—and they are often associated with exotic beauties and landscapes, the political trend is to assimilate all ethnic groups within China into a "modern" nation-state. This is seen as a workable path to national unity and as a useful device to prostrate the consensus around independentism and autonomist claims, mainly by Uyghurs, Mongolians and Tibetans. Barry Sautman, Professor at Hong Kong University for Science and Technology, argues that, in order to preserve socio-political stability, it would be necessary to increase the extent of preferential policies for minorities, and to put a stronger emphasis on the concept of "multinational state". Sautman argues that the diversity of languages and major difficulties for minority nationals to be integrated into a Han-dominated society are major factors. Because of these disadvantages, the author believes that minority nationals need support and help in their efforts to go through a process of socio-economic integration. Therefore, Sautman firmly believes that scaling down ethnic identity would represent a political mistake from the side of authorities, with the potential of creating chaos in the country. The debate is still ongoing and there is the need to wait to see which position will eventually prevail in Beijing.

A clear-cut sense of ethnic belonging, together with a distinct commonly perceived sense of ethnic divide, is among the most peculiar characteristics of how the Chinese population lives its multidimensional identity in modern China. With nationalism on the rise, Chinese first-hand historical sources highlighting the rich demographic and cultural diversity of the country as the expression of different populations living inside and around the imperial territory, whose identifications mainly followed geographical, religious or even cultural/phenotypical lines, become sensitive. At the same time, the label "Han" has always been employed to define a population linked to a territory which dates back to the origin of Chinese culture, and in this way, the concept of what was Chinese, and what was not, did not clearly emerge. The only outstanding identitarian difference was created between "Hans" and "barbarians", the collective label for peoples living at the outskirts of the imperial territory. In China's imperial past, different namings were arbitrarily applied according to the characteristics of the various populations, with their religion and phenotypical features identified as distinct elements.

Today, ethnicity is a well-established concept in everyone's mind in China. The Chinese population was classified into 56 ethnic groups by the first teams of anthropologists and sociologists who, in the 1950s, were sent from the most famous universities in the country to the different corners of the Chinese territory to carry on a detailed and accurate taxonomy of the populations. Considering the work made by the Soviet Union in their ethnic diverse territory as reference, their task was to produce an accurate classification of peoples on the basis of their cultural characteristics and self-perception. All the rest was politics: Han settlers were transferred to areas with a high concentration of minorities to dilute the strongest ethnic identities, while in other cases scholars were sent to ascribe a certain ethnic group into a broader ethnic category. The fieldworks and methodologies followed for this classificatory work were, in some cases, highly questionable. In those first reports from the field, it is not rare to read sentences like: "We (the team of anthropologists in question) told them they were Zhuang, we kept repeating it every day, and the result was that at the end, we convinced them they were Zhuang". With a new categorization at hand, the government of the new China put a special attention in ensuring that the Han population would be the overwhelming majority (today around 92%), and that territories with a too high concentration of minority nationals would become the destination of consistent numbers of Han nationals. Clever political operations followed, mainly in order to secure the central government from having, inside its national borders, areas with high concentrations of minority nationals and from the eventuality to be forced to face outbreaks of movements claiming self-determination, or even separation. The only two exceptions to this plan, due to their extreme climates, geographical positions and environmental hardships, were Tibet and Xinjiang, where the Han population represented 1 and 6%, respectively (1952 census data). For the Han population, those territories were too harsh to become possible destinations for a new life. This notwithstanding, today Hans became the second largest ethnicity in Xinjiang, and in Tibet their number increased consistently, with traditional Uyghur and Tibetan centers as Turpan and Shigatse already turned into predominantly Han urban settlements.

The development of Xinjiang was characterized by deep inequalities between the Northern and the Southern parts, where clear-cut ethnic differentiations still exist, and since 1949, most of the migrants from Inner China concentrated in the North, where the main connection links and infrastructures were already built. Most of the Han population settled there, where there was the highest concentration of state farms and almost all the regional industrial capacity was gathered. The Southern regions remained overwhelmingly rural, with farmers mainly cultivating small plots on oasis land. Standards of living were much lower than in the North, and numerous districts fell well below the national poverty threshold. For instance, the average rural yearly income for Xinjiang was 684 yuan per head in 1998, but only 200 yuan for the Southern areas (Fig. 6.1).

Fig. 6.1 Rebyia Dasha in Urumqi, the shopping mall established by Rebiya Kadeer, just before the demolition (Picture taken by the author in 2009)

6.2 Ethnic Affiliation and Social Practices

In one of his works, Marco Buttino explains how he started one of his courses at the University of Turin: He asked students to write down the names of five ethnic groups. After having collected all the notes, where all the kinds of identities were listed, from African to Bosnian, he used to ask students: "Which is your ethnic group?" Quite surprisingly, almost all the students did not have a clear answer in their minds: They were basically perceiving themselves as universal citizens, while only other populations were ethnics. The course focus was on ethnic violence, and the close relationship between ethnic construction and conflict was the core of the whole course. Buttino writes that "those who build the conflict are using ethnic categories as tools for social framing and analysis", while the language of the media uncritically adopts this ethnic terminology, unconsciously contributing to the escalation of the conflict. As mentioned, the circumstantialist/instrumentalist models maintain that ethnicities are "constructed" by rational actors who calculate their objective interests, and then make decisions concerning association and/or political mobilization with others. At the same time, several anecdotes about Xinjiang reveal that Uyghurs adopt ethno-biological, and therefore "primordialist", models concerning the acquisition/transmission of ethnic statuses. This can be explained by considering those main social practices related to ethnic affiliation.

China is a multi-ethnic country, and ethnic data are written on personal documents of each Chinese citizen, from ID cards to membership cards. In the case of citizens of Uyghur ethnicity, the simple transliteration of their names and surnames into Mandarin Chinese reveals their ethnic origin. In any public office, government bureau, official location, ethnicity is easily traced since it is listed as the third item in any official paper after "name" and "sex". It is then considered and presented as an inborn feature of any human being. In the case of Uyghurs, phenotypical characteristics are also at stake: They have very different appearances, they are mistaken for foreigners, thus can be immediately identified by Hans. This fact does not entail any obvious discriminatory attitude, but it makes the feeling of being "outsider" grow. This "being different" becomes relevant also in private occasions, for example checking-in at hotels, looking for a job, for a house or in any circumstance where there is the need to negotiate on an equal footing. In common street and legal disputes, the fact of being Uyghur is always a disadvantage, and when Uyghurs are involved in this kind of disputes and skirmishes, observers and other people involved uncritically point at them as troublemakers, or when there is a reimbursement or a vindication at stake, Uyghurs usually have more hardships in claiming respect for their requests. Being Muslim is also an issue: for instance, Uyghurs cannot eat in restaurants run by non-Uyghurs; if they want to be observant, they need to pray five times a day, and these religious customs, which are highly connoted in China, have a direct impact on their interaction with other Chinese citizens, making "Uyghur ethnicity" a synonym of traditionalism and insignificance. Moreover, venues where Uyghurs gather (schools, marketplaces, restaurants and so on) have a higher number of camera installed and some police vans stationed.

The aim of the first classificatory missions already mentioned before, carried on by Chinese anthropologists together with Soviet advisors, was to assign an ethnic identity to each Chinese citizen, and to make citizens "absorb" this identity. After that first labeling process, what followed was a systematic operation for "constructing nationalities", providing them with indigenous traditions, ethnic histories and cultures, festivals and an overall national rhetoric. This operation is well explained in Terry Martin work on policies toward ethnic minorities in the Soviet Union, the Affirmative Action Empire. Generations of people conscious of their ethnicity followed, up to the point that being "Chinese" without ethnicity is something inconceivable in contemporary Chinese society. To mistake a Uyghur for a Kazakh or Mongol or Hui is considered offensive, to assume him/her as Han is blasphemy. At the same time, Uyghurs get questioned every day at checkpoints, bus stations, airports, hotels, when they want to rent houses or buy a car, inside and outside Xinjiang. The ethnic stigma becomes then a burden, and, while Uyghurs usually feel proud and self-confident in their "ethnic clothes", I heard several of them declaring, when asked about their ethnicity orally or on the phone, that they were Hui, mainly in restaurants or in student dormitories and hotels when they visit friends, as well as when they have to buy something expensive or to rent houses. I then tried to understand the reason why they lie, and also made an effort to grasp their feelings and see if there was not a sense of frustration in being forced to deny their own identity and ethnicity. Quite surprisingly, no sense of frustration nor similar feelings emerged, but they explained that claiming to be Hui makes things easier: In this way, the counterpart knows they are Muslim, at the same time not feeling immediately disappointed by the fact that they have to deal with Uyghurs and all what this ethnic label represents. Also surprisingly, the ethnic label can easily become a cage, even within the same ethnic community. It happens to hear Uyghurs confidentially saying: "I would like to move to a place where there are no Uyghurs at all", or "If I can get the passport, I just leave China and get easily adjusted to any condition abroad". This is what usually happens with Uyghurs who leave China; they tend to stay abroad, unless their relatives who are still in China do not strongly oppose such a decision. Their distrust toward services such as the medical system in Xinjiang and their overall perplexity over the Chinese state and system makes them tend to go abroad to give birth, to get a better health insurance or simply to find a job, in an environment which they feel more fair and respective of their rights. Uyghurs live in a traditional clan-based society, in which socio-economic interactions, including marriages, revolve around the enlarged family environment. Those who live in Inner China or abroad, once back in their home villages feel constrained and often criticize what they consider the traditionalism and backwardness of their relatives and acquaintances. When possible, they try to help the younger members of the family to leave the villages and find a job abroad. This kind of situations is more and more frequent in a society which is rapidly changing its traditional patterns of social interactions to become more consumerist and globalized. In an environment where kinship and neighbors' relations are gradually loosening, it is easier for younger generations to be fascinated by new lifestyles, the environment of the enlarged Uyghur family becomes too limited, and young people look for opportunities to study and work in Inner China and abroad without considering too much the views of the families. In this framework, ethnicity becomes a burden, and some Uyghurs do not even hesitate to become Party members in order to get better jobs and a higher status. According to the fieldworks carried on by Ilham Tohti, Professor of Economics at Minzu University of China, the number of Uyghurs who buy Kazakh, Hui or even Han ethnicity for their children is growing, as well as of those living abroad, mainly in Central Asian countries, who change nationality as soon as the chance arises. In this framework, the process of turning China into a nation-state is helped by the perception of ethnicity as an "identitarian cage", which, up to a certain extent, is growing more and more strong among Uyghur youngsters.

This trend stands in overt contrast to the decades-long and still in force government mind-set focused on ethnicity, which assumes ethnic affiliation as a factor inborn to each human being, an idea which is still dominant in Chinese society. At the same time, social change and a less religious environment make the concept of ethnic identity a more uncertain and blurred one, at the point that it can happen to meet Uyghur girls going to study to Inner China wearing leggings and tight clothes, with accessories with verses from the Koran and hearings shaped as Catholic crosses. These trends make the shift from an essentialist view of ethnicity toward an instrumental perspective, at both the individual and collective level, easier.

6.3 Affirmative Action and Preferential Policies for Minorities

Imperial China was populated by different communities with diverse origins, histories, cultures and religions, with their customs and habits generally all accepted and tolerated under the wide-brimmed imperial umbrella. In historical sources written by court literati, non-Han people were named with eponyms indicating their geographic origin, physical appearance, special characteristics or even alimentary and business habits. At the time, real national minorities and ethnic awareness did not exist. In this framework, affirmative action as it has been explained by Thierry Martin can be understood as the process of creation of ethnicities by the central state, mainly through a classificatory work, an administrative, fiscal and legal system including them, the creation of minorities' histories and traditions, the finalization of different cultural characteristics and folk traditions, and their related political patronage. This means that, without the Chinese state, no Uyghurs, Tibetans or Mongols would exist as they do today, and their respective histories would have taken different directions. Without the political will of establishing a multinational state, and the respective academic and scholarly engagement to create it, the 56 ethnic groups of today's China would not exist in the shape they have today, and at the same time, the level of control over the Chinese population would not be so tight. In this sense, the Affirmative Action Empire, a relevant work on Soviet policies on ethnic minorities, can still be taken as reference for the Chinese situation. In this outstanding work, Martin underlines how "the Soviet Union was the world's first Affirmative Action Empire. Russia's new revolutionary government was the first of the old European multi-ethnic states to confront the rising tide of nationalism and respond by systematically promoting the national consciousness of its ethnic minorities and establishing for them many of the characteristic institutional forms of the nation-state" (p. 1). What happens in China cannot be compared to the Soviet initiatives, but, at the same time, the current form of Tibetan and Uyghur nationalisms could arise only as a result of the Chinese political stance toward non-Han populations, and of the preferential policies implemented by Beijing toward its minority nationals. On the other side, the construction of a Uyghur tradition by a Uyghur élite supported by the central power, together with the conception of a separate history and a peculiar folklore, is at the core of the whole nationalist operation. A suitable example is that of the newly established "Doppa festival", a Uyghur cultural event conceived by part of the Uyghur cultural élite both in Xinjiang and in Inner China, which saw its first edition in 2010, and rapidly became popular among the Uyghur wider population, and it started to be rooted in the Uyghur ethnic and national consciousness. The doppa is the traditional headgear for men, a symbol of religious and cultural commitment, an object which distinguishes the Uyghurs from all the other Muslim populations of Central Asia. During the festival, which takes place for one day in the month of April, all Uyghur men wear the doppa, which today is rarely used among youngsters, and meet in previously fixed venues like theaters and restaurants, where readings and performances such as meshrep take place. The festival has a multiple meaning: It bolsters the use of doppas among young Uyghur men, creates a moment of national unity during which Uyghurs meet altogether and listen to readings of Uyghur poetry and literature, reinforces the sense of being "Uyghur", and represents an important moment of reunion among Uyghurs who live in alien contexts like urban environments in Inner and coastal China. The historical roots and evidences of this kind of cultural events are questionable, but the whole operation works as a binding agent for different interests, at the same time being welcomed by the Uyghur broader population. Just as reference, historical, deeply rooted and hearth-felt festivals like that which were taking place at Ordam Mazar for three days every spring, close to Kashgar, have been forbidden by the authorities since the 1990s.

Bibliography

Barth, Fredrik (1998), *Ethnic Groups and Boundaries*, Waveland.

Buttino, Marco (1997), *L'URSS a pezzi. Nazionalismi e conflitto etnico nel crollo del regime sovietico*, Paravia.

Buttino, Marco (2003), *La Rivoluzione Capovolta. L'Asia Centrale tra il crollo dell'impero zarista e la formazione dell'Urss*, L'Ancora del Mediterraneo.

Buttino, Marco (2007), "Tra l'Urss e le colonie. L'uso di categorie collettive, appunti di ricerca" (Between the Soviet Union and the Colonies: The Adoption of Collective Categories, Research Notes), article published in the website of the Italian Society for the Study of Contemporary History (http://www.sissco.it/fileadmin/user_upload/Attivita/Convegni/identita_collettive/buttino.rtf).

Buttino, Marco, C. Ercolessi, and A. Triulzi (2000), *Uomini in armi. Costruzione etnica e violenza politica*, L'ancora del Mediterraneo.

Geertz, Clifford (1963), *Peddlers and Princes: Social Development and Economic Change in Two Indonesian Towns*, University of Chicago Press.

Gil-White, F. J. (1999), "How Thick Is Blood? The Plot Thickens ... If Ethnic Actors Are Primordialists, What Remains of the Circumstantialist/ Primordialist Controversy?" *Ethnic and Racial Studies*, 22(5): 789–820.

Gil-White, F. J. (2001), "Are Ethnic Groups Biological 'Species' to the Human Brain?: Essentialism in Our Cognition of Some Social Categories", *Current Anthropology*, 42(4): 515–554.

Grosby, Steven (1994), "The Verdict of History: The Inexpungeable Tie of Primordiality—A Response to Eller and Coughlan", *Ethnic and Racial Studies*, 17(1): 164–171.

Isaacs, Harold (1975), "Basic Group Identity: The Idols of the Tribe," in N. Glazer and D. P. Moynihan (eds.), *Ethnicity: Theory and Experience*, Harvard University Press, pp. 29–52.

Leach Edmund (1973), *Political Systems of Highland Burma: A Study of Kachin Social Structure*, LSE Monographs on Social Anthropology, Berg Publishers.

Ma, Rong (2008), *Ethnic Relations in China*, China Tibetology Publishing House.

Martin, Terry (2001), *The Affirmative Action Empire: Nations and Nationalism in the Soviet Union 1923–1939*, Cornell University Press.

Moerman, Michael (1965), "Who Are the Lue? Ethnic Identity in a Complex Society", *The American Anthropologist*, 67: 1215–1230.

Nagata, J. (1981), "In Defense of Ethnic Boundaries: The Changing Myths and Charters of Malay Identity", in C. F. Keyes (ed.), *Ethnic Change*, University of Washington Press.

Shils, Edward (1957), "Primordial, Personal, Sacred and Civil Ties: Some Particular Observations on the Relationship of Sociological Research and Theory", *The British Journal of Sociology*, 8(2): 130–145.

Stack, John F. (ed.) (1986), *The Primordial Challenge*, Greenwood Press.

CHAPTER 7

Conclusions: The CCP and a "Bridge Society" in XUAR—Ethnicity as a Tool for Social Engineering and Stratification

The development trajectory in Xinjiang Uyghur Autonomous Region shows that the economic path of a specific area depends substantially on the support received by the institutions and powers in charge. In the case of Xinjiang, Northern Xinjiang's economy was chosen for central support since the Qing Dynasty, while Southern Xinjiang lagged behind as the area did not enjoy any kind of sustenance. This generated a sort of path dependence mechanism which became importantly evident today. While Northern Xinjiang continues to grow and to be supported by the central, regional and local governments, Southern Xinjiang does not enjoy a systemic public backing and its development depends on the intentions and engagement of individual cadres and officers. As the central government did not change the focus of its investments and of support over the centuries, this course has never been inverted, and as a result, once very important and economically flourishing oases such as Khotan and Yarkand became secondary settlements in Southern Xinjiang. Their administrative status was also downgraded, for instance, Yarkand—which was bigger and more important than Kashgar until the Qing Dynasty—lost the status of prefecture and became a county within the Kashgar Prefecture. If we look at the dynamics of land appropriation in the rural areas of the Kashgar Prefecture, and at how farmers are persuaded to leave their fields and homes to local authorities, we understand how weak is the institutional presence in Southern Xinjiang, and how much of arbitrary policy-making is left to certain powerful individual actors. The

A. Cappelletti, *Socio-Economic Development in Xinjiang Uyghur Autonomous Region*,
https://doi.org/10.1007/978-981-15-1536-1_7

voice of farmers is heard as long as the farmer is close to a Party cadre, or either has connections in the government. This situation is the result of a long-term neglect of the needs of the region's South, where under-development, poverty and a general sense of being abandoned created conflicts and tensions, reported by international media until 2014, when the central government decided to adopt drastic measures to cope with the "Nanjiang[1] problem" and move forward with the construction of a national identity.

These regional patterns of uneven development caused a series of important problems of unemployment in the Southern part of the region, from where young Uyghurs started to migrate to urban centers in Xinjiang and in China in search for jobs. This young unskilled work-force started to be employed in low-end jobs in the cities (mainly in construction, transportation, restaurants and hotels), and according to Professor Ilham Tohti, they had the chance to develop the awareness of being B-series citizens and, at a certain point, fight for their rights.[2] This process did not happen because of the too low level of education of these migrants, and because the political climate became much more tense with the Xi-Wen administration. The level of education of Uyghurs is not comparable with that of the Hans, and this has a spillover impact on a range of issues such as HIV infections, unemployment and street criminality, as it is illustrated in this book's chapter on social development in Xinjiang.

A major factor impacting socio-economic development is represented by a sense of uncertainty related to what is legal and what is not. Uyghurs are currently undergoing continuous security checks, both on the streets and in their private lives; the degree of surveillance is very high and the employment of high-tech equipment makes it more invasive; ethnic discrimination is attested in hotels (Uyghurs are not accepted in a number of hotels), housing (house owners do not easily rent apartments to Uyghurs), access to credit (banks do not easily issue mortgages or loans to Uyghurs), mobility (difficulties to get the passport), and so on; and a general sense of stigma is perceived among the Uyghur population just for being Uyghur. Moreover, venues where Uyghurs

[1] Nanjiang 南疆 is the current way to define Southern Xinjiang.

[2] The 2009 riots have been mainly caused by young Uyghur migrants to Urumqi who wanted to claim their right to get access to the same services and benefits guaranteed to the rest of the Chinese population.

Award to a village household for being in line with the Party directions (DSCN 3466)

gather—in Xinjiang and all across China—such as mosques, restaurants and marketplaces are constantly patrolled by police vans. The fact that Uyghurs can be taken to ideological reeducation facilities—or "vocational education centers"—from one day to the other and kept there for up to two years, or sometimes more, without knowing when they will be out, makes the whole situation even more complex.

7.1 Human Development Index and "Capability Approach"

If we look at the progression of the HDI values in Xinjiang Uyghur Autonomous Region, we can argue that figures are consistent with our fieldwork findings: While China has been ranked at the 101st position since the second half of the first decade of the twenty-first century and jumped to the 86th position in the rankings in 2017, in 2008 Xinjiang was listed with a numerical value of 0.774 (medium), ranking 21st among the 31 Chinese provinces, autonomous regions and municipalities, and, in 2017, it reached the 18th position together with Henan Province, the same HDI of the state of Suriname in South Africa.

In the first Human Development Report issued in 1997, titled *China—Human Development Report, Human Development and Poverty Alleviation*, the region ranked 15th, while its GDP index ranking was 14th. In 1999, the region raised in its GDP ranking to the 12th position and remained 15th for its HDI value. In 2002, the ranking was still stable at the 15th position, and in 2005, there was an improvement to the 14th position. This is in line with Wiemer's analysis published in 2004, where the author argues that the region's economic performance was extraordinarily effective in comparison with that of other Western and central provinces and regions of China. In 2008, the region dropped to the 21st position, while its GDP ranking was still relatively high, at the 15th position. In 2010, the situation was still stable, with an HDI index still lagging behind the achievements of China's Eastern and Southern provinces. As mentioned, Wiemer (2004) is the author who analyses how these fluctuations started and developed. The abrupt decrease in the HDI ranking in 2008, when the GDP remained high and stable along the years, represents an interesting case for further analysis and supports those political economists who argue that "economic growth" does not necessary means "development".[3] Economic growth might well be a necessary condition for economic development but not a sufficient one. While the GDP per capita might be rising, poverty might be on the rise, inequality in the distribution of income as well and massive environmental damage might be occurring.[4]

The HDI represents a possibility to conceive a definition of economic development: as a multidimensional figure, it involves indicators related to per capita GDP, but mainly incorporates other factors. These are aimed at understanding whether people are put in the conditions and have the instruments and possibilities to improve their situations in the future. The capability approach[5] is the core concept of the HDI. In Xinjiang, growth is currently on the rise due to the progress of the BRI, the establishment of SEZs and to the development programs financed by

[3] Mainly Al Haq and Sen.

[4] Nixson (2001, p. 15).

[5] See Al Haq.

Beijing, but the majority of its population, mainly those of Uyghur ethnicity, lack the same capabilities which Han residents enjoy. In the specific case of our research focus, this development gap is due to the lack of institutional support; ethnic discrimination; and lack of Uyghur participation in the decision-making processes and of "good governance" in general terms. Lack of "good governance" at the local level, which depends on the weakness of institutions, seems to be a major cause of intraregional development disparities. The responsibilities of Uyghur elites in this situation are explored later in this conclusive chapter.

7.2 Summary of Fieldwork Findings

In both Kashgar and Shihezi, the HDI value is on a rising trend. The index does not allow us to understand whether inequalities are still an issue, as data are not disaggregated along ethnic lines: Fieldwork outcomes give us the possibility for a more in-depth and meticulous analysis which can in some ways replace the breakup of data. Therefore, only through the fieldwork it has been possible to better understand the dynamics underpinning the "selective" still existing inequalities.

The HDI in the Kashgar Prefecture denotes a gradually rising trend, and the increase rate is faster than the Shihezi one. This can be understood by considering the influx of capitals and investments into the prefecture's coffers, as well as the growing number of development, infrastructural and industrial projects which are being implemented in the area, mainly after the establishment of the SEZ in 2010 and the launch of the BRI in 2013. The HDI in Shihezi sub-prefectural municipality remains stable: The development of the city dates back to the 1980s, when it was selected by the central and regional governments as a vanguard for the economic and political development in the whole region. The HDI is now increasing slowly, since the development of Shihezi is already consolidated and on track. This notwithstanding, during our fieldwork we had the opportunity to test and better understand to what extent the observed HDI trends correspond to what happens in the field. On the basis of the collected information (both quantitative and qualitative), and mainly from interview outcomes, we could assess a striking difference in self-perceptions about development and capabilities. This difference follows the ethnic affiliation of the respondents: The almost entirety of respondents of Uyghur ethnicity declared their dissatisfaction about their achievements and capabilities. The rest of Uyghur respondents expressed their satisfaction, in the same way as their Han counterparts: The discriminating factor between the two groups is the CCP membership and the position held in the local administration. We named this small part of the Uyghur population, corresponding to an approximate 2.5% of the total, as "bridge society", mainly for its role as a sort of bridge between Beijing and Uyghur peoples, and for its being in charge of keeping the status quo. This co-opted élite in Xinjiang shall be object of further research. The main factor of inequality is therefore ethnicity, which comes out as a label revealing an individual or a group socio-economic status. Ethnicity is here understood not as an essentialist concept inborn into every human being, making him a product of tradition, history and generational ethnic affiliation, but only a political tool to better control a large population. "Uyghur" means "backward", "thief", "cheater", "dirty" and "grill maker". This labeling of a certain ethnic group is a useful expedient to alienate all the other ethnicities' sympathy and to avoid a potential coalition of different social/ethnic groups against the central power. The same dynamics and political actions at the central level could be observed in the former Soviet Union.

Here below we will try to list, not in order of importance, the main factors determining inequality in Xinjiang:

1. Ethnic identity
2. Class affiliation
3. Family affiliation and socio-political guanxi
4. *Danwei*
5. Party membership
6. Level of assimilation and adoption of government-promoted political and cultural values
7. Level of education and individual/group awareness
8. Religion
9. Hukou
10. Age (mainly for male Uyghurs)
11. Gender

The identity and label "Uyghur" is already an indicator of inequality within individuals and communities. Just to mention an example, a young Uyghur who moves from a remote and poor village in Xinjiang to a big city like Shanghai or Beijing to look for job opportunities and a better life, eventually finds himself trapped in a society which allows him to raise the social ladder only up to a certain extent, and after a certain point she/he does not have the possibility to move forward. She/he can find a poorly paid position in the construction or service sectors, but it is very difficult, due to discrimination and low educational attainments, to hope moving from that position onward. The discrimination is evident in a number of fields, such as housing, mobility and job opportunities. A Han in the same conditions has more or less the same problems, but can take the challenge to step up the socio-economic ladder. In the case of a secularized Uyghur with a good education, studies abroad, knowledge of foreign languages and of how to move within Chinese society, the situation can be different but not substantially. The Uyghur can move forward together with his/her Han counterparts, get a good position, but when the situation becomes competitive because an enhancement of power and status get into the picture, the Uyghur has no chance to get the better of his Han counterparts. This situation cuts across all social strata within Chinese society, including government officials, Party cadres, academics and so on. In terms of capabilities, a Uyghur has real and perceived limitations which are increasingly incapacitating than those that a Han faces, regardless of the degree of sinification. The lack of valid political representatives and intellectual voices in Uyghur society, the co-opted élite and the "bridge society", working to maintain the status quo, are preventing the development of any process of self-awareness. The political control implemented by Beijing, as well as maintaining Uyghurs at the lower level of society (according to some respondents sometimes it happens on purpose), is all factors which help reaffirming the social role within the echelons of Chinese society.

Our findings are therefore in line with the concept of "internal colonialism" as it has been put forward by Michael Hechter, the backbone of social relations can be identified in power struggle, with consequent domination, oppression and subjection of one group over the others. Hechter emphasizes the severe social dualism which apparently exists as a result of the exploitation of subjected groups. The dominant group at the top is not a source of structural change, but, rather, a preserver of the structure which allows to continue reaping the benefits of such a set of social relations, and the exploited community is partly responsible for this situation, especially its "bridge society". In other words, internal colonialism refers to structural arrangements typified by a relatively small dominant group which controls the allocation of resources and the articulation of power (in this case, Beijing and its representatives), and a large, subjected mass composed of various groups with unarticulated interests largely divorced from participation in the development process and blocked from means of social mobility.

7.3 Ethnic Perspectives: Who Benefits?

The ethnic perspective comes out as the concept defining inequality, where the meaning of the term "inequality" is broad enough to include differences in capabilities and a basic imbalance in the relations and modes of production. The Chinese society in Xinjiang is divided into clusters which have and share, on different extents, the power, and groupings with a limited control on resources and with no political representation.

Actors who mainly benefit from the adoption of ethnic categories are: (1) the Chinese central government and the CCP, for which ethnicities are a way to ensure political and social stability, and provide a tool to better control the population; (2) Han population in key positions, an elite supported and listened by the central government (even if part of the Han population perceives a sort of discrimination: Preferential policies for minorities are seen as strong social benefits, even though indirectly, affect Hans negatively); and (3) "bridge society", composed by hybrid identities, minority nationals who are a new elite, CCP officials and cadres, personnel inside Chinese institutions.

7.3.1 The Bridge Society

History of élite co-optation in Xinjiang Uyghur Autonomous Region dates back to the Qing Dynasty, when the whole region was conquered by the imperial troops after the conflicts with the Zunghar tribes on the North of the Tarim Basin, and the defeat of the Sufi khojas in the South. The territorial conquest of 1759 represents a starting point for a new form of administration and bureaucracy in the region. When the territory corresponding to today's Xinjiang was annexed, a discourse on the historical meaning of that conquest started, opening the way to the construction of national foundations, and of a national identity of its inhabitants. While these concepts were put forward, theorized and already accepted in the West, they were still new in Far-East Asia. This process required middlemen able to mediate among the several interests of different actors and to help the Manchu establishment to deal with "foreign" populations by increasing the level of mutual understanding, and the subsequent implementation of an assimilatory process promoted by Beijing. Those first Uyghur middlemen who were employed were called *beg*, and they operated under the supervision of the Manchu and Mongol *amban*. They could be considered as precursors of that "bridge society" which helps Beijing to rule today's Xinjiang. Part of the Uyghur society became then an essential active actor in the strategic policy carried on by the Chinese imperial court first, and government later, for the control of its Northwestern border region and populations. The "bridge society" is basically composed by Uyghurs who occupy high-level positions, such as CCP officials, people working in the government or in government-related bodies, scholars at universities and research institutes, intellectuals with close connections to Chinese institutions, students and migrant workers in Inner China's urban centers.

These middlemen, or negotiators, have characteristics such as a hybrid identity; a high degree of sinification; thoughts in line with the central government policies; they retain only some marginal features of their own culture; share the same life standards, expectations and aims of their Han colleagues and wish to be accepted and welcomed by the Han society. They can also have completely opposite features: Apparently traditional and conservative, with a low degree of assimilation, act as reference for their peoples; they use of terms like "original", "traditional", "inborn" with an essentialist meaning; they do not have a broad political vision, nor cultural tools to understand and question the concept of ethnic identity; and they are essentialist, and sometimes racist and easily corruptible.

Ethnic identity thus shapes society in its multilayered structure: It defines power and its actors, becomes a category of exclusion and creates, by itself, the categories of power. In this "ethnic context", the interests and goals of several actors intermingle and define, step by step, the socio-economic status of its components. These actors interact in a complex dynamic which is hard to detect for those who are not familiar with the specific socio-economic context. While we identified one of those actors, a Uyghur élite which acts as one of the fundamental players in this "game", and which is an active/passive tool of a political power with a deep strategic vision, at the same time we also tried to sketch two profiles of those people belonging to this co-opted élite. This said, a major analysis of what we tentatively call "bridge society" remains to be done, as well as a study on all the political and social actors who, in different ways, and not always with the same weight, contribute to making "ethnicity" a dangerous social weapon.

It is thanks to the collaboration of these "bridge profiles" that the central government can argue that a harmonious society has been established in today's Xinjiang.

7.4 Theoretical Implications: A Social Pact Between Beijing and the "Bridge Society"

The original hypothesis of this work was that historical, cultural, political and religious diversity could represent fundamental factors hindering mutual understanding, communication and peaceful coexistence among diverse ethnicities sharing the same territory. This hypothesis, which basically considered diversity as an obstacle, emerged from a preliminary analysis of the problem, which considered the Hans as the dominant group, with power and economic resources to control and manage the far Western border region, and the Uyghurs, weak and discriminated, are marginalized and not involved in the developmental dynamics interesting the area, passive spectators vis-a-vis the massive influx of capitals and migrant workforce coming from Inner China. In this complex and tense context, any kind of policy could be easily read as discriminative and detrimental for Uyghurs, a contribution to push them down to the weakest positions of Xinjiang and Chinese society. I looked at diversity, mainly cultural incommunicability, as the main source of the so-called Xinjiang problem.

During the fieldworks, I handled a variety of material, from interviews outcomes to official documents and statistics, and, thanks to a more accurate and attentive study, the initial interpretative approach focused on the so-called ethnic question started to be more centered on the dynamics underlying inequalities: Distribution of resources, class and power struggle, together with corruption, clearly emerged as factors generating disparities, unbalances masked under the label of ethnic conflict. In this in-depth analysis, what I call a "bridge society" is composed by Uyghur officers, cadres, scholars and common people who support the Chinese government in its endeavors in Xinjiang, guaranteeing in this way the constant reconfirmation of a "social pact" and helping to maintain the status quo. This concept has not been considered yet by Uyghur scholars, intellectuals and politicians well inside the national and international debates, even if it emerges as the backbone of the dominant Han leadership.

The stages of the research, which implied a substantial change of the original interpretative approach and understanding, can be listed as follows.

1. In-depth fieldwork and familiarization with Uyghur society with participant observation activities
2. Fieldworks and surveys realized as consultant for the Sino-German Poverty Alleviation Programme Xinjiang
3. Academic and research activities at Minzu University of China conducted from September 2010 to October 2012
4. Research and fieldwork activity with Uyghur scholars
5. Conversations with Uyghurs in Beijing and with hybrid identity *minkaohan* 民考汉
6. Familiarization with venues where peoples of different ethnicities meet and interact
7. Anthropological and historical documents and studies
8. In-depth interviews with Uyghur middle-class members in Beijing and Xinjiang
9. In-depth interviews with Uyghur intellectuals, scholars, academics, CCP officials and farmers.

Through these steps, I was able to better identify those deep dynamics underlying socio-economic inequalities, and a number of aspects in the current disparities started to be more clear, while the different levels of interaction between Hans and Uyghurs gradually became more visible. A new interpretative perspective with "ethnicity" as key concept but with a circumstantialist meaning emerged.

7.4.1 Original Hypothesis

ETHNICITY

means *essential* cultural, geographical, historical, linguistic and phonotypical differences

↓

Hans and the Chinese government make

NO EFFORT TO LISTEN TO UYGHURS AND TO UNDERSTAND, ACCEPT, PROTECT WHAT IS DIFFERENT

↓

UYGHURS CLAIM

respect of culture and traditions, Muslim religion, language differences, more autonomy, and, in some cases, independence

↓

NO EFFORT TO START A DIALOGUE BY THE HAN SIDE

BUT

IMPOSITION OF A HAN DEVELOPMENT MODEL AND INSTITUTIONAL OPPRESSION ON UYGHURS

↓

REGIONAL INEQUALITIES

unequal distribution of resources, preferential policies, cultural and religious discrimination

↓

SPORADIC CLASHES

Baren 1990

Ghulja 1997

Urumqi 2009

Kashgar 2011

Beijing 2013

Urumqi 2014

Kunming 2014

7.4.2 Current Thesis

STEADY SOCIAL PACT

"dominant group" and an elite among the "subjected people"—a *bridge society*—interact in a power dynamic in which they are allies in sharing resources and performing social control

↓

REGIONAL INEQUALITIES FOLLOWING ETHNIC LINES

(gradual reassessment of Uyghur history and culture, political measures to assimilate Uyghurs, unequal redistribution of resources, discrimination in the job market, etc.)

↓

USE OF A CIRCUMSTANTIALIST CONCEPT OF "ETHNICITY" TO JUSTIFY POVERTY

(the claim is "they are poor and marginalized" because they are "Uyghurs", and, by being Uyghurs, they are poor and marginalized)

↓

CLAIMS BY PART OF UYGHUR SOCIETY: EQUAL RIGHTS, REAL AUTONOMY

against discrimination, racism, socio-economic and political segregation

↓

STRUMENTALIZATION OF ETHNICITY
BOTH BY THE HAN POWER AND THE "BRIDGE SOCIETY"
to keep the status quo

↓

LACK OF GOOD GOVERNANCE AT THE LOCAL LEVEL:
NO REAL POLITICAL REPRESENTATION, NO INTELLECTUAL VOICES
NO DIALOGUE—HARDENING OF POSITIONS
(top-down political processes; repression; tensions)

↓

CLASHES—PERIODICAL BUT CONSTANT INSTABILITY
(arrests; political turmoil; ideological reeducation)

The understanding of hybrid identities and cross-cultural experiences permeating Xinjiang society maintains that ethnicity is still the main factor of socio-political inequality, but not as an essentialist tract of people's identity, but as a political tool adopted by both Uyghurs and Hans in framing their reciprocal understanding, their relationship with the power, and their interaction with different environments on different levels. As the research core concept, ethnicity as such changed and transformed its intrinsic sense and semantics. The discriminant of inequality is still ethnic affiliation as a category empty of essentialist meaning and full of political sense. Beyond cultural diversity, Uyghur is a label for "poor, not educated, backward, and narrow-minded". Han is the label for "modern, educated, powerful, rich and farsighted". The most elucidative materials were interviews and observations which revealed that for Uyghurs the two labels are interchangeable according to the specific situation and environment. For instance, it was not rare to see local officials and professors of Uyghur ethnicity who were not different from their Han counterparts in terms of behavior, values and expectations. When interviewed, part of the authorities who claimed to be of Uyghur ethnicity answered questions about traditions, history and personal expectations, with the same understandings and comments as those of their Han counterparts. The perceptions of some Uyghur local authorities belonging to the CCP were the same as those of their Han counterparts. Employed as a concept deprived of its essentialist sense, Uyghur ethnicity becomes then a socio-political label adopted to classify those individuals belonging to the lower levels of the social ladder and with specific characteristics in terms of socio-economic background and capabilities. To summarize, we can reasonably argue that a steady social pact is one of the main mechanisms behind persisting inequalities, a "social contract" tacitly stipulated between Beijing and a small part of the Uyghur population which we call "bridge society", aimed at the conservation of the status quo and at guaranteeing a long-lasting control and power from the center, in return of special status and opportunities for them and for their offspring, mainly in terms of jobs, socio-political positions, economic benefits and opportunities.

Bibliography

Hechter, Michael (1987), *Internal Colonialism: the Celtic Fringe in British National Development*, University of California Press.

Nixson, Frederick (2001), *Development Economics: Studies in Economics and Business*, Heinemann.

Ul Haq, Mahbub (1976), *The Poverty Curtain: Choices for the Third World*, Columbia University Press.

Ul Haq, Mahbub (1996), *Reflections on Human Development*, Oxford University Press.

Wiemer, Calla (2004), "The Economy of Xinjiang", in Starr Frederick, *China's Muslim Borderland*, M. E. Sharpe.

Woodhouse, Keith Mako (2018), *The Ecocentrists: A History of Radical Environmentalism*, Columbia University Press.

Appendix 1: Questionnaires

Questionnaire for Residents in Kashgar/Shihezi

1) ***General information***

age
gender
nationality
origins
family status (married/not married-nationality of the eventual partner; children-nationality)
occupation
religion
educational degree (if belonging to a national minority, minkaohan or minkaomin)

2) ***Social services***

2.1. When you or a member of your family has a **health** problem, how do you try to solve it?
2.2. When you or a member of your family need to find a **job**, which institution you address to (if any)?

A. Cappelletti, *Socio-Economic Development in Xinjiang Uyghur Autonomous Region*,
https://doi.org/10.1007/978-981-15-1536-1

2.3. When you or a member of your family need money, what do normally you do?
2.4. Which kind of loans or credits or facilitations you have access to as a Shihezi/Kashgar citizen?
2.5. When you need to enroll children of your family at **school**, what do normally you do?
2.6. Do you or members of your family practice some **sports**?
2.7. In case you have more children than the allowed ones, what do you do?
2.8. Which is your idea of social services? Are they effective in your territory? Do you think they satisfy your and your community needs?
2.9. Did you notice any change in the provision of social services in the last ten years? If yes, which are the main ones?
2.10. In your opinion, should it be the state or the community leaders to provide social services?
2.11. Which are your hopes and your requests for the future?

3) ***Social environment and restrictions***

3.1. Are you satisfied about the supply of **basic services**, like communication system, water, sanitary equipment, electricity and heating?
3.2. Do you have the **passport**? If not, why?
- Which kind of documents and administrative procedures you need to go through in order to get the passport?
- do you usually travel outside the city/the region/China?

3.3. (for Muslims believers) Do you usually go to the mosque? If yes, how often a week? If not, why?
3.4. What could you say about the **housing** policy? What could you say about the education and **language** policy?
3.5. What could you say about **environmental** problems in Shihezi/Kashgar?
3.6. Do you think that the government development plans can help the social development of the region? If not, why? If yes, how?
3.7. What about the neighbor relationship with non-Han and non-Uyghur people?

4) ***Community leadership and organisation***

4.1. In your opinion, which are the most important aspects and elements of your community life?
4.2. Thinking of these aspects and elements, which are the major changes occurred in the last 10 years?
4.3. Which changes would you consider positive and which ones would you consider negative?
4.4. When it happens that in your community there are problems, do you tend to express them or try to solve them from inside?
4.5. In case you decide to complain about public services, which is your counterpart?
4.6. In case you decide to find a solution within your community, who are your direct referents?
4.7. Talking about the concept of "social development", what does it remind you without having time to reflect on it?
4.8. In your perspective, which categories would you include in the idea of "social development"?
4.9. Thinking about this idea from your own perspective, would you say there have been changes in your own community during the last 10 years? If yes, which ones?

5) ***Knowledge about Kashgar/Shihezi***

5.1. Have you ever been to Kashgar/Shihezi?
5.2. If yes, what do you think of the social conditions there in comparison with Kashgar/Shihezi?
5.3. If not, what is your knowledge about Kashgar prefecture/Shihezi?

Questionnaire for Officials and Local Authorities in the Kashgar Prefecture/Shihezi

1. What is the meaning of the development projects you are implementing in the area under your administration? Do you think it is useful for raise the living standard and general awareness of the people on their right to have services and to improve their conditions?

2. Which have been the criteria you followed for allocating the fundings of the development projects? Could you provide us with copies of the documents explaining the criteria your County/Township/Village used for such allocations?
3. Could you provide us with any document and material related to the socio-economic conditions of the people under your supervision?
4. How people respond to the implementation of the Beijing-sponsored and regionally funded development programs?
5. How do you usually inform farmers on the development projects' aims and contents?
6. Do you, or members of your family, benefit from these development programs? If yes, how?
7. Do you have any suggestions on the way to improve the effectiveness of the development projects in your area?
8. Are residents paying any fee in order to benefit from the allocation of funding?
9. Do you receive a good support from your direct supervisors?
10. On the basis of your experience and observations, which are the main problems existing in your project areas? Could you briefly elaborate on it?
11. Do you have expectations about the development programs? If yes, which kind of benefits would you expect to receive?
12. Do you think that residents involved in the project are committed to its aim and spirit? If you would need to make an assessment of the level of commitment, how committed would you say they are from 1 to 10?
13. Would you have some suggestions to improve the overall project implementation in your area?

Questionnaire for Professors and University Personnel in Shihezi/Kashgar

1) ***General information***

age
gender
residence (hukou and temporary residence)

nationality
origins
religion
minkaohan or minkaomin
family status (married/not married-nationality of the eventual partner; children- nationality)
department of affiliation and univeristy position
study career
family income (approximately)

2) ***Shihezi University/Kashgar Teachers' College and Xinjiang social environment***

2.1. Was it a choice to work/teach at Shihezi university/Kashgar Teachers' College?
2.2. Which are the courses you are teaching?
2.3. Which is your work at home?
2.4. What do you think of the study curriculum at Shihezi University/ Kashgar Teachers' College?
2.5. What do you think of the students' level? Do you think there are differences between Han and students belonging to minority nationalities?
2.6. And about the textbooks you are using during your courses?
2.7. Which is the relationship between the university and the bingtuan?
2.8. Are there exchange academic programs with other national universities?
2.9. Are there exchange academic programs with foreign universities?
2.10. Is the university receiving ad hoc fundings from the Ministry of Education and from the central government?
2.11. Which are the living conditions for professors/administrative employees?
2.12. Why do you think Shihezi university/Kashgar Teachers' College students are mainly Han/Uyghurs?
2.13. According to your study and cultural background, what do you think of the national minorities/majority living in Xinjiang, mainly the Uyghur minority/Han majority?
2.14. Are you satisfied of your teaching here?

2.15. Talking about Xinjiang, which kind of factors would you include in the concept of "social development"?
2.16. What do you think about social development in Xinjiang?
2.17. What can you say if you compare your life here and your life in your homeplace?
2.18. Do you often travel outside of Shihezi/Kashgar, around Xinjiang?
2.19. Are you satisfied of the life in Shihezi/Kashgar and Xinjiang in general?
2.20. How do you see the future progress of your professional career?
2.21. Do you have the possibility to respect the customs and uses of your nationality?
2.22. Do you think that the government development plans can help social development of the region? If not, why? If yes, in which way?
2.23. What would say if I would ask you to compare the socio-economic development of Kashgar and Shihezi?

3) ***Knowledge about Kashgar/Shihezi***

3.1. Have you ever been to Kashgar/Shihezi?
3.2. If yes, what do you think of the social conditions there in comparison with Shihezi/Kashgar?
3.3. If not, what is your knowledge about Kashgar prefecture/Shihezi?

Questionnaire for University Students in Shihezi/Kashgar

1) ***General information***

age
gender
residence (hukou and temporary residence)
nationality
origins
religion
minkaohan or minkaomin (if the interviewed belongs to a minoriy nationality)

family status (married/not married-nationality of the eventual partner; children-nationality)
univeristy course
study career
scholarship or self-paying student
family income (approximately)

2) ***Shihezi University and Xinjiang social environment***

2.1. Did you choose yourself Shihezi university/Kashgar Teachers' College or where you sent here according to the results of the national examinations or parents' choice?
2.2. Which are the courses you are following?
2.3. Which courses do you prefer?
2.4. Which is your general opinion about Shihezi University?
2.5. What do you think about the textbooks you are using during your courses?
2.6. What is the relationship between Shihezi university/Kashgar Teachers' College and foreign universities?
2.7. How do you relate Shihezi university/Kashgar Teachers' College to the bingtuan?
2.8. Which are the living conditions in the campus?
2.9. Why Shihezi university/Kashgar Teachers' College students are mainly Han?
2.10. According to your study and cultural background, what do you think of the national minorities/national majority living in Xinjiang, mainly the Uyghur minority/Han majority?
2.11. Are you satisfied about your studying here?
2.12. Do you have the chance to respect the customs and uses of your nationality?
2.13. Which kind of factors would you include in the concept of "social development"?
2.14. What do you think about social development in Xinjiang?
2.15. What can you say if you compare your life here and your life in your hometown?
2.16. Do you often travel outside of Shihezi/Kashgar, around Xinjiang?
2.17. Are you satisfied of the life in Shihezi/Kashgar and Xinjiang in general?

2.18. Which is the field you would like to work in after graduation, or job would you like to do? Where would you like to work?
2.19. Do you think that the government development plans can help the social and economic development of the region? If not, why? If yes, in which way?

3) ***Knowledge about Kashgar/Shihezi***

3.1. Have you ever been to Kashgar/Shihezi?
3.2. If yes, what do you think of the social conditions there in comparison with Shihezi/Kashgar?
3.3. If not, what is your knowledge about Kashgar prefecture/Shihezi?

Appendix 2: Acronyms and Abbreviations

CASS	Chinese Academy of Social Sciences
CCP	Chinese Communist Party
CCPCC	Chinese Communist Party Central Committee
CECC	Congressional-Executive Commission on China
CSWs	Commercial Sex Workers
ETDZ	Economic and Technological Development Zone
FIEs	Foreign Invested Enterprises
FYP	Five-Year Plan
GDP	Gross Domestic Product
HDI	Human Development Index
HDRs	Human Development Reports
ICE	Istituto nazionale per il Commercio Estero
IDUs	Injection Drug Users
JVs	Joint Ventures
Ltd	Limited Company
NATO	North Atlantic Treaty Organisation
PLA	People's Liberation Army
Rmb	Ren Min Bi (Chinese national currency – 10 Rmb approximately correspond to 0,7 €)
SCO	Shanghai Cooperation Organisation
SEZs	Special Economic Zones

A. Cappelletti, *Socio-Economic Development in Xinjiang Uyghur Autonomous Region*,
https://doi.org/10.1007/978-981-15-1536-1

SOEs State Owned Enterprises
SWAT Special Weapons And Tactics
SY Statistical Yearbook
TAR Tibetan Autonomous Region
TIP Turkestan Islamic Party
UHRP Uyghur Human Rights Project
UNDP United Nations Development Project
US United States
XJPCC Xinjiang Production and Construction Corps
XJSY Xinjiang Statistical Yearbook
XUAR Xinjiang Uyghur Autonomous Region
WB World Bank
WRB Water Resources Bureau
WUC World Uyghur Congress
XJSY Xinjiang Statistical Yearbook
XUAR Xinjiang Uyghur Autonomous Region

Appendix 3: Place Names in the Kashgar Prefecture

	Original name (Uyghur)	Chinese translation
1.	Konasheher county	Shufu county
2.	Yengiösteng	Yingwusitan
3.	Yengihisar county	Yingjisha county
4.	Cholpan	Qiaolepan
5.	Yopurgha county	Yuepuhu county
6.	Siyek	Seyeke
7.	Terim	Tielimu
8.	Peyzawat county	Jiashı county
9.	Shaptul	Xiaputuli
10.	Yengisheher county	Shule county
11.	Aral	Alali
12.	Yandurma	Yangdaman
13.	Akto county	Aketao county
14.	Barin	Baren

A. Cappelletti, *Socio-Economic Development in Xinjiang Uyghur Autonomous Region*,
https://doi.org/10.1007/978-981-15-1536-1

Index

A. Cappelletti, *Socio-Economic Development in Xinjiang Uyghur Autonomous Region*,
https://doi.org/10.1007/978-981-15-1536-1

The manufacturer's authorised representative in the EU is Springer Nature Customer Service Centre GmbH, Europaplatz 3, 69115 Heidelberg, Germany. If you have any concerns regarding our products, please contact ProductSafety@springernature.com

Printed and bound by CPI Group (UK) Ltd, Croydon, CR0 4YY
25/09/2026
02222897-0013